Dave Taylor

SAMS
Teach Yourself
Unix
in 24 Hours

THIRD EDITION

SAMS

201 West 103rd St., Indianapolis, Indiana, 46290 USA

Sams Teach Yourself Unix in 24 Hours, Third Edition

Copyright © 2001 by Sams Publishing

International Standard Book Number: 0-672-32127-0

Library of Congress Catalog Card Number: 2001087590

Printed in the United States of America

First Printing: April 2001

04   03   02   01   4   3   2   1

Trademarks

Warning and Disclaimer

ASSOCIATE PUBLISHER
Jeff Koch

ACQUISITIONS EDITOR
Katie Purdum

DEVELOPMENT EDITOR
Hugh Vandivier

MANAGING EDITOR
Matt Purcell

PROJECT EDITOR
Andy Beaster

COPY EDITOR
Cynthia Fields

INDEXER
Sandy Henselmeier

PROOFREADER
Benjamin Berg

TECHNICAL EDITOR
Tim Hicks

TEAM COORDINATOR
Vicki Harding

INTERIOR DESIGNER
Gary Adair

COVER DESIGNER
Aren Howell

Contents at a Glance

Contents

Appendix

About the Authors

Dave Taylor is president of Intuitive Systems, a strategic and tactical consulting firm working with dot-com startups, and currently serves on the board of three Internet startups. Founder of startups The Internet Mall and iTrack, he has been involved with Unix and the Internet since 1980, having created the popular Elm Mail System and Embot mail autoresponder. A prolific author, he has been published more than 1,000 times, and his most recent books include the best-selling *Creating Cool HTML 4.0 Web Pages* and *The eAuction Insider*.

Previous positions include being a research scientist at HP Palo Alto Laboratories and senior reviews editor of *SunWorld/Advanced Systems* magazine. He has contributed software to the official 4.4 release of Berkeley Unix (BSD), and his programs are found in all versions of Linux and other popular Unix variants.

Dave has a bachelor's degree in computer science (University of California at San Diego, 1984) and a master's degree in educational computing (Purdue University, 1995), and he teaches Internet and interface design courses at San Jose State University's Professional Development Program. His official home page on the Web is `http://www.intuitive.com/taylor`, and his e-mail address for the past 15 years has been `taylor@intuitive.com`.

About the Technical Editor

Tim Hicks is a senior Unix engineer for HomeSide Lending, Inc. He is an HP Certified IT Professional in HP-UX Systems Administration and has been working extensively with HP-UX 10.10 - 11.00 as well as some work with Solaris 8 and AIX 4.1 for five years. He has in-depth knowledge and experience with Highly Available Clusters using HP's MC/ServiceGuard and HP-UX 11.00 with Sybase and Oracle. Mr. Hicks graduated from Florida State University with a B.S. in finance and a B.S. in management information systems in '94 and '96 respectively.

Dedication

To the lights of my life: Linda, Ashley, and Gareth

Acknowledgments

However you slice it, you can't write a book locked in a cave (even if there's a DSL line and fancy computer therein), and this book has evolved over many years, starting out its life as an interactive Unix tutorial book I was writing for Sun Microsystems. In the interim, a number of people have added their spices to the stew, most notably my co-author for the first and second editions of *Teach Yourself Unix in 24 Hours*, James C. Armstrong, Jr.

In this new third edition, I've been delighted by the cooperative and talented team at Sams Publishing, again, and would like to specifically thank both Kathryn Purdum and Andrew Beaster. Thanks also to Tim Hicks for his close and precise technical editing skills, and generally for keeping me on my toes. Although he wasn't directly in the loop, my agent, Christian Crumlish of Waterside, offered some sage advice on the terms of the deal, too.

Finally, I would like to acknowledge and thank my family for letting me sneak into my office night after night, working on the book and updating each and every chapter. I wouldn't trade them in, even for a 1GHz PC! :-)

Tell Us What You Think!

As the reader of this book, *you* are our most important critic and commentator. We value your opinion and want to know what we're doing right, what we could do better, what areas you'd like to see us publish in, and any other words of wisdom you're willing to pass our way.

As an associate publisher for Sams, I welcome your comments. You can fax, e-mail, or write me directly to let me know what you did or didn't like about this book—as well as what we can do to make our books stronger.

Please note that I cannot help you with technical problems related to the topic of this book, and that due to the high volume of mail I receive, I might not be able to reply to every message.

When you write, please be sure to include this book's title and author as well as your name and phone or fax number. I will carefully review your comments and share them with the author and editors who worked on the book.

Fax: 317-581-4770
E-mail: feedback@samspublishing.com
Mail: Jeff Koch
          Associate Publisher
          Sams Publishing
          201 West 103rd Street
          Indianapolis, IN 46290 USA

Introduction

Welcome to the third edition of *Sams Teach Yourself Unix in 24 Hours*! This book has been designed to be helpful as a guide as well as a tutorial for both beginning users and those with previous Unix experience. The reader of this book is assumed to be intelligent, but no familiarity with Unix is expected or required.

Does Each Chapter Take an Hour?

You can learn the concepts in each of the 24 lessons in one hour. If you want to experiment with what you learn in each lesson, you might take longer than an hour. However, all the concepts presented here are straightforward. If you are familiar with Windows applications or the Macintosh, you will be able to progress more quickly through the lessons.

What If I Take Longer Than 24 Hours?

Since the publication of the first edition of this book, I've received a considerable amount of praise and positive feedback, but the one message that has always been a surprise is "I finished your book, but it took me a lot longer than 24 hours." Now you can read here, direct from the author: It's okay! Take your time and make sure you try everything as you go along. Learning and remembering is more important than speed. And if you do finish it all in 24 hours, let me know!

How to Use This Book

This book is designed to teach you topics in one-hour lessons. All the books in the *Sams Teach Yourself* series enable you to start working and become productive with the product as quickly as possible. This book will do that for you!

Each hour, or lesson, starts with an overview of the topic to inform you of what to expect in that lesson. The overview helps you determine the nature of the lesson and whether the lesson is relevant to your needs.

Main Section

Each lesson has a main section that discusses the lesson topic in a clear, concise manner by breaking the topic down into logical components and explaining each component clearly.

Interspersed in each lesson are special elements, called Notes, Tips, and Cautions, to provide additional information.

Notes are designed to clarify the concept that is being discussed. They elaborate on the subject, and if you are comfortable with your understanding of the subject, you can bypass them without danger.

Tips inform you of tricks or elements that are easily missed by most computer users. You can skip them, but often Tips show you an easier way to do a task.

A Caution deserves at least as much attention as a Tip because Cautions point out a problematic element of the topic being discussed. Ignoring the information contained in the Caution could have adverse effects on the task at hand. These are the most important special elements in this book.

Tasks

This book offers another special element called a Task. These step-by-step exercises are designed to walk you quickly through the most important skills you can learn in Unix. Each Task has three parts: Description, Action, and Summary.

Workshops

The Workshop section at the end of each lesson provides Key Terms and Exercises that reinforce concepts you learned in the lesson and help you apply them in new situations. You can skip this section, but we recommend that you go through the exercises to see how the concepts can be applied to other common tasks. The Key Terms also are compiled in one alphabetized list in the Glossary at the end of the book.

HOUR 1

What Is This Unix Stuff?

Welcome to *Sams Teach Yourself Unix in 24 Hours, Third Edition!* This hour starts you toward becoming a Unix expert. Our goal for the first hour is to introduce you to some history of Unix and teach you where to find help online.

Goals for This Hour

In the first hour, you will learn

- The history of Unix
- Why it's called Unix
- What multiuser systems are all about
- The difference between Unix and other operating systems
- About command-line interpreters and how users interact with Unix
- How to use man pages, Unix's online reference material
- Other ways to find help in Unix

What Is Unix?

Unix is a computer operating system, a control program that works with users to run programs, manage resources, and communicate with other computer systems. Several people can use a Unix computer at the same time; hence Unix is called a *multiuser* system. Any of these users can also run multiple programs at the same time; hence Unix is called *multitasking*. Because Unix is such a pastiche—a patchwork of development—it's a lot more than just an operating system. Unix has more than 250 individual commands. These range from simple commands for copying a file, for example, to the quite complex: those used in high-speed networking, file-revision management, and software development.

Most notably, Unix is a multichoice system. As an example, Unix has three different primary command-line–based user interfaces (in Unix, the command-line user interface is called a *shell*): the Bourne shell, the C shell_, and the Korn shell. In addition, a number of graphical interfaces exist too, including Motif, OpenLook, and Gnome. Often, soon after you learn to accomplish a task with a particular command, you discover a second or third way to do that task. This is simultaneously the greatest strength of Unix and a source of frustration for both new and current users.

Why are all these choices such a big deal? Think about why Microsoft Windows and the Apple Macintosh interfaces are considered so easy to use. Both are designed to give the user less power. Both have dramatically fewer commands and precious little overlap in commands: You can't click a button and find out how many of your Windows files are over a certain size, and you can't drag a Mac file icon around to duplicate it in its own directory. The advantage to these interfaces is that, in either system, you can learn the one-and-only way to do a task and be confident that you're as sophisticated in doing that task as the next person is. It's easy. It's quick to learn. It's exactly how the experts do it, too.

Unix, by contrast, is much more like a spoken language, with commands acting as verbs, command options (which you learn about later in this lesson) acting as adjectives, and the more complex command sequences acting akin to sentences. How you do a specific task can, therefore, be completely different from how your Unix-expert friend does the same task. Worse, some specific commands in Unix have many different versions, partly because of the variations from different Unix vendors. (You've heard of these variations and vendors, I'll bet: Linux from Red Hat [and many others], Solaris from Sun, System V Release 4 [pronounce that "system five release four" or, to sound like an ace, "ess-vee-are-four"], and BSD Unix [pronounced "bee-ess-dee"] from the University of California at Berkeley, HP-UX from Hewlett-Packard, and AIX from International Business Machines, are some of the primary players. Each is a little different from the others.)

1

Another contributor to the sprawl of modern Unix is the energy of the Unix programming community; plenty of Unix users decide to write a new version of a command to solve slightly different problems, thus spawning many versions of a command.

Given the multichoice nature of Unix, I promise to teach you the most popular Unix commands, and, if alternatives exist, I will teach you about those too. The goal of this book is for you to learn Unix and to be able to work alongside longtime Unix folk as a peer, sharing your expertise with them and continuing to learn about the system and its commands from them and from other sources.

> I must admit that I too am guilty of rewriting various Unix commands, including those for an electronic mail system, a simple line-oriented editor, a text formatter, a programming language interpreter, a calendar manager, and even slightly different versions of the file-listing command ls and the remove-files command rm. As a programmer, I found that trying to duplicate the functionality of a particular command or utility was a wonderful way to learn more about Unix and programming.

A Brief History of Unix

To understand why the Unix operating system has so many commands and why it's not only the premier multiuser, multitasking operating system, but also the most successful and the most powerful multichoice system for computers, you'll have to travel back in time. You'll need to learn where Unix was designed, the goals of the original programmers, and what has happened to Unix in the subsequent decades.

Unlike DOS, Windows, OS/2, the Macintosh, NT, VMS, MVS, and just about any other operating system, Unix was designed by a couple of programmers as a fun project. It evolved through the efforts of hundreds of programmers, each of whom was exploring their own ideas of particular aspects of OS design and user interaction. In this regard, Unix is not like other operating systems, needless to say!

It all started back in the late 1960s in a dark and stormy laboratory deep in the recesses of the American Telephone and Telegraph (AT&T) corporate facility in New Jersey. Working with the Massachusetts Institute of Technology, AT&T Bell Labs was co-developing a massive, monolithic operating system called Multics. On the Bell Labs team were Ken Thompson, Dennis Ritchie, Brian Kernighan, and other people in the Computer Science Research Group who would prove to be key contributors to the new Unix operating system.

When 1969 rolled around, Bell Labs was becoming increasingly disillusioned with Multics, an overly slow and expensive system that ran on General Electric mainframe computers that themselves were expensive to run and rapidly becoming obsolete. The problem was that Thompson and the group really liked the capabilities that Multics offered, particularly the individual-user environment and multiple-user aspects.

In that same year, Thompson wrote a computer game called Space Travel, first on Multics, then on the GECOS (GE computer operating system). The game was a simulation of the movement of the major bodies of the solar system, with the player guiding a ship, observing the scenery, and attempting to land on the various planets and moons. The game wasn't much fun on the GE computer, however, because performance was jerky and irregular, and, more importantly, it cost almost $100 in computing time for each game.

In his quest to improve the game, Thompson found a little-used Digital Equipment Corporation PDP-7, and with some help from Ritchie, he rewrote the game for the PDP-7. Development was done on the GE mainframe and hand-carried to the PDP-7 on paper tape.

After he'd explored some of the capabilities of the PDP-7, Thompson couldn't resist building on the game, starting with an implementation of an earlier file system he'd designed, and then adding processes, simple file utilities (cp, mv), and a command interpreter that he called a *shell*. It wasn't until the following year that the newly created system acquired its name, Unix, which Brian Kernighan suggested as a pun on Multics.

The Thompson file system was built around the low-level concept of *i-nodes*, linked blocks of information that together compose the contents of a file or program. These i-nodes were kept in a list called the *i-list*, subdirectories, and special types of files that described devices and acted as the actual device driver for user interaction. What was missing in this earliest form of Unix were *pathnames*. No slash (/) was present, and subdirectories were referenced through a confusing combination of file links that proved too complex, causing users to stop using subdirectories. Another limitation in this early version was that directories couldn't be added while the system was running but had to be added to the pre-load configuration.

In 1970, Thompson's group requested and received a Digital PDP-11 system for the purpose of creating a system for editing and formatting text. It was such an early unit that the first disk did not arrive at Bell Labs until four months after the CPU showed up. The first important program on Unix was the text-formatting program roff, which—keep with me now—was inspired by McIlroy's BCPL program on Multics, which in turn had been inspired by an earlier program called runoff on the CTSS operating system.

The initial customer was the Patent Department inside the Labs, a group that needed a system for preparing patent applications. There, Unix was a dramatic success, and it didn't take long for others inside Bell Labs to begin clamoring for their own Unix computer systems.

The C Programming Language

Now that you've learned some history about Unix, let's talk a bit about the C programming language, the programming language that is integral to the Unix system.

In 1969, the original Unix had a very low-level assembly language compiler available for writing programs; all the PDP-7 work was done in this primitive language. Just before the PDP-11 arrived, McIlroy ported a language called TMG to the PDP-7, which Thompson then tried to use to write a FORTRAN compiler. That didn't work, and instead he produced a language called B. Two years later, in 1971, Ritchie created the first version of a new programming language based on B, a language he called C. By 1973, the entire Unix system had been rewritten in C for portability and speed.

Unix Becomes Popular

In the 1970s, AT&T hadn't yet been split up into the many regional operating companies known today, and the company was prohibited from selling the new Unix system. Hoping for the best, Bell Labs distributed Unix to colleges and universities for a nominal charge. These institutions also were happily buying the inexpensive and powerful PDP-11 computer systems—a perfect match. Before long, Unix was the research and software-development operating system of choice.

The Unix of today is not, however, the product of a couple of inspired programmers at Bell Labs. Many other organizations and institutions contributed significant additions to the system as it evolved from its early beginnings and grew into the monster it is today. Most important were the C shell, TCP/IP networking, vi editor, Berkeley Fast File System, and sendmail electronic mail-routing software from the Computer Science Research Group of the University of California at Berkeley. Also important were the early versions of UUCP and Usenet from the University of Maryland, University of Delaware, and Duke University. After dropping Multics development completely, MIT didn't come into the Unix picture until the early 1980s, when it developed the X Window System as part of its successful Athena project. Ten years and four releases later, X is the predominant windowing system standard on all Unix systems, and it is the basis of Gnome, Motif, OpenWindows, and Open Desktop.

Gradually, large corporations have become directly involved with the evolutionary process, notably Hewlett-Packard, Sun Microsystems, and Digital Equipment

Corporation. Smaller companies have started to get into the action, too, with Unix available from Apple for the Macintosh (it's the underpinning of Mac OS X) and from Red Hat, Debian, and many other vendors for PCs.

Today, Unix runs on all sizes of computers, from humble PC laptops to powerful desktop-visualization workstations, and even to supercomputers that require special cooling fluids to prevent them from burning up while working. It's a long way from Space Travel, a game that, ironically, isn't part of Unix anymore.

What's All This About Multiuser Systems?

Among the many *multi* words you learned earlier was one that directly concerns how you interact with the computer: multiuser. The goal of a multiuser system is for all users to feel as though they've been given their own personal computer, their own individual Unix system, although they actually are working within a large system. To accomplish this, each user is given an *account*—usually based on the person's last name, his initials, or another unique naming scheme—and a home directory, the default place where his files are saved. This leads to a bit of a puzzle: When you're working on the system, how does the system know that you're you? What's to stop someone else from masquerading as you, going into your files, prying into private letters, altering memos, or worse?

On a Macintosh or PC, anyone can walk up to your computer when you're not around, flip the power switch, and pry, and you can't do much about it. You can add some security software, but security isn't a fundamental part of the system, which results in an awkward fit between system and software. For a computer sitting on your desk in your office, though, that's okay; the system is not a shared multiuser system, so verifying who you are when you turn on the computer isn't critical. If you have that computer attached to a network, you might have it configured to prompt for a password before you can get to your desktop.

But Unix is a system designed for multiple users, so it is very important that the system can confirm your identity in a manner that precludes others from masquerading as you. As a result, all accounts have passwords associated with them—as with a PIN for a bank card, keep it a secret!—and when you use your password in combination with your account, the computer can be pretty sure that you are who you're claiming to be. For obvious reasons, when you're finished using the computer, you always should remember to end your session, or, in effect, to turn off your virtual personal computer when you're done.

In the next hour, you learn your first Unix commands. At the top of the list are commands to log in to the system, enter your password, and change your password to be memorable and highly secure.

Cracking Open the Shell

Another unusual feature of Unix systems, especially for those of you who come from either the Macintosh or the Windows environments, is that Unix is designed to be a command-line–based system rather than a more graphically based (picture-oriented) system. That's a mixed blessing. It makes Unix harder to learn, but the system is considerably more powerful than fiddling with a mouse to drag little pictures about on the screen. In Unix parlance, a command-line interpreter is called a shell, and you'll see that various shells are available, differing in both syntax and capabilities.

Graphical interfaces to Unix are built within the X Window System environment. Notable ones are Motif, OpenWindows, Gnome, and Open Desktop. Even with the best of these, however, the command-line heart of Unix still shines through, and in my experience, it's impossible really to use all the power that Unix offers without turning to a shell.

If you're used to writing letters to your friends and family or even mere shopping lists, you won't have any problem with a command-line interface: It's a command program that you tell what to do. When you type specific instructions and press the Enter key, the computer leaps into action and immediately performs whatever command you've specified, even if it's dangerous, such as the command sequence that requests the system to "remove all my files."

> Throughout this book, I refer to pressing the Return key, but your keyboard might have this key labeled as "Enter" or marked with a left-pointing, specially shaped arrow. These all mean the same thing.

In Windows, you might move a file from one folder to another by opening the folder, opening the destination folder, fiddling around for a while to be sure that you can see both folders onscreen at the same time, and then clicking and dragging the specific file from one place to the other. In Unix it's much easier: Typing the following simple command does the trick:

```
cp folder1/file folder2
```

This command automatically ensures the file has the same name in the destination directory also.

This might not seem much of a boon, but imagine the situation where you want to move all files with names that start with the word project or end with the suffix .c (C program files). This could be quite tricky and could take a lot of patience with a graphical interface. Unix, however, makes it easy:

```
cp project* *.c folder2
```

Soon you not only will understand this command, but also will be able to compose your own examples!

Getting Help

Throughout this book, the focus is on the most important and valuable flags and options for the commands covered. That's all well and good, but how do you find out about the other alternatives that might actually work better for your use? That's where the Unix *man pages* come in. You will learn how to browse them to find the information desired.

Task 1.1: Man Pages, Unix Online Reference

DESCRIPTION It's not news to you that Unix is a very complex operating system, with hundreds of commands that can be combined to execute thousands of possible actions. Most commands have a considerable number of options, and all seem to have some subtlety or other that it's important to know. But how do you figure all this out? You need to look up commands in the Unix online documentation set. Containing purely reference materials, the Unix *man pages* (*man* is short for *manual*) cover every command available.

To search for a man page, enter man followed by the name of the command to find. Many sites also have a table of contents for the man pages (it's called a whatis database, for obscure historical reasons). You can use the all-important -k flag for keyword searches to find the name of a command if you know what it should do but you just can't remember what it's called. The -k option will give you a list of manual pages that refer to the keyword you specify.

A *flag* or *switch* is a command-line option, an option that changes the behavior of the command you're using. In this instance, man displays the man page for the specified command, but if you modify its behavior with the -k flag, it instead searches the command documentation database to identify which subsets relate to the keyword you've specified. We'll use the word *flag* to denote these command line options throughout the book.

A command performs a basic task, which can be modified by adding flags to the end of the command when you enter it on the command line. These flags are described in the man pages. For example, to use the -k flag for man, enter this:

% **man -k**

The command apropos is available on most Unix systems and is often just an alias to man -k. If it's not on your system, you can create it by adding the line alias apropos='man -k \!' to your .profile file.

The Unix man pages are organized into nine sections, as shown in Table 1.1. This table is organized for System V, but it generally holds true for Linux and Berkeley systems too, with these few changes: BSD has I/O and special files in Section 4, administrative files in Section 5, and miscellaneous files in Section 7. Some BSD systems also split user commands into further categories: Section 1C for intersystem communications and Section 1G for commands used primarily for graphics and computer-aided design. Man pages in different sections might have the same name, so you might need to specify in which section to find the page. In addition, sometimes you'll be looking for a user-level command and find a match in section 2 or 3. Those aren't what you seek; they're specifically for Unix programmers, as you can see in the table.

TABLE 1.1   System V Unix Man Page Organization

Section	Category
1	User commands
1M	System maintenance commands
2	System calls
3	Library routines
4	Administrative files
5	Miscellaneous
6	Games
7	I/O and special files
8	Administrative commands

ACTION

1. The mkdir man page is succinct and exemplary:

   % **man mkdir**

   ```
   MKDIR(1)                FreeBSD General Commands Manual
   MKDIR(1)

   NAME
        mkdir - make directories

   SYNOPSIS
        mkdir [-p] [-m mode] directory_name ...

   DESCRIPTION
        Mkdir creates the directories named as operands, in the order
   ➥specified,
        using mode rwxrwxrwx (0777) as modified by the current umask(2).

        The options are as follows:

        -m      Set the file permission bits of the final created directory to
                the specified mode.  The mode argument can be in any of the
   ➥for-
                mats specified to the chmod(1) command.  If a symbolic mode is
                specified, the operation characters ``+'' and ``-'' are inter-
                preted relative to an initial mode of ``a=rwx''.

        -p      Create intermediate directories as required.  If this option
   ➥is
                not specified, the full path prefix of each operand must
   ➥already
                exist.  Intermediate directories are created with permission
   ➥bits
                of rwxrwxrwx (0777) as modified by the current umask, plus
   ➥write
                and search permission for the owner.

        The user must have write permission in the parent directory.

   DIAGNOSTICS
        The mkdir utility exits 0 on success, and >0 if an error occurs.

   SEE ALSO
        rmdir(1)

   STANDARDS
        The mkdir utility is expected to be IEEE Std1003.2 (``POSIX.2'')
   ```

```
compatible.

HISTORY
      A mkdir command appeared in Version 1 AT&T UNIX.

BSD                              January 25, 1994
1
%
```

> Notice in the example that in the first line, the command itself is in boldface type, but everything else is not bold. Throughout this book, whenever an example contains both user input and Unix output, the user input will be bold so that you can spot easily what you are supposed to enter.

The very first line of the output tells me that it's found the mkdir command in Section 1 (user commands) of the man pages, with the middle phrase, FreeBSD General Commands Manual, indicating that I'm running on a version of Unix called FreeBSD. The NAME section always details the name of the command and a one-line summary of what it does. SYNOPSIS explains how to use the command, including all possible command flags and options.

DESCRIPTION is where all the meaningful information is, and it can run on for dozens of pages, explaining how complex commands such as csh or vi work. SEE ALSO suggests other commands that are related in some way. The Revision line at the bottom is different on each version of man, and it indicates the last time, presumably, that this document was revised.

2. The same man page from a Sun workstation is quite different:

```
% man mkdir
MKDIR(1)                     USER COMMANDS                     MKDIR(1)

NAME
      mkdir - make a directory

SYNOPSIS
      mkdir [ -p ] dirname...

DESCRIPTION
      mkdir creates directories.  Standard entries, `.',  for  the
      directory itself, and `..' for its parent, are made automat-
      ically.

      The -p flag allows missing parent directories to be  created
      as needed.
```

> With the exception of the set-gid bit, the current umask(2V)
> setting determines the mode in which directories are
> created. The new directory inherits the set-gid bit of the
> parent directory. Modes may be modified after creation by
> using chmod(1V).
>
> mkdir requires write permission in the parent directory.
>
> SEE ALSO
>   chmod(1V), rm(1), mkdir(2V), umask(2V)
>
> Sun Release 4.1   Last change: 22 August 1989   1
> %

Notice that a flag is in the FreeBSD version of mkdir that isn't in this version of
the SunOS command: the -m flag. More importantly, note that the flag is shown in
square brackets within the SYNOPSIS section. By convention, square brackets in this
section mean that the flag is optional. From the SEE ALSO section, you can see that
the engineers at Sun have a very different idea about what other commands might
be worth viewing!

3. One thing I always forget on Sun systems is the command that lets me format a
   floppy disk. That's exactly where the apropos command comes in handy:

```
% apropos floppy
fd (4S)                 - disk driver for Floppy Disk Controllers
%
```

That's not quite what I want, unfortunately. Because it's in Section 4 (note that the
word in parentheses is 4S, not 1), this document will describe the disk driver rather
than any command to work with floppy disks.

I can look up the disk command instead:

```
% man -k disk
acctdisk, acctdusg, accton, acctwtmp (8)    - overview of accounting
➥and miscellaneous accounting
 commands
add_client (8)           - create a diskless network bootable NFS
➥client on a server
chargefee, ckpacct, dodisk, lastlogin, monacct, nulladm, prctmp,
➥prdaily,prtacct, runacct, shutacct, startup, turnacct (8) - shell
➥procedures for accounting
client (8)               - add or remove diskless Sun386i systems
df (1V)                  - report free disk space on file systems
diskusg (8)              - generate disk accounting data by user
dkctl (8)                - control special disk operations
dkinfo (8)               - report information about a disk's geometry and
➥partitioning
dkio (4S)                - generic disk control operations
du (1L)                  - summarize disk usage
```

```
du (1V)                   - display the number of disk blocks used per
➥directory or file
fastboot, fasthalt (8)    - reboot/halt the system while disabling disk
➥checking
fd (4S)                   - disk driver for Floppy Disk Controllers
fdformat (1)              - format diskettes for use with SunOS
format (8S)               - disk partitioning and maintenance utility
fsync (2)                 - synchronize a file's in-core state with
➥that on disk
fusage (8)                - RFS disk access profiler
id (4S)                   - disk driver for IPI disk controllers
installboot (8S)          - install bootblocks in a disk partition
pnpboot, pnp.s386 (8C)    - pnp diskless boot service
quota (1)                 - display a user's disk quota and usage
quotactl (2)              - manipulate disk quotas
root (4S)                 - pseudo-driver for Sun386i root disk
sd (4S)                   - driver for SCSI disk devices
sync (1)                  - update the super block; force changed
➥blocks to the disk
xd (4S)                   - Disk driver for Xylogics 7053 SMD Disk
[ic:cc]Controller
xy (4S)                   - Disk driver for Xylogics 450 and 451 SMD
➥Disk Controllers
%
```

Notice the ➥ character at the beginning of some of the lines in this example. This character does not appear on your screen. It's a typographical convention used in the book because the number of characters that can be
displayed by Unix on a line of your screen is greater than the number of
characters that can appear (legibly) on a line in this book. The ➥ indicates
that the text following it is actually part of the preceding line on your
screen.

This yields quite a few choices! To trim the list down to just those that are in
Section 1 (the user commands section), I use an output stream filter called grep—
you'll learn more about grep in chapter five.

```
% man -k disk | grep '(1'
df (1V)                   - report free disk space on file systems
du (1L)                   - summarize disk usage
du (1V)                   - display the number of disk blocks used per
➥directory or file
fdformat (1)              - format diskettes for use with SunOS
quota (1)                 - display a user's disk quota and usage
sync (1)                  - update the super block; force changed
➥blocks to the disk
%
```

That's better! The command I was looking for is fdformat.

4. To learn a succinct snippet of information about a Unix command, you can check to see whether your system has the whatis utility. You can even ask it to describe itself (a bit of a philosophical conundrum):

```
% whatis whatis
whatis (1)               - display a one-line summary about a keyword
%
```

In fact, this is the line from the NAME field of the relevant man page. The whatis command is different from the apropos command because it considers only command names rather than all words in the command description line:

```
% whatis cd
cd (1)                   - change working directory
%
```

Now see what apropos does:

```
% apropos cd
bcd, ppt (6)             - convert to antique media
cd (1)                   - change working directory
cdplayer (6)             - CD-ROM audio demo program
cdromio (4S)             - CDROM control operations
draw, bdraw, cdraw (6)   - interactive graphics drawing
fcdcmd, fcd (1)          - change client's current working directory
➥in the FSP database
getacinfo, getacdir, getacflg, getacmin, setac, endac (3)   - get
➥audit control file information
ipallocd (8C)            - Ethernet-to-IP address allocator
mp, madd, msub, mult, mdiv, mcmp, min, mout, pow, gcd, rpow, itom,
➥xtom, mtox, mfree (3X)   - multiple precision integer arithmetic
rexecd, in.rexecd (8C)   - remote execution server
sccs-cdc, cdc (1)        - change the delta commentary of an SCCS
➥delta
sr (4S)                  - driver for CDROM SCSI controller
termios, tcgetattr, tcsetattr, tcsendbreak, tcdrain, tcflush, tcflow,
➥cfgetospeed, cfgetispeed, cfsetispeed, cfsetospeed (3V) - get and
➥set terminal attributes, line control, get and set baud rate, get
➥and set terminal foreground process group ID
tin, rtin, cdtin, tind (1)   - A threaded Netnews reader
uid_allocd, gid_allocd (8C)   - UID and GID allocator daemons
%
```

5. One problem with man is that it really isn't too sophisticated. As you can see in the example in step 4, apropos (which, recall, is man -k) lists a line more than once if more than one man page matches the specified pattern. You can create your own apropos alias to improve the command:

```
% alias apropos="man -k \!* | uniq"
% apropos cd
bcd, ppt (6)             - convert to antique media
```

```
cd (1)                        - change working directory
cdplayer (6)                  - CD-ROM audio demo program
cdromio (4S)                  - CDROM control operations
draw, bdraw, cdraw (6)        - interactive graphics drawing
fcdcmd, fcd (1)               - change client's current working directory
⇒in the FSP database
getacinfo, getacdir, getacflg, getacmin, setac, endac (3)    - get
⇒audit control file information
ipallocd (8C)                 - Ethernet-to-IP address allocator
mp, madd, msub, mult, mdiv, mcmp, min, mout, pow, gcd, rpow, itom,
⇒xtom, mtox, mfree (3X)     - multiple precision integer arithmetic
rexecd, in.rexecd (8C)  - remote execution server
sccs-cdc, cdc (1)             - change the delta commentary of an SCCS
⇒delta
sr (4S)                       - driver for CDROM SCSI controller
termios, tcgetattr, tcsetattr, tcsendbreak, tcdrain, tcflush, tcflow,
⇒cfgetospeed, cfgetispeed, cfsetispeed, cfsetospeed (3V) - get and
⇒set terminal attributes, line control, get and set baud rate, get
⇒and set terminal foreground process group ID
tin, rtin, cdtin, tind (1)  - A threaded Netnews reader
uid_allocd, gid_allocd (8C)  - UID and GID allocator daemons
%
```

That's better, but I'd like to have the command tell me about only user commands because I don't care much about file formats, games, or miscellaneous commands when I'm looking for a command. I'll try this:

```
% alias apropos="man -k \!* | uniq | grep 1"
% apropos cd
cd (1)                        - change working directory
fcdcmd, fcd (1)               - change client's current working directory
⇒in the FSP database
sccs-cdc, cdc (1)             - change the delta commentary of an SCCS
⇒delta
tin, rtin, cdtin, tind (1)  - A threaded Netnews reader
%
```

That's much better.

6. I'd like to look up one more command—sort—before I'm done here.

```
% man sort

SORT(1)                                                       SORT(1)


NAME
      sort - sort lines of text files

SYNOPSIS
      sort  [-cmus] [-t separator] [-o output-file] [-T tempdir]
```

```
[-bdfiMnr] [+POS1 [-POS2]] [-k POS1[,POS2]] [file...]
sort {--help,--version}
```

DESCRIPTION
      This manual page documents the GNU version of sort. sort
      sorts, merges, or compares all the lines from the given
      files, or the standard input if no files are given.   A
      file name of `-' means standard input. By default, sort
      writes the results to the standard output.

      sort has three modes of operation: sort (the default),
      merge, and check for sortedness. The following options
      change the operation mode:

    -c   Check whether the given files are already sorted:
           if they are not all sorted, print an error message
           and exit with a status of 1.

    -m   Merge the given files by sorting them as a group.
           Each input file should already be individually
           sorted. It always works to sort instead of merge;
           merging is provided because it is faster, in the
           case where it works.

      A pair of lines is compared as follows: if any key fields
      have been specified, sort compares each pair of fields, in
      the order specified on the command line, according to the
      associated ordering options, until a difference is found
      or no fields are left.
--More-- _

On almost every system, the man command feeds output through a program so that information won't scroll by faster than you can read it. You also can save the output of a man command to a file if you'd like to study the information in detail.

Notice in the sort man page that many options exist to the sort command (certainly more than discussed in this book). As you learn Unix, if you find areas about which you'd like more information, or if you need a capability that doesn't seem to be available, check the man page. There just might be a flag for what you seek.

You can obtain lots of valuable information by reading the introduction to each section of the man pages. Use man 1 intro to read the introduction to Section 1, for example.

If your version of man doesn't stop at the bottom of each page, you can remedy the situation using alias man='man \!* | more'.

SUMMARY Unix was one of the very first operating systems to include online documentation. The man pages are an invaluable reference. Most of them are poorly written, unfortunately, and precious few include examples of actual usage. However, as a quick reminder of flags and options, or as an easy way to find out the capabilities of a command, `man` is great. I encourage you to explore the man pages and perhaps even read the man page on the `man` command itself.

Task 1.2: Other Ways to Find Help in Unix

DESCRIPTION Reading the man pages is really the best way to learn about what's going on with Unix commands, but some alternatives also can prove helpful. Some systems have a `help` command. Many Unix utilities make information available with the `-h`, `-help` or `-?` flag too. Finally, one trick you can try is to feed a set of gibberish flags to a command, which sometimes generates an error and a helpful message reminding you of what possible options the command accepts.

ACTION

1. At the University Tech Computing Center, the support team has installed a `help` command:

```
% help
Look in a printed manual, if you can, for general help. You should
➥have  someone show you some things and then read one of the tutorial
papers
(e.g., UNIX for Beginners or An Introduction to the C Shell) to get
started. Printed manuals covering all aspects of Unix are on sale at the
bookstore.

Most of the material in the printed manuals is also available online
via "man" and similar commands; for instance:

apropos keyword - lists commands relevant to keyword
whatis filename - lists commands involving filename
man command - prints out the manual entry for a command
help command - prints out the pocket guide entry for a command
➥are helpful; other basic commands are:
cat - display a file on the screen
date - print the date and time
du - summarize disk space usage
edit - text editor (beginner)
ex - text editor (intermediate)
finger - user information lookup program
learn - interactive self-paced tutorial on Unix
--More(40%)-- _
```

Your system might have something similar. However, be careful if you're running on an HP-UX system, as its help command isn't intended to enlighten shell users.

2. Some commands offer helpful output if you specify the -h flag:

```
% ls -h
usage: ls [ -acdfgilqrstu1ACLFR ] name ...
%
```

Then again, others don't:

```
% ls -h
Global.Software   Mail/       Src/        history.usenet.Z
Interactive.Unix  News/       bin/        testme
%
```

A few commands offer lots of output when you use the -h flag:

```
% elm -h
Possible Starting Arguments for ELM program:
arg     Meaning
-a      Arrow - use the arrow pointer regardless
-c      Checkalias - check the given aliases only
-dn     Debug - set debug level to 'n'
-fx     Folder - read folder 'x' rather than incoming mailbox
-h      Help - give this list of options
-k      Keypad - enable HP 2622 terminal keyboard
-K      Keypad&softkeys - enable use of softkeys + "-k"
-m      Menu - Turn off menu, using more of the screen
-sx     Subject 'x' - for batchmailing
-V      Enable sendmail voyeur mode.
-v      Print out ELM version information.
-w      Supress warning messages...
-z      Zero - don't enter ELM if no mail is pending
%
```

Unfortunately, there isn't a command flag common to all Unix utilities that lists the possible command flags.

3. Sometimes you can obtain help from a program by incurring its wrath. You can specify a set of flags that are impossible, unavailable, or just plain puzzling. I always use -xyz because they're uncommon flags:

```
% man -xyz
man: unknown option `-x', use `-h' for help
```

Okay, I'll try it:

```
% man -h
man: usage [-S | -t | -w] [-ac] [-m path] [-M path] [section] pages
man: usage -k [-ac] [-m path] [-M path] [section] keywords
man: usage -f [-ac] [-m path] [-M path] [section] names
man: usage -h
man: usage -V
```

```
a          display all manpages for names
c          cat (rather than page) manual pages
f          find whatis entries for pages by these names
names      names to search for in whatis
h          print this help message
k          find whatis entries by keywords
keywords   keywords to search for in whatis
m path     add to the standard man path directories
M path     override standard man path directories
S          display only SYNOPSIS section of pages
t          find the source (rather than the formatted page)
V          show version information
w          only output which pages we would display
section    section for the manual to search
pages      pages to locate
%
```

For every command that does something marginally helpful, there are a half-dozen commands that give useless, and amusingly different, output for these flags:

```
% bc -xyz
unrecognizable argument
% cal -xyz
Bad argument
% file -xyz
-xyz:   No such file or directory
% grep -xyz
grep: unknown flag
%
```

You can't rely on programs being helpful about them, but you can rely on the man page being available for just about everything on the system.

SUMMARY As much as I'd like to tell you that a wide variety of useful and interesting information is available within Unix on the commands therein, in reality, Unix has man pages but precious little else. Furthermore, some commands installed locally might not even have man page entries, which leaves you to puzzle out how they work. If you encounter commands that are undocumented, I recommend that you ask your system administrator or vendor what's going on and why there's no further information on the program.

Some vendors are addressing this problem in innovative, if somewhat limited, ways. Sun Microsystems, for example, offers its complete documentation set, including all tutorials, user guides, and man pages, on a single CD-ROM. AnswerBook, as it's called, is helpful, but has some limitations, not the least of which is that you must have a CD-ROM drive and keep the disc in the drive at all times.

Summary

In this first hour, the goal was for you to learn a bit about Unix, where it came from, and how it differs from other operating systems that you might have used in the past. You also learned about the need for security on a multiuser system and how a password helps maintain that security, so that your files aren't easily read, altered, or removed by anyone but you.

You also learned what a command shell, or command-line interpreter, is all about, how it differs from graphically oriented interface systems such as the Macintosh and Windows, and how it's not only easy to use, but considerably more powerful than dragging and dropping little pictures.

Finally, you learned about getting help on Unix. Although there aren't many options, you do have the manual pages available, as well as the command-line arguments and `apropos`.

Workshop

The Workshop summarizes the key terms you learned and poses some questions about the topics presented in this chapter. It also provides you with a preview of what you will learn in the next hour.

Key Terms

account   This is the official one-word name by which the Unix system knows you. Mine is `taylor`.

arguments   Not any type of domestic dispute, arguments are the set of options and filenames specified to Unix commands. When you use a command such as `vi test.c`, all words other than the command name itself (`vi`) are arguments, or parameters to the program.

command   Each program in Unix is also known as a command: The two words are interchangeable.

i-list   See **i-node**.

i-node   The Unix file system is like a huge notebook full of sheets of information. Each file is like an index tab, indicating where the file starts in the notebook and how many sheets are used. The tabs are called i-nodes, and the list of tabs (the index to the notebook) is the i-list.

man page   Each standard Unix command comes with some basic online documentation that describes its function. This online documentation for a command is called a man page. Usually, the man page lists the command-line flags and some error conditions.

multitasking   A multitasking computer is one that actually can run more than one program, or task, at a time. By contrast, most personal computers lock you into a single program that you must exit before you launch another.

multiuser   Computers intended to have more than a single person working on them simultaneously are designed to support multiple users, hence the term *multiuser*. By contrast, personal computers are almost always single-user because someone else can't be running a program or editing a file while you are using the computer for your own work.

pathname   Unix is split into a wide variety of different directories and subdirectories, often across multiple hard disks and even multiple computers. So that the system needn't search laboriously through the entire mess each time you request a program, the set of directories you reference are stored as your search path, and the location of any specific command is known as its *pathname*.

shell   To interact with Unix, you type in commands to the command-line interpreter, which is known in Unix as the *shell*, or *command shell*. It's the underlying environment in which you work with the Unix system.

Exercises

Each hour concludes with a set of questions for you to contemplate. Here's a warning up front: Not all the questions have a definitive answer. After all, you are learning about a multichoice operating system!

1. Name the three *multi* concepts that are at the heart of Unix's power.

2. Is Unix more like a grid of streets, letting you pick your route from point A to point B, or more like a directed highway with only one option? How does this compare with other systems you've used?

3. Systems that support multiple users always ask you to say who you are when you begin using the system. What's the most important thing to remember when you're finished using the system?

4. If you're used to graphical interfaces, try to think of a few tasks that you feel are more easily accomplished by moving icons than by typing commands. Write those tasks on a separate paper, and in a few days, pull that paper out and see whether you still feel that way.

5. Think of a few instances in which you needed to give a person written instructions. Was that easier than giving spoken instructions or drawing a picture? Was it harder?

Preview of the Next Hour

In the next hour, you learn how to log in to the system at the login prompt (`login:`) and how to log out of the system. You learn how to use the `passwd` command to change your password, how to use the `id` command to find out who the computer thinks you are, and lots more!

HOUR 2

Getting onto the System and Using the Command Line

This is the second hour of Unix lessons, so it's time for you to log in to the system and try some commands. This hour focuses on learning the basics of interacting with your Unix machine.

Goals for This Hour

In this hour, you will learn how to

- Log in and log out of the system
- Change your password with the `passwd` command
- Choose a memorable and secure password
- Find out who the computer thinks you are
- Find out who else is on the system

- Find out what everyone is doing on the system
- Check the current date and time

This hour introduces many commands, so it's very important that you have a Unix system available on which you can work through all examples. Most examples have been taken from a Sun workstation running Solaris, a variant of Unix System V Release 4, and have been double-checked on a BSD-based system. Any variance between the two is noted, and if you have a Unix system available, odds are good that it's based on either AT&T System V or Berkeley Unix.

Beginning Your Session

Before you can start interacting with the Unix command shell of your choice, you'll need to learn how to log in to your account. The good news is that it's easy! Let's have a look.

Task 2.1: Logging In and Out of the System

DESCRIPTION Because Unix is a multiuser system, you need to start by finding a terminal, a computer, or some other way to access the system. I use a Macintosh and a modem to dial up various systems by telephone. You might have a similar approach, you might have a terminal directly connected to the Unix computer on your desk or in your office, or you might have the Unix system itself on your desk. Regardless of how you connect to your Unix system, the first thing you'll see on the screen will look something like this:

```
4.3BSD DYNIX (mentor.utech.edu) 5:38pm on Fri, 8 Dec 2000
login:
```

No matter how you access Unix, you will need to go through the login process. The first line indicates what variant of Unix the system is running (DYNIX is Unix on Sequent computers), the actual name of the computer system, and the current time and date. The second line asks for your login, your account name. If what you see varies from this, you'll still end up with the login: prompt where you need to type in your account name.

ACTION

1. Connect your terminal or PC to the Unix system until the point where you see a login prompt (login:) on your screen similar to that in the preceding example, using the phone and modem to dial up the computer if you need to.

   It would be nice if computers could keep track of users by simply using full names so that I could enter Dave Taylor at the login prompt. Alas, like the Internal

Revenue Service, the Department of Motor Vehicles, and many other agencies, Unix—rather than using names—assigns each user a unique identifier. This identifier is called an *account name*, has eight characters or fewer, and is usually based on the user's first or last name, although it can be any combination of letters and numbers. I have two account names, or logins, on the systems I use: `taylor` and, on another machine where someone already had that account name, `dataylor`.

2. You should know your account name on the Unix system. Perhaps your account name is on a paper with your initial password, both assigned by the Unix system administrator. If you do not have this information, you need to track it down before you can go further. Some accounts might not have an initial password; that means that you won't have to enter one the first time you log in to the system. In a few minutes, you will learn how you can give yourself the password of your choice by using a Unix command called `passwd`.

3. At the login prompt, enter your account name. *Be particularly careful to use all lowercase letters* unless specified otherwise by your administrator (for example, the accounts `taylor`, `Taylor`, and `TAYLOR` are all different to Unix).

    ```
    login: taylor
    Password:
    ```

    After you've entered your account name, the system moves the cursor to the next line and prompts you for your password. When you enter your password, the system won't echo it (that is, won't display it) on the screen. That's okay. Lack of an echo doesn't mean anything is broken; instead, this is a security measure to ensure that even if people are looking over your shoulder, they can't learn your secret password by watching your screen. Be certain to type your password correctly, because you won't see what you've typed to correct it.

4. If you enter either your login or your password incorrectly, the system complains with an error message:

    ```
    login: taylor
    Password:
    Login incorrect
    login:
    ```

Most systems give you three or four attempts to get both your login and your password correct, so try again. Don't forget to enter your account name at the login prompt each time.

5. After you've successfully entered your account name and password, you are shown some information about the system, some news for users, and an indication of whether you have electronic mail. The specifics will vary, but here's an example of what I see when I log in to my account:

```
login: taylor
Password:
Last login: Thu Dec 7 17:00:23 on ttyAe
You have mail.
%
```

> The percent sign is Unix's way of telling you that it's ready for you to enter some commands. The percent sign is the equivalent of an enlisted soldier saluting and saying, "Ready for duty!" or an employee saying, "What shall I do now, boss?"

Your system might be configured so that you have some slightly different prompt here. The possibilities include a $ for the Korn or Bourne shells, your current location in the file system, the current time, the command-index number (which you'll learn about when you learn how to teach the Unix command-line interpreter to adapt to your work style, rather than vice versa), and the name of the computer system itself. Here are some examples:

```
[/users/taylor] :
(mentor) 33 :
taylor@mentor %
```

Your prompt might not look exactly like any of these, but it has one unique characteristic: It is at the beginning of the line on which your cursor sits, and it reappears each time you've completed working with any Unix program.

6. At this point, you're ready to enter your first Unix command, exit, to sign off from the computer system. Try it. On my system, entering exit shuts down all my programs and hangs up the telephone connection. On other systems, it returns the login prompt. Many Unix systems offer a pithy quote as you leave, too.

```
% exit
He who hesitates is lost.
4.3BSD DYNIX (mentor.utech.edu) 5:38pm on Thu, 7 Dec, 2000
login:
```

You might be able to end your session by pressing Ctrl-D. Some shells will catch this and prompt you to determine whether you want to end your session; others will exit. The Ctrl-D character is actually an end-of-file character; it may be different on your system.

2

7. If you have a direct connection to the computer, odds are very good that logging out causes the system to prompt for another account name, enabling the next person to use the system. If you dialed up the system with a modem, you probably will see something more like the following example. After being disconnected, you'll be able to shut down your computer.

```
% exit
Did you lose your keys again?

DISCONNECTED
```

Unix is *case sensitive*, so the exit command is not the same as EXIT. If you enter a command all in uppercase, the system won't find it and instead will respond with the complaint command not found.

SUMMARY At this point, you've overcome the toughest part of Unix. You have an account, know the password, have logged in to the system, and have entered a simple command telling the computer what you want to do, and the computer has done it!

Task 2.2: Changing Passwords with `passwd`

DESCRIPTION Having logged in to a Unix system, you can clearly see that many differences exist between Unix and a PC or Macintosh personal computer. Certainly the style of interaction is different. With Unix command lines, the keyboard becomes the exclusive method of instructing the computer what to do, and the mouse sits idle, waiting for something to happen. One of the greatest differences is that Unix is a multiuser system, as you learned in the preceding hour. As you learn more about Unix, you'll find that this characteristic has an impact on various tasks and commands. The next Unix command you learn is one that exists because of the multiuser nature of Unix: passwd.

With the passwd command, you can change the password associated with your individual account name. As with the personal identification number (PIN) for your automated-teller machine, the value of your password is directly related to how secret it remains.

Unix is careful about the whole process of changing passwords. It requires you to enter your current password to prove you're really you. Imagine that you are at a computer center and have to leave the room to make a quick phone call. Without much effort, a prankster could lean over and quickly change your environment or even delete some critical files! That's why you should log out if you're not going to be near your system, and that's also why passwords are never echoed in Unix.

ACTION

1. Consider what happens when I use the `passwd` command to change the password associated with my account:

```
% passwd
Changing password for taylor.
Old password:
New passwd:
Retype new passwd:
%
```

2. Notice that I never received any visual confirmation that the password I actually entered was the same as the password I thought I entered. This is not as dangerous as it seems, though, because if I had made any typographical errors, the password I entered the second time (when the system said `Retype new passwd:`) wouldn't have matched the first. In a no-match situation, the system would have warned me that the information I supplied was inconsistent:

```
% passwd
Changing password for taylor.
Old password:
New passwd:
Retype new passwd:
Mismatch - password unchanged.
%
```

SUMMARY After you change the password, don't forget it. To reset it to a known value if you don't know the current password requires the assistance of a system administrator or other operator. Remembering your password can be a Catch-22, though: You don't want to write down the password because that reduces its secrecy, but you don't want to forget it, either. You want to be sure that you pick a good password, too, as described in Task 2.3.

Task 2.3: Picking a Secure Password

DESCRIPTION If you're an aficionado of old movies, you are familiar with the thrillers in which the hoods break into an office and spin the dial on the safe a few times, snicker a bit about how the boss shouldn't have chosen his daughter's birthday as the combination, and crank open the safe. (If you're really familiar with the genre, you recall films in which the criminals rifle the desk drawers and find the combination of the safe taped to the underside of a drawer as a fail-safe, or a failed safe, as the case may be. Hitchcock's great film *Marnie* has just such a scene.) The moral is that you always should choose good secret passwords or combinations and keep them secure.

For computers, security is tougher because, in less than an hour, a fast computer system can test all the words in an English dictionary against your account password. If your password is *kitten* or, worse yet, your account name, any semi-competent bad guy could be in your account and messing with your files in no time.

Many of the more modern Unix systems have some *heuristics*, or smarts, built in to the passwd command; the heuristics check to determine whether what you've entered is reasonably secure.

The tests performed typically answer these questions:

- Is the proposed password at least six characters long? (A longer password is more secure.)
- Does it have both digits and letters? (A mix of both is better.)
- Does it mix upper- and lowercase letters? (A mix is better.)
- Is it in the online dictionary? (You should avoid common words.)
- Is it a name or word associated with the account? (Dave would be a bad password for my account taylor because my full name on the system is Dave Taylor).

Some versions of the passwd program are more sophisticated, and some less, but generally these questions offer a good guideline for picking a secure password.

ACTION

1. An easy way to choose memorable and secure passwords is to think of them as small sentences rather than as a single word with some characters surrounding it. If you're a fan of Alexander Dumas and *The Three Musketeers*, then "All for one and one for all!" is a familiar cry, but it's also the basis for a couple of great passwords. Easily remembered derivations might be all4one or one4all.

2. If you've been in the service, you might have the U.S. Army jingle stuck in your head: "Be All You Can Be." It would make a great password, `ballucanb`. You might have a self-referential password: `account4me` or `MySekrit` would work. If you're ex-Vice President Dan Quayle, `1Potatoe` could be a memorable choice (`potatoe` by itself wouldn't be particularly secure because it lacks digits and lacks uppercase letters, and because it's a simple variation on a word in the online dictionary).

3. Another way to choose passwords is to find acronyms that have special meaning to you. Don't choose simple ones—remember, short ones aren't going to be secure. But, if you have always heard that "Real programmers don't eat quiche!" then `Rpdeq!` could be a complex password that you'll easily remember.

4. Many systems you use every day require numeric passwords to verify your identity, including the automated-teller machine (with its PIN), government agencies (with the Social Security number), and the Department of Motor Vehicles (your driver's license number or vehicle license). Each of these actually is a poor Unix password: It's too easy for someone to find out your license number or Social Security number.

> The important thing is that you come up with a strategy of your own for choosing a password that is both memorable and secure. Then, keep the password in your head rather than write it down.

SUMMARY Why be so paranoid? For a small Unix system that will sit on your desk in your office and won't have any other users, a high level of concern for security is, to be honest, unnecessary. As with driving a car, though, it's never too early to learn good habits. Any system that has dial-up access or direct-computer–network access—you might need to use such a system—is a likely target for delinquents who relish the intellectual challenge of breaking into an account and then altering and destroying files and programs purely for amusement.

The best way to avoid trouble is to develop good security habits now when you're first learning about Unix. Learn how to recognize what makes a good, secure password; pick one for your account; and keep it a secret.

With that in mind, log in again to your Unix system and try changing your password. First, change it to `easy` and see whether the program warns you that `easy` is too short or otherwise a poor choice. Then, try entering two different secret passwords to see whether the program notices the difference. Finally, pick a good password, using the preceding guidelines and suggestions, and change your account password to be more secure.

Seeing What's Going On Around You

You're logged in, looking at the command prompt, and ready to delve into this Unix thing. Great! Let's have a look.

Task 2.4: Who Are You?

DESCRIPTION While you're logged in to the system, you can learn a few more Unix commands, including a couple that can answer a philosophical conundrum that has bothered men and women of thought for thousands of years: Who am I?

ACTION

1. The easiest way to find out "who you are" is to enter the whoami command:

```
% whoami
taylor
%
```

Try it on your system. The command lists the account name associated with the current login.

2. Ninety-nine percent of the commands you type with Unix don't change if you modify the punctuation and spacing. With whoami, however, adding spaces to transform the statement into proper English—that is, entering who am I—dramatically changes the result. On my system, I get the following results:

```
% who am i
mentor.utech.edu!taylor      ttyp4    Feb 8 14:34
%
```

This tells me quite a bit about my identity on the computer, including the name of the computer itself, my account name, and where and when I logged in. Try the command on your system and see what results you get.

In this example, mentor is a *hostname*—the name of the computer I am logged in to—and utech.edu is the full *domain name*—the address of mentor. The exclamation point (!) separates the domain name from my account name, taylor. The ttyp4 (pronounced "tee-tee-why-pea-four") is the current communication line I'm using to access mentor, and 5 October at 2:34pm is when I logged in to mentor today.

Unix is full of oddities that are based on historical precedent. One is "tty" to describe a computer or terminal line. This comes from the earliest Unix systems in which Digital Equipment Corporation teletypewriters would be hooked up as interactive devices. The teletypewriters quickly received the nickname "tty," and all these years later, when people wouldn't dream of hooking up a teletypewriter, the line is still known as a tty line.

3. One of the most dramatic influences Unix systems have had on the computing community is the propensity for users to work together on a network, hooked up by telephone lines and modems (the predominant method until the middle to late 1980s) or by high-speed network connections to the Internet (a more common type of connection today). Regardless of the connection, however, you can see that each computer needs a unique identifier to distinguish it from others on the network. In the early days of Unix, systems had unique hostnames, but as hundreds of systems have grown into the hundreds-of-thousands, this has proved to be an unworkable solution.

4. The alternative was what's called a domain-based naming scheme, where systems are assigned unique names within specific subsets of the overall network. Consider the output that was shown in step 2, for example:

```
mentor.utech.edu!taylor     ttyp4    Feb 11 14:34
```

The computer I use is within the `.edu` domain (read the hostname and domain— `mentor.utech.edu`—from right to left), meaning that the computer is located at an educational institute. Then, within the educational institute subset of the network, `utech` is a unique descriptor, and, therefore, if other UTech universities existed, they couldn't use the same top-level domain name. Finally, `mentor` is the name of the computer itself.

5. As with learning to read addresses on envelopes, learning to read domain names can unlock much information about a computer and its location. For example, `lib.stanford.edu` is the library computer at Stanford University, and `ccgate.infoworld.com` tells you that the computer is at InfoWorld, a commercial computer site, and that its hostname is `ccgate`. You learn more about this later when you learn how to use electronic mail to communicate with people throughout the Internet.

6. Another way to find out who you are in Unix is the `id` command. The purpose of this command is to tell you what group or groups you're in and the numeric

identifier for your account name (known as your *user ID number* or *user ID*). Enter
id and see what you get. I get the following result:

```
% id
uid=211(taylor)  gid=50(users0) groups=50(users0)
%
```

> If you enter id and the computer returns a different result or indicates that
> you need to specify a filename, don't panic. On many Berkeley-derived sys-
> tems, the id command is used to obtain low-level information about files.

7. In this example, you can see that my account name is taylor and that the numeric
   equivalent, the user ID, is 211. (Here it's abbreviated as uid—pronounce it "you-
   eye-dee" to sound like a Unix expert). Just as the account name is unique on a system, so also is the user ID. Fortunately, you rarely, if ever, need to know these
   numbers, so focus on the account name and group name.

8. Next, you can see that my group ID (or gid) is 50, and that group number 50 is
   known as the users0 group. Finally, users0 is the only group to which I belong.

   On another system, I am a member of two different groups:

```
% id
uid=103(taylor) gid=10(staff) groups=10(staff),44(ftp)
%
```

   Although I have the same account name on this system (taylor), you can see that
   my user ID and group ID are both different from the earlier example. Note also
   that I'm a member of two groups: the staff group, with a group ID of 10, and the
   ftp group, with a group ID of 44.

SUMMARY Later, you learn how to set protection modes on your files so that people in your
group can read your files, but those not in your group are barred from access.
You've now learned a couple of different ways to have Unix give you some information
about your account.

Task 2.5: Finding Out What Other Users Are Logged In to the System

DESCRIPTION The next philosophical puzzle that you can solve with Unix is "Who else is
there?" The answer, however, is rather restricted, limited to only those people
currently logged in to the computer at the same time. Three commands are available to
get you this information, based on how much you'd like to learn about the other users:
users, who, and w.

1. The simplest of the commands is the `users` command, which lists the account names of all people using the system:

```
% users
david mark taylor
%
```

In this example, `david` and `mark` are also logged in to the system with me. Try this on your computer and see what other users—if any—are logged in to your computer system.

2. A command that you've encountered earlier in this hour can be used to find out who is logged on to the system, what line they're on, and how long they've been logged in. That command is `who`:

```
% who
taylor    ttyp0    Oct  8 14:10    (limbo)
david     ttyp2    Oct  4 09:08    (calliope)
mark      ttyp4    Oct  8 12:09    (dent)
%
```

Here, you can see that three people are logged in, taylor (me), david, and mark. Further, you can now see that david is logged in by connection ttyp2 and has been connected since October 4 at 9:08 a.m. He is connected from a system called calliope. You can see that mark has been connected since just after noon on October 8 on line ttyp4 and is coming from a computer called dent. Note that I have been logged in since 14:10, which is 24-hour time for 2:10 p.m. Unix doesn't always indicate a.m. or p.m.

The `user` and `who` commands can tell you who is using the system at any particular moment, but how do you find out what they're doing?

Task 2.6: What Is Everyone Doing on the Computer?

To find out what everyone else is doing, there's a third command, `w`, that serves as a combination of "Who are they?" and "What are they doing?"

1. Consider the following output from the `w` command:

```
% w
2:12pm  up 7 days,  5:28,  3 users, load average: 0.33, 0.33, 0.02
User      tty        login@  idle  JCPU  PCPU  what
taylor    ttyp0      2:10pm               2          w
```

```
david    ttyp2   Mon 9am  2:11   2:04   1:13  xfax
mark     ttyp4   12:09pm  2:03                -csh
%
```

This is a much more complex command, offering more information than either users or who. Notice that the output is broken into different areas. The first line summarizes the status of the system and, rather cryptically, the number of programs that the computer is running at one time. Finally, for each user, the output indicates the username, the tty, when the user logged in to the system, how long it's been since the user has done anything (in minutes and seconds), the combined CPU time of all jobs the user has run, and the amount of CPU time taken by the current job. The last field tells you what you wanted to know in the first place: What are the users doing?

In this example, the current time is 2:12 p.m., and the system has been up for 7 days, 5 hours, and 28 minutes. Currently 3 users are logged in, and the system is very quiet, with an average of 0.33 jobs submitted (or programs started) in the last minute; 0.33, on average, in the last 5 minutes; and 0.02 jobs in the last 15 minutes.

User taylor is the only user actively using the computer (that is, who has no idle time) and is using the w command. User david is running a program called xfax, which has gone for quite awhile without any input from the user (2 hours and 11 minutes of idle time). The program already has used 1 minute and 13 seconds of CPU time, and overall, david has used over 2 minutes of CPU time. User mark has a C shell running, -csh. (The leading dash indicates that this is the program that the computer launched automatically when mark logged in. This is akin to how the system automatically launches the Finder on a Macintosh.) User mark hasn't actually done anything yet: Notice there is no accumulated computer time for that account.

2. Now it's your turn. Try the w command on your system and see what kind of output you get. Try to interpret all the information based on the explanation here. One thing is certain: Your account should have the w command listed as what you're doing.

SUMMARY   On a multiuser Unix system, the w command gives you a quick and easy way to see what's going on.

Task 2.7: Checking the Current Date and Time

DESCRIPTION   You've learned how to orient yourself on a Unix system, and you are able now to figure out who you are, who else is on the system, and what everyone is doing. What about the current time and date?

ACTION

1. Logic suggests that `time` shows the current time, and `date` the current date; but this is Unix, and logic doesn't always apply. In fact, consider what happens when I enter `time` on my system:

```
% time
14.5u 17.0s 29:13 1% 172+217io 160pf+1w
%
```

The output is cryptic to the extreme and definitely not what you're interested in finding out. Instead, the program is showing how much user time, system time, and CPU time has been used by the command interpreter itself, broken down by input/output operations and more. (The `time` command is more useful than it looks, particularly if you're a programmer.)

2. Well, `time` didn't work, so what about `date`?

```
% date
Tue  Oct 5 15:03:41 EST 1993
%
```

That's more like it!

3. Try the `date` command on your computer and see whether the output agrees with your watch.

SUMMARY How do you think `date` keeps track of the time and date when you've turned the computer off? Does the computer know the correct time if you unplug it for a few hours? (I hope so. Almost all computers today have little batteries inside for just this purpose.)

Summary

This hour focused on giving you the skills required to log in to a Unix system, figure out who you are and what groups you're in, change your password, and log out again. You also learned how to list the other users of the system, find out what Unix commands they're using, and check the date and time.

Workshop

The Workshop summarizes the key terms you learned and poses some questions about the topics presented in this chapter. It also provides you with a preview of what you will learn in the next hour.

Key Terms

account name   This is the official one-word name by which the Unix system knows you: mine is `taylor`. (See also **account** in Hour 1, "What Is This Unix Stuff?")

domain name   Unix systems on the Internet, or any other network, are assigned a domain within which they exist. This is typically the company (for example, `sun.com` for Sun Microsystems) or institution (for example, `lsu.edu` for Louisiana State University). The domain name is always the entire host address, except the hostname itself. (See also **hostname**.)

flags   Arguments given to a Unix command that are intended to alter its behavior are called *flags*. They're always prefaced by a single dash. As an example, the command line `ls -l /tmp` has `ls` as the command itself, `-l` as the flag to the command, and `/tmp` as the argument.

heuristic   A set of well-defined steps or a procedure for accomplishing a specific task.

hostname   Unix computers all have unique names assigned by the local administration team. The computers I use are `limbo`, `well`, `netcom`, and `mentor`, for example. Enter `hostname` to see what your system is called.

login   A synonym for account name, this also can refer to the actual process of connecting to the Unix system and entering your account name and password to your account.

user ID   A synonym for account name.

Exercises

1. Why can't you have the same account name as another user? How about user ID? Can you have the same `uid` as someone else on the system?

2. Which of the following are good passwords, based on the guidelines you've learned in this hour?

foobar	4myMUM	Blk&Blu
234334	Laurie	Hi!
2cool.	rolyat	j j kim

3. Are the results of the two commands `who am i` and `whoami` different? If so, explain how. Which do you think you'd rather use when you're on a new computer?

4. List the three Unix commands to find out who is logged in to the system. Talk about the differences between the commands.

5. One of the commands in the answer to question 4 indicates how long the system has been running (in the example, it had been running for seven days). What value do you think there is for keeping track of this information?

6. If you can figure out what other people are doing on the computer, they can figure out what you're doing too. Does that bother you?

Preview of the Next Hour

The next hour focuses on the Unix hierarchical file system. You learn about how the system is organized, how it differs from Windows and Macintosh hierarchical file systems, the difference between relative and absolute filenames, and the mysterious . and .. directories. You also learn about the env, pwd, and cd commands, and the HOME and PATH environment variables.

Hour 3

Moving About the File System

This third hour focuses on the Unix hierarchical file system. You learn how the system is organized, how it differs from the Macintosh and Windows hierarchical file systems, the difference between relative and absolute filenames, and the mysterious . and .. directories. You also learn about the env, pwd, and cd commands and the HOME and PATH environment variables.

Goals for This Hour

In this hour, you will learn

- What a hierarchical file system is all about
- How the Unix file system is organized
- How Mac and PC file systems differ from Unix
- The difference between relative and absolute filenames
- About hidden files in Unix

- About the special directories . and ..
- About the env command
- About user environment variables, PATH and HOME
- How to find where you are with pwd
- How to move to another location with cd

The preceding hour introduced many Unix commands, but this hour takes a more theoretical approach, focusing on the Unix file system, how it's organized, and how you can navigate it. This hour focuses on the environment that tags along with you as you move about, particularly the HOME and PATH variables. After that is explained, you learn about the env command as an easy way to show environment variables, and you learn the pwd and cd pair of commands for moving about directly.

What a Hierarchical File System Is All About

In a nutshell, a hierarchy is a system organized by graded categorization. A familiar example is the organizational structure of a company, where workers report to supervisors and supervisors report to middle managers. Middle managers, in turn, report to senior managers, and senior managers report to vice-presidents, who report to the president of the company. Graphically, this hierarchy looks as shown in Figure 3.1.

FIGURE 3.1

A typical organizational hierarchy.

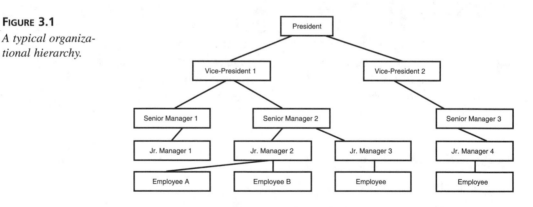

You've doubtless seen this type of illustration before, and you know that a higher position indicates more control. Each position is controlled by the next highest position or row. The president is top dog of the organization, but each subsequent manager is also in control of his or her own small fiefdom.

To understand how a file system has a similar organization, imagine each of the managers in the illustration as a file folder and each of the employees as a piece of paper, filed in a particular folder. Open any file cabinet, and you probably see things organized this way: Filed papers are placed in labeled folders, and often these folders are filed in groups under specific topics. The drawer might then have a specific label to distinguish it from other drawers in the cabinet, and so on.

That's exactly what a hierarchical file system is all about. You want to have your files located in the most appropriate place in the file system, whether at the very top, in a folder, or in a nested series of folders. With careful usage, a hierarchical file system can contain thousands of files and still allow users to find any individual file quickly.

On my computer, the chapters of this book are organized in a hierarchical fashion, as shown in Figure 3.2.

FIGURE 3.2

File organization for the chapters of Sams Teach Yourself Unix in 24 Hours, Third Edition.

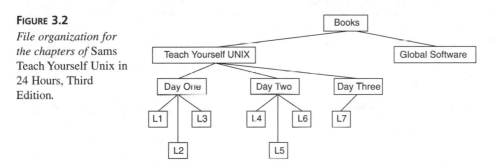

Task 3.1: The Unix File System Organization

DESCRIPTION A key concept enabling the Unix hierarchical file system to be so effective is that anything that is not a folder is a file. Programs are files in Unix, device drivers are files, documents and spreadsheets are files, your keyboard is represented as a file, your display is a file, and even your tty line and mouse are files.

What this means is that as Unix has developed, it has avoided becoming an ungainly mess. Unix does not have hundreds of cryptic files stuck at the top (this is still a problem in DOS) or tucked away in confusing folders within the System Folder (as with the Macintosh).

The top level of the Unix file structure (/) is known as the *root* directory or *slash* directory, and it always has a certain set of subdirectories, including bin, dev, etc, lib, mnt, tmp, and usr. There can be a lot more, however. The following code shows files found at the top level of the mentor file system (the system I work on). Typically, Unix directories are shown followed by a slash in the listing.

```
AA          boot        flags       rf          userb       var
OLD         core        gendynix    stand       userc
archive     dev         lib         sys         users
ats         diag        lost+found  tftpboot    usere
backup      dynix       mnt         tmp         users
bin         etc         net         usera       usr
```

You can obtain a listing of the files and directories in your own top-level directory by using the ls -F / command. (You'll learn all about the ls command in the next hour. For now, just be sure that you enter exactly what's shown in the example.)

On a different computer system, here's what I see when I enter that command:

```
% ls -F /
Mail/           export/         public/
News/           home/           reviews/
add_swap/       kadb*           sbin/
apps/           layout          sys@
archives/       lib@            tftpboot/
bin@            lost+found/     tmp/
boot            mnt/            usr/
cdrom/          net/            utilities/
chess/          news/           var/
dev/            nntpserver      vmunix*
etc/            pcfs/
```

In this example, any filename that ends with a slash (/) is a folder (Unix calls these *directories*). Any filename that ends with an asterisk (*) is a program. Anything ending with the at sign (@) is a *symbolic link*, and everything else is a normal, plain file.

As you can see from these two examples, and as you'll immediately find when you try the command yourself, there is much variation in how different Unix systems organize the top-level directory. There are some directories and files in common, and once you start examining the contents of specific directories, you'll find that hundreds of programs and files always show up in the same place from Unix to Unix.

It's as if you were working as a file clerk at a new law firm. Although this firm might have a specific approach to filing information, the approach can be similar to the filing system of other firms where you have worked in the past. If you know the underlying organization, you can quickly pick up the specifics of a particular organization.

ACTION

1. Try the command ls -F / on your computer system, and identify, as previously explained, each of the directories in your resultant listing.

The output of the previous ls command shows the files and directories in the top level of your system. Next, you learn what the commonly found directories are.

The bin Directory

In Unix parlance, programs are considered *executables* because users can execute them. (In this case, *execute* is a synonym for *run*, not an indication that you get to wander about murdering innocent applications!) When the program has been compiled, it is translated from source code into what's called a *binary* format. Add the two together, and you have a common Unix description for an application—an executable binary.

It's no surprise that the original Unix developers decided to have a directory labeled binaries to store all the executable programs on the system. Remember the primitive teletypewriter discussed earlier? Having a slow system to talk with the computer had many ramifications you might not expect. The single most obvious one was that everything became quite concise. There were no lengthy words like binaries or listfiles, but rather succinct abbreviations: bin and ls are, respectively, the Unix equivalents.

The bin directory is where all the executable binaries were kept in early Unix. Over time, as more and more executables were added to Unix, having all the executables in one place proved unmanageable, and the bin directory split into multiple parts (/bin, /sbin, /usr/bin).

The dev Directory

Among the most important portions of any computer are its device drivers. Without them, you wouldn't have any information on your screen (the information arrives courtesy of the display device driver). You wouldn't be able to enter information (the information is read and given to the system by the keyboard device driver), and you wouldn't be able to use your floppy disk drive (managed by the floppy device driver).

Remember, everything in Unix is a file. Every component of the system, from the keyboard driver to the hard disk, is a file.

Earlier, you learned how almost anything in Unix is considered a file in the file system, and the dev directory is an example. All device drivers—often numbering into the hundreds—are stored as separate files in the standard Unix dev (devices) directory. Pronounce this directory name "dev," not "dee-ee-vee."

The etc Directory

Unix administration can be quite complex, involving management of user accounts, the file system, security, device drivers, hardware configurations, and more. To help, Unix designates the etc directory as the storage place for all administrative files and information.

3

Pronounce the directory name "ee-tea-sea," "et-sea," or "etcetera." All three pronunciations are common.

The `lib` Directory

Like your own community, Unix has a central storage place for function and procedural libraries. These specific executables are included with specific programs, allowing programs to offer features and capabilities otherwise unavailable. The idea is that if programs want to include certain features, they can reference only the shared copy in the Unix library rather than having a new, unique copy.

Many of the more recent Unix systems also support what's called *dynamic linking*, where the library of functions is included on-the-fly as you start the program. The wrinkle is that instead of the library reference being resolved when the program is created, it's resolved only when you actually run the program itself.

Pronounce the directory name "libe" or "lib" (to rhyme with the word *bib*).

The `lost+found` Directory

With multiple users running many different programs simultaneously, it's been a challenge over the years to develop a file system that can remain synchronized with the activity of the computer. Various parts of the Unix *kernel*—the brains of the system—help with this problem. When files are recovered after any sort of problem or failure, they are placed here, in the `lost+found` directory, if the kernel cannot ascertain the proper location in the file system. This directory should be empty almost all the time.

This directory is commonly pronounced "lost and found" rather than "lost plus found."

The `mnt` and `sys` Directories

The `mnt` (pronounced "em-en-tea") and `sys` (pronounced "sis") directories are safely ignored by Unix users. The `mnt` directory is intended to be a common place to mount external media—hard disks, removable cartridge drives, and so on—in Unix. On many systems, though not all, `sys` contains files indicating the system configuration.

The `tmp` Directory

A directory that you can't ignore, the `tmp` directory—say "temp"—is used by many of the programs in Unix as a temporary file-storage space. If you're editing a file, for example, the editor makes a copy of the file, saves it in `tmp`, and you work directly with that, saving the new file back to your original only when you've completed your work.

On most systems, `tmp` ends up littered with various files and executables left by programs that don't remove their own temporary files. On one system I use, it's not uncommon to find 10–30 megabytes of files wasting space.

Even so, if you're manipulating files or working with copies of files, `tmp` is the best place to keep the temporary copies. Indeed, on some Unix workstations, `tmp` actually can be the fastest device on the computer, allowing for dramatic performance improvements over working with files directly in your home directory.

The usr Directory

The last of the standard directories at the top level of the Unix file system hierarchy is the `usr`—pronounced "user"—directory. Originally, this directory was intended to be the central storage place for all user-related commands. Today, however, many companies have their own interpretation, and there's no telling what you'll find in this directory.

 Standard practice is that /usr contains Unix operating-system binaries.

Other Miscellaneous Stuff at the Top Level

In addition to all the directories previously listed, various other directories and files commonly occur in Unix systems. Some files might have slight variations in name on your computer, so when you compare your listing to the following files and directories, be alert for possible alternative spellings.

A file you must have in order to bring up Unix at all is one usually called `unix` or `vmunix`, or named after the specific version of Unix on the computer. The file contains the actual Unix operating system. The file must have a specific name and must be found at the top level of the file system. Hand-in-hand with the operating system is another file called `boot`, which helps during initial startup of the hardware.

Notice on one of the previous listings that the files `boot` and `dynix` appear. (DYNIX is the name of the particular variant of Unix used on Sequent computers.) By comparison, the listing from the Sun Microsystems workstation shows `boot` and `vmunix` as the two files.

Another directory you might find in your own top-level listing is `diag`—pronounced "dye-ag"—which acts as a storehouse for diagnostic and maintenance programs. If you have any programs within this directory, it's best not to try them out without proper training!

3

The *home directory*, /home, also sometimes called *users*, is a central place for organizing all files owned by specific users. Listing this directory is usually an easy way to find out what accounts are on the system, too, because by convention each individual account directory is named after the user's account name. On one system I use, my account is taylor, and my individual account directory is also called taylor. Home directories are always created by the system administrator.

The net directory, if set up correctly, is a handy shortcut for accessing other computers on your network.

The tftpboot directory is a relatively new feature of Unix. The letters stand for "trivial file transfer protocol boot." Don't let the name confuse you, though; this directory contains versions of the kernel suitable for X Window System–based terminals and diskless workstations to run Unix.

Some Unix systems have directories named for specific types of peripherals that can be attached. On the Sun workstation, you can see examples with the directories cdrom and pcfs. The former is for a CD-ROM drive and the latter for DOS-format floppy disks.

Many more directories are in Unix, but this will give you an idea of how things are organized.

Directory Separator Characters

If you look at the organizational chart presented earlier in this hour (refer to Figure 3.1), you see that employees are identified simply as "employee" where possible. Because each has a unique path upward to the president, each has a unique identifier if all components of the path upward are specified.

For example, the rightmost of the four employees could be described as "Employee managed by Jr. Manager 4, managed by Senior Manager 3, managed by Vice-President 2, managed by the President." Using a single character, instead of "managed by," can considerably shorten the description: Employee/Jr. Manager 4/Senior Manager 3/Vice-President 2/President. Now consider the same path specified from the very top of the organization downward: President/Vice-President 2/Senior Manager 3/Jr. Manager 4/Employee.

Because only one person is at the top, that person can be safely dropped from the path without losing the uniqueness of the descriptor: /Vice-President 2/Senior Manager 3/Jr. Manager 4/Employee.

In this example, the / (pronounce it "slash") is serving as a *directory separator character*, a convenient shorthand to indicate different directories in a path.

The idea of using a single character isn't unique to Unix, but using the slash is unusual. On the Macintosh, the system uses a colon to separate directories in a pathname. (Next time you're on a Mac, try saving a file called test:file and see what happens.) DOS uses a backslash: \DOS indicates the DOS directory at the top level. The characters /tmp indicate the tmp directory at the top level of the Unix file system, and :Apps is a folder called Apps at the top of the Macintosh file system.

On the Macintosh, you rarely encounter the directory delineator because the system has a completely graphical interface. Windows also offers a similar level of freedom from having to worry about much of this complexity, although you'll still need to remember whether "A:" is your floppy disk or hard disk drive.

The Difference Between Relative and Absolute Filenames

Specifying the exact location of a file in a hierarchy to ensure that the filename is unique is known in Unix parlance as specifying its *absolute filename*. That is, regardless of where you are within the file system, the absolute filename always specifies a particular file. By contrast, relative filenames are not unique descriptors.

To understand, consider the files shown in Figure 3.3.

FIGURE 3.3

A simple hierarchy of files.

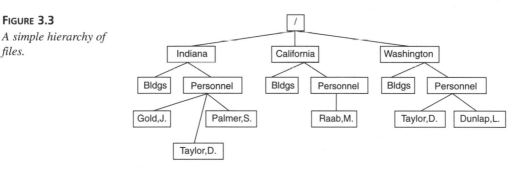

If you are currently looking at the information in the Indiana directory, Bldgs uniquely describes one file: the Bldgs file in the Indiana directory. That same name, however, refers to a different file if you are in the California or Washington directories. Similarly, the directory Personnel leaves you with three possible choices until you also specify which state you're interested in.

As a possible scenario, imagine you're reading through the Bldgs file for Washington and some people come into your office, interrupting your work. After a few minutes of talk, they comment about an entry in the `Bldgs` file in `California`. You turn to your Unix system and bring up the `Bldgs` file, and it's the wrong file. Why? You're still in the `Washington` directory.

These problems arise because of the lack of specificity of *relative filenames*. Relative filenames describe files that are referenced relative to an assumed position in the file system. In Figure 3.3, even `Personnel/Taylor,D.` isn't unique because that can be found in both `Indiana` and `Washington`.

To avoid these problems, you can apply the technique you learned earlier, specifying all elements of the directory path from the top down. To look at the `Bldgs` file for `California`, you could simply specify `/California/Bldgs`. To check the `Taylor,D.` employee in `Indiana`, you'd use `/Indiana/Personnel/Taylor,D.`, which is different, you'll notice, from `/Washington/Personnel/Taylor,D.`.

Learning the difference between these two notations is crucial to surviving the complexity of the hierarchical file system used with Unix. Without it, you'll spend half your time verifying that you are where you think you are, or, worse, not moving about at all, not taking advantage of the organizational capabilities.

If you're ever in doubt as to where you are or what file you're working with in Unix, simply specify its absolute filename. You always can differentiate between the two by looking at the very first character: If it's a slash, you've got an absolute filename (because the filename is rooted to the very top level of the file system). If you don't have a slash as the first character, the filename's a relative filename.

Earlier I told you that in the `/home` directory at the top level of Unix, I have a home directory called `taylor`. In absolute filename terms, I'd properly say that I have `/home/taylor` as a unique directory.

 To add to the confusion, most Unix people don't pronounce the slashes, particularly if the first component of the filename is a well-known directory. I would pronounce `/home/taylor` as "home taylor," but I would usually pronounce `/newt/awk/test` as "slash newt awk test." When in doubt, pronounce the slash.

As you learn more about Unix, particularly about how to navigate in the file system, you'll find that a clear understanding of the difference between a relative and absolute filename proves invaluable. The rule of thumb is that if a filename begins with `/`, it's absolute.

Task 3.2: Hidden Files in Unix

DESCRIPTION One of the best aspects of living in an area for a long time, frequenting the same shops and visiting the same restaurants, is that the people who work at each place learn your name and preferences. Many Unix applications can perform the same trick, remembering your preferred style of interaction, what files you last worked with, which lines you've edited, and more, through *preference files*.

On the Macintosh, because it's a single-user system, there's a folder within the System Folder called Preferences, which is a central storage place for preference files, organized by application. On my Macintosh, for example, I have about 75 different preference files in this directory, enabling me to have all my programs remember the defaults I prefer.

Unix must support many users at once, so Unix preference files can't be stored in a central spot in the file system. Otherwise, how would the system distinguish between your preferences and those of your colleagues? To avoid this problem, all Unix applications store their preference files in your home directory.

Programs want to be able to keep their own internal preferences and status stored in your directory, but these aren't for you to work with or alter. If you use DOS, you're probably familiar with how Windows solves this problem: Certain files are hidden and do not show up when you use DIR, in DOS, or the File Manager to list files in a directory.

Macintosh people don't realize it, but the Macintosh also has lots of hidden files. On the topmost level of the Macintosh file system, for example, the following files are present, albeit hidden from normal display: AppleShare PDS, Deleted File Record, Desktop, Desktop DB, and Desktop DF. Displaying hidden files on the Macintosh is very difficult, as it is with Windows.

Fortunately, the Unix rule for hiding files is much easier than that for either the Mac or PC. No secret status flag reminds the system not to display the file when listing directories. Instead, the rule is simple, any filename starting with a dot (.) is called a *hidden file*.

> A *hidden file* is any file with a dot as the first character of the filename.

If the filename or directory name begins with a dot, it won't show up in normal listings of that directory. If the filename or directory name has any other character as the first character of the name, it lists normally.

ACTION

1. Knowing that, turn to your computer and enter the `ls` command to list all the files and directories in your home directory.

```
% ls -F
Archives/       Mail/           RUMORS.18Sept   mailing.lists
InfoWorld/      News/           bin/            newlists
LISTS           OWL/            iecc.list       src/
%
```

2. You can see that I have 12 items in my own directory, seven directories (the directory names have a slash as the last character because of the `-F`, remember) and five files. Files have minimal rules for naming, too. Avoid slashes, spaces, and tabs, and you'll be fine.

3. Without an explicit direction to the contrary, Unix is going to let the hidden files remain hidden. To add the hidden files to the listing, you just need to add a `-a` flag to the command. Turn to your computer and try this command to see what hidden files are present in your directory. These are my results:

```
% ls -aF
./              .gopherrc       .oldnewsrc      .sig            RUMORS.18Sep
../             .history*       .plan           Archives/       bin/
.Agenda         .info           .pnewsexpert    InfoWorld/      iecc.list
.aconfigrc      .letter         .report         LISTS           mail.lists
.article        .login          .rm-timestamp   Mail/           newlists
.cshrc          .mailrc         .rnlast         News/           src/
.elm/           .newsrc         .rnsoft         OWL/
%
```

Many dot files tend to follow the format of a dot, followed by the name of the program that owns the file, with `rc` as the suffix. In my directory, you can see six dot files that follow this convention: `.aconfigrc`, `.cshrc`, `.gopherrc`, `.mailrc`, `.newsrc`, and `.oldnewsrc`.

SUMMARY Because of the particular rules of hidden files in Unix, they are often called dot files, and you can see that I have 23 dot files and directories in my directory.

The `rc` suffix tells you that this file is a configuration file for that particular utility. For instance, `.cshrc` is the configuration file for the C shell and is executed every time the C shell (`/bin/csh`) is executed. You can define aliases for C shell commands and a special search path, for example.

> Because it's important to convey the specific filename of a dot file, pronunciation is a little different from elsewhere in Unix. The name .gopherrc would be spoken as "dot gopher are sea," and .mailrc would be "dot mail are sea." If you can't pronounce the program name, odds are good that no one else can either, so .cshrc is "dot sea ess aitch are sea."

Other programs create many different dot files and try to retain a consistent naming scheme. You can see that .rnlast and .rnsoft are both from the rn program, but it's difficult to know simply from the filenames that .article, .letter, .newsrc, .oldnewsrc, and .pnewsexpert are all also referenced by the rn program. Recognizing this problem, some application authors designed their applications to create a dot directory, with all preference files neatly tucked into that one spot. The elm program does that with its .elm hidden directory.

Some files are directly named after the programs that use them: the .Agenda file is used by the agenda program, and .info is used by the info program. Those almost have a rule of their own, but it's impossible to distinguish them from .login, from the sh program; .plan for the finger program; .rm-timestamp from a custom program of my own; and I frankly have no idea what program created the .report file!

This should give you an idea of the various ways that Unix programs name and use hidden files. As an exercise, list all the dot files in your home directory and try to figure out which program created each file. Check by looking in the index of this book to see whether a program by that name exists, if it's a ".xxx" file. If you can't figure out which programs created which files, you're not alone. Keep the list handy; refer to it as you learn more about Unix while exploring *Sams Teach Yourself Unix in 24 Hours, Third Edition*, and by the time you're done, you'll know exactly how to find out which programs created which dot files.

Task 3.3: The Special Directories . and ..

DESCRIPTION I haven't mentioned two dot directories, although they show up in my listing and most certainly show up in your listing too. They are dot and dot dot (. and ..), and they're shorthand directory names that can be terrifically convenient.

The *dot* directory is shorthand for the current location in the directory hierarchy; the *dot-dot* directory moves you up one level, to the parent directory.

Consider again the list of files shown in Figure 3.3. If you were looking at the files in the California Personnel directory (best specified as /California/Personnel) and wanted to check quickly an entry in the Bldgs file for California, either you'd have to use the absolute filename and enter the lengthy ls /California/Bldgs, or, with the new short-hand directories, you could enter ls ../Bldgs.

As directories move ever deeper into the directory hierarchy, the dot-dot notation can save you much typing time. For example, what if the different states and related files were all located in my home directory /home/taylor, in a new directory called business? In that case, the absolute filename for employee Raab,M. in California would be /home/taylor/business/California/Personnel/Raab,M., which is unwieldy and a great deal to type if you want to hop up one level and check on the buildings database in Indiana!

You can use more than one dot-dot notation in a filename too, so if you're looking at the Raab,M. file and want to check on Dunlap,L., you could save typing in the full filename by instead using ../../../Washington/Personnel/Dunlap,L.. Look at Figure 3.3 to see how that would work, tracing back one level for each dot-dot in the filename.

This explains why the dot-dot shorthand is helpful, but what about the single-dot notation that simply specifies the current directory?

I haven't stated it explicitly yet, but you've probably figured out that one ramification of the Unix file system organization, with its capability to place applications anywhere in the file system, is that the system needs some way to know where to look for particular applications. Just as if you were looking for something in a public library, in Unix, having an understanding of its organization and a strategy for searching is imperative for success and speed.

Unix uses an ordered list of directories called a *search path* for this purpose. The search path typically lists five or six different directories on the system where the computer checks for any application you request.

The question that arises is, "What happens if your own personal copy of an application has the same name as a standard system application?" The answer is that the system always finds the standard application first, if its directory is listed earlier in the search path.

To avoid this pitfall, use the dot notation, forcing the system to look in the current directory rather than search for the application. If you wanted your own version of the ls command, for example, you'd need to enter ./ls to ensure that Unix uses your version rather than the standard version.

ACTION

1. Enter ./ls on your computer and watch what happens.
2. Enter ls without the dot notation, and you'll instantly see how the computer searches through various directories in the search path, finds the ls program, and executes it, automatically.

SUMMARY When you learn about cd (change directory) later in this hour, you also will learn other uses of the dot-dot directory, but the greatest value of the dot directory is that you can use it to force the system to look in the current directory and nowhere else for any file specified.

Task 3.4: The env Command

DESCRIPTION You've learned much about the foundations of the Unix file system and how applications remember your preferences through hidden dot files. There's another way, however, that the system remembers specifics about you, and that's through your *user environment*. The user environment is a collection of specially named variables that have specific values.

ACTION

1. To view your environment, you can use the env command. Here's what I see when I enter the env command on my system:

```
% env
HOME=/home/taylor
SHELL=/bin/csh
TERM=vt100
PATH=/home/taylor/bin:/bin:/usr/bin:/usr/ucb:/usr/local/bin:
➥/usr/unsup/bin:.
MAIL=/usr/spool/mail/taylor
LOGNAME=taylor
TZ=EST5
%
```

SUMMARY Try it yourself and compare your values with mine. You might find that you have more defined in your environment than I do because your Unix system uses your environment to keep track of more information.

Here we see some of the standard environment variables. Table 3.1 describes what they do.

3

TABLE 3.1 Common Shell Environment Variables and What They Do

Variable	Description
HOME	The directory where you log in and store all your personal files
SHELL	The program you run as your command-line interpreter
TERM	The type of terminal emulation you need to provide cursor graphics
PATH	A list of directories searched when you enter a command
MAIL	The file where your incoming mail is stored
LOGNAME	Your login name
TZ	The time zone on your system

Many Unix systems offer the printenv command instead of env. If you enter env and the system complains that it can't find the env command, try using printenv instead. All examples here work with either env or printenv.

Task 3.5: PATH and HOME

DESCRIPTION The two most important values in your environment are the name of your home directory (HOME) and your search path (PATH). Your home directory (as it's known) is the name of the directory that you always begin your Unix session within.

The PATH environment variable lists the set of directories, in left-to-right order, that the system searches to find commands and applications you request. You can see from the example that my search path tells the computer to start looking in the /home/taylor/bin directory, and then sequentially try /bin, /usr/bin, /usr/ucb, /usr/local/bin, /usr/unsup/bin, and . before concluding that it can't find the requested command. Without a PATH, the shell wouldn't be able to find any of the many, many Unix commands: As a minimum, you always should have /bin and /usr/bin.

ACTION

1. You can use the echo command to list specific environment variables too. Enter echo $PATH and echo $HOME. When I do so, I get the following results:

```
% echo $PATH
/home/taylor/bin:/bin:/usr/bin:/usr/ucb:/usr/local/bin:/usr/unsup/
➥bin:.
% echo $HOME
/home/taylor
%
```

Your PATH value is probably similar, although certainly not identical, to mine, and your HOME is /home/*accountname* or similar (*accountname* is your account name).

Task 3.6: Find Where You Are with pwd

DESCRIPTION So far you've learned a lot about how the file system works but not much about how to move around in the file system. With any trip, the first and most important step is to find out your current location—that is, the directory in which you are currently working. In Unix, the command pwd tells you the *present working directory*.

ACTION

1. Enter pwd. The output should be identical to the output you saw when you entered env HOME because you're still in your home directory.

```
% echo $HOME
/home/taylor
% pwd
/home/taylor
%
```

SUMMARY Think of pwd as a compass, always capable of telling you where you are. It also tells you the names of all directories above you because it always lists your current location as an absolute directory name.   •

Task 3.7: Moving to Another Location with cd

DESCRIPTION The other half of the dynamic duo is the cd command, which is used to change directories. The format of this command is simple, too: cd *new-directory* (where *new-directory* is the name of the new directory you want).

ACTION

1. Try moving to the very top level of the file system and entering pwd to see whether the computer agrees that you've moved.
```
% cd /
% pwd
/
%
```

2. Notice that cd doesn't produce any output. Many Unix commands operate silently like this, unless an error is encountered. The system then indicates the problem.

You can see what an error looks like by trying to change your location to a nonexistent directory. Try the /taylor directory to see what happens!

```
% cd /taylor
/taylor: No such file or directory
%
```

3. Enter cd without specifying a directory. What happens? I get the following result:

```
% cd
% pwd
/home/taylor
%
```

4. Here's where the HOME environment variable comes into play. Without any directory specified, cd moves you back to your home directory automatically. If you get lost, it's a fast shorthand way to move to a known location without fuss.

Remember the dot-dot notation for moving up a level in the directory hierarchy? Here's where it also proves exceptionally useful. Use the cd command without any arguments to move to your home directory, and then use pwd to ensure that's where you've ended up.

5. Now, move up one level by using cd .. and check the results with pwd:

```
% cd
% pwd
/home/taylor
% cd ..
% pwd
/home
%
```

6. Use the ls -C -F command to list all the directories contained at this point in the file system. Beware, though; on large systems, this directory could easily have hundreds of different directories. On one system I use, almost 550 different directories are on one level above my home directory in the file system!

```
% ls -F
armstrong/   christine/   guest/     laura/   matthewm/   shane/
bruce/       david/       higgins/   mac/     rank/       taylor/
cedric/      green/       kane/      mark/    shalini/    vicki/
%
```

SUMMARY Try using a combination of cd and pwd to move about your file system, and remember that without any arguments, cd always zips you right back to your home directory.

Summary

This hour focused on the Unix hierarchical file system. You've learned the organization of a hierarchical file system, how Unix differs from Macintosh and DOS systems, and how Unix remembers preferences with its hidden dot files. This hour also explained the difference between relative and absolute filenames, and you've learned about the . and .. directories. You learned four new commands: `env` to list your current environment, `echo` to show a particular value, `cd` to change directories, and `pwd` to find your present working directory location.

Workshop

The Workshop summarizes the key terms you learned and poses some questions about the topics presented in this chapter. It also provides you with a preview of what you will learn in the next hour.

Key Terms

absolute filename   Any filename that begins with a leading slash (/); these always uniquely describe a single file in the file system.

binary   A file format that is intended for the computer to work with directly rather than for humans to peruse. See also **executable**.

device driver   All peripherals attached to the computer are called *devices* in Unix, and each has a control program always associated with it, called a *device driver*. Examples are the device drivers for the display, keyboard, mouse, and all hard disks.

directory   A type of Unix file used to group other files. Files and directories can be placed inside other directories, to build a hierarchical system.

directory separator character   On a hierarchical file system, there must be some way to specify which items are directories and which is the actual filename itself. This becomes particularly true when you're working with absolute filenames. In Unix, the directory separator character is the slash (/), so a filename like `/tmp/testme` is easily interpreted as a file called `testme` in a directory called `tmp`.

dot   A shorthand notation for the current directory.

dot dot   A shorthand notation for the directory one level higher up in the hierarchical file system from the current location.

dot file   A configuration file used by one or more programs. These files are called dot files because the first letter of the filename is a dot, as in `.profile` or `.login`. Because they're dot files, the `ls` command doesn't list them by default, making them also hidden files in Unix. See also **hidden file**.

dynamic linking   Although most Unix systems require all necessary utilities and library routines (such as the routines for reading information from the keyboard and displaying it to the screen) to be plugged into a program when it's built (known in Unix parlance as *static linking*), some of the more sophisticated systems can delay this inclusion until you actually need to run the program. In this case, the utilities and libraries are linked when you start the program, and this is called *dynamic linking*.

executable   A file that has been set up so that Unix can run it as a program. This is also shorthand for a binary file. You also sometimes see the phrase *binary executable*, which is the same thing. See also **binary**.

hidden file   By default, the Unix file-listing command `ls` shows only files whose first letter isn't a dot (that is, those files that aren't dot files). All dot files, therefore, are hidden files, and you can safely ignore them without any problems. Later, you learn how to view these hidden files. See also **dot file**.

home directory   This is your private directory, and is also where you start out when you log in to the system.

kernel   The underlying core of the Unix operating system itself. This is akin to the concrete foundation under a modern skyscraper.

preference file   These are what dot files (hidden files) really are: They contain your individual preferences for many of the Unix commands you use.

relative filename   Any filename that does not begin with a slash (/) is a filename whose exact meaning depends on where you are in the file system. For example, the file `test` might exist in both your home directory and in the root directory: `/test` is an absolute filename and leaves no question which version is being used, but `test` could refer to either copy, depending on your current directory.

root directory   The directory at the very top of the file system hierarchy, also known as *slash*.

search path   A list of directories used to find a command. When a user enters a command `ls`, the shell looks in each directory in the search path to find a file `ls`, either until it is found or the list is exhausted.

slash   The root directory.

symbolic link   A file that contains a pointer to another file rather than contents of its own. This can also be a directory that points to another directory rather than having files of its own. A useful way to have multiple names for a single program or to allow multiple people to share a single copy of a file.

user environment   A set of values that describe the user's current location and modify the behavior of commands.

working directory   The directory where the user is working.

Exercises

1. Can you think of information you work with daily that's organized in a hierarchical fashion? Is a public library organized hierarchically?

2. Which of the following files are hidden files and directories according to Unix?

   ```
   .test    hide-me    ,test    .cshrc
   ../      .dot.      dot      .HiMom
   ```

3. What programs most likely created the following dot files and dot directories?

   ```
   .cshrc     .rnsoft    .exrc     .print
   .tmp334    .excel/    .letter   .vi-expert
   ```

4. In the following list, circle the items that are absolute filenames:

   ```
   /Personnel/Taylor,D.
   /home/taylor/business/California
   ../..
   Recipe:Gazpacho
   ```

5. Referring to the list of directories found on all Unix systems (/bin, /dev, /etc, /lib, /lost+found, /mnt, /sys, /tmp, /usr), use cd and pwd to double-check that they are all present on your own Unix machine.

Preview of the Next Hour

In the next hour, you learn all about the ls command that you've been using, including an extensive discussion of command flags. The command touch enables you to create your own files, and du and df help you learn how much disk space is used and how much is available, respectively. You also learn how to use a valuable if somewhat esoteric Unix command, compress, which helps you minimize your disk-space usage.

HOUR 4

Listing Files and Managing Disk Usage

This hour introduces you to the ls command, one of the most commonly used commands in Unix. The discussion includes more than a dozen different command options, or flags. You also learn how to use the touch command to create files, how to use the du command to see how much disk space you're using, and how to use the df command to see how much disk space is available. Finally, the compress command can help you minimize your disk space usage, particularly on files you do not use very often.

Goals for This Hour

In this hour, you will learn

- All about the ls command
- About special ls command flags
- How to create files with touch
- How to check disk space usage with du

- How to check available disk space with df
- How to shrink big files with compress

Your first hours focused on some basic Unix commands, particularly those for interacting with the system to accomplish common tasks. In this hour, you expand that knowledge by analyzing characteristics of the system you're using, and you learn a raft of commands that let you create your own Unix workspace. You also learn more about the Unix file system and how Unix interprets command lines. In addition to the cd and pwd commands that you learned in the preceding hour, you learn how to use ls to wander in the file system and see what files are kept where.

Unlike in the Windows and Macintosh operating systems, information about the Unix system is often difficult to obtain. In this hour, you learn easy ways to ascertain how much disk space you're using with the du command. You also learn how to interpret the oft-confusing output of the df command, which enables you to see instantly how much total disk space is available on your Unix system.

This hour concludes with a discussion of the compress command, which enables you to shrink the size of any file or set of files.

The ls Command

This section introduces you to the ls command, which enables you to examine the file system and see what files are kept where.

Task 4.1: All About the ls Command

DESCRIPTION From the examples in the preceding hour, you've already figured out that the command used to list files and directories in Unix is the ls command.

All operating systems have a similar command, a way to see what's in the current location. In DOS, for example, you're no doubt familiar with the DIR command. DOS also has command flags, which are denoted by a leading slash before the specific option. For example, DIR /W produces a directory listing in wide-display format. The DIR command has quite a few other options and capabilities.

Listing the files in a directory is a pretty simple task, so why all the different options? You've already seen some examples, including ls -a, which lists hidden dot files. The answer is that there are many different ways to look at files and directories, as you will learn.

ACTION

1. The best way to learn what ls can do is to go ahead and use it. Turn to your computer, log in to your account, and try each command as it's explained.

2. The most basic use of ls is to list files. The command ls lists all the files and directories in the present working directory (recall that you can check what directory you're in with the pwd command at any time).

```
% ls
Archives        Mail            RUMORS.18Sept   mailing.lists
InfoWorld       News            bin             newels
LISTS           OWL             iecc.list       src
```

Notice that the files are sorted alphabetically from top to bottom, left to right. This is the default, known as *column-first order* because it sorts downward, then across. You should also note how things are sorted in Unix: The system differentiates between uppercase and lowercase letters, unlike DOS. (The Macintosh remembers whether you use uppercase or lowercase letters for naming files, but it can't distinguish between them internally. Try it. Name one file TEST and another file test the next time you use a Macintosh.)

> Some of the Unix and Linux versions available for the PC have an ls that behaves slightly differently and can list all files in a single column rather than in multiple columns. If your PC does this, you can use the -C flag to ls to force multiple columns.

SUMMARY It's important that you always remember to typeUnix commands in lowercase letters, unless you know that the particular command is actually uppercase; remember that Unix treats Archives and archives as different filenames. Also, avoid entering your account name in uppercase when you log in. Unix has some old compatibility features that make using the system much more difficult if you use an all-uppercase login. If you ever accidentally log in with all uppercase, log out and try again in lowercase.

Task 4.2: Having ls Tell You More

DESCRIPTION Without options, the ls command offers relatively little information. Questions you might still have about your directory include these: How big are the files? Which are files, and which are directories? How old are they? What hidden files do you have?

ACTION

1. Start by entering `ls -s` to indicate file sizes:

```
% ls -s
total 403
    1 Archives     1 Mail      5 RUMORS.18Sept  280 mailing.lists
    1 InfoWorld    1 News      1 bin             2 newels
  108 LISTS        1 OWL       4 iecc.list       1 src
```

2. To ascertain the size of each file or directory listed, you can use the `-s` flag with `ls`. The size indicated is the number of kilobytes, rounded upward, for each file. The first line of the listing also indicates the total amount of disk space used, in kilobytes, for the contents of this directory. The summary number does not, however, include the contents of any subdirectories, so it's deceptively small.

> A kilobyte is 1,024 bytes of information, a byte being a single character. The preceding paragraph, for example, contains slightly more than 400 characters. Unix works in units of a *block* of information, which, depending on which version of Unix you're using, is either 1 kilobyte or 512 bytes. Most Unix systems now work with a 1 kilobyte block. When you use the `-s` flag, you're being shown how many of these blocks each file contains.

3. Here is a further definition of what occurs when you use the `-s` flag: `ls -s` indicates the number of blocks each file or directory occupies. You then can use simple calculations to convert blocks into bytes. For example, the `ls` command indicates that the `LISTS` file in my home directory occupies 108 blocks. A quick calculation of block size × number of blocks reveals that the maximum file size of `LISTS` is 110,592 bytes.

   You can always estimate size by multiplying the number of blocks by 1,000. Be aware, however, that in large files, the difference between 1,000 and 1,024 is significant enough to introduce an error into your calculation. As an example, `bigfile` is more than 3 megabytes in size (a megabyte is 1,024 kilobytes, which is 1,024 bytes, so a megabyte is 1,024×1,024, or 1,048,576 bytes):

```
% ls -s bigfile
3648 bigfile
```

4. The file actually occupies 3,727,360 bytes. If I estimated its size by multiplying the number of blocks (3,648 as seen from the preceding command) by 1,000 (which equals 3,648,000 bytes), I'd have underestimated its size by 79,360 bytes. (Remember, blocks × 1,000 is simply an easy estimate!)

The preceding example reveals something else about the `ls` command. You can specify individual files or directories you're interested in viewing and avoid having to see all files and directories in your current location.

Depending on what shell you're using, and what version of Unix you have, you might be able to press the Tab key while entering a filename and have it automatically completed. Try it; if you have this shortcut, it's great!

5. You can specify as many files or directories as you like, and separate them by spaces:

```
% ls -s LISTS iecc.list newels
 108 LISTS       4 iecc.list    2 newels
```

In the preceding hour, you learned that Unix identifies each file that begins with a dot (.) as a hidden file. Your home directory is probably littered with dot files, which retain preferences, status information, and other data. To list these hidden files, use the `-a` flag to `ls`:

```
% ls -a
.               gopherrc     .oldnewsrc     .sig          RUMORS.18Sept
..              .history     .plan          Archives      bin
.Agenda         .info        .pnewsexpert   InfoWorld     iecc.list
.aconfigrc      .letter      .report        LISTS         mailing.lists
.article        .login       .rm-timestamp  Mail          newels
.cshrc          .mailrc      .rnlast        News          src
.elm            .newsrc      .rnsoft        OWL
```

You can see that this directory contains more dot files than regular files and directories. That's not uncommon in a Unix home directory. However, it's rare to find any dot files other than the standard dot and dot-dot directories (those are in every directory in the entire file system) in directories other than your home directory. (These dot files are typically created by applications you use, and they should be edited with care.)

6. You used another flag to the `ls` command—the `-F` flag—in the preceding hour. Do you remember what it does?

```
% ls -F
Archives/       Mail/        RUMORS.18Sept  mailing.lists
InfoWorld@      News/        bin/           newels
LISTS           OWL/         iecc.list      src/
```

4

Adding the -F flag to ls appends suffixes to certain filenames so that you can ascertain more easily what types of files they are. Three different suffixes can be added, as shown in Table 4.1.

TABLE 4.1 Filename Suffixes Appended by `ls -F`

Suffix	Example	Meaning
/	Mail/	Mail is a directory.
*	prog*	prog is an executable program.
@	bin@	bin is a symbolic link to another file or directory.

7. If you're familiar with the Macintosh and have used MacOS 8 or a more recent version of the operating system, you may recall the new feature that enables the user to create and use an alias. An alias is a file that does not contain information, but acts, instead, as a pointer to the actual information files. Aliases can exist either for specific files or for folders. Windows folk know this as a "shortcut" file.

Unix has offered a similar feature forever, which in Unix jargon is called a *symbolic link*. A symbolic link, such as bin in Table 4.1, contains the name of another file or directory rather than any contents of its own. If you could peek inside, it might look like bin = @/usr/bin. Every time someone tries to look at bin, the system shows the contents of /usr/bin instead.

You'll learn more about symbolic links and how they help you organize your files in Hour 6, "Creating, Moving, Renaming, and Deleting Files and Directories." For now, just remember that if you see an @ after a filename, it's a link to another spot in the file system.

8. A useful flag for ls (one that might not be available in your version of Unix) is the -m flag. This flag outputs the files as a comma-separated list. If there are many files, -m can be a quick and easy way to see what's available:

```
% ls -m
Archives, InfoWorld, LISTS, Mail, News, OWL, RUMORS.18Sept,
bin, iecc.list, mailing.lists, newels, src
```

SUMMARY Sometime you might want to list each of your files on a separate line, perhaps for a printout you want to annotate. You've learned that the -C flag forces recalcitrant versions of ls to output in multiple columns. Unfortunately, the opposite behavior isn't obtained by use of a lowercase c. (Unix should be so consistent!) Instead, use the -1 flag to indicate that you want one column of output. Try it.

Task 4.3: Combining Flags

DESCRIPTION The different flags you've learned so far are summarized in Table 4.2.

TABLE 4.2 Some Useful Flags to `ls`

Flag	Meaning
-a	List all files, including any dot files.
-F	Indicate file types; / = directory, * = executable.
-m	Show files as a comma-separated list.
-s	Show size of files, in blocks (typically, 1 block = 1,024 bytes).
-C	Force multiple-column output on listings.
-1	Force single-column output on listings.

What if you want a list, generated with the `-F` conventions, that simultaneously shows you all files and indicates their types?

ACTION

1. Combining flags in Unix is easy. All you have to do is run them together in a sequence of characters, and prefix the whole thing with a dash:

```
% ls -aF
./              .gopherrc       .oldnewsrc      .sig
../             .history*       .plan           Archives/
.Agenda         .info           .pnewsexpert    InfoWorld/
.aconfigrc      .letter         .report         LISTS
.article        .login          .rm-timestamp   Mail/
.cshrc          .mailrc         .rnlast         News/
.elm/           .newsrc         .rnsoft         OWL/
```

2. Sometimes it's more convenient to keep all the flags separate. This is fine, as long as each flag is prefixed by its own dash:

```
% ls -s -F
total 403
    1 Archives/      1 Mail/         5 RUMORS.18Sept   280
↪mailing.lists
    1 InfoWorld/     1 News/         1 bin/            2 newels
  108 LISTS          1 OWL/          4 iecc.list       1 src/
```

3. Try some of these combinations on your own computer. Also try to list a flag more than once (for example, `ls -sss -s`), or list flags in different orders.

SUMMARY Very few Unix commands care about the order in which flags are listed. Because it's the presence or absence of a flag that's important, listing a flag more than once also doesn't make any difference.

Task 4.4: Listing Other Directories Without Changing Location

DESCRIPTION Every time I try to do any research in the library, I find myself spending hours and hours there, but it seems to me that I do less research than I think I should. That's because most of my time is for the tasks between the specifics of my research: finding the location of the next book, and finding the book itself.

If `ls` constrained you to listing only the directory you were in, it would hobble you in a similar way. Using only `ls` would slow you down dramatically and force you to use `cd` to move around each time.

Instead, just as you can specify certain files by using `ls`, you can specify certain directories you're interested in viewing.

ACTION

1. Try this yourself. List `/usr` on your system:

```
% ls -F /usr
5bin/           diag/          lddrv/          share/          ucbinclude@
5include/       dict/          lib/            source/         ucblib@
5lib/           etc/           local/          spool@          xpg2bin/
acc/            export/        lost+found/     src@            xpg2include/
acctlog*        games/         man@            stand@          xpg2lib/
adm@            hack/          mdec@           sys@
bin/            hosts/         old/            system/
boot@           include/       pub@            tmp@
demo/           kvm/           sccs/           ucb/
```

You probably have different files and directories listed in your own `/usr` directory. Remember, @ files are symbolic links in the listing, too.

2. You can also specify more than one directory:

```
% ls /usr/local /home/taylor
/home/taylor:
Global.Software    Mail/           Src/                    history.usenet.Z
Interactive.Unix   News/           bin/
/usr/local/:
T/              emacs/         ftp/            lists/          motd~
admin/          emacs-18.59/   gnubin/         lost+found/     netcom/
bin/            etc/           include/        man/            policy/
cat/            faq/           info/           menu/           src/
doc/            forms/         lib/            motd            tmp/
```

In this example, the `ls` command also sorted the directories before listing them. I specified that I wanted to see `/usr/local` and then `/home/taylor`, but it presented the directories in opposite order.

> I've never been able to figure out how `ls` sorts directories when you ask for more than one to be listed—it's not an alphabetical listing. Consider it a mystery. Remember that if you must have the output in a specific order, you can use the `ls` command twice in a row.

3. Here's where the dot-dot shorthand for the parent directory can come in handy. Try it yourself:

```
% ls -m ..
armstrong, bruce, cedric, christine, david, green,
guest, higgins, james, kane, laura, mac, mark,
rank, shalini, shane, taylor, Vicki
```

If you were down one branch of the file system and wanted to look at some files down another branch, you could easily find yourself using the command `ls ../Indiana/Personnel` or `ls -s ../../source`.

4. There's a problem here, however. You've seen that you can specify filenames to look at those files, and directory names to look at the contents of those directories, but what if you're interested in the directory itself, not in its contents? I might want to list just two directories—not the contents, just the directory names themselves, as shown here:

```
% ls -F
Archives/      Mail/           RUMORS.18Sept  mailing.lists
InfoWorld/     News/           bin/           newlists
LISTS          OWL/            iecc.list      src/
% ls -s LISTS Mail newlists
 108 LISTS          2 newlists
Mail:
total 705
  8 cennamo     27 ean_houts      4 kcs     21 mark    7 sartin
 28 dan_sommer   2 gordon_haight 34 lehman   5 raf     3 shelf
 14 decc        48 harrism       64 mac      7 rock   20 steve
  3 druby       14 james         92 mailbox  5 rustle 18 tai
```

4

5. The problem is that ls doesn't know that you want to look at Mail unless you tell it not to look inside the directories specified. The command flag needed is -d, which forces ls to list directories rather than their contents. The same ls command, but with the -d flag, has dramatically different output:

```
% ls -ds LISTS Mail newlists
 108 LISTS           1 Mail/          2 newlists
```

Try some of these flags on your own system, and watch how they work together.

SUMMARY To list a file or directory, you can specify it to ls. Directories, however, reveal their contents, unless you also include the -d flag.

Special ls Command Flags

It should be clear to you that Unix is the ultimate toolbox. Even some of the simplest commands have dozens of different options. On one system I use, ls has more than 20 different flags.

Task 4.5: Changing the Sort Order in ls

DESCRIPTION What if you wanted to look at files, but wanted them to show up in a directory sorting order different from the default (that is, column-first order)? How could you change the sort order in ls?

ACTION

1. The -x flag sorts across, listing the output in columns, or first-row order (entries are sorted across, then down):

```
% ls -a
.                    .elm            .plan          Global.Software
..                   .forward        .pnewsexpert   Interactive.Unix
.Pnews.header        .ircmotd        .rnlast        Mail
.accinfo             .login          .rnlock        News
.article             .logout         .rnsoft        Src
.cshrc               .newsrc         .sig           bin
.delgroups           .oldnewsrc      .tin           history.usenet.Z
% ls -x -a
.                    ..              .Pnews.header  .accinfo
.article             .cshrc          .delgroups     .elm
.forward             .ircmotd        .login         .logout
.newsrc              .oldnewsrc      .plan          .pnewsexpert
.rnlast              .rnlock         .rnsoft        .sig
.tin                 Global.Software Interactive.Unix Mail
News                 Src             bin            history.usenet.Z
```

2. Even more ways exist to sort files in `ls`. If you want to sort by most recently accessed to least recently accessed, you use the `-t` flag:

```
% ls -a -t
./                  ../             .rnlock           .cshrc
.newsrc             News/           .rnlast           .sig
.oldnewsrc          .tin/           .rnsoft           .plan
.article            .ircmotd        Interactive.Unix  Mail/
.elm/               .delgroups      .accinfo*         .Pnews.header*
.forward            .login          Src/              .pnewsexpert
history.usenet.Z    bin/            Global.Software   .logout
```

From this output, you can see that the most recently accessed files are `.newsrc` and `.oldnewsrc`, and that it's been quite a while since `.logout` was touched. Try using the `-t` flag on your system to see which files you've been accessing and which you haven't.

3. So far, you know three different approaches to sorting files within the `ls` command: column-first order, row-first order, and most recently accessed-first order. But more options exist in `ls` than just these three; the `-r` flag reverses any sorting order.

```
% ls
Global.Software     Mail/           Src/              history.usenet.Z
Interactive.Unix    News/           bin/
% ls -r
history.usenet.Z    Src/            Mail/             Global.Software
bin/                News/           Interactive.Unix
```

4. Things can become confusing when you combine some of these flags. Try to list the contents of the directory that is one level above the current directory, sorted so the most recently accessed file is last in the list. At the same time, indicate which items are directories and the size of each file.

```
% ls -r -t -F -s ..
total 150
    2 bruce/      2 rank/        2 kane/       14 higgins/
    2 laura/      2 christine/   2 shane/       6 mac/
    2 cedric      2 peggy/       4 patrickb/   10 mark/
    2 james@      4 taylor/      4 green/       6 armstrong/
    2 vicki/      2 guest/       6 shalini/     4 david/
```

SUMMARY A better and easier way to type the preceding command would be to bundle flags into the single argument `ls  -rtFs ..`, which would work just as well, and you'd look like an expert!

4

Task 4.6: Listing Directory Trees Recursively in 1s

DESCRIPTION In case things aren't yet complicated enough with 1s, two more important valuable flags are available. One is the -R flag, which causes 1s to recursively list directories below the current or specified directory. (If you are familiar with DOS, you can think of using the -R flag as the same as the tree command in DOS.) If you think of listing files as a numbered set of steps, recursion is simply adding a step—the rule is if this file is a directory, list it too—to the list.

ACTION

1. When I use the -R flag, here's what I see:

```
% ls -R
Global.Software    Mail/      Src/       history.usenet.Z
Interactive.Unix   News/      bin/
Mail:
Folders/  Netnews/
Mail/Folders:
mail.sent  mailbox    steinman    tucker
Mail/Netnews:
postings
News:
uptodate   volts
Src:
sum-up.c
bin:
Pnews*    punt*    submit*
```

Try it yourself.

Notice that 1s lists the current directory and then alphabetically lists the contents of all subdirectories. Notice also that the Mail directory has two directories within it and that those are also listed here.

SUMMARY Viewing all files and directories below a certain point in the file system can be a valuable way to look for files (although you'll soon learn better tools for finding files). If you aren't careful, though, you can get hundreds or thousands of lines of information streaming across your screen. Do not enter a command such as 1s -R / unless you have time to sit and watch information fly past.

If you try to list the contents of a directory when you don't have permission to access the information, 1s warns you with an error message:

```
% ls ../marv
../marv unreadable
```

Now ask for a recursive listing, with indications of file type and size, of the directory /etc, and see what's there. The listing will include many files and subdirectories, but they should be easy to wade through due to all the notations ls uses to indicate files and directories.

Task 4.7: Long Listing Format in ls

DESCRIPTION You've seen how to estimate the size of a file by using the -s flag to find the number of blocks it occupies. To find the exact size of a file in bytes, use the -l flag. (Use a lowercase letter L. The numeral 1 produces single-column output, as you've already learned).

ACTION

1. The first long listing shows information for the LISTS file.

```
% ls -l LISTS
-rw------- 1 taylor     106020 Oct  8 15:17 LISTS
```

The output is explained in Figure 4.1.

FIGURE 4.1
The meaning of the -l output for a file.

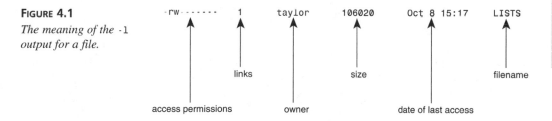

4

SUMMARY For each file and directory in the Unix file system, the owner, size, name, number of other files pointing to it (links), and access permissions are recorded. The creation, modification, and access times and dates are also recorded for each file. The modification time is the default time used for the -t sorting option and listed by the ls long format.

Permissions Strings

Interpreting permissions strings is a complex issue because Unix has a sophisticated security model. Security revolves around three different types of user: the owner of the file, the group of which that the file is a part, and everyone else.

The first character of the permissions string, identified in Figure 4.1 as *access permissions*, indicates the kind of file. The two most common values are d for directories and - for regular files. Be aware that there are many other file types that you'll rarely, if ever, see.

The following nine characters in the permissions string indicate what type of access is allowed for different users. From left to right, these characters show what access is allowed for the owner of the file, the group that owns the file, and everyone else.

Figure 4.2 shows how to break down the permissions string for the LISTS file into individual components.

FIGURE 4.2
Reading access permissions for LISTS.

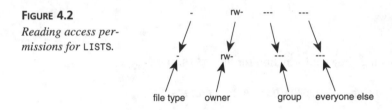

Each permissions string is identically composed of three components—permission for reading, writing, and execution—as shown in Figure 4.3.

FIGURE 4.3
Elements of a permissions string.

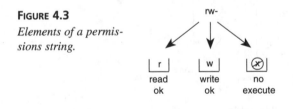

Armed with this information—specifically, knowing that a - character means that the specific permission is denied—you can see that ls shows that the owner of the file, taylor as illustrated in Figure 4.1, has read and write permission. Nobody else either in taylor's group or in any other group has permission to view, edit, or run the file.

Earlier you learned that just about everything in Unix ends up as a file in the file system, whether it's an application, a device driver, or a directory. The system keeps track of whether a file is executable because that's one way it knows whether LISTS is the name of a file or the name of an application.

Task 4.8: Long Listing Format for Directories in `ls`

DESCRIPTION   The long form of a directory listing is almost identical to a file listing, but the permissions string is interpreted in a very different manner.

ACTION

1. Here is an example of a long directory listing:

```
% ls -l -d Example
drwxr-x---  2 taylor        1024 Sep 30 10:50 Example/
```

Remember that you must have both read and execute permissions for a directory. If you have either read or execute permission but not both, the directory will not be usable (as though you had neither permission). Write permission, of course, enables the user to alter the contents of the directory or add new files to the directory.

2. The `Example` directory breaks down for interpretation as shown in Figure 4.4.

FIGURE 4.4
Elements of directory permissions.

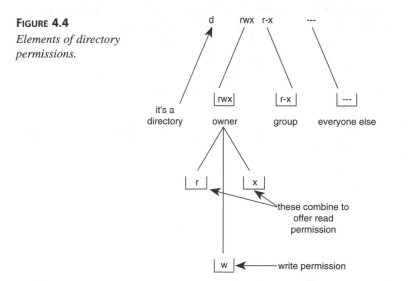

>
> I've never understood the nuances of a directory with read but not execute permission, or vice versa, and explanations from other people have never proven to be correct. It's okay, though, because I've never seen a directory on a Unix system that was anything other than ---, r-x, or rwx.

3. Now try using the `-l` flag yourself. Move to your home directory, and enter `ls -l` as shown here:

```
% ls -l
total 403
drwx------  2 taylor      512 Sep 30 10:38 Archives/
drwx------  3 taylor      512 Oct  1 08:23 InfoWorld/
-rw-------  1 taylor   106020 Oct  8 15:17 LISTS
drwx------  2 taylor     1024 Sep 30 10:50 Mail/
drwx------  2 taylor      512 Oct  6 09:36 News/
drwx------  2 taylor      512 Sep 30 10:51 OWL/
-rw-------  1 taylor     4643 Sep 20 10:49 RUMORS.18Sept
drwx------  2 taylor      512 Oct  1 09:53 bin/
-rw-------  1 taylor     3843 Oct  6 18:02 iecc.list
-rw-rw----  1 taylor   280232 Oct  6 09:57 mailing.lists
-rw-rw----  1 taylor     1031 Oct  7 15:44 newlists
drwx------  2 taylor      512 Sep 14 22:14 src/
```

The size of a directory is usually in increments of 512 bytes. The second field, the "link," is an interesting and little-known value when a directory is being listed. Instead of counting up the number of other files that point to the file, (that is, the number of files that have a link to the current file), the second field indicates the number of directories that are contained in that specific directory. Remember that all directories have dot and dot-dot, so the minimum value is always 2.

4. Consider the following example of a directory listing:

```
% ls -Fa
./                .gopherrc        .oldnewsrc       .sig             OWL/
../               .history*        .plan            Archives/
➥RUMORS.18Sept
.Agenda           .info            .pnewsexpert     Cancelled.mail  bin/
.aconfigrc        .letter          .report          InfoWorld/
➥iecc.list
.article          .login           .rm-timestamp    LISTS
➥mailing.lists
.cshrc            .mailrc          .rnlast          Mail/
➥newlists
.elm/             .newsrc          .rnsoft          News/            src/
% ls -ld .
drwx------ 10 taylor     1024 Oct 10 16:00 ./
```

5. Try entering `ls -ld` . and see whether it correctly identifies the number of directories in your home directory. Move to other directories and see whether the listing agrees with your own count of directories.

SUMMARY   The output from the `ls -l` command is unquestionably complex and packed with information. Interpretation of permissions strings is an important part of understanding and being able to use Unix, and more explanation is offered in subsequent hours.

Table 4.3 summarizes the many different command flags for ls that you have learned in this hour.

TABLE 4.3   Summary of Command Flags for ls

Flag	Meaning
-1	Force single-column output on listings.
-a	List all files, including any dot files.
-C	Force multiple-column output on listings.
-d	List directories rather than their contents.
-F	Indicate file types; / = directory, * = executable.
-l	Generate a long listing of files and directories.
-m	Show files as a comma-separated list.
-r	Reverse the order of any file sorting.
-R	Recursively show directories and their contents.
-s	Show size of files, in blocks (typically 1 block = 1,024 bytes).
-t	Sort output in most-recently modified order.
-x	Sort output in row-first order.

Without a doubt, ls is one of the most powerful and, therefore, also one of the most confusing commands in Unix. The best way for you to learn how all the flags work together is to experiment with different combinations.

Task 4.9: Creating Files with the touch Command

DESCRIPTION At this point, you have various Unix tools that help you move through the file system and learn about specific files. The touch command is the first command that helps you create new files on the system, independent of any program other than the shell itself. This can prove very helpful for organizing a new collection of files, for example.

The main reason that touch is used in Unix is to force the last-modified time of a file to be updated, as the following example demonstrates:

```
% ls -l iecc.list
-rw-------  1 taylor        3843 Oct  6 18:02 iecc.list
% touch iecc.list
% ls -l iecc.list
-rw-------  1 taylor        3843 Oct 10 16:22 iecc.list
```

Because the touch command changes modification times of files, anything that sorts files based on modification time will, of course, alter the position of that file when the file is altered by touch.

ACTION

1. Consider the following output:

```
% ls -t
mailing.lists   LISTS          News/          OWL/           src/
Cancelled.mail  newlists       bin/           Mail/
RUMORS.18Sept   iecc.list      InfoWorld/     Archives/
% touch iecc.list
% ls -t
iecc.list       RUMORS.18Sept  News/          OWL/           src/
mailing.lists   LISTS          bin/           Mail/
Cancelled.mail  newlists       InfoWorld/     Archives/
```

You probably will not use touch for this purpose very often.

2. If you try to use the touch command on a file that doesn't exist, the program creates the file:

```
% ls
Archives/       LISTS          OWL/           iecc.list      src/
Cancelled.mail  Mail/          RUMORS.18Sept  mailing.lists
InfoWorld/      News/          bin/           newlists
% touch new.file
% ls
Archives/       LISTS          OWL/           iecc.list
➥newlists
Cancelled.mail  Mail/          RUMORS.18Sept  mailing.lists  src/
InfoWorld/      News/          bin/           new.file
% ls -l new.file
-rw-rw----  1 taylor         0 Oct 10 16:28 new.file
```

The new file has zero bytes, as can be seen by the ls -l output. Notice that by default the files are created with read and write permission for the user and anyone in the user's group. You learn in another hour how to specify, by using the umask command, your own default permission for files.

SUMMARY You won't need touch very often, but it's valuable to know.

Task 4.10: Checking Disk Space Usage with du

DESCRIPTION One advantage that Windows and Macintosh systems have over Unix is they make it easy to find out how much disk space you're using and how much remains available. On a Macintosh, viewing folders by size shows disk space used, and the top of any Finder window shows available space. In DOS it's even easier; both items are listed at the end of the output from a DIR command:

```
C> DIR .BAT
 Volume in drive C is MS-DOS_5
 Volume Serial Number is 197A-A8D7
 Directory of C:\
AUTOEXEC BAT        142 02-28-96    8:19p
CSH      BAT         36 12-22-97    3:01p
        2 file(s)            178 bytes
                        5120000 bytes free
```

In this DOS example, you can see that the files listed take up 178 bytes, and that there are 5,120,000 bytes (about 5 megabytes, or 5MB) available on the hard drive.

Like a close-mouthed police informant, Unix never volunteers any information, so you need to learn two new commands. The du, disk usage, command is used to find out how much disk space is used; the df, disk free, command is used to find out how much space is available.

ACTION

4

1. The du command lists the size, in kilobytes, of all directories at or below the current point in the file system.

```
% du
11      ./OWL
38      ./.elm
20      ./Archives
14      ./InfoWorld/PIMS
28      ./InfoWorld
710     ./Mail
191     ./News
25      ./bin
35      ./src
.
```

Notice that du went two levels deep to find the InfoWorld/PIMS subdirectory, adding its size to the size indicated for the InfoWorld directory. At the very end, it lists 1,627 kilobytes as the size of the dot directory—the current directory. As you know, 1,024 kilobytes is a megabyte. Through division, you'll find that this directory is taking up 1.5MB of disk space.

2. If you are interested in only the grand total, you can use the -s flag to output just a summary of the information.

```
% du -s
.
```

Of course, you can look anywhere on the file system, but the more subdirectories there are, the longer it takes.

3. Error messages with du are possible:

```
% du -s /etc
/etc/shadow: Permission denied
4417    /etc
```

In this example, one of the directories within the /etc directory has a permissions set denying access:

```
% ls -ld /etc/shadow
drwx------  2 root           512 Oct 10 16:34 /etc/shadow/
```

The du command summarizes disk usage only for the files and directories it can read, so regardless of the size of the shadow directory, I'd still have the 4,417 kilobytes size indicated.

4. Although by default du lists only the sizes of directories, it also computes the size of all files. If you're interested in that information, you can, by adding the -a flag, have the program list it for all files.

```
% cd InfoWorld
% du -a
9        ./PIM.review.Z
5        ./Expert.opinion.Z
4        ./PIMS/proposal.txt.Z
1        ./PIMS/task1.txt.Z
2        ./PIMS/task2.txt.Z
2        ./PIMS/task3.txt.Z
2        ./PIMS/task4.txt.Z
2        ./PIMS/task5.txt.Z
2        ./PIMS/task6.txt.Z
1        ./PIMS/contact.info.Z
14       ./PIMS
.
```

The problems of the -a flag for du are similar to those for the -R flag for ls. There might be more files in a directory than you care to view.

Task 4.11: Checking Available Disk Space with df

DESCRIPTION   Figuring out how much disk space is available on the overall Unix system is difficult for everyone except experts. The df command is used for this task, but it doesn't summarize its results—the user must add the column of numbers.

ACTION

1. This is the system's response to the df command:

```
% df
Filesystem          kbytes    used    avail capacity  Mounted
/dev/zd0a            17259   14514     1019    93%     /
/dev/zd8d           185379  143995    22846    86%     /userf
/dev/zd7d           185379   12984   153857     8%     /tmp
/dev/zd3f           385689  307148    39971    88%     /users
/dev/zd3g           367635  232468    98403    70%     /userc
/dev/zd2f           385689  306189    40931    88%     /usere
/dev/zd2g           367635  207234   123637    63%     /userb
/dev/zd1g           301823  223027    48613    82%     /usera
/dev/zd5c           371507  314532    19824    94%     /usr
/dev/zd0h           236820  159641    53497    75%     /usr/src
/dev/zd0g           254987   36844   192644    16%     /var
```

You end up with lots of information, but it's not easily added quickly to find the total space available. Nonetheless, the output offers quite a bit of information.

2. Because I know that my home directory is on the disk /users, I can simply look for that directory in the rightmost column to find out that I'm using the hard disk /dev/zd3f. I can see that 385,689 kilobytes are on the disk, and 88% of the disk is used, which means that 307,148 kilobytes are used and 39,971 kilobytes, or only about 38MB, are unused.

3. Some Unix systems have relatively few separate computer disks hooked up, making the df output more readable. The df output is explained in Figure 4.5.

FIGURE 4.5

Understanding df output.

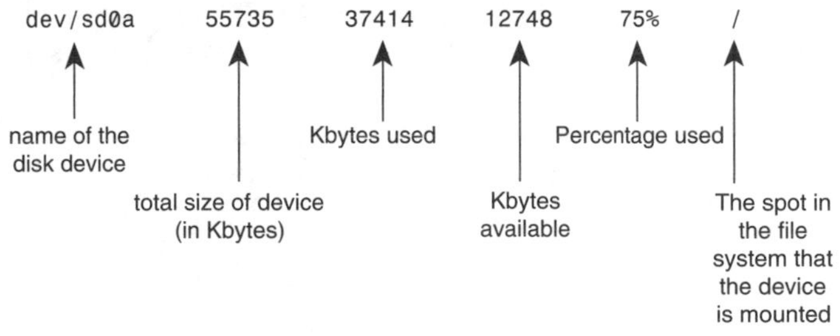

```
dev/sd0a        55735       37414       12748      75%       /
```

name of the disk device — total size of device (in Kbytes) — Kbytes used — Kbytes available — Percentage used — The spot in the file system that the device is mounted

```
% df
Filesystem          kbytes    used    avail capacity  Mounted
/dev/sd0a            55735   37414    12748    75%     /
/dev/sd2b          187195  153569    14907    91%     /usr
/dev/sd1a           55688   43089     7031    86%     /utils
```

4

You can add the columns to find that the system has a total of about 300MB of disk space (55,735 + 187,195 + 55,688), of which 230MB are used. The remaining space is therefore 33MB, or 16% of the total disk size.

4. Many modern Unix systems have a -h flag (some man pages refer to this as the *human readable output* flag!) which offers a much more useful output format. Here's an example from yet another computer system:

```
% df -h
Filesystem     Size   Used   Avail  Capacity  Mounted on
/dev/sd0a      15G    2.1G   13G    14%       /
/dev/sd1a      15G    157M   15G    1%        /web
```

SUMMARY   Try using the du and df commands on your system to determine how much disk space is available on both the overall system and the disk you're using for your home directory. Then use du to identify how much space your files and directories are occupying.

Task 4.12: Shrinking Big Files with the compress Program

DESCRIPTION   Now that you can determine how much space you're using with the files in your directory, you're ready to learn how to save space without removing any files. Unix has a built-in program—the compress program—that offers this capability.

ACTION

1. In this simple example, the compress program is given a list of filenames and then compresses each of the files, renaming them with a .Z suffix, which indicates that they are compressed.

```
% ls -l LISTS
-rw-------  1 taylor        106020 Oct 10 13:47 LISTS
% compress LISTS
% ls -l LISTS.Z
-rw-------  1 taylor         44103 Oct 10 13:47 LISTS.Z
```

Compressing the LISTS file has reduced its size from 106 kilobytes to a little more than 44 kilobytes (a savings of almost 60% in disk space). If you expect to have large files on your system that you won't access very often, using the compress program can save lots of disk space.

2. Using `compress` on bigger files can show even greater savings:

```
% ls -l huge.file
-rwxrwxrwx  1 root       3727360 Sep 27 14:03 huge.file
% compress huge.file
% ls -l huge.file.Z
-rwxrwxrwx  1 taylor     2121950 Sep 27 14:03 huge.file.Z
```

In this example, it took a powerful Sun computer with no other users exactly 20 seconds to compress `huge.file`. This single command was able to free over 1.5MB of disk space. If you're using a PC to run Unix, or if you are on a system with many users (which you can easily ascertain by using the w command), it might take a significant amount of time to compress files.

3. To reverse the operation, use the companion command `uncompress`, and specify either the current name of the file (that is, with the `.Z` suffix) or the name of the file before it was compressed (that is, without the `.Z` suffix).

```
% uncompress LISTS
% ls -l LISTS
-rw-------  1 taylor      106020 Oct 10 13:47 LISTS
```

Why would you compress files? You would do so to save file space. Before you use any of the compressed files, though, you must uncompress them, so the compress utility is best used with large files you won't need for a while.

4

4. For information on how well the `compress` program shrank your files, you can add a `-v` flag to the program for verbose output:

```
% compress -v huge.file
huge.file: Compression: 43.15% -- replaced with huge.file.Z
```

 Try using the `compress` program on some of the files in your directory, being careful not to compress any files (particularly preference or dot files) that might be required to run programs.

Summary

Most of this hour was spent learning about the powerful and complex `ls` command and its many ways of listing files and directories. You also learned how to combine command flags to reduce typing. You learned how to use the `touch` command to create new files and update the modification time on older files, if needed. The hour continued with a discussion of how to ascertain the amount of disk space you're using and how much space is left, using the du and df commands respectively. Finally, you learned how the compress command can keep you from running out of space by ensuring that infrequently used files are stored in the minimum space needed.

Workshop

The Workshop summarizes the key terms you learned and poses some questions about the topics presented in this chapter. It also provides you with a preview of what you will learn in the next hour.

Key Terms

access permission   The set of accesses (read, write, and execute) allowed for each of the three classes of users (owner, group, and everyone else) for each file or directory on the system.

block   At its most fundamental, a block is like a sheet of information in the virtual notebook that represents the disk: A disk is typically composed of many tens, or hundreds, of thousands of blocks of information, each 512 bytes in size. You also might read the explanation of **i-node** in the glossary at the back of the book to learn more about how disks are structured in Unix.

column-first order   When you have a list of items that are listed in columns and span multiple lines, column-first order is a sorting strategy in which items are sorted so that the items are in alphabetical order down the first column. The sorting continues at the top of the second column, then the third column, and so on. The alternative strategy is **row-first order**.

permissions strings   The string that represents the access permissions.

row-first order   In contrast to column-first order, this is when items are sorted in rows so that the first item of each column in a row is in alphabetical order from left to right, then the second line contains the next set of items, and so on.

Exercises

1. Try using the du command on different directories to see how much disk space each requires. If you encounter errors with file permissions, use ls -ld to list the permissions of the directory in question.

2. Why would you want all the different types of sorting alternatives available with ls? Can you think of situations in which each would be useful?

3. Use a combination of the `ls -t` and `touch` commands to create a few new files. Then update their modification times so that in a most recently modified listing of files, the first file you created shows up ahead of the second file you created.

4. Try using the `du -s ..` command from your home directory. Before you try it, however, what do you think will happen?

5. Use `df` and `bc` or `dc` to figure out the amounts of disk space used and available on your system.

6. Use the `compress` command to shrink a file in `/tmp` or your home directory. Use the `-v` flag to learn how much the file was compressed, and then restore the file to its original condition.

Preview of the Next Hour

The next hour is a bit easier. It offers further explanation of the various information given by the `ls` command and a discussion of file ownership, including how to change the owner and group of any file or directory. You will learn about the `chmod` command, which can change the specific set of permissions associated with any file or directory, and the `umask` command, which can control the modes that new files are given upon creation.

4

Hour 5

Ownership and Permissions

This hour focuses on teaching the basics of Unix file permissions. Topics include setting and modifying file permissions with `chmod`, analyzing file permissions as shown by the `ls -l` command, and setting up default file permissions with the `umask` command. Permission is only half the puzzle, however, and you also learn about file ownership and group ownership, and how to change either for any file or directory.

Goals for This Hour

In this hour, you will learn how to

- Understand file permissions settings
- Understand directory permissions settings
- Modify file and directory permissions with `chmod`
- Set new file permissions with `chmod`

- Establish default file and directory permissions with umask
- Identify the owner and group for any file or directory

The preceding hour contained the first tutorial dealing with the permissions of a file or directory using the -l option with ls. If you haven't read that hour recently, it would help to review the material. In this hour, you learn about another option to ls that tells Unix to show the group and owner of files or directories. Two more commands are introduced and discussed in detail: chmod for changing the permissions of a file and umask for defining default permissions.

Working with File Permissions

As you have seen in examples throughout the book, Unix treats all directories as files; they have their own size (independent of their contents), their own permissions strings, and more. As a result, unless it's an important difference, from here on I talk about files with the intention of referring to files and directories both. Logic will confirm whether commands can apply to both, or to files only, or to directories only. (For example, you can't edit a directory and you can't store files inside other files.)

Task 5.1: Understanding File Permissions Settings

DESCRIPTION   In the past hour you learned a bit about how to interpret the information that ls offers on file permissions when ls is used with the -l flag. Consider the following example:

```
% ls -l
total 403
drwx------   2 taylor        512 Sep 30 10:38 Archives/
drwx------   3 taylor        512 Oct  1 08:23 InfoWorld/
-rw-------   1 taylor     106020 Oct 10 13:47 LISTS
drwx------   2 taylor       1024 Sep 30 10:50 Mail/
drwx------   2 taylor        512 Oct  6 09:36 News/
drwx------   2 taylor        512 Sep 30 10:51 OWL/
-rw-------   1 taylor       4643 Oct 10 14:01 RUMORS.18Sept
drwx------   2 taylor        512 Oct 10 19:09 bin/
-rw-------   1 taylor       3843 Oct 10 16:22 iecc.list
-rw-rw-r--   1 taylor     280232 Oct 10 16:22 mailing.lists
-rw-rw----   1 taylor       1031 Oct  7 15:44 newlists
drwx------   2 taylor        512 Oct 10 19:09 src/
```

The first item of information on each line is what is key here. You learned in the preceding hour that the first item is called the permissions string or, more succinctly, permissions. It also is sometimes referred to as the *mode* or *permissions mode* of the file, a mnemonic that can be valuable for remembering how to change permissions.

The permissions can be broken into four parts: type, owner, group, and world permissions. The first character indicates the file type: d is a directory and - is a regular file. Various other types of files are in Unix, each indicated by the first letter of its permissions string, as summarized in Table 5.1. You can safely ignore, however, any file that isn't either a regular file or a directory.

TABLE 5.1   The ls File Type Indicators

Letter	Indicated File Type
d	Directory
b	Block-type special file
c	Character-type special file
l	Symbolic link
p	Pipe
s	Socket
-	Regular file

The next nine letters in the permissions string are broken into three groups of three each—representing the owner, group, and everyone else—as shown in Figure 5.1.

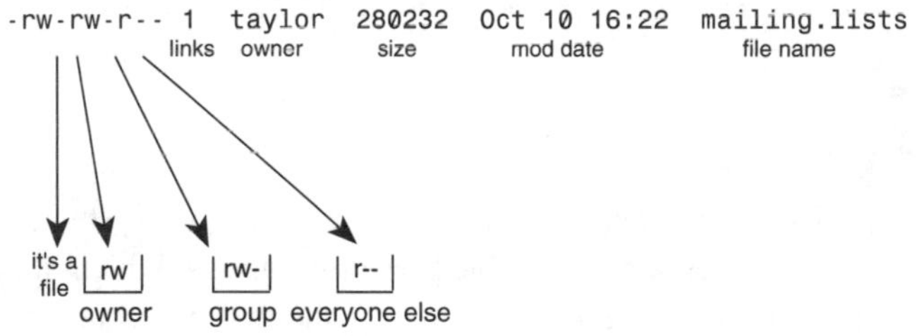

FIGURE 5.1
Interpreting file permissions.

```
-rw-rw-r-- 1  taylor  280232  Oct 10 16:22  mailing.lists
           links owner  size    mod date      file name
```

it's a file | rw | rw- | r--
owner group everyone else

To understand what the permissions actually mean to the computer system, remember that Unix treats everything as a file. If you install an application, it's just like everything else, with one exception: The system knows that an application is executable. A letter to your Mum is a regular file, but if you were to tell Unix that it was executable, the system would merrily try to run it as a program (and fail).

Three primary types of permission exist for files: read, write, and execute. Read permission enables users to examine the contents of the file with various programs, but they cannot alter, modify, or delete any information. They can copy the file to a directory where they have write permission and then edit the new version.

Write permission is the next step up. Users with write access to a file can add information to the file. If you have write permission and read permission for a file, you can edit the file: The read permission enables you to view the contents, and the write permission enables you to alter them. With write permission only, you'd be able to add information to the file, but you wouldn't be able to view the contents of the file at any time. Admittedly, write-only permission is unusual in Unix, but you might see it for log files, which are files that track activity on the system. Imagine if each time anyone logged in to your Unix system the computer recorded the fact, noting who logged in, where they logged in from, and the current time and date. Armed with that information, you could ascertain who last logged in, who uses dial-up phone lines, and who uses the computer the most. (In fact, a Unix command does just that. It's called last.)

So far you've learned that you can have files with read-only permission, read-write permission, and write-only permission. The third type of access permission is execute, noted by ls with an x in the third slot of the permissions string. You can set any file to be executable; shell scripts, Perl, and other interpreted languages are text files that are executed.

```
% ls -l bin
total 57
-rwx------  1 taylor       1507 Aug 17 13:27 bounce.msg
-rwxrwx---  1 taylor      32916 Oct 10 19:09 calc
-rwx------  1 taylor      18567 Sep 14 22:14 fixit
-rw-------  1 taylor        334 Oct  1 09:53 punt
-rwx------  1 taylor       3424 Sep 10 22:27 rumor.mill.sh
```

ACTION

1. Try listing the files in the directory /etc on your system, and see whether you can identify which are executable files or programs, which are directories, which are symbolic links (denoted with an l as the first character of the permissions string; they're files that point to other files, or directories that point to other directories), and which are regular files.

2. Execute permission is slightly different from either read or write permission. Any file with execute permission can be treated like a program. You enter the name of the file on the command line, and if the directory is in your PATH, the file is executed.

```
% pwd
/home/taylor
% echo $PATH
/home/taylor/bin:/bin:/usr/bin:/usr/ucb:/usr/local:/usr/local/bin:
% ls -l bin/say.hi
-rwxrwx---  1 taylor          9 Oct 11 13:32 bin/say.hi
% say.hi
hi
```

You can now see the importance of your search PATH. Without a search PATH, the system wouldn't be able to find any commands, and you'd be left with a barely functional system. You can also see the purpose of checking the executable permission status. I'm going to jump ahead a bit to show you one use of the chmod (change mode/permission) program so that you can see what happens if I remove the execute permission from the say.hi program with the -x flag:

```
% chmod -x bin/say.hi
% ls -l bin/say.hi
-rw-rw----  1 taylor          9 Oct 11 13:32 bin/say.hi
% say.hi
/home/taylor/bin/say.hi: Permission denied.
```

This time Unix searched through my search path, found a file that matched the name of the program I requested, and then ascertained that it wasn't executable. The resultant error message: Permission denied.

3. Now try entering say.hi on your computer system. You'll get a different error message, Command not found, which tells you that Unix searched all the directories in your search path but couldn't find a match anywhere.

4. Check your PATH and find a directory that you can add files in. You'll probably have a bin directory in your home directory on the list, as I have /home/taylor/bin in my search path. If you don't, use mkdir bin to create one. It's a good place to add a file using the touch command:

```
% echo $PATH
/home/taylor/bin:/bin:/usr/bin:/usr/ucb:/usr/local:/usr/local/bin:
% touch bin/my.new.cmd
% ls -l bin
-rw-rw----  1 taylor          0 Oct 11 15:07 my.new.cmd
```

5. Now try to actually execute the command by entering its name directly:

```
% my.new.cmd
/home/taylor/bin/my.new.cmd: Permission denied.
```

If you're using the C Shell as your command interpreter, it probably won't find the new command you just created. This is because, to speed things up, it keeps an internal table of where different commands are found in your search path. You need to force the program to rebuild its table, and you can do that with the simple command rehash. If, when you enter the filename, you don't get permission denied but instead see Command not found, enter rehash and try again.

6. Finally, use chmod to add execute permission to the file, and try executing it one more time:

```
% chmod +x bin/my.new.cmd
% ls -l bin/my.new.cmd
-rwxrw----   1 taylor            0 Oct 11 15:07 bin/my.new.cmd
% my.new.cmd
%
```

Voila! You've created your first Unix command, an achievement, even though it doesn't do much. You can now see how the search path and the Unix philosophy of having applications be identical to regular files, except for the permission, can be invaluable as you learn how to customize your environment.

SUMMARY Execute permission enables the user to run the file as if it were a program. Execute permission is independent of other permissions granted—or denied—so it's perfectly feasible to have a program with read and execute permission, but no write permission. (After all, you wouldn't want others altering the program itself.) You also can have programs with execute permission only. This means that users can run the application, but they can't examine it to see how it works or copy it. (Copying requires the ability to read the file.)

> Though actual programs with execute-only permission work fine, a special class of programs called *shell scripts* fail. Shell scripts act like a Unix command-line macro facility, which enables you to easily save a series of commands in a file and then run them as a single program. To work, however, the shell must be able to read the file and execute it too, so shell scripts always require both read and execute permission.

There are clearly quite a few permutations on the three different permissions: read, write, and execute. In practice, a few occur most commonly, as listed in Table 5.2.

TABLE 5.2   The Most Common File Permissions

Permission	Meaning
---	No access is allowed
r--	Read-only access
r-x	Read and execute access, for programs and shell scripts
rw-	Read and write access, for files
rwx	All access allowed, for programs

These permissions have different meanings when applied to directories, but `---` always indicates that no one can access the file in question.

Interpretation of the following few examples should help:

```
-rw-------  1 taylor      3843 Oct 10 16:22 iecc.list
-rw-rw-r--  1 taylor    280232 Oct 10 16:22 mailing.lists
-rw-rw----  1 taylor      1031 Oct  7 15:44 newlists
-rwxr-x---  1 taylor        64 Oct  9 09:31 the.script
```

The first file, `iecc.list`, has read and write permission for the owner (`taylor`) and is off-limits to all other users. The file `mailing.lists` offers similar access to the file owner (`taylor`) and to the group, but offers read-only access to everyone else on the system. The third file, `newlists`, provides read and write access to both the file owner and group, but no access to anyone not in the group.

The fourth file on the list, `the.script`, is a program that can be run by both the owner and group members, read (or copied) by both the owner and the group, and written (altered) by the owner. In practice, this probably would be a shell script, as described earlier, and these permissions would enable the owner (`taylor`) to use an editor to modify the commands therein. Other members of the group could read and use the shell script but would be denied access to change it.

Task 5.2: Directory Permissions Settings

DESCRIPTION Directories are similar to files in how you interpret the permissions strings. The differences occur because of the unique purpose of directories, namely to store other files or directories. I always think of directories as bins or boxes. You can examine the box itself, or you can look at what's inside.

In many ways, Unix treats directories simply as files in the file system, where the content of the file is a list of the files and directories stored within, rather than a letter, program, or shopping list.

The difference, of course, is that when you operate with directories, you're operating both with the directory itself and, implicitly, with its contents. By analogy, when you fiddle with a box full of toys, you're not altering just the state of the box itself, but also potentially the toys within.

Three permissions are possible for a directory, just as for a file: read, write, and execute. The easiest is write permission. If a directory has write permission enabled, you can add new items and remove items from the directory. It's like owning the box; you can do what you'd like with the toys inside.

5

The interaction between read and execute permission with a directory is confusing. There are two types of operations you perform on a directory: listing the contents of the directory (usually with ls) and examining specific known files within the directory.

ACTION

1. Start by listing a directory, using the -d flag:

    ```
    % ls -ld testme
    dr-x------  2 taylor         512 Oct 11 17:03 testme/
    % ls -l testme
    total 0
    -rw-rw----  1 taylor           0 Oct 11 17:03 file
    % ls -l testme/file
    -rw-rw----  1 taylor           0 Oct 11 17:03 testme/file
    ```

    For a directory with both read and execute permission, you can see that it's easy to list the directory, find out the files therein, and list specific files within the directory.

2. Read permission on a directory enables you to read the "table of contents" of the directory, but, by itself, does not allow you to examine any of the files therein. By itself, read permission is rather bizarre:

    ```
    % ls -ld testme
    dr--------  2 taylor         512 Oct 11 17:03 testme/
    % ls -l testme
    testme/file not found
    total 0
    % ls -l testme/file
    testme/file not found
    ```

    Notice that the system indicated the name of the file contained in the testme directory. When I tried to list the file explicitly, however, the system couldn't find the file.

3. Compare this with the situation when you have execute permission—which enables you to examine the files within the directory—but you don't have read permission, and you are prevented from viewing the table of contents of the directory itself:

    ```
    % ls -ld testme
    d--x------  2 taylor         512 Oct 11 17:03 testme/
    % ls -l testme
    testme unreadable
    % ls -l testme/file
    -rw-rw----  1 taylor           0 Oct 11 17:03 testme/file
    ```

With execute-only permission, you can set up directories so that people who know the names of files contained in the directories can access those files, but people without that knowledge cannot list the directory to learn the filenames.

4. I've actually never seen anyone have a directory in Unix with execute-only permission, and certainly you would never expect to see one set to read-only. It would be nice if Unix would warn you if you set a directory to have one permission and not the other. However, Unix won't do that. So, remember for directories always to be sure that you have both read and execute permissions set. Table 5.3 summarizes the most common directory permissions.

TABLE 5.3 The Most Common Directory Permissions

Permission	Meaning
- - -	No access allowed to directory
r - x	Read-only access, no modification allowed
rwx	All access allowed

5. One interesting permutation of directory permissions is for a directory that's write-only. Unfortunately, the write-only permission doesn't do what you'd hope, that is, enable people to add files to the directory without being able to see what the directory already contains. Instead, it is functionally identical to having it set for no access permission at all.

At the beginning of this hour, I used `ls` to list various files and directories in my home directory:

```
% ls -l
total 403
drwx------  2 taylor          512 Sep 30 10:38 Archives/
drwx------  3 taylor          512 Oct  1 08:23 InfoWorld/
-rw-------  1 taylor       106020 Oct 10 13:47 LISTS
drwx------  2 taylor         1024 Sep 30 10:50 Mail/
drwx------  2 taylor          512 Oct  6 09:36 News/
drwx------  2 taylor          512 Sep 30 10:51 OWL/
-rw-------  1 taylor         4643 Oct 10 14:01 RUMORS.18Sept
drwx------  2 taylor          512 Oct 10 19:09 bin/
-rw-------  1 taylor         3843 Oct 10 16:22 iecc.list
-rw-rw-r--  1 taylor       280232 Oct 10 16:22 mailing.lists
-rw-rw----  1 taylor         1031 Oct  7 15:44 newlists
drwx------  2 taylor          512 Oct 10 19:09 src/
```

Now you can see that all my directories are set so that I have list, examine, and modify (read, execute, and write, respectively) capability for myself, and no access is allowed for anyone else.

6. The very top-level directory is more interesting, with various directories and permissions.

```
% ls -l /
-rw-r--r--   1 root         61440 Nov 29  1991 boot
drwxr-xr-x   4 root         23552 Sep 27 11:31 dev
-r--r--r--   1 root        686753 Aug 27 21:58 dynix
drwxr-xr-x   6 root          3072 Oct 11 16:30 etc
drwxr-xr-x   2 root          8192 Apr 12  1991 lost+found
lrwxr-xr-x   1 root             7 Jul 28  1988 sys -> usr/sys
drwxrwxrwx  65 root         12800 Oct 11 17:33 tmp
drwxr-xr-x 753 root         14848 Oct  5 10:07 usera
drwxr-xr-x 317 root         13312 Oct  5 10:17 userb
drwxr-xr-x 626 root         13312 Oct  8 13:02 userc
drwxr-xr-x 534 root         10752 Sep 30 13:06 users
drwxr-xr-x  34 root          1024 Oct  1 09:10 usr
drwxr-xr-x   5 root          1024 Oct  1 09:20 var
```

Clearly, this machine has a lot of users. Notice that the link count for usera, userb, userc, and users is each in the hundreds. The dev directory has read and execute permissions for everyone and write permission for the owner (root). Indeed, all the directories at this level are identical except for tmp, which has read, write, and execute permission for all users on the system.

7. Did you notice the listing for the sys directory buried in that output?

```
lrwxr-xr-x  1 root             7 Jul 28  1988 sys -> usr/sys
```

From the information in Table 5.1, you know that because the first letter of the permissions string is a l that the directory is a symbolic link. The filename shows just the specifics of the link, indicating that sys points to the directory usr/sys. In fact, if you count the number of letters in the name usr/sys, you'll find that it exactly matches the size of the sys link entry too.

8. Try using ls -l / yourself. You should be able to understand the permissions of any file or directory that you encounter.

SUMMARY Permissions of files and directories will prove easier as you work with Unix more.

Task 5.3: Modifying File and Directory Permissions with chmod

DESCRIPTION Now that you can list directory permissions and understand what they mean, how about learning a Unix command that lets you change them to meet your needs? You've already had a sneak preview of the command: chmod. The mnemonic is "change mode," and it derives from early Unix folk talking about permission modes of files. You can remember it by thinking of it as a shortened form of change permission modes.

To sound like a Unix expert, pronounce chmod as "ch-mod," "ch" like the beginning of child, and "mod" to rhyme with *cod*.

The chmod command enables you to specify permissions in two different ways: symbolically or numerically. Symbolic notation is most commonly used to modify existing permissions, whereas numeric format always replaces any existing permission with the new value specified. In this task, you learn about symbolic notation, and the next task focuses on the powerful numeric format.

Symbolic notation for chmod is a bit like having a menu of different choices, enabling you to pick the combination that best fits your requirements. Figure 5.2 shows the menus.

FIGURE 5.2

The menu of symbolic chmod *values.*

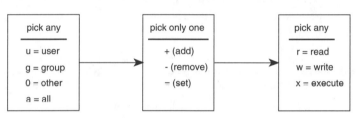

The command chmod is like a smorgasbord where you can choose any combination of items from either the first or last boxes, and place your choice from the center box between them.

For example, if you wanted to add write permission to the file test for everyone in your group, you would, working backward from that description, choose g for group, + for add, and w for write. The finished Unix command would be chmod g+w test.

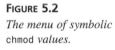

When you have an account assigned to you, you have a unique user name, but you are also included in one or more groups. Group permissions let other people working on the same project share information without opening up the information to the rest of the world.

If you decided to take away read and execute permission for everyone not in your group, you could use chmod o-rx test to accomplish the task.

5

ACTION

1. Turn to your computer and, using `touch` and `ls`, try changing permissions and see what happens. I'll do the same:

   ```
   % touch test
   % ls -l test
   -rw-r--r--  1 taylor          0 Oct 11 18:29 test
   ```

2. The first modification I want to make is that people in my group should be able to read and write to the file. I'll add write permission for group members:

   ```
   % chmod g+w test
   % ls -l test
   -rw-rw-r--  1 taylor          0 Oct 11 18:29 test
   ```

3. But then my boss reminds me that everyone in the group should have all access permissions. Okay, I'll do so.

   ```
   % chmod g+x test
   % ls -l test
   -rw-rwxr--  1 taylor          0 Oct 11 18:29 test
   ```

   I also could have done that with `chmod g=rwx`, of course.

4. Wait a second. This `test` file is just for my own use, and nobody in my group should be looking at it anyway. I'll change it back.

   ```
   % chmod o-r test
   % chmod g-rwx test
   % ls -l test
   -rw-------  1 taylor          0 Oct 11 18:29 test
   ```

   Great. Now the file is set so that I can read and write it, but nobody else can touch it, read it, modify it, or anything else.

5. If I relented a bit, I could easily add, with one last `chmod` command, read-only permission for everyone:

   ```
   % chmod a+r test
   % ls -l test
   -rw-r--r--  1 taylor          0 Oct 11 18:29 test
   ```

SUMMARY Permissions in Unix are based on a concentric access model from Multics. (In Hour 1, "What Is This Unix Stuff?" you learned that the name Unix is also a pun on Multics.) Figure 5.3 illustrates this concept.

As a result, it's incredibly rare to see a file where the owner doesn't have the most access to a file. It'd be like buying a car and letting everyone but you drive it—rather silly. Similarly, members of the group are given better or equal permission to everyone else on the machine. You would never see `r--r--rwx` as a permissions string.

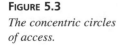

FIGURE 5.3
The concentric circles of access.

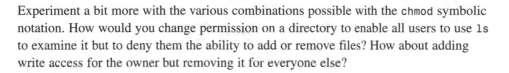

Experiment a bit more with the various combinations possible with the chmod symbolic notation. How would you change permission on a directory to enable all users to use ls to examine it but to deny them the ability to add or remove files? How about adding write access for the owner but removing it for everyone else?

Task 5.4: Setting New File Permissions with chmod

DESCRIPTION The second form of input that chmod accepts is absolute numeric values for permissions. Before you can learn how to use this notation, you have to learn a bit about different numbering systems.

The numbering system you're familiar with, the one you use to balance your checkbook and check the receipt from the market, is in decimal form, or base 10. This means that each digit—from right to left—has the value of the digit raised by a power of 10, based on the digit's location in the number. Figure 5.4 shows what the number 5,783 is in decimal form.

FIGURE 5.4
Interpreting decimal numbers.

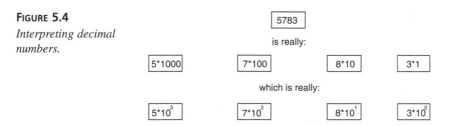

You can see that in a base-10 numbering system, the value of a number is the sum of the value of each digit multiplied by the numeric base raised to the *n*th power. The *n* is the number of spaces the digit is away from the rightmost digit. That is, in the number 5,783, you know that the 7 is worth more than just 7, because it's two spaces away from the rightmost digit (the 3). Therefore, its value is the numeric base (10) raised to the *n*th power, where *n* is 2 (it's two spaces away). Ten to the second power equals 100 ($10^2 = 100$), and when you multiply that by 7, sure enough, you find that the 7 is worth 700 in this number.

What does all this have to do with the chmod command? At its most fundamental, Unix permissions are a series of on/off switches. Does the group have write permission? One equals yes, zero equals no. A binary system is one in which each digit can have only two values: on or off, 1 or 0, yes or no. Therefore, you can easily and uniquely describe any permissions string as a series of zeros and ones, as a binary number. Figure 5.5 demonstrates this.

FIGURE 5.5
Permissions as binary numbers.

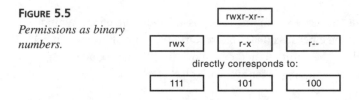

The convention is that if a letter is present, the binary digit is a 1—that permission is permitted—and if no letter is present, the digit is a zero. Thus, r-xr----- can be described as 101100000, and r--r--r-- can be described in binary as 100100100.

You've already learned that the nine-character permissions string is really just a three-character permissions string duplicated thrice for the three different types of user (the owner, group, and everyone else). That means that you can focus on learning how to translate a single tri-character permissions substring into binary and extrapolate for more than one permission. Table 5.4 lists all possible permissions and their binary equivalents.

TABLE 5.4 Permissions and Binary Equivalents

Permissions String	Binary Equivalent
- - -	000
- -x	001
-w-	010
-wx	011
r--	100
r-x	101
rw-	110
rwx	111

Knowing how to interpret decimal numbers using the rather complex formula presented earlier, you should not be surprised that the decimal equivalent of any binary number can be obtained by the same technique. Figure 5.6 shows how, with the binary equivalent of the r-x permission.

FIGURE 5.6

Expressing r-x as a single digit.

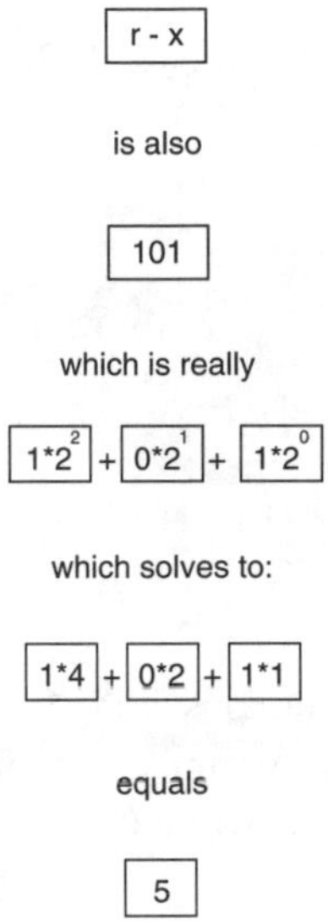

r-x

is also

101

which is really

$$1*2^2 + 0*2^1 + 1*2^0$$

which solves to:

$$1*4 + 0*2 + 1*1$$

equals

5

If r-x is equal to 5, it stands to reason that each of the possible three-character permissions has a single-digit equivalent, and Table 5.5 expands Table 5.4 to include the single-digit equivalents.

TABLE 5.5   Permissions and Numeric Equivalents

Permissions String	Binary Equivalent	Decimal Equivalent
- - -	000	0
- - x	001	1
- w -	010	2
- w x	011	3
r - -	100	4
r - x	101	5
r w -	110	6
r w x	111	7

5

The value of having a single digit to describe any of the seven different permission states should be obvious. Using only three digits, you now can fully express any possible combination of permissions for any file or directory in Unix—one digit for the owner permission, one for group, and a one for everyone else. Figure 5.7 shows how to take a full permissions string and translate it into its three-digit numeric equivalent.

Note: if this math is a bit intimidating, remember that r=4, w=2, and x=1, so, for example, rwx = 4+2+1 = 7 and r-x = 4+1 = 5.

FIGURE 5.7

Translating a full permissions string into its numeric equivalent.

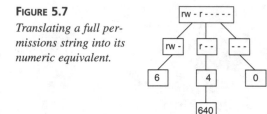

From this illustration, you can see how the permissions string `rw-r-----` (read and write permission for the owner, read permission for the group, and no access allowed for everyone else) is exactly equivalent to the numeric string 640.

ACTION

1. Try to create numeric strings on your own, using Table 5.4 to help. Turn to your computer and use `ls` to display some listings. Break each permissions string into three groups of three letters, and figure out the numeric equivalents. Here are some examples from the `ls -F` listing of my home directory:

   `drwx------  2 taylor        512 Sep 30 10:38 Archives/`

   For `Archives/`, the equivalent numeric permission is 700.

   `-rw-------  1 taylor     106020 Oct 10 13:47 LISTS`

   For `LISTS`, the equivalent numeric permission is 600.

   `-rw-rw-r--  1 taylor     280232 Oct 10 16:22 mailing.lists`

   For `mailing.lists`, the equivalent numeric permission is 664.

   `-rw-rw----  1 taylor       1031 Oct  7 15:44 newlists`

   For `newlists`, the equivalent numeric permission is 660.

SUMMARY One last step is required before you can try using the numeric permissions strings with `chmod`. You need to be able to work backward to determine a permission that you'd like to set, and determine the numeric equivalent for that permission.

Task 5.5: Calculating Numeric Permissions Strings

DESCRIPTION For example, if you wanted to have a directory set so that you have all access, people in your group can look at the contents but not modify anything, and everyone else is shut out, how would you do it?

All permissions for yourself means you want read+write+execute for owner (or numeric permission 7); read and listing permission for others in the group means read+execute for group (numeric permission 5); and no permission for everyone else, numeric permission 0. Put the three together and you have the answer, 750.

That's the trick of working with chmod in numeric mode. You specify the absolute permissions you want as a three-digit number, and the system sets the permissions on the file or directory appropriately.

The absolute concept is important with this form of chmod. You cannot use the chmod numeric form to add or remove permissions from a file or directory. It is usable only for reassigning the permissions string of a file or directory.

The good news is that, as you learned earlier in this hour, there are a relatively small number of commonly used file permissions, summarized in Table 5.6.

TABLE 5.6   Common Permissions and Their Numeric Equivalents

Permission	Numeric	Used With
`---------`	000	All types
`r--------`	400	Files
`r--r--r--`	444	Files
`rw-------`	600	Files
`rw-r--r--`	644	Files
`rw-rw-r--`	664	Files
`rw-rw-rw-`	666	Files
`rwx------`	700	Programs and directories
`rwxr-x---`	750	Programs and directories
`rwxr-xr-x`	755	Programs and directories

5

ACTION

1. Turn to your computer and try using the numeric mode of chmod, along with ls, to
    display the actual permissions to learn for yourself how this works.

    ```
    % touch example
    % ls -l example
    -rw-rw----  1 taylor          0 Oct 12 10:16 example
    ```

    By default, files are created in my directory with mode 660.

2. To take away read and write permission for people in my group, I'd replace the 660
    permission with what numeric permissions string? I'd use 600:

    ```
    % chmod 600 example
    % ls -l example
    -rw-------  1 taylor          0 Oct 12 10:16 example
    ```

3. What if I change my mind and want to open up the file for everyone to read or
    write? I'd use 666:

    ```
    % chmod 666 example
    % ls -l example
    -rw-rw-rw-  1 taylor          0 Oct 12 10:16 example
    ```

4. Finally, pretend that example is actually a directory. What numeric mode would I
    specify to enable everyone to use ls in the directory and enable only the owner to
    add or delete files? I'd use 755:

    ```
    % chmod 755 example
    % ls -l example
    -rwxr-xr-x  1 taylor          0 Oct 12 10:16 example
    ```

SUMMARY You've looked at both the numeric mode and the symbolic mode for defining
permissions. Having learned both, which do you prefer?

> Somehow I've never gotten the hang of symbolic mode, so I almost always
> use the numeric mode for chmod. The only exception is when I want to add
> or delete simple permissions. Then, I use something like chmod +r test to
> add read permission. Part of the problem is that I don't think of the user of
> the file but rather the owner, and specifying o+r causes chmod to change
> permission for others. It's important, therefore, that you remember that files
> have users so you remember u for user, and that everyone not in the group
> is other so you remember o. Otherwise, learn the numeric shortcut!

File permissions and modes are one of the most complex aspects of Unix. You can tell— it's taken two hours to explain it fully. It's very important that you spend the time really to understand how the permissions strings relate to directory permissions, how to read the output of ls, and how to change modes using both styles of the chmod command. It will be time well spent.

Task 5.6: Establishing Default File and Directory Permissions with the umask Command

DESCRIPTION When I've created files, they've had read+write permission for the owner and group, but no access allowed for anyone else. When you create files on your system, you might find that the default permissions are different.

The controlling variable behind the default permissions is called the *file creation mask*, or umask for short.

Inexplicably, umask doesn't always list its value as a three-digit number, but you can find its value in the same way you figured out the numeric permissions strings for chmod. For example, when I enter umask, the system indicates that my umask setting is 07. A leading zero has been dropped, so the actual value is 007, a value that British MI6 could no doubt appreciate!

But 007 doesn't mean that the default file is created with read+write+execute for everyone else and no permissions for the owner or group. It means quite the opposite, literally.

The umask command is a filter through which permissions are pushed to ascertain what remains. Figure 5.8 demonstrates how this works.

Think of your mask as a series of boxes: If the value is true, the information can't exude through the box. If the value is false, it can. Your mask is therefore the direct opposite to how you want your permissions to be set. In Figure 5.8, I want to have 770 as the default permission for any new file or directory I create, so I want to specify the exact opposite of that, 007. Sure enough, with this umask value, when I create new files the default permission allows read and write access to the owner and group, but no access to anyone else.

Things are a bit trickier than that. You've probably already asked yourself, Why, if I have 007 as my mask (which results in 770 as the default permissions), do my files have 660 as the actual default permission?

The reason is that Unix tries to be smart about the execute permission setting. If I create a directory, Unix knows that execute permission is important, and so it grants it. However, for some files (particularly text files), execute permission doesn't make sense, so Unix actually masks it out internally.

5

FIGURE 5.8

Interpreting the umask *value.*

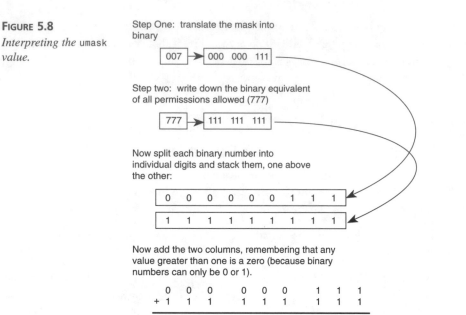

Step One: translate the mask into binary

007 → 000 000 111

Step two: write down the binary equivalent of all permisssions allowed (777)

777 → 111 111 111

Now split each binary number into individual digits and stack them, one above the other:

0	0	0	0	0	0	1	1	1
1	1	1	1	1	1	1	1	1

Now add the two columns, remembering that any value greater than one is a zero (because binary numbers can only be 0 or 1).

```
    0  0  0     0  0  0     1  1  1
 +  1  1  1     1  1  1     1  1  1
   ──────────────────────────────────
    1  1  1     1  1  1     0  0  0
```

And translate that back to a decimal value:

7 7 0

default creation permission

Another way to look at this is that any time you create a file containing information, the original mask that the system uses to compare against your umask is not 777 (not rwxrwxrwx, to put it another way) but rather 666 (rw-rw-rw-). This is in recognition of the unlikely case that you'll want to execute the new file.

The good news is that you now know an easy way to set the execute permission for a file if the system gets it wrong: chmod +x *filename* does the trick.

ACTION

1. Turn to your computer and check your umask setting, and then alternate between changing its values and creating new files with touch.

    ```
    % umask
    07
    % touch test.07
    % ls -l test.07
    -rw-rw----  1 taylor          0 Oct 12 14:38 test.07
    ```

2. To change the value of your umask, add the numeric value of the desired mask to the command line:

```
% umask 077
```

This changes my umask value from 007 (------rwx, which produces a 770 default permission: rwxrwx---) to 077 (---rwxrwx, which produces a 700 default permission: rwx------). Before you look at the following listing, what would you expect this modification to mean? Remember that you should read it as the exact opposite of how you want the default permissions.

```
% touch test.077
% ls -l test.077
-rw------- 1 taylor          0 Oct 12 14:38 test.077
```

Is that what you expected?

3. What would you have as your umask if you wanted to have the default permission keep files private to just the owner and make them read-only?

You can work through this problem in reverse. If you want r-x------ as the default permission (because the system takes care of whether execute permission is needed, based on file type), write down the opposite permission, which is -w-rwxrwx. Translate that to a binary number, 010 111 111, and then to a three-digit value, 277 (010=2, 111=7, 111=7). That's the answer. The value 277 is the correct umask value to ensure that files you create are read-only for yourself and off-limits to everyone else.

```
% umask 277
% touch test.277
% ls -l test.277
-r-------- 1 taylor          0 Oct 12 14:39 test.277
```

4. What if you wanted to have files created with the default permission being read-only for everyone, read-write for the group, but read-only for the owner? Again, work backward. The desired permission is r-xrwxr-x, so create the opposite value (-w-----w-), translate it into binary (010 000 010), and then translate that into a three-digit value: 202 (010=2, 000=0, 010=2).

> As a rule of thumb, it's best to leave the execute permission enabled when building umask values so the system doesn't err when creating directories.

SUMMARY The umask is something set once and left alone. If you've tried various experiments on your computer, remember to restore your umask back to a sensible value to avoid future problems (though each time you log in to the system it's reset to your default value).

5

In the next hour, you learn how to use the mkdir command to create new directories, and you see how the umask value affects default directory access permissions.

Task 5.7: Identifying Owner and Group for Any File or Directory

DESCRIPTION One of the many items of information that the ls command displays when used with the -l flag is the owner of the file or directory. So far, all the files and directories in your home directory have been owned by you, with the probable exception of the .. directory, which is owned by whoever owns the directory above your home.

In other words, when you enter ls -l, you should see your account name as the owner for every file in the listing.

If you're collaborating with another user, however, there might well be times when you'll want to change the owner of a file or directory after you've created and modified it. The first step in accomplishing this is to identify the owner and group.

Identifying the owner is easy; ls lists that by default. But how do you identify the group of which the file or directory is a part?

ACTION

1. The ls command can show the group membership of any file or directory by addition of a new command flag, -g. By itself, -g doesn't alter the output of ls, but when used with the -l flag, it adds a column of information to the listing. Try it on your system. Here is an example:

```
% ls -lg /tmp
-rw-r--r--  1 root      root           0 Oct 12 14:52 sh145
drwxr-xr-x  2 shakes    root         512 Oct 12 07:23 shakes/
-rw-------  1 meademd   com435         0 Oct 12 14:46 snd.12
-rw-------  1 dessy     stuprsac    1191 Oct 12 14:57 snd.15
-rw-------  1 steen     utech          1 Oct 12 10:28 snd.17
-rw-r-----  1 jsmith    utech     258908 Oct 12 12:37 sol2
```

 On many System V-based systems, the output of ls -l always shows user and group. The –g flag actually turns off this display!

Both owners and groups vary for each of the files and directories in this small listing. Notice that files can have different owners while having the same group. (There are two examples here: sh145 and the shakes directory, and snd.17 and sol2.)

2. Directories where there are often a wide variety of owners for directories are the directories above your own home directory and the `tmp` directory, as you can see in step 1. Examine both on your system and identify both the owner and group of all files. For files in the same group you're in (with the `id` command, you can find which group or groups you are in) but not owned by you, you'll need to check which of the three permission values to identify your own access privileges.

SUMMARY Files and directories have both owners and groups, although the group is ultimately less important than the owner, particularly where permissions and access are involved.

Summary

In this hour, you learned the basics of Unix file permissions, including how to set and modify file permissions with `chmod` and how to analyze file permissions as shown by the `ls -l` command. You also learned about translating between numeric bases (binary and decimal) and how to convert permissions strings into numeric values. Both are foundations for the `umask` command, which you learned to interpret and alter as desired.

Workshop

The Workshop summarizes the key terms you learned and poses some questions about the topics presented in this chapter. It also provides you with a preview of what you will learn in the next hour.

Key Terms

file creation mask When files are created in Unix, they inherit a default set of access permissions. These defaults are under the control of the user and are known as the file creation mask.

mode A shorthand way of saying permissions mode.

permissions mode The set of accesses (read, write, and execute) allowed for each of the three classes of users (owner, group, and everyone else) for each file or directory on the system. This is a synonym for access permission.

shell script A collection of shell commands in a file.

5

Exercises

1. In what situations might the following file permissions be useful?

   r--rw-r--   r--r--rw-

   rw--w--w-   -w--w--w-

   rwxr-xr-x   r-x--x--x

2. Translate the six file permissions strings in step 1 into their binary and numeric equivalents.

3. Explain what the following umask values would make the default permissions for newly created files:

007	077	777
111	222	733
272	544	754

4. Count the number of groups that are represented by group membership of files in the tmp directory on your system. Use id to see whether you're a member of any of them.

5. Which of the following directories could you modify, if the id command listed the following information? Which could you view using the ls command?

```
% id
uid=19(smith) gid=50(users) groups=50(users)
% ls -lgF
drw-r--r--  2 root      users       512 Oct 12 14:52 sh/
drwxr-xr-x  2 shakes    root        512 Oct 12 07:23 shakes/
drw-------  2 meademd   com435     1024 Oct 12 14:46 tmp/
drwxr-x---  3 smith     users       512 Oct 12 12:37 viewer/
drwx------  3 jin       users       512 Oct 12 12:37 Zot!/
```

Preview of the Next Hour

In the next hour, you learn the various Unix file-manipulation commands, including how to copy files, how to move them to new directories, and how to create new directories. You also learn how to remove files and directories as well as about the dangers of file removal on Unix.

Hour **6**

Creating, Moving, Renaming, and Deleting Files and Directories

In this hour, you learn the basic Unix file-manipulation commands. These commands will explain how to create directories with `mkdir`, remove directories with `rmdir`, use `cp` and `mv` to move files about in the file system, and use `rm` to remove files. The `rm` command has its dangers: You learn that there isn't an "unremove" command in Unix, and you also learn how to circumvent the possible dangers that lurk in the program.

Goals for This Hour

In this hour, you will learn how to

- Create new directories using `mkdir`
- Copy files to new locations using `cp`
- Move files to new locations using `mv`

- Rename files using mv
- Remove directories using rmdir
- Remove files using rm
- Minimize the danger of using the rm command

This hour introduces several tremendously powerful commands that enable you to create a custom file-system hierarchy (or wreak unintentional havoc on your files). As you learn these commands, you also learn hints and ideas on how best to use the Unix file system to keep your files neat and organized. Not only are these simple Unix commands, all new in this hour, found in all variants of Unix, both BSD-based and System V-based, but they also can be added to the MS-DOS world through utilities such as the MKS Toolkit from Mortice-Kern Systems.

Manipulating the Unix File System

You know how to find out what files are where in the file system using ls, but there are also various incredibly useful commands that let you manipulate and modify files, directories, and the file system itself. That's what we'll focus on here.

Task 6.1: Creating New Directories Using mkdir

DESCRIPTION One important aspect of Unix that has been emphasized continually in this book is that the Unix file system is hierarchical. The Unix file system includes directories containing files and directories, each directory of which can contain yet more files and directories. Your own home directory, however, probably doesn't contain any directories (except . and .. of course), which prevents you from exploiting what I call the virtual file cabinet of the file system.

The command for creating directories is actually one of the least complex and most mnemonic (for Unix, anyway) in this book: mkdir, called "make directory."

Pronounce the mkdir command as "make dir."

ACTION

1. Turn to your computer, move to your home directory, and examine the files and directories there. Here's an example:

```
% cd
% ls -F
Archives/               OWL/                    rumors.26Oct.Z
InfoWorld/              PubAccessLists.Z        rumors.5Nov.Z
LISTS                   bin/                    src/
Mail/                   educ
News/                   mailing.lists.bitnet.Z
```

2. To create a directory, specify what you'd like to name the directory and where you'd like to locate it in the file system (the default location is your current working directory):

```
% mkdir NEWDIR
% ls -F
Archives/               News/                   mailing.lists.bitnet.Z
InfoWorld/              OWL/                    rumors.26Oct.Z
LISTS                   PubAccessLists.Z        rumors.5Nov.Z
Mail/                   bin/                    src/
NEWDIR/                 educ
```

> Although Unix is very flexible about file and directory names, as a general rule you'll want to avoid spaces, tabs, control characters, and the / character.

3. That's all there is to it. You've created your first Unix directory, and you can now list it with ls to see what it looks like:

```
% ls -ld NEWDIR
drwxrwx---  2 taylor            24 Nov  5 10:48 NEWDIR/
% ls -la NEWDIR
total 2
drwxrwx---  2 taylor            24 Nov  5 10:48 ./
drwx------ 11 taylor          1024 Nov  5 10:48 ../
```

Not surprisingly, the directory is empty other than the two default entries of . (the directory itself) and .. (the parent directory, your home directory).

4. Look closely at the permissions of the directory. Remember that the permissions are a result of your umask setting. As you learned in the preceding hour, changing

6

the umask setting changes the default directory permissions. Then, when you create a new directory, the new permissions will be in place:

```
% umask
07
% umask 0
% mkdir NEWDIR2
% ls -ld NEWDIR2
drwxrwxrwx  2 taylor            24 Nov  5 10:53 NEWDIR2/
% umask 222
% mkdir NEWDIR3
% ls -ld NEWDIR3
dr-xr-xr-x  2 taylor            24 Nov  5 10:54 NEWDIR3/
```

5. What happens if you try to create a directory with a name that has already been used?

```
% mkdir NEWDIR
mkdir: NEWDIR: File exists
```

6. To create a directory someplace other than your current location, prefix the new directory name with a location:

```
% mkdir /tmp/testme
% ls -l /tmp
-rwx------  1 zhongqi     22724 Nov  4 21:33 /tmp/a.out*
-rw-------  1 xujia       95594 Nov  4 23:10 /tmp/active.10122
-rw-r--r--  1 beast         572 Nov  5 05:59 /tmp/anon1
-rw-rw----  1 root            0 Nov  5 10:30 /tmp/bar.report
-rw-------  1 qsc             0 Nov  5 00:18 /tmp/lh013813
-rwx------  1 steen       24953 Nov  5 10:40 /tmp/mbox.steen*
-rwx------  1 techman      3711 Nov  5 10:45 /tmp/mbox.techman*
-rw-r--r--  1 root       997536 Nov  5 10:58 /tmp/quotas
-rw-------  1 zhongqi    163579 Nov  4 20:16 /tmp/sp500.1
drwxrwx---  2 taylor         24 Nov  5 10:56 testme/
-rw-r--r--  1 aru            90 Nov  5 02:55 /tmp/trouble21972
```

SUMMARY Like other basic Unix utilities, most variations of Unix have no arguments for mkdir so it is quite easy to use. Some variants offer one or more flags, most commonly -m mode to specify permissions, and -p to have mkdir create any intermediate directories required. Keep two things in mind: You must have write permission to the current directory if you're creating a new directory, and you should ensure that the name of the directory is not the same as (or, to avoid confusion, similar to) a directory name that already exists.

Task 6.2: Copying Files to New Locations Using cp

DESCRIPTION One of the most basic operations in any system is moving files, the modern-office computer equivalent of paper shuffling. On a computer, moving files is a simple matter of using one or two commands: You can move a file to a different location, or you can create a copy of the file and move the copy to a different location.

Windows has an interesting strategy for differentiating between moving and copying. If you drag a file to another location on the same device (a hard disk, for example), by default the computer moves the file to that location. If you drag the file to a location on a different device (from a floppy to a hard disk, for instance), the computer automatically copies the file, placing the new, identically named copy on the device.

Unix lacks this subtlety. Instead, Unix lets you choose which of the two operations you'd like to perform. The two commands are typically succinct Unix mnemonics: mv to move files, and cp to copy files. The mv command also serves the dual duty of enabling you to rename files.

> Pronounce cp as "sea pea." When you talk about copying a file, however, say "copy." Similarly, pronounce mv as "em vee," but when you speak of moving a file, say "move."

I find myself using cp more than mv because it offers a slightly safer way to organize files: If I get confused and rename it such that it steps on another file (you'll see what I mean in a moment), I still have original copies of all the files.

ACTION

1. The format of a cp command is to specify first the name of the file you want to copy and then the new filename. Both names should be either relative filenames (that is, without a leading slash or other indication of the directory) or absolute filenames. Start out by making a copy of your .login file, naming the new copy login.copy:

```
% cp .login login.copy
% ls -ld .login login.copy
-rw-------  1 taylor        1858 Oct 12 21:20 .login
-rw-------  1 taylor        1858 Nov  5 12:08 login.copy
```

   You can see that the new file is identical in size and permissions but that it has a more recent creation date, which certainly makes sense.

2. What happens if you try to copy a directory?

```
% cp olddir newdir
cp: olddir: Is a directory (not copied).
```

   Generally, Unix won't permit you to use the cp command to copy directories.

6

> I found that this command worked—sort of—on one machine I have used.
> The system's response to the cp command indicated that something peculiar
> was happening with the following message:
>
> `cp: .: Is a directory (copying as plain file)`
>
> But the system also created newdir as a regular, executable file. You may
> find that your system reacts in this manner, but you probably do not have
> any use for it. On the other hand, you might find that your version of cp
> includes the useful -R command, which instructs it to recursively copy all
> files and directories below the specified location.

3. The cp command is quite powerful, and it can copy many files at once if you specify a directory as the destination rather than specifying a new filename. Further, if you specify a directory destination, the program automatically will create new files and assign them the same names as the original files.

First, you need to create a second file to work with:

```
% cp .profile profile.copy
```

Now try it yourself. Here is what I did:

```
% cp login.copy profile.copy NEWDIR
% ls -l NEWDIR
total 4
-rw-------  1 taylor        1178 Nov  5 12:18 profile.copy
-rw-------  1 taylor        1858 Nov  5 12:18 login.copy
```

SUMMARY You can use the cp command to copy an original file as a new file or to a specific directory (the format being cp *original-file new-file-or-directory*), and you can copy many files to a directory (cp *list-of-files new-directory*). With the -R flag that many versions of cp offer, you can recursively copy all files and directories below the specified directory. Experiment with creating new directories using mkdir and copying the files into the new locations. Use ls to confirm that the originals aren't removed as you go along.

On some Unix systems, a lowercase "r" gives you a recursive copy. You can check with the man cp command, of course.

Task 6.3: Moving Files to New Locations Using mv

DESCRIPTION Whereas cp leaves the original file intact, making a sort of electronic equivalent of a photocopy, mv functions like a more traditional desk: Papers are moved from one location to another. Rather than creating multiple copies of the files you're copying, mv physically relocates them from the old directory to the new.

ACTION

1. You use `mv` almost the same way that you use `cp`:

```
% ls -l login.copy
-rw------- 1 taylor        1858 Nov  5 12:08 login.copy
% mv login.copy new.login
% ls -l login.copy new.login
login.copy not found
-rw------- 1 taylor        1858 Nov  5 12:08 new.login
```

2. Also, you move a group of files together using `mv` almost the same way you do it using `cp`:

```
% cd NEWDIR
% ls
profile.copy  login.copy
% mv profile.copy login.copy ..
% ls -l
total 0
% ls -F ..
Archives/           OWL/                 mailing.lists.bitnet.Z
InfoWorld/          PubAccessLists.Z      new.login
LISTS               bin/                 rumors.26Oct.Z
Mail/               profile.copy          rumors.5Nov.Z
NEWDIR/             educ                 src/
News/               login.copy
```

3. Because you can use `mv` to rename files or directories, you can relocate the new directory NEWDIR. However, you cannot use `mv` to relocate the dot directory because you're inside it:

```
% mv . new.dot
mv: .: rename: Invalid argument
```

4. Both `mv` and `cp` can be dangerous. Carefully consider the following example before trying either `mv` or `cp` on your own computer:

```
% ls -l login.copy profile.copy
-rw------- 1 taylor        1178 Nov  5 12:38 profile.copy
-rw------- 1 taylor        1858 Nov  5 12:37 login.copy
% cp profile.copy login.copy
% ls -l login.copy profile.copy
-rw------- 1 taylor        1178 Nov  5 12:38 profile.copy
-rw------- 1 taylor        1178 Nov  5 12:38 login.copy
```

Without bothering to warn me, Unix copied the file `profile.copy` over the existing file `login.copy`. Notice that after the `cp` operation occurred, both files had the same size and modification dates.

6

The mv command will cause the same problem:

```
% ls -l profile.copy login.copy
-rw------- 1 taylor        1178 Nov  5 12:42 profile.copy
-rw------- 1 taylor        1858 Nov  5 12:42 login.copy
% mv profile.copy login.copy
% ls -l profile.copy login.copy
profile.copy not found
-rw------- 1 taylor        1178 Nov  5 12:42 login.copy
```

The good news is that you can set up Unix so it won't overwrite files. The bad news is that for some reason many systems don't default to this behavior. If your system is configured reasonably, when you try either of the two preceding dangerous examples, the system's response is remove login.copy?. You can either press the Y key to replace the old file or press Enter to change your mind. If your system cannot be set up to respond this way, you can use the -i flag to both cp and mv to avoid this problem. Later, you learn how to permanently fix this problem with a shell alias.

SUMMARY Together, mv and cp are the dynamic duo of Unix file organization. These commands enable you to put the information you want where you want it, leaving duplicates behind if desired.

Task 6.4: Renaming Files with mv

DESCRIPTION Both Windows and Macintosh systems have easy ways to rename files. In DOS, you can use RENAME to accomplish the task. On the Mac, you can select the name under the file icon and enter a new filename. On Windows, you right-click the icon and choose Rename from the pop-up menu.

Unix has neither option. To rename files, you use the mv command, which, in essence, moves the old name to the new name. It's a bit confusing, but it works.

ACTION

1. Rename the file profile.copy with your own first name. Here's an example:
   ```
   % ls -l profile.copy
   -rw------- 1 taylor        1178 Nov  5 13:00 profile.copy
   % mv profile.copy dave
   % ls -l dave
   -rw------- 1 taylor        1178 Nov  5 13:00 dave
   ```

2. Rename a directory too:

```
% ls -ld NEWDIR
drwxrwx---  2 taylor          512 Nov  5 12:32 NEWDIR/
% mv NEWDIR New.Sample.Directory
% ls -ld New.Sample.Directory
drwxrwx---  2 taylor          512 Nov  5 12:32 New.Sample.Directory/
```

3. Be careful! Just as moving files with cp and mv can carelessly overwrite existing files, renaming files using mv can overwrite existing files:

```
% mv dave login.copy
```

If you try to use mv to rename a directory with a name that already has been assigned to a file, the command fails:

```
% mv New.Sample.Directory dave
mv: New.Sample.Directory: rename: Not a directory
```

The reverse situation works fine because the file is moved into the directory as expected. It's the subtlety of using the mv command to rename files.

4. If you assign a new directory a name that belongs to an existing directory, some versions of mv will happily overwrite the existing directory and name the new one as requested:

```
% mkdir testdir
% mv New.Sample.Directory testdir
```

 SUMMARY Being able to rename files is another important part of building a useful Unix virtual file cabinet for you. Some major dangers are involved, however, so tread carefully and always use ls in conjunction with cp and mv to ensure that in the process you don't overwrite or replace an existing file.

Task 6.5: Removing Directories with `rmdir`

DESCRIPTION Now that you can create directories with the mkdir command, it's time to learn how to remove directories using the rmdir command.

ACTION

1. With rmdir, you can remove any directory for which you have appropriate permissions:

```
% mkdir test
% ls -l test
total 0
% rmdir test
```

Note that the output of ls shows there are no files in the test directory.

6

2. The `rmdir` command removes only directories that are empty:

```
% mkdir test
% touch test/sample.file
% ls -l test
total 0
-rw-rw----  1 taylor            0 Nov  5 14:00 sample.file
% rmdir test
rmdir: test: Directory not empty
```

To remove a directory, you must first remove all files therein using the `rm` command. In this example, `test` still has files in it. Note: some versions of `rmdir` offer a `-p` flag which will recursively remove all directories and subdirectories from right-to-left until it encounters a non-empty directory.

3. Permissions are important, too. Consider what happens when I try to remove a directory that I don't have permission to touch:

```
% rmdir /tmp
rmdir: /tmp: Permission denied
% ls -l /tmp
drwxrwxrwt 81 root         15872 Nov  5 14:07 /tmp
```

The permissions of the parent directory, rather than the directory you're trying to remove, are the important considerations.

SUMMARY There's no way to restore a directory you've removed, so be careful and think through what you're doing. The good news is that, because with `rmdir` you can't remove a directory having anything in it (a second reason the attempt in the preceding example to remove `/tmp` would have failed), you're reasonably safe from major gaffes. You are not safe, however, with the next command, `rm`, because it will remove anything.

Task 6.6: Removing Files Using `rm`

DESCRIPTION The `rm` command is the most dangerous command in Unix. Lacking any sort of archival or restoration feature, the `rm` command removes files permanently. It's like throwing a document into a shredder instead of into a dustbin.

ACTION

1. Removing a file using `rm` is easy. Here's an example:

```
% ls -l login.copy
-rw-------  1 taylor          1178 Nov  5 13:00 login.copy
% rm login.copy
% ls -l login.copy
login.copy not found
```

If you decide that you removed the wrong file and actually wanted to keep the login.copy file, it's too late. You're out of luck.

2. You can remove more than one file at a time by specifying each of the files to the rm command:

```
% ls -F
Archives/              PubAccessLists.Z      new.login
InfoWorld/             bin/                  rumors.26Oct.Z
LISTS                  profile.copy           rumors.5Nov.Z
Mail/                  educ                  src/
News/                  login.copy            test/
OWL/                   mailing.lists.bitnet.Z testdir/
% rm profile.copy login.copy new.login
% ls -F
Archives/              OWL/                  rumors.26Oct.Z
InfoWorld/             PubAccessLists.Z      rumors.5Nov.Z
LISTS                  bin/                  src/
Mail/                  educ                  test/
News/                  mailing.lists.bitnet.Z testdir/
```

3. Fortunately, rm does have a command flag that to some degree helps avoid accidental file removal. When you use the -i flag to rm (the i stands for *interactive* in this case), the system will ask you whether you're sure you want to remove the file:

```
% touch testme
% rm -i testme
rm: remove testme? n
% ls testme
testme
% rm -i testme
rm: remove testme? y
% ls testme
testme not found
```

Note that n is *no* and y is *yes*. Delete the file.

4. Another flag that is often useful for rm, but is very dangerous, is the -r flag for recursive deletion of files (a *recursive command* repeatedly invokes itself). When the -r flag to rm is used, Unix will remove any specified directory along with all its contents:

```
% ls -ld test ; ls -lR test
drwxrwxrwx  3 taylor         512 Nov  5 15:32 test
total 1
-rw-rw----  1 taylor           0 Nov  5 15:32 alpha
drwxrwx---  2 taylor         512 Nov  5 15:32 test2

test/test2:
total 0
-rw-rw----  1 taylor           0 Nov  5 15:32 file1
```

6

```
% rm -r test
% ls -ld test
test not found
```

Without any warning or indication that it was going to do something so drastic, entering rm -r test caused not just the test directory, but all files and directories inside it as well, to be removed.

> This latest example demonstrates that you can give several commands in a single Unix command line. To do this, separate the commands with a semi-colon. Instead of giving the commands ls -ld test and ls -lR test on separate lines, I opted for the more efficient ls -ld test; ls -lR test, which executes the commands one after the other.

SUMMARY The Unix equivalent of the paper shredder, the rm command allows easy removal of files. With the -r flag, you can even clean out an entire directory. Nothing can be retrieved after the fact, however, so use great caution.

Task 6.7: Minimizing the Danger of the rm Command

DESCRIPTION At this point, you might be wondering why I am making such a big deal of the rm command and the fact that it does what it is advertised to do—that is, remove files. The answer is that learning a bit of paranoia now can save you immense grief in the future. It can prevent you from destroying a file full of information you really needed to save.

For Windows, commercial programs (Norton Utilities, for instance) exist that can retrieve accidentally removed files. The trash can on the Macintosh can be clicked open and the files retrieved with ease. If the trash can is emptied after a file is accidentally discarded, a program such as Symantec Utilities for the Macintosh can be used to restore files.

Unix just doesn't have that capability, though, and files that are removed are gone forever.

The only exception is if you work on a Unix system that has an automatic, reliable backup schedule. In such a case, you might be able to retrieve from a storage tape an older version of your file (maybe).

That said, you can do a few things to lessen the danger of using rm and yet give yourself the ability to remove unwanted files.

ACTION

1. You can use a shorthand, a *shell alias*, to attach the `-i` flag automatically to each use of `rm`. To do this, ascertain what type of login shell you're running, which you can do most easily by using the following command. (Don't worry about what it all does right now. You learn about the `grep` command a few hours from now.)

```
% grep taylor /etc/passwd
taylor:?:19989:1412:Dave Taylor:/users/taylor:/bin/csh
```

The last word on the line is what's important. The `/etc/passwd` file is one of the database files Unix uses to track accounts. Each line in the file is called a *password entry* or *password file entry*. On my password entry, you can see that the login shell specified is `/bin/csh`. If you try this and you don't have an identical entry, you should have `/bin/sh` or `/bin/ksh`.

2. If your entry is `/bin/csh`, enter exactly what is shown here:

```
% echo "alias rm /bin/rm -I" >> ~/.profile
% source ~/.profile
```

Now `rm` includes the `-i` flag each time it's used:

```
% touch testme
% rm testme
rm: remove testme? N
```

3. If your entry is `/bin/ksh` or `/bin/bash`, enter exactly what is shown here, paying particular attention to the two different quotation-mark characters used in the example:

```
$ echo 'alias rm="/bin/rm -I"' >> ~/.profile
$ . ~/.profile
```

Now `rm` includes the `-i` flag each time it's used.

> One thing to pay special attention to is the difference between the single quote (`'`), the double quote (`"`), and the backquote (`` ` ``). Unix interprets each differently, although single and double quotes are often interchangeable. The backquotes, also known as grave accents, are more unusual and delineate commands within other commands.

6

4. If your entry is `/bin/sh`, you cannot program your system to include the `-i` flag each time `rm` is used. The Bourne shell, as `sh` is known, is the original command shell of Unix. The Bourne shell lacks an alias feature, a feature that both the Korn

shell (ksh) and the C shell (csh) include. As a result, I recommend that you change your login shell to one of these alternatives, if available.

To see what's available, look in the /bin directory on your machine for the specific shells:

```
% ls -l /bin/sh /bin/ksh /bin/csh
-rwxr-xr-x  1 root        102400 Apr  8  1991 /bin/csh*
-rwxr-xr-x  1 root        139264 Jul 26 14:35 /bin/ksh*
-rwxr-xr-x  1 root         28672 Oct 10  1991 /bin/sh*
```

Most of the examples in this book focus on the Korn Shell because I think it's the easiest of the shells to use. To change your login shell you'll need to e-mail your system administrator with the request, though some versions of Unix offer the chsh (change shell) command for just this purpose. If yours does, use man chsh to learn more about how to use it. Now you can go back to step 2 and set up a Korn shell alias. This will help you avoid mischief with the rm command.

SUMMARY The best way to avoid trouble with any of these commands is to learn to be just a bit paranoid about them. Before you remove a file, make sure it's the one you want to remove. Before you remove a directory, make doubly sure that it doesn't contain any files you might want. Before you rename a file or directory, double-check to see whether renaming it is going to cause any trouble.

Take your time with the commands you learned in this hour, and you should be fine. Even in the worst case, you will hopefully have the safety net of a backup performed by a system administrator, but don't rely on it.

Summary

You now have completed six hours of Unix instruction, and you are armed with enough commands to cause trouble and make Unix do what you want it to do. In this hour, you learned the differences between cp and mv for moving files and how to use mv to rename both files and directories. You also learned how to create directories with the mkdir command and how to remove them with the rmdir command. And you learned about the rm command for removing files and directories, and how to avoid getting into too much trouble with it.

Finally, if you were really paying attention, you learned how to identify which login shell you're using (csh, ksh, or sh).

Workshop

The Workshop summarizes the key terms you learned and poses some questions about the topics presented in this chapter. It also provides you with a preview of what you will learn in the next hour.

Key Terms

password entry   For each account on the Unix system, there is an entry in the account database known as the *password file*. This also contains an encrypted copy of the account `password`. This set of information for an individual account is known as the *password entry*.

recursive command   A command that repeatedly invokes itself.

shell alias   Most Unix shells have a convenient way for you to create abbreviations for commonly used commands or series of commands, known as shell aliases. For example, if I always found myself typing `ls -F`, an alias can let me type just `ls` and have the shell automatically add the `-F` flag each time.

Exercises

1. What are the differences between `cp` and `mv`?

2. If you were installing a program from a floppy disk onto a hard disk, would you use `cp` or `mv`?

3. If you know DOS, this question is for you. Although DOS has a `RENAME` command, it doesn't have both `COPY` and `MOVE`. Which of these two do you think DOS includes? Why?

4. Try using `mkdir` to create a directory. What happens and why?

5. You've noticed that both `rmdir` and `rm -r` can be used to remove directories. Which is safer to use?

6. The `rm` command has another flag that wasn't discussed in this hour. The `-f` flag forces removal of files regardless of permission (assuming you're the owner, that is). In combination with the `-r` flag, this can be amazingly destructive. Why?

Preview of the Next Hour

The seventh hour introduces the useful `file` command, which indicates the contents of any file in the Unix file system. With `file`, you will explore various directories in the Unix file system to see what the command reveals about different system and personal files. Then, when you've found some files worth reading, you will learn about `cat`, `more`, and `pg`, which are different ways of looking at the contents of a file.

6

HOUR 7

Looking into Files

By this point, you've learned a considerable number of Unix commands and a lot about the operating and file systems. This hour focuses on Unix tools to help you ascertain what types of files you've been seeing in all the different directories. It then introduces five powerful tools for examining the content of files.

Goals for This Hour

In this hour, you will learn how to

- Use `file` to identify file types
- Explore Unix directories with `file`
- Peek at the first few lines with `head`
- View the last few lines with `tail`
- View the contents of files with `cat`
- View larger files with `more`

This hour begins with a tool to help ensure that the files you're about to view are intended for human perusal and then explores many of the commands available to view the contents of the file in various ways.

Looking Inside Files

You've learned how to manipulate files and directories, so now it's time to find out what kind of information is contained within these files and to look inside the files.

Task 7.1: Using `file` to Identify File Types

DESCRIPTION One of the most undervalued commands in Unix is `file`, which is often neglected and collecting dust in an unused virtual corner of the system. The `file` command is a program that can easily offer you an idea as to the contents of a file by looking at the first few lines.

Unfortunately, a problem exists with the `file` command: It isn't 100% accurate. The program relies on a combination of the permissions of a file, the filename, and an analysis of the first few lines of the text. If you had a text file that started out looking like a C program or that had execute permission enabled, `file` might well identify it as an executable program rather than an English text file.

 You can determine how accurate your version of `file` is by checking the size of its database of file types. You can do this with the Unix command `wc -l /etc/magic`. The number of entries in the database should be at least 100. If you have many fewer than this number, you're probably going to have trouble. If you have considerably more, you might have a very accurate version of `file` at your fingertips! Remember, however, that even if it's relatively small, `file` can still offer invaluable suggestions regarding file content.

ACTION

1. Start by logging in to your account and using the `ls` command to find a file or two to check:

```
% ls -F
Archives/               OWL/                    rumors.26Oct.Z
InfoWorld/              PubAccessLists.Z        rumors.5Nov.Z
LISTS                   bin/                    src/
Mail/                   educ                    temp/
News/                   mailing.lists.bitnet.Z
```

Next, enter the `file` command, listing each of the files you'd like the program to analyze:

```
% file LISTS educ rumors.26Oct.Z src
LISTS:  ascii text
educ:   ascii text
rumors.26Oct.Z: block compressed 16 bit code data
src:    directory
```

From this example, you can see that `file` correctly identifies `src` as a directory, offers considerable information on the compressed file `rumors.26Oct.Z`, and tags both `LISTS` and `educ` as plain ASCII text files.

 ASCII is the *American Standard Code for Information Interchange*, and it means that the file contains the letters of the English alphabet, punctuation, and numbers, but not much else. There are no multiple typefaces, italics, or underlined passages, and there are no graphics. It's the lowest common denominator of text in Unix.

2. Now try using the asterisk (*), a Unix wildcard (wildcards are explained in Hour 9, "Wildcards and Regular Expressions"), to have the program analyze all files in your home directory:

```
% file *
Global.Software:      English text
Interactive.Unix:     mail folder
Mail:         directory
News:         directory
Src:          directory
bin:          directory
history.usenet.Z:     compressed data block compressed 16 bits
```

The asterisk (*) is a special character in Unix. Used by itself, it tells the system to substitute the names of all the files in the current directory.

This time you can begin to see how `file` can help differentiate files. Using this command, I am now reminded that the file `Global.Software` is English text, but `Interactive.Unix` is actually an old electronic mail message. (`file` can't differentiate between a single mail message and a multiple-message folder, so it always errs on the side of saying that the file is a mail folder.)

3. Mail folders are actually problematic for the `file` command. On one of the systems I use, the `file` command doesn't know what mail messages are, so asking it to analyze mail folders results in a demonstration of how accuracy is related to the size of the `file` database.

7

On a Sun system, I asked `file` to analyze two mail folders, with the following results:

```
% file Mail/mailbox Mail/sent
Mail/mailbox:   mail folder
Mail/sent: mail folder
```

Almost identical files on a Berkeley Unix system, however, have very different results when analyzed:

```
% file Mail/mailbox Mail/sent Mail/netnews
Mail/mailbox:        ascii text
Mail/sent:       shell commands
Mail/netnews:        English text
```

Not only does the Berkeley version of Unix not identify the files correctly, it doesn't even misidentify them consistently.

4. Another example of the `file` command's limitations is how it interacts with file permissions. Use `cp` to create a new file and work through this example to see how your `file` command interprets the various changes:

```
% cp .cshrc test
% file test
test: shell commands
% chmod +x test
% file test
test: shell script
```

Adding execute permission to this file caused this version of `file` to identify it as a shell script rather than shell commands.

 SUMMARY Don't misinterpret the results of these examples as proof that the `file` command is useless and that you shouldn't use it. Quite the opposite is true. Unix has neither a specific file-naming convention (Windows has its three-letter filename suffixes) nor indication of file ownership by icon (Macintosh does this with creator information added by each program). As a result, it's vital that you have a tool for helping ascertain file types without actually opening the file.

Why not just look at the contents? The best way to figure out the answer to this question is to accidentally display the contents of an executable file on the screen. You'll see it's quite a mess, loaded with special control characters that can be best described as making your screen go berserk.

Task 7.2: Exploring Unix Directories with `file`

DESCRIPTION Now that you know how to work with the `file` command, it's time to wander through the Unix file system, learning more about types of files that tend to be found in specific directories. Your system might vary slightly—it'll certainly have more files in some directories than what I show here in the examples, but you'll quickly see that `file` can offer some valuable insight into the contents of files.

ACTION

1. First things first. Take a look at the files found in the very top level of the file system, in / (slash):

```
% cd /
% ls -F
-No _rm_ star  boot       flags/      rhf@        userb/
OLD/           core       gendynix    stand/      userc/
archive/       dev/       lib@        sys@        userd/
ats/           diag@      lost+found/ tftpboot@   usere/
backup/        dynix      mnt/        tmp/        users/
bin@           etc/       net/        usera/      usr/
% file boot core gendynix tftpboot
boot:   SYMMETRY i386 stand alone executable version 1
core:   core from getty
gendynix:       SYMMETRY i386 stand alone executable not
➥stripped version 1
tftpboot:       symbolic link to /usr/tftpboot
```

This example is from a Sequent computer running DYNIX, the Sequent's version of Unix, based on Berkeley 4.3 BSD with some AT&T System V extensions. It's the same machine that has such problems identifying mail folders.

Executable binaries are explained in detail by the `file` command on this computer: `boot` is listed as SYMMETRY i386 stand alone executable version 1. The specifics aren't vital to understand: The most important word to see in this output is executable, indicating that the file is the result of compiling a program. The format is SYMMETRY i386, version 1, and the file requires no libraries or other files to execute—it's standalone.

For `gendynix`, the format is similar, but one snippet of information is added that isn't indicated for boot: The executable file hasn't been stripped.

Stripping a file doesn't mean that you peel its clothes off, but rather that various information included in most executables to help identify and isolate problems (for example, debug) has been removed to save space.

7

When a program dies unexpectedly in Unix, the operating system tries to leave a snapshot of the memory that the program was using, to aid in debugging. Wading through these core files can be quite difficult—it's usually reserved for a few experts at each site—but some useful information is still inside. The best, and simplest, way to check it is with the `file` command. The listing in step 1 shows that `file` recognized the file core as a crashed program memory image. It further extracted the name of the program, `getty`, that originally failed, causing the program to fail. When this failure happens, Unix creates an image of the program in memory at the time of failure, which is called a *core dump*.

The fourth of the listings offers an easy way to understand symbolic links, indicated in `ls  -F` output with the special suffix @, as shown in the preceding example with `tftpboot@`. Using `file`, you can see that the file `tftpboot` in the root directory is actually a symbolic link to a file with the same name elsewhere in the file system, `/usr/tftpboot`.

2. There are differences in output formats on different machines. The following example shows what the same command would generate on a Sun Microsystems workstation, examining analogous files:

```
% file boot core kadb tmp
boot:           sparc executable
core:           core file from 'popper'
kadb:           sparc executable not stripped
tmp:            symbolic link to /var/tmp
```

The Sun computer offers the same information, but fewer specifics about executable binaries. In this case, Sun workstations are built around SPARC chips (just like PCs are built around Intel chips), so the executables are identified as `sparc executable`.

3. Are you ready for another directory of weird files? It's time to move into the `/lib` directory to see what's there.

Entering `ls` will demonstrate quickly that there are many files in this directory! The `file` command can tell you about any of them. On my Sun computer, I asked for information on a few select files, many of which you might also have on yours:

```
% file lib.b lib300.a diffh sendmail
lib.b:          c program text
lib300.a:       archive random library
diffh:          sparc pure dynamically linked executable not stripped
sendmail:       sparc demand paged dynamically linked set-uid executable
```

The first file, `lib.b`, demonstrates that the `file` command works regardless of the name of a file: Standard naming for C program files specifies that they end with the characters `.c`, as in `test.c`. So, without `file`, you might never have suspected that lib.b is a C program. The second file is an actual program library and is identified here as an archive random library, meaning that it's an archive and that the information within can be accessed in random order (by appropriate programs).

The third file is an executable, demonstrating another way that file can indicate programs on a Sun workstation. The sendmail program is an interesting program: It's an executable, but it has some new information you haven't seen before. The set-uid indicates that the program is set up so that when anyone runs it, sendmail runs as the user who owns the file, not the user who launched the program. A quick ls can reveal a bit more about this:

```
% ls -l /lib/sendmail
-r-sr-x--x  1 root        155648 Sep 14 09:11 /lib/sendmail
```

Notice here that the fourth character of the permissions string is an s rather than the expected x for an executable. Also check the owner of the file in this listing. Combined, the two mean that when anyone runs this program, sendmail actually will set itself to a different user ID (root in this case) and have that set of access permissions. Having sendmail run with root permissions is how you can send electronic mail to someone else without fuss, but you can't view his or her mailbox.

SUMMARY The good news is that you don't have to worry a bit about what files are in /lib, /etc, or any other directory other than your own home directory. Thousands of happy Unix folk busily work each day without ever realizing that these other directories exist, let alone knowing what's in them.

What's important here is that you have learned that the file command identifies special Unix system files of various types. It can be a very helpful tool when you are looking around in the file system and even when you are trying to determine what's what in your own directory.

Task 7.3: Peeking at the First Few Lines with head

DESCRIPTION Now that you have the tools needed to move about in the file system, to double-check where you are, and to identify the different types of files, it's time to learn about some of the many tools Unix offers for viewing the contents of files. The first on the list is head, a simple program for viewing the first 10 lines of any file.

The head program is more versatile than it sounds: You can use it to view up to the first few hundred lines of a very long file, actually. To specify the number of lines you want to see, you need to indicate how many as a starting argument, prefixing the number of lines desired with a dash.

This command, head, is the first of a number of Unix commands that tend to work with their own variant on the regular rules of starting arguments. Instead of a typical Unix command argument of -133 to specify 33 lines, head uses -33 to specify the same information.

ACTION

1. Start by moving back into your home directory and viewing the first few lines of your .cshrc file (or use .profile if you don't have a .cshrc file):

```
% cd
% head .cshrc
#
# Default user .cshrc file (/bin/csh initialization).

set host=limbo

set path=(. ~/bin /bin /usr/bin /usr/ucb /usr/local /etc
/usr/etc/usr/local/bin /usr/unsup/bin)

# Set up C shell environment:

alias  diff     '/usr/bin/diff -c -w'
```

The contents of your own .cshrc file will doubtless be different, but notice that the program lists only the first few lines of the file.

2. To specify a different number of lines, use the -*n* format (where *n* is the number of lines). I'll look at just the first four lines of the .login file:

```
% head -4 .login
#
# @(#) $Revision: 62.2 $

setenv TERM vt100
```

3. You also can easily check multiple files by specifying them to the program:

```
% head -3 .newsrc /etc/passwd
==> .newsrc <==
misc.forsale.computers.mac: 1-14536
utech.student-orgs! 1
general! 1-546

==> /etc/passwd <==
root:?:0:0: root,,,,:/:/bin/csh
news:?:6:11:USENET News,,,,:/usr/spool/news:/bin/ksh
ingres:*?:7:519:INGRES Manager,,,,:/usr/ingres:/bin/csh
```

4. More importantly, head, and other Unix commands, can work also as part of a *pipeline*, where the output of one program is the input of the next. The special symbol for creating Unix pipelines is the pipe character (|). Pipes are read left to right, so you can easily have the output of who, for example, feed into head, offering powerful new possibilities. Perhaps you want to see just the first five people logged in to the computer right now. Try this:

```
% who | head -5
root       console Nov  9 07:31
mccool     ttyaO   Nov 10 14:25
millekl2 ttyaP   Nov 10 14:58
paulwhit ttyaR   Nov 10 14:50
bobweir  ttyaS   Nov 10 14:49
Broken pipe
```

Pipelines are one of the most powerful features of Unix, and I have many examples of how to use them to great effect throughout the remainder of this book.

5. Here is one last thing. Find an executable—/boot will do fine—and enter **head -1 /boot**. Watch what happens. Or, if you'd like to preserve your sanity, take it from me that the random junk thrown on your screen is plenty to cause your telnet or terminal program to get quite confused and possibly even crash.

The point isn't to have that happen to your system, but rather to remind you that using file to confirm the file type for unfamiliar files can save you lots of grief and frustration!

SUMMARY The simplest of programs for viewing the contents of a file, head, is easy to use, is efficient, and works as part of a pipeline too. The remainder of this hour focuses on other tools in Unix that offer other ways to view the contents of text and ASCII files.

Task 7.4: Viewing the Last Few Lines with `tail`

DESCRIPTION The head program shows you the first 10 lines of the file you specify. What would you expect tail to do, then? I hope you guessed the right answer: It shows the last 10 lines of a file. Like head, tail also understands the same format for specifying the number of lines to view.

ACTION

1. Start out viewing the last 12 lines of your .cshrc file:

```
% tail -12 .cshrc

set noclobber history=100 system=filec
umask 007
```

7

```
    setprompt
endif

# special aliases:

alias info        ssinfo
alias ssinfo      'echo "connecting..." ; rlogin oasis'
```

2. Next, the last four lines of the file LISTS in my home directory can be shown with the following command line:

```
% tail -5 LISTS
            College of Education
            Arizona State University
            Tempe, AZ 85287-2411
            602-965-2692
```

Don't get too hung up trying to figure out what's inside my files; I'm not even sure myself sometimes.

3. Here's one to think about. You can use head to view the first *n* lines of a file, and tail to view the last *n* lines of a file. Can you figure out a way to combine the two so that you can see just the 10th, 11th, and 12th lines of a file?

```
% head -12 .cshrc | tail -3
alias  diff      '/usr/bin/diff -c -w'
alias  from      'frm -n'
alias  ll        'ls -l'
```

It's easy with Unix command pipelines!

 SUMMARY Combining the two commands head and tail can give you considerable power in viewing specific slices of a file on the Unix system. Try combining them in different ways for different effects.

Task 7.5: Viewing the Contents of Files with cat

DESCRIPTION Both head and tail offer the capability to view a piece of a file, either the top or the bottom, but neither lets you conveniently see the entire file, regardless of length. For this job, the cat program is the right choice.

 The cat program got its name from its function in the early versions of Unix; its function was to concatenate (or join together) multiple files. It isn't, unfortunately, any homage to feline pets or anything so exotic!

The cat program also has a valuable secret capability: Through use of the -v flag, you can use cat to display any file on the system, executable or otherwise, with all characters that normally would not be printed (or would drive your screen bonkers) displayed in a special format I call *control key notation*. In control key notation, each non-printing character is represented as ^*n*, where *n* is a printable letter or symbol. A character with the value of zero (also referred to as a *null* or *null character*) is displayed as ^@, a character with the value 1 is ^A, a character with the value 2 is ^B, and so on.

Another cat flag that can be useful for certain files is -s, which suppresses multiple blank lines from a file. It isn't immediately obvious how that could help, but some files (particularly log files from system programs) can have a screenful (or more) of blank lines. To avoid having to watch them all fly past, you can use cat -s to chop 'em down to a single blank line.

ACTION

1. Move back to your home directory again, and use cat to display the complete contents of your .cshrc file:

```
% cd
% cat .cshrc
#
# Default user .cshrc file (/bin/csh initialization).

set path=(. ~/bin /bin /usr/bin /usr/ucb /usr/local /etc
/usr/etc/usr/local/bin /usr/unsup/bin )

# Set up C shell environment:

alias   diff      '/usr/bin/diff -c -w'
alias   from      'frm -n'
alias   ll        'ls -l'
alias   ls        '/bin/ls -F'
alias   mail      Mail
alias   mailq     '/usr/lib/sendmail -bp'

alias   newaliases 'echo you mean newalias...'

alias   rd        'readmsg $ | page'
alias   rn        '/usr/local/bin/rn -d$HOME -L -M -m -e -S -/'

# and some special stuff if we're in an interactive shell

if ( $?prompt ) then            # shell is interactive.
```

7

```
alias  cd            'chdir \!* ; setprompt'
alias  env           'printenv'
alias  setprompt     'set prompt="$system ($cwd:t) \! : "'

set noclobber history=100 system=limbo filec
umask 007

setprompt
endif

# special aliases:

alias info      ssinfo
alias ssinfo    'echo "connecting..." ; rlogin oasis'
```

Don't be too concerned if the content of your .cshrc file (or mine) doesn't make any sense to you. You are slated to learn about the content of this file within a few hours, and, yes, it is complex.

You can see that cat is pretty simple to use. If you specify more than one filename to the program, it lists the filenames in the order you specify. You can even list the contents of a file multiple times by specifying the same filename on the command line multiple times.

2. The cat program also can be used as part of a pipeline. Compare the following command with my earlier usage of head and tail:

```
% cat LISTS | tail -5
          College of Education
          Arizona State University
          Tempe, AZ 85287-2411
          602-965-2692
```

3. Now find an executable file, and try cat -v in combination with head to get a glimpse of the contents therein:

```
% cat -v /bin/ls | head -1
M-k"^@^@^@M-^@^@^@^@^P^@^@M-45^@^@^@^@^@^@M-l^P^@^@^@^@^@
➡^@^@^@^@^@^@^@^@
^@^@^@^@^@^@^@^@^@^@^@^@^@^@^@^@^@^@^@^@^@^@^@^@^@^@^@^@
➡^@^@^@^@^@^@^@^@
^@^@^@^@^@^@^@^@^@^@^@^@^@^@^@^@^@^@^@^@^@^@^@^@^@^@^@^@
➡^@^@^@^@^@^@^@^@
^@^@^@^@^@^@^@^@^@^@^@^@^A^@^@^@@$Header: crt0.c 1.4 87/04/23
➡$^@^@@(#)Copy
right (C) 1984 XXXXXXX Computer Systems, Inc.  All rights reserved.
➡^@M-^KM-NM-^KM-
tM-^MF^DM-^KM-XM-^K^F@M-^M^DM-^E^@^@^@^@M-^KM-S^AM-BM-^I^U^@M-^@^@
➡^@SM-^?6M-hw^T^@^@M-
^CM-D^HM-^?5^@M-^@^@^@SM-^?6M-h&^@^@^@M-^CM-D^LPM-h)[^@^@YM-tM-^PM-
➡^PM-^PM-k^BM-IM-CUM-
```

```
^KM-1M-kM-yM-^PM-^PM-^PM
-k^BM-IM-CUM-^KM-1M-kM-yM-^PM-^PM-^PUM-^KM-1M-^CM-1^XWVSM-^K
➥u^LM-^K]^HKM-^CM-F^DM-hM
-X^V^@^@M-^EM-@u^FM-^?^EM-1M-^L^@^@h^DM-^M^@^@M-hM-P7^@^
➥@YM-^K^E^DM-^M^@^@-^@NM-
m^@M-^I^E^HM-^M^@^@M-^K^E^DM-^M^@^@^E^P^N^@^@M-^I^E^LM-^
ÂM^@^@M-^C^E^DM-^M^@^@<M-
G^E^PM-^M^@^@P^@^@^@j^AM-hM-%[^@^@YM-^EM-@tNh^TM-^M^@^@h
➥M-HM-^J^@^@M-h12^@^@M-^C
M-D^HM-G^EM-pM-^L^@^@^A^@^@^@M-8^A^@^@^@M-^I^EM-hM-^L^@^
➥@M-ht^S^@^@M-^MEM-nPj^AM
-h]^V^@^@M-^CM-D^H^OM-?EM-r%^@^L^@^@=^@Broken pipe
```

This is complex and confusing, indeed! What's worse, this isn't the entire first line of the executable. You can see that because the data ends with `Broken pipe`. This indicates that a lot more was being fed to `head` than it could process, due to the constraint of having only the first line listed—a line that `head` typically defines as no more than 512 characters long.

SUMMARY The `cat` command is useful for viewing files and is quite easy to use. The problem with it is that if the file you choose to view has more lines than can be displayed on your screen, it will fly past without any way to slow it down. That's where the next command, the `more` command, comes in handy for stepping through files.

Task 7.6: Viewing Larger Files with `more`

DESCRIPTION You can now wander about the file system, find files that might be of interest, check their type with `file`, and even view them with the `cat` command, but what if they're longer than your screen? That's the job of the `more` program, a program that knows how big your screen is and displays the information page by page.

Three primary flags are in `more`:

`-s`	Suppresses multiple blank lines, just like the `-s` flag to `cat`
`-d`	Forces `more` to display friendlier prompts at the bottom of each page
`-c`	Causes the program to clear the screen before displaying each screenful of text

The program also allows you to start at a specific line in the file by using the curious *+n* notation, where *n* is a specific number. Finally, you can start also at the first occurrence of a specific pattern by specifying that pattern to the program in a format similar to *+/pattern* (patterns are defined in Hour 9, "Wildcards and Regular Expressions").

ACTION

1. View the .cshrc file using more:

```
% more ~/.cshrc
#
# Default user .cshrc file (/bin/csh initialization).

set host=limbo

set path=(. ~/bin /bin /usr/bin /usr/ucb /usr/local /etc
/usr/etc /usr/local/bin /usr/unsup/bin)

# Set up C shell environment:

alias  diff      '/usr/bin/diff -c -w'
alias  from      'frm -n'
alias  ll        'ls -l'
alias  ls        '/bin/ls -F'
alias  mail      Mail
alias  mailq     '/usr/lib/sendmail -bp'

alias  newaliases 'echo you mean newalias...'

alias  rd        'readmsg $ | page'
--More--(51%)
```

Unlike previous examples, where the program runs until completed, leaving you back on the command line, more is the first *interactive program* you've encountered. When you see the --More--(51%) prompt, the cursor sits at the end of that line, waiting for you to tell the program what to do. The more program lets you know how far into the file you've viewed,; in the example, you've seen about half of the file (51%).

At this point, quite a variety of commands are available. Press the spacebar to see the next screen of information, until you have seen the entire file.

2. Try starting the program with the 12th line of the file:

```
% more +12 ~/.cshrc
alias  mailq    '/usr/lib/sendmail -bp'

alias  newaliases 'echo you mean newalias...'

alias  rd        'readmsg $ | page'
alias  rn        '/usr/local/bin/rn -d$HOME -L -M -m -e -S -/'

# and some special stuff if we're in an interactive shell
```

```
if ( $?prompt ) then              # shell is interactive.

  alias  cd                 'chdir \!* ; setprompt'
  alias  env                'printenv'
  alias  setprompt          'set prompt="$system ($cwd:t) \! : "'

  set noclobber history=100 filec
  umask 007

  setprompt
endif
--More--(82%)
```

3. You can see that about halfway through the .cshrc file there is a line that contains the word newaliases. I can start more so that the line with this pattern is displayed on the top of the first screenful:

```
% more +/newaliases ~/.cshrc

...skipping
alias  mailq    '/usr/lib/sendmail -bp'

alias  newaliases 'echo you mean newalias...'

alias  rd       'readmsg $ | page'
alias  rn       '/usr/local/bin/rn -d$HOME -L -M -m -e -S -/'

# and some special stuff if we're in an interactive shell

if ( $?prompt ) then              # shell is interactive.

  alias  cd                 'chdir \!* ; setprompt'
  alias  env                'printenv'
  alias  setprompt          'set prompt="$system ($cwd:t) \! : "'

  set noclobber history=100 filec
  umask 007

  setprompt
endif

# special aliases:

alias info       ssinfo
--More--(86%)
```

Actually, notice that the line containing the pattern newaliases shows up as the third line of the first screen, not the first line. That's so that you have a bit of context to the matched line, but it can take some getting used to. Also note that more tells us—with the message ...skipping as the first line—that it's skipping some lines to find the pattern.

4. The list of commands available at the --More-- prompt is quite extensive, as shown in Table 7.1. The sidebar following the table explains what the conventions used in the table mean and how to enter the commands.

TABLE 7.1 Commands Available Within the more Program

Command	Function
[Space]	Press the spacebar to display the next screenful of text.
n[Return]	Display the next n lines (the default is the next line only of text).
h	Display a list of commands available in the more program.
d	Scroll down half a page.
q	Quit the more program.
ns	Skip forward n lines (default is 1).
nf	Skip forward n screenfuls (default is 1).
b or Control-b	Skip backward a screenful of text.
=	Display the current line number.
/pattern	Search for an occurrence of pattern.
n	Search for the next occurrence of the current pattern.
v	Start the vi editor at the current line.
Control-l	(That's a lowercase L.) Redraw the screen.
:f	Display the current filename and line number.

Entering Commands in the more Program

In this table and in the following text, [Space] (the word *space* enclosed in brackets) refers to pressing the spacebar as a command. Likewise, [Return] means you should press the Return key as part of the command.

A hyphen in a command—for example, Ctrl-B—means that you should hold down the first indicated key while you press the second key. The lowercase-letter commands in the table indicate that you should press the corresponding key, the A key for the a command, for example.

Two characters together, but without a hyphen (:f), mean that you should press the appropriate keys in sequence as you would when typing text.

Finally, entries that have an n before the command mean that you can prefix the command with a number, which will let it use that value to modify its action. For example, 3[Return] displays the next three lines of the file, and 250s skips the next 250 lines. Typically, pressing Return after typing a command within more is not necessary.

Try some commands on a file of your own. A good file that will have enough lines to make this interesting is /etc/passwd:

```
% more /etc/passwd
root:?:0:0: root:/:/bin/csh
news:?:6:11:USENET News:/usr/spool/news:/bin/ksh
ingres:*?:7:519:INGRES Manager:/usr/ingres:/bin/csh
usrlimit:?:8:800:(1000 user system):/mnt:/bin/false
vanilla:*?:20:805:Vanilla Account:/mnt:/bin/sh
charon:*?:21:807:The Ferryman:/users/tomb:
actmaint:?:23:809: Maintenance:/usr/adm/actmaint:/bin/ksh
pop:*?:26:819:,,,,:/usr/spool/pop:/bin/csh
lp:*?:70:10:System V Lp Admin:/usr/spool/lp:
trouble:*?:97:501:Trouble Report Facility:/usr/trouble:/usr/msh
postmaster:?:98:504:Mail:/usr/local/adm:/bin/csh
aab:?:513:1233:Robert Townsend:/users/aab:/bin/ksh
billing:?:516:1233:Accounting:/users/billing:/bin/csh
aai:?:520:1233:Pete Cheeseman:/users/aai:/bin/csh
--More--(1%) 60s

...skipping 60 lines

cq:?:843:1233:Rob Tillot:/users/cq:/usr/local/bin/tcsh
robb:?:969:1233:Robb:/users/robb:/usr/local/lib/msh
aok:?:970:1233:B Jacobs:/users/aok:/usr/local/lib/msh
went:?:1040:1233:David Math:/users/went:/bin/csh
aru:?:1076:1233:Raffie:/users/aru:/bin/ksh
varney:?:1094:1233:/users/varney:/bin/csh
brandt:?:1096:1233:Eric Brand:/users/brand:/usr/local/bin/tcsh
ask:?:1098:1233:/users/ask:/bin/csh
asn:?:1101:1233:Ketter Wesley:/users/asn:/usr/local/lib/msh
--More--(2%)
```

This example isn't exactly what you'll see on your screen, because each time you type a command to more, it erases its own prompt and replaces the prompt with the appropriate line of the file. Try pressing [Return] to move down one line, and you'll see what I mean.

Quit more in the middle of viewing this file by typing **q**.

SUMMARY The more program is one of the best general-purpose programs in Unix, offering an easy and powerful tool for perusing files.

Summary

Now that you can add this set of commands to your retinue of Unix expertise, you are most certainly ready to wander about your own computer system, understanding what

7

files are what, where they are, and how to peer inside. You learned about `file` to ascertain type, `head` and `tail` for seeing snippets of files, and `cat` and `more` to help easily view files of any size on your screen.

Workshop

The Workshop summarizes the key terms you learned and poses some questions about the topics presented in this chapter. It also provides you with a preview of what you will learn in the next hour.

Key Terms

block special device   A device driver that controls block-oriented peripherals. A hard disk, for example, is a peripheral that works by reading and writing blocks of information (as distinguished from a character special device). See also **character special device**.

character special device   A device driver that controls a character-oriented peripheral. Your keyboard and display are both character-oriented devices, sending and displaying information on a character-by-character basis. See also **block special device**.

control key notation   A notational convention in Unix that denotes the use of a control key. There are three common conventions: Ctrl-C, ^c, and C-C that all denote the Control-c character, produced by pressing the Control key (labeled Control or Ctrl on your keyboard) and, while holding it down, pressing the c key.

core dump   The image of a command when it executed improperly.

interactive program   An interactive Unix application is one that expects the user to enter information and then responds as appropriate. The `ls` command is not interactive, but the `more` program, which displays text a screenful at a time, is interactive.

major number   For device drivers, the major number identifies the specific type of device in use to the operating system. This is more easily remembered as the device ID number.

minor number   After the device driver is identified to the operating system by its major number, the address of the device in the computer itself (that is, which card slot a peripheral card is plugged into) is indicated by its minor number.

null character   Each character in Unix has a specific value, and any character with a numeric value of zero is known as a null or null character.

pipeline   A series of Unix commands chained by |, the pipe character.

Exercises

1. Many people who use Unix systems tend to stick with file-naming conventions. Indeed, Unix has many of its own, including .c for C source files, .Z for compressed files, and a single dot prefix for dot files. Yet `file` often ignores filenames (test it yourself). Why?

2. Do you remember the television game show "Name That Tune?" If so, you'll recall how contestants had to identify a popular song by hearing just the first few notes. The `file` command is similar; the program must guess at the type of the file by checking only the first few characters. Do you think it would be more accurate if it checked more of the file, or less accurate? (Think about this one.)

3. Use `more` to check some possible file types that can be recognized with the `file` command by peeking in the configuration file `/etc/magic`.

4. How did the `cat` command get its name? Do you find that to be a helpful mnemonic?

5. Here's an oddity: What will this command do?

   ```
   cat LISTS | more
   ```

6. If you were looking at an absolutely huge file, and you were pretty sure that what you wanted was near the bottom, what command would you use, and why?

7. What if the information was near the top?

Preview of the Next Hour

Many special characters are in Unix, as you have doubtless learned by accidentally typing a slash, an asterisk, a question mark, a quotation mark, or just about any other punctuation character. What might surprise you is that they all have different specific meanings. The next hour explains considerably more about how pipelines work and how programs are used as filters. Among the new commands you will learn are `sort`, `wc`, `nl`, `uniq`, and `spell`. You also will learn a new, immensely helpful flag to `cat` that makes cat produce line numbers.

7

HOUR 8

Filters and Piping

If you've ever learned a foreign language, you know that the most common approach is to start by building your vocabulary (almost always including the names of the months, for some reason) and then learning about the rules of sentence construction. The Unix command line is much like a language. Now you've learned many Unix words, so it's time to learn how to put them together as sentences using file redirection, filters, and pipes.

Commands to be added to your vocabulary this hour include wc, sort, and uniq.

Goals for This Hour

In this hour, you will learn

- The secrets of file redirection
- How to count words and lines using wc
- How to remove extraneous lines using uniq
- How to sort information in a file using sort

This hour begins by focusing on one aspect of constructing powerful custom commands in Unix by using file redirection. The introduction of some filters—programs intended to be used as part of command pipes—follows. Next you learn another aspect of creating your own Unix commands using pipelines.

Maximizing the Command Line

Now that you've learned some of the individual words of the Unix command vocabulary, it's time to get into some of the fun and power of the Unix system: combining individual commands into *pipes* or *filters* to perform complex and sophisticated tasks.

Task 8.1: The Secrets of File Redirection

DESCRIPTION So far, all the commands you've learned while teaching yourself Unix have required you to enter information at the command line, and all have produced output on the screen. But, as Gershwin wrote in *Porgy and Bess*, "it ain't necessarily so." In fact, one of the most powerful features of Unix is the capability for the input to come from a file as easily as it can come from the keyboard, and for the output to be saved to a file as easily as it can be displayed on your screen.

The secret is *file redirection*, the use of special commands in Unix that instruct the computer to read from a file, write to a file, or even append information to an existing file. Each of these acts can be accomplished with a file-redirection command in a regular command line: < redirects input, > redirects output, and >> redirects output and appends the information to the existing file. A mnemonic for remembering which is which is to remember that, just as in English, Unix works from left to right, so a character that points to the left (<) changes the input, whereas a character that points right (>) changes the output.

ACTION

1. Log in to your account and create an empty file using the `touch` command:

   ```
   % touch testme
   ```

2. First, use this empty file to learn how to redirect output. Use `ls` to list the files in your directory, saving them all to the newly created file:

   ```
   % ls -l testme
   -rw-rw-r--  1 taylor        0 Nov 15 09:11 testme
   % ls -l > testme
   % ls -l testme
   -rw-rw-r--  1 taylor        120 Nov 15 09:12 testme
   ```

Notice that when you redirected the output, nothing was displayed on the screen; no visual confirmation indicated that it worked. But it did, as you can see by the increased size of the new file.

3. Instead of using `cat` or `more` to view thisfile, try using file redirection:

```
% cat < testme
total 127
drwx------   2 taylor        512 Nov  6 14:20 Archives/
drwx------   3 taylor        512 Nov 16 21:55 InfoWorld/
drwx------   2 taylor       1024 Nov 19 14:14 Mail/
drwx------   2 taylor        512 Oct  6 09:36 News/
drwx------   3 taylor        512 Nov 11 10:48 OWL/
drwx------   2 taylor        512 Oct 13 10:45 bin/
-rw-rw----   1 taylor      57683 Nov 20 20:10 bitnet.lists.Z
-rw-rw----   1 taylor      46195 Nov 20 06:19 drop.text.hqx
-rw-rw----   1 taylor      12556 Nov 16 09:49 keylime.pie
drwx------   2 taylor        512 Oct 13 10:45 src/
drwxrwx---   2 taylor        512 Nov  8 22:20 temp/
-rw-rw----   1 taylor          0 Nov 20 20:21 testme
```

The results are the same as if you had used the `ls` command, but the output file is saved, too. You now can easily print the file or go back to it later to compare the way it looks with the way your files look in the future.

4. Use the `ls` command to add some further information at the bottom of the `testme` file, by using `>>`, the append double-arrow notation:

```
% ls -FC >> testme
```

The `-C` flag to `ls` forces the system to list output in multicolumn mode. Try redirecting the output of `ls  -F` to a file to see what happens without the `-C` flag.

5. It's time for a real-life example. You've finished learning Unix, and your colleagues now consider you an expert. One afternoon, Chrys tells you she has a file in her directory and wants to know what it is, but she can't figure out how to get to it. You try the `file` command, and Unix tells you the file is data. You are a bit puzzled. But then you remember file redirection:

```
% cat -v < mystery.file > visible.mystery.file
```

This command has `cat  -v` take its input from the file `mystery.file` and save its output in `visible.mystery.file`. All the nonprinting characters are transformed, and Chrys can poke through the file at her leisure.

Find a file on your system that `file` reports as a data file, and try using the redirection commands to create a version with all characters printable through the use of `cat  -v`.

SUMMARY You can combine the various forms of file redirection in an infinite number of ways to create custom commands and to process files in various ways. This hour just scratches the surface. Next, you learn about some popular Unix filters and how they can be combined with file redirection to create new versions of existing files. Also, study the example of Chrys's file, which shows the basic steps in all Unix file-redirection operations: Specify the input to the command, specify the command, and specify where the output should go.

Task 8.2: Counting Words and Lines Using wc

DESCRIPTION Writers generally talk about the length of their work in terms of number of words, rather than number of pages. In fact, most magazines and newspapers are laid out according to formulas based on multiplying an average-length word by the number of words in an article.

These people are obsessed with counting the words in their articles, but how do they do it? You can bet they don't count each word themselves. If they're using Unix, they simply use the Unix wc program, which computes a word count for the file. It also can indicate the number of characters (which `ls -1` indicates too) and the number of lines in the file.

ACTION

1. Start by counting the lines, words, and characters in the `testme` file you created earlier in this hour:

```
% wc testme
      4      12      121
% wc < testme
      4      12      121
% cat testme | wc
      4      12      121
```

All three of these commands offer the same result (which probably seems a bit cryptic now). Why do you need to have three ways of doing the same thing? Later, you learn why this flexibility is so helpful. For now, stick to using the first form of the command.

The output is three numbers, which reveal how many lines, words, and characters, respectively, are in the file. You can see that there are 4 lines, 12 words, and 121 characters in `testme`.

2. You can have wc list any one of these counts, or a combination of two, by using different command flags: -w counts words, -c counts characters, and -l counts lines:

```
% wc -w testme
   12 testme
% wc -l testme
    4 testme
% wc -wl testme
       12       4 testme
% wc -lw testme
12 testme
```

3. Now the fun begins. Here's an easy way to find out how many files you have in your home directory:

```
% ls | wc -l
37
```

The ls command lists each file, one per line (because you didn't use the -C flag). The output of that command is fed to wc, which counts the number of lines it's fed. The result is that you can find out how many files you have (37) in your home directory.

4. How about a quick gauge of how many users are on the system?

```
% who | wc -l
   12
```

Notice here that I used the "|" to create a pipe. Why not just use file redirection? Because by creating a pipe, I can feed the output of the first command to a second command, rather than just save it to disk. You'll see that this capability is the essence of pipes, and that they are, in turn, the core of the powerful command-line capabilities of Unix itself.

5. How many accounts are on your computer?

```
% cat /etc/passwd | wc -l
   3877
```

SUMMARY The wc command is a great example of how the simplest of commands, when used in a sophisticated pipeline, can be very powerful.

Task 8.3: Removing Extraneous Lines Using `uniq`

DESCRIPTION Sometimes when you're looking at a file, you'll notice that many duplicate entries exist, either blank lines or, perhaps, lines of repeated information. To clean up these files and shrink their size at the same time, you can use the uniq command, which lists each unique line in the file.

Well, it *sort of* lists each unique line in the file. What `uniq` really does is compare each line it reads with the preceding line. If the lines are the same, `uniq` does not list the second line. You can use flags with `uniq` to get more specific results: `-u` lists only lines that are not repeated, `-d` lists only lines that are repeated (the exact opposite of `-u`), and `-c` adds a count of how many times each line occurred.

ACTION

1. If you use `uniq` on a file that doesn't have any common lines, `uniq` has no effect:

```
% uniq testme
Archives/              OWL/                    keylime.pie
InfoWorld/             bin/                    src/
Mail/                  bitnet.mailing-lists.Z  temp/
News/                  drop.text.hqx           testme
```

2. A trick using the `cat` command is that `cat` lists the contents of each file sequentially, even if you specify the same file over and over again, so you can easily build a file with many lines:

```
% cat testme testme testme > newtest
```

Examine `newtest` to verify that it contains three copies of `testme`, one after the other. (Try using `wc`.)

3. Now you have a file with duplicate lines. Will `uniq` realize that these files have duplicate lines? Use `wc` to find out:

```
% wc newtest
    12   36   363
% uniq newtest | wc
    12   36   363
```

They're the same. Remember, the `uniq` command removes duplicate lines only if they're adjacent.

4. Create a file that has duplicate lines:

```
% tail -1 testme > lastline
% cat lastline lastline lastline lastline > newtest2
% cat newtest2
News/                  drop.text.hqx           testme
News/                  drop.text.hqx           testme
News/                  drop.text.hqx           testme
News/                  drop.text.hqx           testme
```

Now you can see what `uniq` does:

```
% uniq newtest2
News/                  drop.text.hqx           testme
```

5. Obtain a count of the number of occurrences of each line in the file. The `-c` flag does that job:

```
% uniq -c newtest2
     4 News/                          drop.text.hqx              testme
```

This shows that this line occurs four times in the file. Lines that are unique have no number preface.

6. You also can see what the `-d` and `-u` flags do, and how they have opposite actions:

```
% uniq -d newtest2
News/                          drop.text.hqx              testme
% uniq -u newtest2
%
```

Why did the `-u` flag list no output? The answer is that the `-u` flag tells `uniq` to list only those lines that are not repeated in the file. Because the only line in the file is repeated four times, there's nothing to display.

SUMMARY Given this example, you probably think `uniq` is of marginal value, but you will find that it's not uncommon for files to have many blank lines scattered willy-nilly throughout the text. The `uniq` command is a fast, easy, and powerful way to clean up such files.

Task 8.4: Sorting Information in a File Using sort

DESCRIPTION Whereas `wc` is useful at the end of a pipeline of commands, `uniq` is a *filter*, a program that is really designed to be tucked in the middle of a pipeline. Filters, of course, can be placed anywhere in a command line, anywhere that enables them to help direct Unix to do what you want it to do. The common characteristic of all Unix filters is that they can read input from standard input, process it in some manner, and list the results in standard output. With file redirection, standard input and output also can be files. To do this, you can either specify the filenames to the command (usually input only) or use the file-redirection symbols you learned earlier in this hour (<, >, and >>).

> Standard input and standard output are two very common expressions in Unix. When a program is run, the default location for receiving input is called *standard input*. The default location for output is *standard output*. If you are running Unix from a terminal, standard input and output are your terminal.
>
> A third I/O location, *standard error,* also exists in Unix. By default, this is the same as standard output, but you can redirect standard error to a different location than standard output. You learn more about I/O redirection later in the book.

One of the most useful filters is sort, a program that reads information and sorts it alphabetically. You can customize the behavior of this program, as with all Unix programs, to ignore the case of words (for example, to sort Big between apple and cat, rather than before—most sorts put all uppercase letters before the lowercase letters) and to reverse the order of a sort (z to a). The program sort also enables you to sort lists of numbers.

Few flags are available for sort, but they are powerful, as shown in Table 8.1.

TABLE 8.1   Flags for the sort Command

Flag	Function
-b	Ignore leading blanks.
-d	Sort in dictionary order (only letters, digits, and blanks are significant).
-f	Fold uppercase into lowercase; that is, ignore the case of words.
-n	Sort in numerical order.
-r	Reverse the order of the sort.

 To force ls to list output one file per line, you can use the -1 flag (that's the number one, not a lowercase L).

ACTION

1. By default, the ls command sorts the files in a directory in a case-sensitive manner. It first lists those files that begin with uppercase letters and then lists those that begin with lowercase letters:

```
% ls -1F
Archives/
InfoWorld/
Mail/
News/
OWL/
bin/
bitnet.mailing-lists.Z
drop.text.hqx
keylime.pie
src/
temp/
testme
```

To sort filenames alphabetically regardless of case, you can use `sort -f`:

```
% ls -1 | sort -f
Archives/
bin/
bitnet.mailing-lists.Z
drop.text.hqx
InfoWorld/
keylime.pie
Mail/
News/
OWL/
src/
temp/
testme
```

2. How about sorting the lines of a file? You can use the `testme` file you created earlier:

```
% sort < testme
Archives/            OWL/                 keylime.pie
InfoWorld/           bin/                 src/
Mail/                bitnet.mailing-lists.Z  temp/
News/                drop.text.hqx        testme
```

3. Here's a real-life Unix example. Of the files in your home directory, which are the largest? The `ls -s` command indicates the size of each file, in blocks, and `sort -n` sorts numerically:

```
% ls -s | sort -n
total 127
    1 Archives/
    1 InfoWorld/
    1 Mail/
    1 News/
    1 OWL/
    1 bin/
    1 src/
    1 temp/
    1 testme
   13 keylime.pie
   46 drop.text.hqx
   64 bitnet.mailing-lists.Z
```

It would be more convenient if the largest files were listed first in the output. That's where the `-r` flag to reverse the sort order can be useful:

```
% ls -s | sort -nr
   64 bitnet.mailing-lists.Z
   46 drop.text.hqx
   13 keylime.pie
    1 testme
```

```
   1 temp/
   1 src/
   1 bin/
   1 OWL/
   1 News/
   1 Mail/
   1 InfoWorld/
   1 Archives/
total 127
```

4. One more refinement is available to you. Instead of listing all the files, use the head command, and specify that you want to see only the top five entries:

```
% ls -s | sort -nr | head -5
  64 bitnet.mailing-lists.Z
  46 drop.text.hqx
  13 keylime.pie
   1 testme
   1 temp/
```

That's a powerful and complex Unix command, yet it is composed of simple and easy-to-understand components.

SUMMARY Like many of the filters, sort isn't too exciting by itself. As you explore Unix further and learn more about how to combine these simple commands to build sophisticated instructions, you will begin to see their true value.

Summary

You have learned quite a bit in this hour and are continuing down the road to Unix expertise. You learned about file redirection. You can't go wrong by spending time studying this information closely. The concept of using filters and building complex commands by combining simple commands with pipes has been more fully demonstrated here, too. This higher level of Unix command language is what makes Unix so powerful and easy to mold.

This hour hasn't skimped on commands, either. It introduced wc for counting lines, words, and characters in a file (or more than one file; try wc * in your home directory). You also learned to use the uniq and sort commands.

Workshop

The Workshop summarizes the key terms you learned and poses some questions about the topics presented in this chapter. It also provides you with a preview of what you will learn in the next hour.

Key Terms

file redirection   Most Unix programs expect to read their input from the user (standard input) and write their output to the screen (standard output). By use of file redirection, however, input can come from a previously created file, and output can be saved to a file instead of being displayed on the screen.

filter   Filters are a particular type of Unix program that expects to work either with file redirection or as part of a pipeline. These programs read input from standard input, write output to standard output, and often don't have any starting arguments.

standard error   This is the same as standard output, but you can redirect standard error to a different location than standard output.

standard input   Unix programs always default to reading information from the user by reading the keyboard and watching what's typed. With file redirection, input can come from a file, and with pipelines, input can be the result of a previous Unix command.

standard output   When processing information, Unix programs default to displaying the output on the screen itself, also known as standard output. With file redirection, output can easily be saved to a file; with pipelines, output can be sent to other programs.

Exercises

1. The placement of file-redirection characters is important to ensure that the command works correctly. Which of the following do you think will work, and why?

   ```
   < file wc          wc file <          wc < file
   cat file | wc      cat < file | wc    wc | cat
   ```

   Now try them and see whether you're correct.

2. The wc command can be used for many different tasks. Try to imagine a few that would be interesting and helpful to learn (for example, to determine how many users are on the system right now). Try them on your system.

3. Does the file size listed by wc -c always agree with the file size listed by the ls command? With the size indicated by ls -s? If there is any difference, why?

4. What do you think would happen if you tried to sort a list of words by pretending they're all numbers? Try it with the command ls -1 | sort -n to see what happens. Experiment with the variations.

Preview of the Next Hour

The next hour introduces wildcards and regular expressions, and tools to use those powerful concepts. You will learn how these commands can help you extract data from even the most unwieldy files.

You will learn one of the secret Unix commands for those really in the know: the secret-society, pattern-matching program grep. Better yet, you will learn how it got its weird and confusing name!

HOUR 9

Wildcards and Regular Expressions

One of the trickiest aspects of Unix is the concept of wildcards and regular expressions. A *wildcard* is a tool that allows you to "guess" at a filename, or to specify a group of filenames easily. Regular expressions are pattern-matching tools that are different from, and more powerful than, wildcards.

You'll meet the wonderful new command grep and its foundation, regular expressions.

Goals for This Hour

In this hour, you will learn about

- Filename wildcards
- Advanced wildcards
- Regular expressions
- Searching files using grep

- A more powerful grep
- A fast grep

This hour begins by looking at the two pattern-matching tools frequently found in Unix. A foray into commands that use these tools immediately follows.

Finding Needles in Haystacks

One of the most powerful parts of the Unix operating system is its capability to understand complex and sophisticated regular expressions. Combined with wildcards, it's an entire language for describing just what you're looking for or seeking to match, and the grep command offers just the tool you need to exploit this new language.

Task 9.1: Filename Wildcards

DESCRIPTION By now you are doubtless tired of typing every letter of each filename into your system for each example. A better and easier way exists! Just as with the special card in poker that can have any value, Unix has special characters that the various shells (the command-line interpreter programs) all interpret as *wildcards*.

You need to learn two wildcards: * acts as a match for any number and sequence of characters, and ? acts as a match for any single character. In the broadest sense, a lone * acts as a match for all files in the current directory (in other words, ls * is identical to ls), whereas a single ? acts as a match for all one-character-long filenames in a directory (for instance, ls ?, which will list only those filenames that are one character long).

ACTION

1. Start by using ls to list your home directory:

   ```
   % ls -F
   Archives/              OWL/                    keylime.pie
   InfoWorld/             bin/                    src/
   Mail/                  bitnet.mailing-lists.Z  temp/
   News/                  drop.text.hqx           testme
   ```

2. To experiment with wildcards, it's easiest to use the echo command. If you recall, echo repeats anything given to it, but—and here's the secret to its value—the shell interprets anything that is entered before echo sees it. That is, the * is expanded before the shell hands the arguments over to the command.

   ```
   % echo *
   Archives InfoWorld Mail News OWL bin bitnet.mailing-lists.Z
   drop.text.hqx keylime.pie src temp testme
   ```

Using the * wildcard enables me to easily reference all files in the directory. This is quite helpful.

3. A wildcard is even more helpful than the example suggests, because it can be embedded in the middle of a word or otherwise used to limit the number of matches. To see all files that began with the letter t, use t*:

```
% echo t*
temp testme
```

Try echo b* to see all your files that start with the letter *b*.

4. Variations are possible too. I could use wildcards to list all files or directories that end with the letter *s*:

```
% echo *s
Archives News
```

Watch what happens if I try the same command using the ls command rather than the echo command:

```
% ls -F *s
Archives:
Interleaf.story    Tartan.story.Z      nextstep.txt.Z
Opus.story         interactive.txt.Z   rae.assist.infoworld.Z

News:
mailing.lists.usenet  usenet.1              usenet.alt
```

Using the ls command here makes Unix think I want it to list two directories, not just the names of the two files. This is where the -d flag to ls could prove helpful to force a listing of the directories rather than of their contents.

5. Notice that, in the News directory, I have three files with the word usenet somewhere in their names. The wildcard pattern usenet* would match two of the files, and *usenet would match one. A valuable aspect of the * wildcard is that it can match *zero* or more characters, so the pattern *usenet* will match all three file-names:

```
% echo News/*usenet*
News/mailing.lists.usenet News/usenet.1 News/usenet.alt
```

Also notice that wildcards can be embedded in a filename or pathname. In this example, I specified that I was interested in files in the News directory.

6. Could you match a single character? To see how this can be helpful, it's time to move into a different directory, OWL on my system:

```
% cd OWL
% ls -F
Student.config    owl.c       owl.o
WordMap/          owl.data    simple.editor.c
owl*              owl.h       simple.editor.o
```

If I request owl*, which files will be listed?

```
% echo owl*
owl owl.c owl.data owl.h owl.o
```

What do I do if I am interested only in the source, header, and object files, which are here indicated by a .c, .h, or .o suffix? Using a wildcard that matches zero or more letters won't work; I don't want to see owl or owl.data. One possibility would be to use the pattern owl.* (by adding the period, I can eliminate the owl file itself). What I really want, however, is to be able to specify all files that start with the four characters owl. and have exactly one more character. This is a situation in which the ? wildcard works:

```
% echo owl.?
owl.c owl.h owl.o
```

Because no files have exactly one letter following the three letters owl, watch what happens when I specify owl? as the pattern:

```
% echo owl?
echo: No match.
```

This leads to a general observation. If you want to have echo return a question to you (output a question mark), you must do it carefully because the shell interprets the question mark as a wildcard:

```
% echo are you listening?
echo: No match.
```

To accomplish this, you need to surround the entire question with single quotation marks:

```
% echo 'are you listening?'
are you listening?
```

SUMMARY It won't surprise you that more complex ways of using wildcards to build file-name patterns exist. What likely will surprise you is that the vast majority of Unix users don't even know about the * and ? wildcards! This knowledge gives you a definite advantage.

Task 9.2: Advanced Filename Wildcards

DESCRIPTION Earlier, you learned about two special wildcard characters that can help you when you're specifying files for commands in Unix. The first was ?, which matches any single character, and the other was *, which matches zero or more characters.

"Zero or more characters," I can hear you asking. "Why would I need that?" The answer is that sometimes you want to have a pattern that might or might not contain a specific character.

You can use more special wildcards for the shell when specifying filenames, and it's time to learn about another of them. This new notation is known as a *character range*, serving as a wildcard less general than the question mark.

ACTION

1. A pair of square brackets denotes a range of characters, which can be either explicitly listed or indicated as a range with a dash between them. I'll start with a list of files in my current directory:

```
% ls
Archives/     News/        bigfiles     owl.c       src/
InfoWorld/    OWL/         bin/         sample      temp/
Mail/         awkscript    keylime.pie  sample2     tetme
```

If I want to see both `bigfiles` and the `bin` directory, I can use b* as a file pattern:

```
% ls -ld b*
-rw-rw----  1 taylor          165 Dec  3 16:42 bigfiles
drwx------  2 taylor          512 Oct 13 10:45 bin/
```

If I want to see all entries that start with a lowercase letter, I can explicitly type each one:

```
% ls -ld a* b* k* o* s* t*
-rw-rw----  1 taylor          126 Dec  3 16:34 awkscript
-rw-rw----  1 taylor          165 Dec  3 16:42 bigfiles
drwx------  2 taylor          512 Oct 13 10:45 bin/
-rw-rw----  1 taylor        12556 Nov 16 09:49 keylime.pie
-rw-rw----  1 taylor         8729 Dec  2 21:19 owl.c
-rw-rw----  1 taylor          199 Dec  3 16:11 sample
-rw-rw----  1 taylor          207 Dec  3 16:11 sample2
drwx------  2 taylor          512 Oct 13 10:45 src/
drwxrwx---  2 taylor          512 Nov  8 22:20 temp/
-rw-rw----  1 taylor          582 Nov 27 18:29 tetme
```

That's clearly quite awkward. Instead, I can specify a subrange of characters to match. I specify the range by listing them all tucked neatly into a pair of square brackets:

```
% ls -ld [abkost]*
-rw-rw----  1 taylor          126 Dec  3 16:34 awkscript
-rw-rw----  1 taylor          165 Dec  3 16:42 bigfiles
drwx------  2 taylor          512 Oct 13 10:45 bin/
-rw-rw----  1 taylor        12556 Nov 16 09:49 keylime.pie
-rw-rw----  1 taylor         8729 Dec  2 21:19 owl.c
-rw-rw----  1 taylor          199 Dec  3 16:11 sample
-rw-rw----  1 taylor          207 Dec  3 16:11 sample2
drwx------  2 taylor          512 Oct 13 10:45 src/
drwxrwx---  2 taylor          512 Nov  8 22:20 temp/
-rw-rw----  1 taylor          582 Nov 27 18:29 tetme
```

9

In this case, the shell matches all files that start with *a*, *b*, *k*, *o*, *s*, or *t*. This notation is still a bit clunky and would be more so if more files were involved.

2. The solution is to specify a range of characters by putting a hyphen in the middle:

```
% ls -ld [a-z]*
-rw-rw----  1 taylor          126 Dec  3 16:34 awkscript
-rw-rw----  1 taylor          165 Dec  3 16:42 bigfiles
drwx------  2 taylor          512 Oct 13 10:45 bin/
-rw-rw----  1 taylor        12556 Nov 16 09:49 keylime.pie
-rw-rw----  1 taylor         8729 Dec  2 21:19 owl.c
-rw-rw----  1 taylor          199 Dec  3 16:11 sample
-rw-rw----  1 taylor          207 Dec  3 16:11 sample2
drwx------  2 taylor          512 Oct 13 10:45 src/
drwxrwx---  2 taylor          512 Nov  8 22:20 temp/
-rw-rw----  1 taylor          582 Nov 27 18:29 tetme
```

In this example, the shell will match any file that begins with a lowercase letter, ranging from *a* to *z*, as specified.

3. Space is critical in all wildcard patterns, too. Watch what happens if I accidentally add a space between the closing bracket of the range specification and the asterisk following:

```
% ls -CFd [a-z] *
Archives/    News/        bigfiles      owl.c        src/
InfoWorld/   OWL/         bin/          sample       temp/
Mail/        awkscript    keylime.pie   sample2      tetme
```

This time, the shell tried to match all files whose names were one character long and lowercase, and then it tried to match all files that matched the asterisk wildcard, which, of course, included all files in the directory.

4. The combination of character ranges, single-character wildcards, and multicharacter wildcards can be tremendously helpful. If I move to another directory, I can easily search for all files that contain a single digit, a dot, or an underscore in the name:

```
% cd Mail
% ls -F
71075.446     emilyc        mailbox           sartin
72303.2166    gordon_hat    manley            sent
bmcinern      harrism       mark              shalini
bob_gull      j=taylor      marmi             siob_n
cennamo       james         marv              steve
dan_some      jeffv         matt_ruby         tai
dataylor      john_welch    mcwillia          taylor
decc          john_prage    netnews.postings  v892127
disserli      kcs           raf               wcenter
druby         lehman        rexb              windows
dunlaplm      lenz          rock              xd1f
ean_huts      mac           rustle
```

```
% ls *[0-9._]*
71075.446        ean_huts         matt_ruby       xd1f
72303.2166       gordon_hat       netnews.postings
bob_gull         john_welcher     siob_n
dan_some         john_prage       v892127
```

SUMMARY I think that the best way to learn about pervasive features of Unix such as shell filename wildcards is just to use them. If you flip through this book, you immediately notice that the examples are building on earlier information. This will continue to be the case, and the filename range notation shown here will be used again and again, in combination with the asterisk and question mark, to specify groups of files or directories.

Remember that if you want to experiment with filename wildcards, you can most easily use the echo command because it dutifully prints the expanded version of any pattern you specify.

Task 9.3: Searching Files Using grep

DESCRIPTION Two commonly used commands are the key to your becoming a power user and becoming comfortable with the capabilities of the system: the ls command and the grep command. The oddly named grep command makes it easy to find lost files or files that contain specific text.

The grep command not only has a ton of command options but has two variations in Unix systems, too. These variations are egrep, for specifying more complex patterns (regular expressions), and fgrep, for using file-based lists of words as search patterns.

After laborious research and countless hours debating with Unix developers, I am reasonably certain that the derivation of the name grep is as follows: Before this command existed, Unix users would use a crude line-based editor called ed to find matching text. As you know, search patterns in Unix are called regular expressions. To search throughout a file, the user prefixed the command with global. After a match was made, the user wanted to have it listed to the screen with print. To put it all together, the operation was global/*regular expression*/print. That phrase was pretty long, however, so users shortened it to g/re/p. Thereafter, when a command was written, grep seemed to be a natural, if an odd and confusing, name.

You could spend the next 100 pages learning all the obscure and weird options to the grep family of commands. When you boil it down, however, you're probably going to use only the simplest patterns and maybe a useful flag or two. Think of it this way: Just because the English language contains more than 500,000 words (according to the

Oxford English Dictionary) doesn't mean that you must learn them all to communicate effectively.

With this in mind, you'll learn the basics of grep this hour, but you'll pick up more insight into the program's capabilities and options during the next few hours. A few of the most important grep command flags are listed in Table 9.2.

TABLE 9.2   The Most Helpful grep Flags

Flag	Function
-c	List a count of matching lines only.
-i	Ignore the case of the letters in the pattern.
-l	List only the names of files that contain the specified *pattern*.
-n	Include line numbers.

ACTION

1. Begin by making sure you have a test file to work with. The example shows the testme file from the previous uniq examples:

```
% cat testme
Archives/               OWL/                    keylime.pie
InfoWorld/              bin/                    src/
Mail/                   bitnet.mailing-lists.Z  temp/
News/                   drop.text.hqx           testme
```

2. The general form of grep is to specify the command, any flags you want to add, the pattern, and a filename:

```
% grep bitnet testme
Mail/                   bitnet.mailing-lists.Z  temp/
```

As you can see, grep easily pulled out the line in the testme file that contained the pattern bitnet.

3. Be aware that grep finds patterns in a case-sensitive manner:

```
% grep owl testme
%
```

Note that OWL was not found because the pattern specified with the grep command was all lowercase, owl.

But that's where the -i flag can be helpful, which causes grep to ignore case:

```
% grep -i owl testme
Archives/               OWL/                    keylime.pie
```

4. For the next few examples, I'll move into the /etc directory because some files there have many lines. The wc command shows that the file /etc/passwd has almost 4,000 lines:

```
% cd /etc
% wc -l /etc/passwd
   3877
```

My account is taylor. I'll use grep to see my account entry in the password file:

```
% grep taylor /etc/passwd
taylorj:?:1048:1375:James Taylor:/users/taylorj:/bin/csh
mtaylor:?:760:1375:Mary Taylor:/users/mtaylor:/usr/local/bin/tcsh
dataylor:?:375:518:Dave Taylor:/users/dataylor:/usr/local/lib/msh
taylorjr:?:203:1022:James Taylor:/users/taylorjr:/bin/csh
taylorrj:?:668:1042:Robert Taylor:/users/taylorrj:/bin/csh
taylorm:?:862:1508:Melanie Taylor:/users/taylormx:/bin/csh
taylor:?:1989:1412:Dave Taylor:/users/taylor:/bin/csh
```

Try this on your system too.

5. As you can see, many accounts contain the pattern taylor.

You could figure out how many accounts there are with the pipeline "grep taylor /etc/passwd | wc –l", right?

A smarter way to see how often the taylor pattern appears is to use the -c flag to grep, which will indicate how many case-sensitive matches are in the file:

```
% grep -c taylor /etc/passwd
7
```

The command located seven matches. Count matches in the listing in step 4 to confirm this.

6. With 3,877 lines in the password file, it could be interesting to see whether all the Taylors started their accounts at about the same time. (This presumably would mean they all appear in the file at about the same point.) To do this, I'll use the -n flag to number the output lines:

```
% grep -n taylor /etc/passwd
319:taylorj:?:1048:1375:James Taylor:/users/taylorj:/bin/csh
1314:mtaylor:?:760:1375:Mary Taylor:/users/mtaylor:/usr/local/_
➥bin/tcsh
1419:dataylor:?:375:518:Dave Taylor:/users/dataylor:/usr/local/_
➥lib/msh
1547:taylorjr:?:203:1022:James Taylor:/users/taylorjr:/bin/csh
1988:taylorrj:?:668:1042:Robert Taylor:/users/taylorrj:/bin/csh
2133:taylorm:?:8692:1508:Melanie Taylor:/users/taylorm:/bin/csh
3405:taylor:?:1989:1412:Dave Taylor:/users/taylor:/bin/csh
```

Unfortunately, this is an example of a default separator adding incredible confusion to the command output. Normally, a line number followed by a colon would be no problem, but in the passwd file (which is already littered with colons), it's confusing. Compare this output with the output in step 4 with the grep command alone to see what has changed.

You can see that my theory about when the Taylors started their accounts was wrong. If proximity in the passwd file is an indicator that accounts are assigned at similar times, then no Taylors started their accounts even within the same week.

SUMMARY These examples of how to use grep barely scratch the surface of how this powerful and sophisticated command can be used. Explore your own file system using grep to search files for specific patterns.

> Armed with wildcards, you now can try the -l flag to grep, which, as you recall, indicates the names of the files that contain a specified pattern, rather than printing the lines that match the pattern. If I go into my electronic mail archive directory—Mail—I can easily, using the command grep -l -i chicago Mail/*, produces a list of mailboxes that contain Chicago. Try using grep -l to search across all files in your home directory for words or patterns.

Task 9.4: Creating Sophisticated Regular Expressions

DESCRIPTION A regular expression can be as simple as a word to be matched letter for letter, such as *acme*, or as complex as '(^[a-zA-Z]|:wi)', which matches all lines that begin with an upper- or lowercase letter or that contain :wi.

The language of *regular expressions* is full of punctuation characters and letters used in unusual ways. It is important to remember that regular expressions are different from shell wildcard patterns. It's unfortunate, but it's true. In the C shell, for example, a* lists any file that starts with the letter *a*. Regular expressions aren't *left rooted*, which means that you need to specify ^a if you want to match only lines that begin with the letter *a*. The shell pattern a* matches only filenames that start with the letter *a*, and the * has a different interpretation completely when used as part of a regular expression: a* is a pattern that matches zero or more occurrences of the letter *a*. The notation for regular expressions is shown in Table 9.1. The egrep command has additional notation, which you will learn shortly.

TABLE 9.1   Summary of Regular Expression Notation

Notation	Meaning
c	Matches the character c
\c	Forces c to be read as the letter c, not as another meaning the character might have
^	Beginning of the line
$	End of the line
.	Any single character
[xy]	Any single character in the set specified
[^xy]	Any single character not in the set specified
c*	Zero or more occurrences of character c

The notation isn't as complex as it looks in this table. The most important things to remember about regular expressions are that the * denotes zero or more occurrences of the preceding character, and . is any single character. Remember that shell patterns use * to match any set of zero or more characters independent of the preceding character, and ? to match a single character.

ACTION

1. The easy searches with grep are those that search for specific words without any special regular expression notation:

```
% grep taylor /etc/passwd
taylorj:?:1048:1375:James Taylor:/users/taylorj:/bin/csh
mtaylor:?:769:1375:Mary Taylor:/users/mtaylor:/usr/local/bin/tcsh
dataylor:?:375:518:Dave Taylor:/users/dataylor:/usr/local/lib/msh
taylorjr:?:203:1022:James Taylor:/users/taylorjr:/bin/csh
taylorrj:?:662:1042:Robert Taylor:/users/taylorrj:/bin/csh
taylorm:?:869:1508:Melanie Taylor:/users/taylorm:/bin/csh
taylor:?:1989:1412:Dave Taylor:/users/taylor:/bin/csh
```

I searched for all entries in the passwd file that contain the pattern taylor.

2. I've found more matches than I wanted, though. If I'm looking for my own account, I don't want to see all these alternatives. Using the ^ character before the pattern left-roots the pattern:

```
% grep '^taylor' /etc/passwd
taylorj:?:1048:1375:James Taylor:/users/taylorj:/bin/csh
taylorjr:?:203:1022:James Taylor:/users/taylorjr:/bin/csh
taylorrj:?:662:1042:Robert Taylor:/users/taylorrj:/bin/csh
taylorm:?:869:1508:Melanie Taylor:/users/taylorm:/bin/csh
taylor:?:1989:1412:Dave Taylor:/users/taylor:/bin/cshx
```

Now I want to narrow the search further. I want to specify a pattern that says "show me all lines that start with `taylor`, followed by a character that is not a lowercase letter."

3. To accomplish this, I use the `[^xy]` notation, which indicates an *exclusion set*, or set of characters that cannot match the pattern:

```
% grep '^taylor[^a-z]' /etc/passwd
taylor:?:1989:1412:Dave Taylor:/users/taylor:/bin/csh
```

It worked! You can specify a set in two ways: You can either list each character or use a hyphen to specify a range starting with the character to the left of the hyphen and ending with the character to the right of the hyphen. That is, a-z is the range beginning with a and ending with z, and 0-9 includes all digits.

4. To see which accounts were excluded, remove the `^` to search for an *inclusion range*, denoting a set of characters of which one must match the pattern:

```
% grep '^taylor[a-z]' /etc/passwd
taylorj:?:1048:1375:James Taylor:/users/taylorj:/bin/csh
taylorjr:?:203:1022:James Taylor:/users/taylorjr:/bin/csh
taylorrj:?:668:1042:Robert Taylor:/users/taylorrj:/bin/csh
taylormx:?:869:1508:Melanie Taylor:/users/taylorm:/bin/csh
```

5. To see some other examples, I use `head` to view the first 10 lines of the password file:

```
% head /etc/passwd
root:?:0:0:root:/:/bin/csh
news:?:6:11:USENET News:/usr/spool/news:/bin/ksh
ingres:*?:7:519:INGRES Manager:/usr/ingres:/bin/csh
usrlimit:?:8:800:(1000 user system):/mnt:/bin/false
vanilla:*?:20:805:Vanilla Account:/mnt:/bin/sh
charon:*?:21:807:The Ferryman:/users/tomb:
actmaint:?:23:809:Maintenance:/usr/adm/actmaint:/bin/ksh
pop:*?:26:819::/usr/spool/pop:/bin/csh
lp:*?:70:10:Lp Admin:/usr/spool/lp:
trouble:*?:97:501:Report Facility:/usr/mrg/trouble:/usr/local/lib/msh
```

Now I'll specify a pattern that tells `grep` to search for all lines that contain zero or more occurrences of the letter *z*.

```
% grep 'z*' /etc/passwd | head
root:?:0:0:root:/:/bin/csh
news:?:6:11:USENET News:/usr/spool/news:/bin/ksh
ingres:*?:7:519:INGRES Manager:/usr/ingres:/bin/csh
usrlimit:?:8:800:(1000 user system):/mnt:/bin/false
vanilla:*?:20:805:Vanilla Account:/mnt:/bin/sh
charon:*?:21:807:The Ferryman:/users/tomb:
actmaint:?:23:809:Maintenance:/usr/adm/actmaint:/bin/ksh
pop:*?:26:819::/usr/spool/pop:/bin/csh
```

```
lp:*?:70:10:Lp Adminuniverse(att):/usr/spool/lp:
trouble:*?:97:501:Report Facility:/usr/mrg/trouble:/usr/local/lib/msh
Broken pipe
```

The result is identical to the preceding command, but it shouldn't be a surprise. Specifying a pattern that matches zero or more occurrences will match every line! Specifying only the lines that have one or more z's is accomplished with an odd-looking pattern:

```
% grep 'zz*' /etc/passwd | head
marg:?:724:1233:Guyzee:/users/marg:/bin/ksh
axy:?:1272:1233:martinez:/users/axy:/bin/csh
wizard:?:1560:1375:Oz:/users/wizard:/bin/ksh
zhq:?:2377:1318:Zihong:/users/zhq:/bin/csh
mm:?:7152:1233:Michael Kenzie:/users/mm:/bin/ksh
tanzm:?:7368:1140:Zhen Tan:/users/tanzm:/bin/csh
mendozad:?:8176:1233:Don Mendoza:/users/mendozad:/bin/csh
pavz:?:8481:1175:Mary L. Pavzky:/users/pavz:/bin/csh
hurlz:?:9189:1375:Tom Hurley:/users/hurlz:/bin/csh
tulip:?:9222:1375:Liz Richards:/users/tulip:/bin/csh
Broken pipe
```

6. Earlier I found that a couple of lines in the /etc/passwd file were for accounts that didn't specify a login shell. Each line in the password file must have a certain number of colons, and the last character on the line for these accounts will be a colon, an easy grep pattern:

```
% grep ':$' /etc/passwd
charon:*?:21:807:The Ferryman:/users/tomb:
lp:*?:70:10:System V Lp Adminuniverse(att):/usr/spool/lp:
```

7. Consider this. I get a call from my accountant, and I need to find a file containing a message about a $100 outlay of cash to buy some software. I can use grep to search for all files that contain a dollar sign, followed by a one, followed by one or more zeros:

```
% grep '$100*' * */*
Mail/bob_gale:      Unfortunately, our fees are currently $100 per
➥test drive, budgets
Mail/dan_sommer:We also pay $100 for Test Drives, our very short
➥"First Looks" section. We often
Mail/james:has been dropped, so if I ask for $1000 is that way outta
➥line
Mail/john_spragens:time testing things since it's a $100 test drive:
➥I'm willing to
Mail/john_spragens:      Finally, I'd like to request $200 rather than
➥$100 for
Mail/mac:again: expected pricing will be $10,000 - $16,000 and the
➥BriteLite LX with
Mail/mark:I'm promised $1000 / month for a first
```

```
Mail/netnews.postings:  Win Lose or Die, John Gardner (hardback) $10
Mail/netnews.postings:I'd be willing to pay, I dunno, $100 / year for
➡the space? I would
Mail/sent:to panic that they'd want their $10K advance back, but the
➡good news is
Mail/sent:That would be fine.  How about $100 USD for both, to
➡include any
Mail/sent:       Amount: $100.00
```

That's quite a few matches. Notice that among the matches are $1000, $10K, and $10. To match the specific value $100, of course, I can use `$100` as the search pattern.

> You can use the shell to expand files not just in the current directory, but one level deeper into subdirectories, too: * expands your search beyond files in the current directory, and */* expands your search to all files contained one directory below the current point. If you have lots of files, you might occasionally see the error arg list too long; that's where the find command (in Hour 20, "Searching for Information and Files,") proves handy.

This pattern demonstrates the sophistication of Unix with regular expressions. For example, the $ is a special character that can be used to denote the end of a line, but only if it is placed at the end of the pattern. Because I did not place it at the end of the pattern, the grep program correctly interpreted it as the $ character itself.

8. Here's one more example. In the old days, when people were tied to typewriters, an accepted convention for writing required that you put two spaces after the period at the end of a sentence even though only one space followed the period of an abbreviation such as J. D. Salinger. Nowadays, with more text being produced through word processing and desktop publishing, the two-space convention is less accepted, and indeed, when submitting work for publication, I often have to be sure that I don't have two spaces after punctuation lest I get yelled at! The grep command can help ferret out these inappropriate punctuation sequences, fortunately; but the pattern needed is tricky.

To start, I want to see whether, anywhere in a file called dickens.note, I have used a period followed by a single space:

```
% grep '. ' dickens.note
                              A Tale of Two Cities
                                    Preface
When I was acting, with my children and friends, in Mr Wilkie Collins's
drama of The Frozen Deep, I first conceived the main idea of this
```

```
story.  A strong desire came upon me then, to
embody it in my own person;
and I traced out in my fancy, the state of mind of which it would
necessitate the presentation
to an observant spectator, with particular
care and interest.
As the idea became familiar to me, it gradually shaped itself into its
present
form.  Throughout its execution, it has had complete possession of me;
 I have so far verified what
is done and suffered in these pages,
as that I have certainly done and suffered it all myself.
Whenever any reference (however slight) is made here to the condition
of the Danish people before or during the Revolution, it is truly made,
 on the faith of the most trustworthy
witnesses.  It has been one of my hopes to add
something to the popular and picturesque means of
understanding that terrible time, though no one can hope
to add anything to the philosophy of Mr Carlyle's wonderful book.
Tavistock House
November 1859
```

What's happening here? The first line doesn't have a period in it, so why does grep say it matches the pattern? Because in grep, the period is a special character that matches any single character, not just the period. Therefore, my pattern matches any line that contains any character followed by a space.

To avoid this interpretation, I must preface the special character with a backslash (\) if I want it to be read as the . character itself:

```
% grep '\. ' dickens.note
story.  A strong desire came upon me then, to
present form.  Throughout its execution, it has had complete
witnesses.  It has been one of my hopes to add
```

Ahhh, that's better. Notice that all three of these lines have two spaces after each period.

SUMMARY With the relatively small number of notations available in regular expressions, you can create quite a variety of sophisticated patterns to find information in a file.

Task 9.5: For Complex Expressions, Try egrep

DESCRIPTION Sometimes a single regular expression can't locate what you seek. For example, perhaps you're looking for lines that have either of the two patterns. That's where the egrep command proves helpful. The command gets its name from "expression grep," and it has a notational scheme more powerful than that of grep, as shown in Table 9.3.

TABLE 9.3   Regular Expression Notation for egrep

Notation	Meaning
c	Matches the character c
\c	Forces c to be read as the letter c, not as another meaning the character might have
^	Beginning of the line
$	End of the line
.	Any single character
[xy]	Any single character in the set specified
[^xy]	Any single character not in the set specified
c*	Zero or more occurrences of character c
c+	One or more occurrences of character c
c?	Zero or one occurrences of character c
a|b	Either a or b
(a)	Nested regular expression

ACTION

1. Now I'll search the password file to demonstrate egrep. A pattern that seemed a bit weird was the one I used earlier with grep to search for lines containing one or more occurrences of the letter z: 'zz*'. With egrep, this search is much easier:

```
% egrep 'z+' /etc/passwd | head
marg:?:724:1233:Guyzee:/users/marg:/bin/ksh
axy:?:1272:1233:martinez:/users/axy:/bin/csh
wizard:?:1560:1375:Oz:/users/wizard:/bin/ksh
zhq:?:2377:1318:Zihong:/users/zhq:/bin/csh
mm:?:7152:1233:Michael Kenzie:/users/mm:/bin/ksh
tanzm:?:7368:1140:Zhen Tan:/users/tanzm:/bin/csh
mendozad:?:8176:1233:Don Mendoza:/users/mendozad:/bin/csh
pavz:?:8481:1175:Mary L. Pavzky:/users/pavz:/bin/csh
hurlz:?:9189:1375:Tom Hurley:/users/hurlz:/bin/csh
tulip:?:9222:1375:Liz Richards:/users/tulip:/bin/csh
Broken pipe
```

2. To search for lines that have either a z or a q, I can use the following:

```
% egrep '(z|q)' /etc/passwd | head
aaq:?:528:1233:Don Kid:/users/aaq:/bin/csh
abq:?:560:1233:K Laws:/users/abq:/bin/csh
marg:?:724:1233:Guyzee:/users/marg:/bin/ksh
ahq:?:752:1233:Andy Smith:/users/ahq:/bin/csh
cq:?:843:1233:Rob Till:/users/cq:/usr/local/bin/tcsh
axy:?:1272:1233:Alan Yeltsin:/users/axy:/bin/csh
```

```
helenq:?:1489:1297:Helen Schoy:/users/helenq:/bin/csh
wizard:?:1560:1375:Oz:/users/wizard:/bin/ksh
qsc:?:1609:1375:Enid Grim:/users/qsc:/usr/local/bin/tcsh
zhq:?:2377:1318:Zong Qi:/users/zhq:/bin/csh
Broken pipe
```

3. Now I can visit a complicated egrep pattern, and it should make sense to you:

```
% egrep '(^[a-zA-Z]|:wi)' /etc/printcap | head
aglw:\
        :wi=AG 23:wk=multiple Apple LaserWriter IINT:
aglw1:\
        :wi=AG 23:wk=Apple LaserWriter IINT:
aglw2:\
        :wi=AG 23:wk=Apple LaserWriter IINT:
aglw3:\
        :wi=AG 23:wk=Apple LaserWriter IINT:
aglw4:\
        :wi=AG 23:wk=Apple LaserWriter IINT:
Broken pipe
```

Now you can see that the pattern specified looks either for lines that begin (^)with an upper- or lowercase letter ([a-zA-Z]) or for lines that contain the pattern :wi.

SUMMARY Anytime you want to look for lines that contain more than a single pattern, egrep is the best command to use.

Task 9.6: Searching for Multiple Patterns at Once with `fgrep`

DESCRIPTION Sometimes it's helpful to look for many patterns at once. For example, you might want to have a file of patterns and invoke a Unix command that searches for lines which contain any of the patterns in that file. That's where the fgrep, or file-based grep, command comes into play. A file of patterns can contain any pattern that grep would understand (which means, unfortunately, that you can't use the additional notation available in egrep) and is specified with the -f *file* option.

ACTION

1. I use fgrep with wrongwords, an alias and file that contains a list of words I commonly misuse. Here's how it works:

```
% alias wrongwords fgrep -i -f .wrongwords
% cat .wrongwords
effect
affect
insure
```

```
ensure
idea
thought
```

Any time I want to check a file, for example `dickens.note`, to see whether it has any of these commonly misused words, I simply enter the following:

```
% wrongwords dickens.note
drama of The Frozen Deep, I first conceived the main idea of this
As the idea became familiar to me, it gradually shaped itself into its
```

I need to determine whether these are ideas or thoughts. It's a subtle distinction I often forget in my writing. To be fair, Charles Dickens probably got the usage correct in his great work "A Tale of Two Cities."

2. Here's another sample file that contains a couple of words from `wrongwords`:

```
% cat sample3
At the time I was hoping to insure that the cold weather
would avoid our home, so I, perhaps foolishly, stapled the
weatherstripping along the inside of the sliding glass
door in the back room. I was surprised how much affect it
had on our enjoyment of the room, actually.
```

Can you see the two incorrectly used words in that sentence? The `spell` program can't:

```
% spell sample3
```

(use `man spell` to learn more about the Unix `spell` command).

The `wrongwords` alias, on the other hand, can detect these words:

```
% wrongwords sample3
At the time I was hoping to insure that the cold weather
door in the back room. I was surprised how much affect it
```

SUMMARY   You have now met the entire family of `grep` commands. For most of your searches for information, you can use the `grep` command itself. Sometimes, though, it's nice to have options!

Summary

In this hour, you have had a chance to build on the knowledge you're picking up about Unix with your introduction to an exciting and powerful Unix utility: `grep`. Finally, what's a poker hand without some new wildcards? Because suicide kings and one-eyed jacks don't make much sense in Unix, you instead learned how to specify ranges of characters in filename patterns, further ensuring that you can type the minimum number of keys for maximum effect.

Workshop

The Workshop summarizes the key terms you learned and poses some questions about the topics presented in this chapter. It also provides you with a preview of what you will learn in the next hour.

Key Terms

exclusion set   A set of characters the pattern must not contain.

inclusion range   A range of characters a pattern must include.

left rooted   Patterns that must occur at the beginning of a line.

regular expressions   A convenient notation for specifying complex patterns. Notable special characters are ^ to match the beginning of the line and $ to match the end of the line.

wildcards   Special characters that are interpreted by the Unix shell or other programs to have meanings other than the characters themselves. For example, * is a shell wildcard and creates a pattern that matches zero or more characters. When prefaced, for example, with the letter X—X*—this shell pattern will match all files beginning with *X*.

Exercises

1. What wildcard expression would you use to find the following?
   - All files in the /tmp directory
   - All files that contain a w in that directory
   - All files that start with a b, contain an e, and end with .c
   - All files that either start with test or contain the pattern hi (notice that it can be more than one pattern)

2. Create regular expressions to match the following:
   - Lines that contain the words hot and cold (tricky!)
   - Lines that contain the word cat but not cats
   - Lines that begin with a numeral

3. There are two ways that you could have Unix match all lines that contain the words hot and cold: One method uses grep and one uses pipelines. Show both.

   4. Use the `-v` flag with various `grep` commands, and show the command and pattern
      needed to match lines that:
      - Don't contain `cabana`
      - Don't contain either `jazz` or `funk`
      - Don't contain `jazz`, `funk`, `disco`, `blues`, or `ska`.
   5. Use a combination of `ls -1`, `cat -n`, and `grep` to learn the name of the 11th or
      24th file in the `/etc` directory on your system.
   6. Two ways exist to look for lines containing any one of the words `jazz`, `funk`,
      `disco`, `blues`, or `ska`. Show both of them.

Preview of the Next Hour

Starting with the next hour, you learn about another powerful and popular program in the
Unix system, a program so helpful that versions of it exist even on DOS and the
Macintosh today. It fills in the missing piece of your Unix knowledge, and, if what's
been covered so far focuses on the plumbing analogy, this command finally moves you
beyond considering Unix as a typewriter (a tty). What's the program? It's the `vi` screen-
oriented editor. It's another program that deserves a book or two, but in two hours, you
learn the basics of `vi` and enough additional commands to let you work with the program
easily and efficiently.

HOUR 10

An Introduction to the vi Editor

The next few hours focus on full-screen editing tools for Unix. First you'll learn how to use vi to create and modify files. This hour covers the basics, including how to move around in the file and how to insert and delete characters, words, and lines. The next hour adds how to search for specific patterns in the text and how to replace them with other information as desired. In the third hour, you learn to use an alternative Unix editor called emacs.

Goals for This Hour

In this hour, you will learn

- How to start and quit vi
- Simple cursor motion in vi
- How to move by words and pages
- How to insert text into the file
- How to delete text

In some ways, an editor is like another operating system living within Unix; it is so complex that you will need two hours to learn to use vi. If you're used to Windows or Macintosh editors, you'll be unhappy to find that vi doesn't know anything about your mouse. After you spend some time working with vi, however, I promise it will grow on you. By the end of this hour, you will be able to create and modify files on your Unix system to your heart's content.

Editing the Unix Way

You've learned about how to manipulate your files and even peek inside at your leisure, but now it's time to learn the key Unix tool for creating and editing files: vi.

Task 10.1: How to Start and Quit vi

DESCRIPTION You might have noticed that many Unix commands covered so far have one characteristic in common. They all do their work, display their results, and quit. Among the few exceptions is more, in which you work within the specific program environment until you have viewed the entire contents of the file being shown or until you quit. The vi editor is another program in this small category of programs that you move in and use until you explicitly tell the program to quit.

> Where did vi get its name? It's not quite as interesting as some of the earlier, more colorful command names. The vi command is so named because it's the visual interface to the ex editor. It was written by Bill Joy while he was at the University of California at Berkeley.

Before you start vi for the first time, you must learn about two aspects of its behavior. The first is that vi is a *modal* editor. A mode is like an environment. Different modes in vi interpret the same key differently. For example, if you're in *insert mode*, typing a adds an a to the text, whereas in *command mode*, typing a puts you in insert mode because a is the key abbreviation for the append command. If you ever get confused about what mode you're in, press the Escape key on your keyboard. Pressing Escape always returns you to the command mode (and if you're already in command mode, it simply beeps to remind you of that fact).

When you are in command mode, you can manage your document; this includes the capability to change text, rearrange it, and delete it. Insert mode is when you are adding text directly into your document from the keyboard.

> In vi, the Return key is a specific command (meaning to move to the beginning of the next line). As a result, you never need to press Return to have vi process your command.

> emacs is a *modeless* editor. In emacs, the A key always adds the letter *a* to the file. You indicate all commands in emacs by holding down the Control key while pressing the command key; for example, Control-C deletes a character.

10

The second important characteristic of vi is that it's a screen-oriented program. It must know what kind of terminal, computer, or system you are using to work with Unix. This probably won't be a problem for you because most systems are set up so that the default terminal type matches the terminal or communications program you're using. In this hour, you learn how to recognize when vi cannot figure out what terminal you're using and what to do about it.

You can start vi in various ways, and you learn about lots of helpful alternatives later this hour. Right now, let's learn the basics. The vi command, by itself, starts the editor, ready for you to create a new file. The vi command with a filename starts vi with the specified file so that you can modify that file immediately.

Let's get started!

ACTION

1. To begin, enter vi at the prompt. If all is working well, the screen will clear, the first character on each line will become a tilde (~), and the cursor will be sitting at the upper-left corner of the screen:

   ```
   % vi
   ```

~
~
~
~
~
~
~
~
~

> I will show you only the portion of the screen that is relevant to the command being discussed for vi, rather than show you the entire screen each time. When the full screen is required to explain something, it will appear. A smooth edge will indicate the edge of the screen, and a jagged edge will indicate that the rest of the display has been omitted.

Type a colon. Doing so moves the cursor to the bottom of the screen and replaces the last tilde with the colon:

~
~
~
~
~
~
~
~
:_

Type q and press the Return key, and you should be back at the shell prompt:

```
~
~
~
~
~
~
~
:q
%
```

2. If that operation worked without a problem, skip to step 3. If the operation did not
work, you received the unknown-terminal-type error message. You might see this
on your screen:

```
% vi
"unknown": Unknown terminal type
I don't know what type of terminal you are on. All I have is
➥"unknown"
[using open mode]

_
```

Alternatively, you might see this:

```
% vi
Visual needs addressible cursor or upline capability
:
```

Don't panic. You can fix this problem. The first step is to get back to the shell
prompt. To do this, do exactly what you did in step 1: Type :q followed by the
Return key. You should then see this:

```
% vi
"unknown": Unknown terminal type
I don't know what type of terminal you are on. All I have is
➥"unknown"
[using open mode]
:q
%
```

The problem here is that vi needs to know the type of terminal you're using, but it
can't figure that out on its own. Therefore, you need to tell the operating system by
setting the TERM environment variable. If you know what kind of terminal you have,
use the value associated with the terminal; otherwise, try the default of vt100:

```
% setenv TERM vt100
```

10

If you have the $ prompt, which means you're using the Bourne shell (sh) or Korn shell (ksh), rather than the C shell (csh), try this:

```
$ set TERM=vt100 ; export TERM
```

Either way, you can now try entering vi again, and it should work.

If it does work, append the command (whichever of these two commands was successful for you) to your .profile file if you use ksh or sh, or .login file if you use csh. You can do this by entering whichever of the following commands is appropriate for your system:

```
% echo "setenv TERM vt100" >> .login
```

or

```
$ echo "set TERM=vt100 ; export TERM" >> .profile
```

This way, the next time you log in, the system will remember what kind of terminal you're using.

> vi and other screen commands use a Unix package called curses to control the screen. Like most Unix applications, curses is not designed for a specific configuration; instead, it is designed to be device independent. Therefore, to work on a specific device, you need to give it some additional information—in this case, the terminal type.
>
> If vt100 didn't work, it's time to talk with your system administrator about the problem or to call your Unix vendor to find out what the specific value should be. If you are connected through a modem or other line and you actually are using a terminal emulator or communications package, you might also try using ansi as a TERM setting. If that fails, call the company that makes your software and learn what terminal type the communications program is emulating.

3. Great! You have successfully launched vi, seen what it looks like, and even entered the most important command: the quit command. Now create a simple file and start vi so that it shows you the contents of the file:

```
% ls -1F > demo
% vi demo
```

```
total 29
drwx------  2 taylor      512 Nov 21 10:39 Archives/
drwx------  3 taylor      512 Dec  3 02:03 InfoWorld/
drwx------  2 taylor     1024 Dec  3 01:43 Mail/
drwx------  2 taylor      512 Oct  6 09:36 News/
drwx------  4 taylor      512 Dec  2 22:08 OWL/
-rw-rw----  1 taylor      126 Dec  3 16:34 awkscript
-rw-rw----  1 taylor      165 Dec  3 16:42 bigfiles
drwx------  2 taylor      512 Oct 13 10:45 bin/
-rw-rw----  1 taylor        0 Dec  3 22:26 demo
-rw-rw----  1 taylor    12556 Nov 16 09:49 keylime.pie
-rw-rw----  1 taylor     8729 Dec  2 21:19 owl.c
-rw-rw----  1 taylor      199 Dec  3 16:11 sample
-rw-rw----  1 taylor      207 Dec  3 16:11 sample2
drwx------  2 taylor      512 Oct 13 10:45 src/
drwxrwx---  2 taylor      512 Nov  8 22:20 temp/
-rw-rw----  1 taylor      582 Nov 27 18:29 tetme
~
~
~
~
~
~
"demo" 17 lines, 846 characters
```

You can see that vi reads the file specified on the command line. In this example, my file is 17 lines long, but my screen can hold 25 lines. To show that some lines lack any text, vi uses the tilde on a line by itself. Finally, note that, at the bottom, the program shows the name of the file, the number of lines it found in the file, and the total number of characters.

Type :q again to quit vi and return to the command line for now. When you type the colon, the cursor will jump down to the bottom line and wait for the q as it did before.

SUMMARY   You have learned the most basic command in vi—the :q command—and survived the experience. It's all downhill from here.

Task 10.2: Simple Cursor Motion in vi

DESCRIPTION   Getting to a file isn't much good if you can't actually move around in it. So let's learn how to use the cursor control keys in vi. To move left one character, type h. To move up, type k. To move down, type j, and to move right a single character, type l (lowercase L). You can also move left one character by pressing the Backspace key, and you can move to the beginning of the next line with the Return key.

ACTION

1. Launch vi again, specifying the demo file:

   % **vi demo**

```
total 29
drwx------  2 taylor       512 Nov 21 10:39 Archives/
drwx------  3 taylor       512 Dec  3 02:03 InfoWorld/
drwx------  2 taylor      1024 Dec  3 01:43 Mail/
drwx------  2 taylor       512 Oct  6 09:36 News/
drwx------  4 taylor       512 Dec  2 22:08 OWL/
-rw-rw----  1 taylor       126 Dec  3 16:34 awkscript
-rw-rw----  1 taylor       165 Dec  3 16:42 bigfiles
drwx------  2 taylor       512 Oct 13 10:45 bin/
-rw-rw----  1 taylor         0 Dec  3 22:26 demo
-rw-rw----  1 taylor     12556 Nov 16 09:49 keylime.pie
-rw-rw----  1 taylor      8729 Dec  2 21:19 owl.c
-rw-rw----  1 taylor       199 Dec  3 16:11 sample
-rw-rw----  1 taylor       207 Dec  3 16:11 sample2
drwx------  2 taylor       512 Oct 13 10:45 src/
drwxrwx---  2 taylor       512 Nov  8 22:20 temp/
-rw-rw----  1 taylor       582 Nov 27 18:29 tetme
~
~
~
~
~
~
~
"demo" 17 lines, 846 characters
```

   You should see the cursor sitting on top of the t in total on the first line or perhaps flashing underneath the t character. Perhaps you have a flashing-box cursor or one that shows up in a different color. In any case, that's your starting spot in the file.

2. Type h once to try to move left. The cursor stays in the same spot, and vi beeps to remind you that you can't move left any farther on the line. Try the k key to try to move up; the same thing will happen.

   Now try typing j to move down a character:

```
total 29
drwx------  2 taylor       512 Nov 21 10:39 Archives/
drwx------  3 taylor       512 Dec  3 02:03 InfoWorld/
drwx------  2 taylor      1024 Dec  3 01:43 Mail/
```

Now the cursor is on the d directory indicator of the second line of the file.

Type k to move back up to the original starting spot.

3. Using the four cursor-control keys—the h, j, k, and 1 keys—move around in the
    file for a little bit until you are comfortable with what's happening on the screen.
    Now try using the Backspace and Return keys to see how they help you move
    around.

4. Move to the middle of a line:

```
total 29
drwx------  2 taylor       512 Nov 21 10:39 Archives/
drwx------  3 taylor       512 Dec  3 02:03 InfoWorld/
drwx------  2 taylor      1024 Dec  3 01:43 Mail/
```

Here, I'm at the middle digit in the file size of the second file in the listing. Here
are a couple of new cursor motion keys: the 0 (zero) key moves the cursor to the
beginning of the line, and $ moves it to the end of the line. First, I type 0:

```
total 29
drwx------  2 taylor       512 Nov 21 10:39 Archives/
drwx------  3 taylor       512 Dec  3 02:03 InfoWorld/
drwx------  2 taylor      1024 Dec  3 01:43 Mail/
```

Now I type $ to move to the end of the line:

```
total 29
drwx------  2 taylor       512 Nov 21 10:39 Archives/
drwx------  3 taylor       512 Dec  3 02:03 InfoWorld/
drwx------  2 taylor      1024 Dec  3 01:43 Mail/
```

10

5. If you have arrow keys on your keyboard, try using them to see whether they work the same way that the h, j, k, and l keys work. If the arrow keys don't move you about, they might have shifted you into insert mode. If you type characters and they're added to the file, you need to press the Escape key (or Esc, depending on your keyboard) to return to command mode. Let's wrap this up by leaving this edit session. Because vi now knows that you have modified the file, it will try to ensure that you don't quit without saving the changes:

```
~
~
:q
No write since last change (:quit! overrides)
```

Use :q! (shorthand for :quit) to quit without saving the changes.

> In general, if you try to use a colon command in vi and the program complains that it might do something bad, try the command again, followed by an exclamation point. I like to think of this as saying, "Do it anyway!"

Stay in this file for the next task if you'd like, or use :q to quit.

SUMMARY Moving about a file using these six simple key commands is, on a small scale, much like the entire process of using the vi editor when working with files. Stick with these simple commands until you're comfortable moving around, and you will be well on your way to becoming proficient using vi.

Task 10.3: Moving by Words and Pages

DESCRIPTION Earlier, in the description of the emacs editor, I commented that because it's always in insert mode, all commands must include the Control key. Well, it turns out that vi has its share of control-key commands, commands that require you to hold down the Control key and press another key. In this section, you learn about Ctrl-f, Ctrl-b, Ctrl-u, and Ctrl-d. These move you forward or backward a screen, and up or down half a screen of text, respectively.

I toss a few more commands into the pot, too: w moves you forward word by word, b moves you backward word by word, and the uppercase versions of these two commands have very similar, but not identical, functions.

ACTION

1. To see how this works, you need to create a file that is longer than the size of your
   screen. An easy way to do this is to save the output of a common command to a
   file over and over until the file is long enough. The system I use has many users, so
   I needed to use the who command just once. You might have to append the output
   of who to the big.output file a couple of times before the file is longer than 24
   lines. (You can check using wc, of course.)

```
% who > big.output; wc -l big.output
   40
% vi big.output
```

```
leungtc   ttyrV   Dec  1 18:27   (magenta)
tuyinhwa  ttyrX   Dec  3 22:38   (expert)
hollenst  ttyrZ   Dec  3 22:14   (dov)
brandt    ttyrb   Nov 28 23:03   (age)
holmes    ttyrj   Dec  3 21:59   (age)
yuxi      ttyrn   Dec  1 14:19   (pc115)
frodo     ttyro   Dec  3 22:01   (mentor)
labeck    ttyrt   Dec  3 22:02   (dov)
chenlx2   ttyru   Dec  3 21:53   (mentor)
leungtc   ttys0   Nov 28 15:11   (gold)
chinese   ttys2   Dec  3 22:53   (excalibur)
cdemmert  ttys5   Dec  3 23:00   (mentor)
yuenca    ttys6   Dec  3 23:00   (mentor)
janitor   ttys7   Dec  3 18:18   (age)
mathisbp  ttys8   Dec  3 23:17   (dov)
janitor   ttys9   Dec  3 18:18   (age)
cs541     ttysC   Dec  2 15:16   (solaria)
yansong   ttysL   Dec  1 14:44   (math)
mdps      ttysO   Nov 30 19:39   (localhost)
md        ttysU   Dec  2 08:45   (muller)
jac       ttysa   Dec  3 18:18   (localhost)
eichsted  ttysb   Dec  3 23:21   (pc1)
sweett    ttysc   Dec  3 22:40   (dov)
"big.output" 40 lines, 1659 characters
```

10

Because I have only a 25-line display and the output is 40 lines long (you can see that on the status line at the bottom), there is more information in this file than the screen can display at once.

2. To see the next screenful, press Ctrl-f.

I press Control-f and get the following output:

```
eichsted ttysb   Dec  3 23:21   (pc1)
sweett   ttysc   Dec  3 22:40   (dov)
wellman  ttysd   Dec  3 23:01   (dov)
tuttleno ttyse   Dec  3 23:03   (indyvax)
wu       ttysf   Dec  3 23:10   (term01)
daurismj ttysg   Dec  3 23:10   (dov)
cs414    ttysh   Dec  3 23:12   (xds)
cq       ttysi   Dec  3 23:13   (expert)
cdemmert ttysk   Dec  3 22:37   (xsun22)
jrlee    ttysn   Dec  3 22:53   (mac1)
fitzgejs ttyso   Dec  3 23:18   (dov)
doerrhb  ttysp   Dec  3 23:20   (dov)
cdemmert ttysq   Dec  3 23:00   (xsun22)
frazierw ttysr   Dec  3 23:01   (dov)
buckeye  ttyss   Dec  3 23:20   (mac2)
mtaylor  ttyst   Dec  3 23:22   (dov)
look     ttysu   Dec  3 23:12   (age)
janitor  ttysw   Dec  3 18:29   (age)
ajones   ttysx   Dec  3 23:23   (rass)
~
~
~
~
```

Notice that the entire screen was rewritten and that the familiar tilde characters have appeared again to let me know that I have reached the end of the file.

By default, vi has a two-line overlap when you move from screen to screen. If you look carefully, you can see that both eichsted and sweett show up on both screens of data. This doesn't mean that they appear twice in the file; rather, vi is trying to help me not get lost while I wander through the file.

3. Now, what do you think will happen if I press Control-u?

```
leungtc  ttys0   Nov 28 15:11   (gold)
chinese  ttys2   Dec  3 22:53   (excalibur)
cdemmert ttys5   Dec  3 23:00   (mentor)
yuenca   ttys6   Dec  3 23:00   (mentor)
janitor  ttys7   Dec  3 18:18   (age)
mathisbp ttys8   Dec  3 23:17   (dov)
janitor  ttys9   Dec  3 18:18   (age)
cs541    ttysC   Dec  2 15:16   (solaria)
yansong  ttysL   Dec  1 14:44   (math)
mdps     ttysO   Nov 30 19:39   (localhost)
md       ttysU   Dec  2 08:45   (muller)
jac      ttysa   Dec  3 18:18   (localhost)
eichsted ttysb   Dec  3 23:21   (pc1)
sweett   ttysc   Dec  3 22:40   (dov)
wellman  ttysd   Dec  3 23:01   (dov)
tuttleno ttyse   Dec  3 23:03   (indyvax)
wu       ttysf   Dec  3 23:10   (term01)
daurismj ttysg   Dec  3 23:10   (dov)
cs414    ttysh   Dec  3 23:12   (xds)
cq       ttysi   Dec  3 23:13   (expert)
cdemmert ttysk   Dec  3 22:37   (xsun22)
jrlee    ttysn   Dec  3 22:53   (mac1)
fitzgejs ttyso   Dec  3 23:18   (dov)
```

10

The command has moved me up half a screen. Notice the location of `eichsted` and `sweett` now. Instead of the text being replaced at once, as when I used Control-f, the text was scrolled downward a line at a time, each new line being added as the program went along. The Control-u command might work either way—one line or an entire screen at a time—for you.

4. Now it's time to try moving around in this file word by word. Type the w key once to see what happens:

```
leungtc  ttys0   Nov 28 15:11   (gold)
chinese  ttys2   Dec  3 22:53   (excalibur)
cdemmert ttys5   Dec  3 23:00   (mentor)
```

Now type w six times more, noting that the cursor stops three times in the field to indicate what time the user logged in to the system (15:11 in this listing). Now your cursor should be sitting on the parenthesized field:

```
leungtc   ttys0   Nov 28 15:11   (gold)
chinese   ttys2   Dec  3 22:53   (excalibur)
cdemmert  ttys5   Dec  3 23:00   (mentor)
```

5. It's time to move backward. Type b a few times; your cursor moves backward to the beginning of each word.

   What happens if you try to move backward and you're already on the first word, or if you try to move forward with the w command and you're already on the last word of the line? Let's find out.

6. Using the various keys you've learned, move back to the beginning of the line that starts with leungtc, which you used in instruction 4:

```
leungtc   ttys0   Nov 28 15:11   (gold)
chinese   ttys2   Dec  3 22:53   (excalibur)
cdemmert  ttys5   Dec  3 23:00   (mentor)
```

This time, type W (uppercase W, not lowercase w) to move through this line. Can you see the difference? Notice what happens when you hit the time field and the parenthesized words. Instead of typing w seven times to move to the left parenthesis before gold, you can type W only five times.

7. Try moving backward using the B command. Notice that the B command differs from the b command the same way in which the W command differs from the w command.

SUMMARY Moving about by words, both forward and backward, being able to zip through half screens or full screens at a time, and being able to zero in on specific spots with the h, j, k, and l cursor-motion keys give you quite a range of motion. Practice using these commands in various combinations to get your cursor to specific characters in your sample file.

Task 10.4: Inserting Text into the File Using i, a, o, and 0

DESCRIPTION Being able to move around in a file is useful. The real function of an editor, however, is to enable you to easily add and remove—in editor parlance, insert and delete—information. The vi editor has a special insert mode, which you must use to add to the contents of the file. Four possible ways exist to shift into insert mode, and you learn about all of them in this unit.

The first way to switch to insert mode is to type the letter i, which, mnemonically enough, inserts text into the file. The other commands that accomplish more or less the same thing are a, to append text to the file; o, to open a line below the current line; and 0, to open a line above the current line.

ACTION

1. For this task, you need to start with a clean file, so quit from the big.output editing session and start vi again, this time specifying a nonexistent file called buckaroo:

   ```
   % vi buckaroo
   ```

```
~
~
~
~
~
~
~
~
~
~
~
~
~
~
~
~
~
~
~
~
~
"buckaroo" [New file]
```

   Notice that vi reminds you that this file doesn't exist; the bottom of the screen says New file, instead of indicating the number of lines and characters.

2. Now it's time to try using insert mode. Try to insert a k into the file by typing k once:

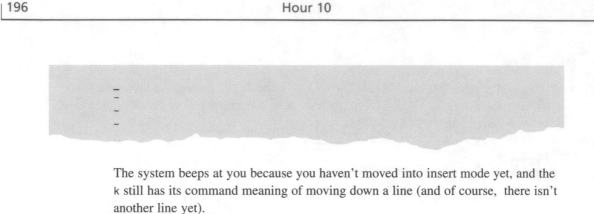

```
    ~
    ~
    ~
```

The system beeps at you because you haven't moved into insert mode yet, and the k still has its command meaning of moving down a line (and of course, there isn't another line yet).

Type i to move into insert mode, and then type k again:

```
k_
~
~
~
```

There you go! You've added a character to the file.

3. Press the Backspace key, which will move the cursor over the letter k:

```
k
~
~
~
```

Now see what happens when you press Escape to leave insert mode and return to the vi command mode:

```
   _
~
~
~
```

Notice that the k vanished when you pressed Escape. That's because vi only saves text you've entered to the left of or above the cursor, not the letter the cursor is resting on.

4. Now move back into insert mode by typing i, and enter a few sentences from a favorite book of mine.

> Movie buffs perhaps will recognize that the text used in this hour comes
> from the book *Buckaroo Banzai*. The cult film *The Adventures of Buckaroo
> Banzai Across the Eighth Dimension* is based on this very fun book.

```
"He's not even here," went the conservation.
"Banzai."
"Where is he?"
"At a hotpsial in El paso."
"What? Why werent' we informed? What's wrong with him?"_
~
~
```

10

I've deliberately left some typing errors in the text here. Fixing them will demonstrate some important features of the vi editor. If you fixed them as you went
along, that's okay, and if you added errors of your own, that's okay too!

Press Escape to leave insert mode. Press Escape a second time to ensure that it
worked; remember that vi beeps to remind you that you're already in command
mode.

5. Use the cursor motion keys (h, j, k, and l) to move the cursor to any point on the
    first line:

```
 "He's not even here," went the conservation.
"Banzai."
"Where is he?"
"At the hotpsial in El paso."
"What? Why werent' we informed? What's wrong with him?"
~
~
```

It turns out that I forgot a line of dialog between the line I'm on and the word
Banzai. One way to enter the line would be to move to the beginning of the line
"Banzai.", insert the new text, and press Return before pressing Escape to quit
insert mode. But vi has a special command "o" to open a line immediately below
the current line for inserting text. Type o and follow along:

```
"He's not even here," went the conservation.
_
"Banzai."
"Where is he?"
"At the hotpsial in El paso."
"What? Why werent' we informed? What's wrong with him?"
~
~
```

Now type the missing text:

```
"He's not even here," went the conservation.
"Who?"_
"Banzai."
"Where is he?"
"At the hotpsial in El paso."
"What? Why werent' we informed? What's wrong with him?"
~
~
```

That's it. Press Escape to return to command mode.

6. The problem with the snippet of dialog we're using is that there's no way to figure out who is talking. Adding a line above this dialog helps identify the speakers. Again, use cursor motion keys to place the cursor on the top line:

```
"He's not _even here," went the conservation.
"Who?"
"Banzai."
"Where is he?"
"At the hotpsial in El paso."
"What? Why werent' we informed? What's wrong with him?"
~
~
```

Now you face a dilemma. You want to open a line for new text, but you want the line to be above the current line, not below it. It happens that vi can do that too. Instead of using the o command, use its big brother O. When I type O, here's what I see:

```
_
"He's not even here," went the conservation.
"Who?"
"Banzai."
"Where is he?"
"At the hotpsial in El paso."
"What? Why werent' we informed? What's wrong with him?"
~
~
```

Type the new sentence and then press Escape.

```
I found myself stealing a peek at my own watch and overheard
General Catbird's
aide give him the latest._
"He's not even here," went the conservation.
"Who?"
"Banzai."
"Where is he?"
"At the hotpsial in El paso."
"What? Why werent' we informed? What's wrong with him?"
~
~
```

Now the dialog makes a bit more sense. The conversation, overheard by the narrator, takes place between the general and his aide.

7. I missed a couple of words in one of the lines, so the next task is to insert them. Use the cursor keys to move the cursor to the seventh line, just after the word Where:

```
I found myself stealing a peek at my own watch and overheard
General Catbird's
aide give him the latest.
"He's not even here," went the conservation.
"Who?"
"Banzai."
"Where_is he?"
"At the hotpsial in El paso."
"What? Why werent' we informed? What's wrong with him?"
~
~
```

At this juncture, I need to add the words `the hell` to make the sentence a bit stronger (and correct). I can use `i` to insert the text, but then I end up with a trailing space. Instead, I can add text immediately after the current cursor location by using the a command to append, or insert, the information. When I type a, the cursor moves one character to the right:

```
I found myself stealing a peek at my own watch and overheard
General Catbird's
aide give him the latest.
"He's not even here," went the conservation.
"Who?"
"Banzai."
"Where is he?"
"At the hotpsial in El paso."
"What? Why werent' we informed? What's wrong with him?"
~
~
```

Here's where `vi` can be difficult to use. I'm in insert mode, but there's no way for me to know that. When I type the letters I want to add, the screen shows that they are appended, but what if I thought I was in insert mode when I actually was in command mode? One trick I could use to ensure I'm in insert mode is to type the command a second time. If the letter a shows up in the text, I simply would backspace over it; now I would know that I'm in append mode. When I'm done entering the new characters, and I'm still in insert mode, here's what my screen looks like:

```
I found myself stealing a peek at my own watch and overheard
General Catbird's
aide give him the latest.
"He's not even here," went the conservation.
"Who?"
"Banzai."
"Where the hell is he?"
"At the hotpsial in El paso."
"What? Why werent' we informed? What's wrong with him?"
~
~
```

Notice that the cursor always stayed on the `i` in `is` throughout this operation. Press Escape to return to command mode. Notice that the cursor finally hops off the `i` and moves left one character.

> To differentiate between the i and a commands, remember that the insert command always adds the new information immediately before the character that the cursor is sitting on, whereas the append command adds the information immediately to the right of the current cursor position.

8. With this in mind, try to fix the apostrophe problem in the word werent' on the last line. Move the cursor to the n in that word:

```
"Where the hell is he?"
"At the hotpsial in El paso."
"What? Why werent' we informed? What's wrong with him?"
~
```

To add the apostrophe immediately after the current character, do you want to use the insert command (i) or the append (a) command? If you said "append," give yourself a pat on the back! Type a to append the apostrophe:

```
"Where the hell is he?"
"At the hotpsial in El paso."
"What? Why werent' we informed? What's wrong with him?"
~
```

Type ' once and then press Escape.

9. Quit vi using :q, and the program reminds you that you haven't saved your changes to this new file:

```
~
~
No write since last change (:quit! overrides)
```

To write the changes, you need a new command, so I'll give you a preview of a set of colon commands you learn later in this hour. Type : (the colon character), which moves the cursor to the bottom of the screen.

```
 ~
 ~
 :_
```

Now type w to write out (save) the file, and then press the Return key:

```
 ~
 ~
"buckaroo" 9 lines, 277 characters
```

It's okay to leave vi now. I'll use :q to quit, and I'm safely back at the command prompt. A quick cat confirms that the tildes were not included in the file itself:

```
% cat buckaroo
I found myself stealing a peek at my own watch and overheard
General Catbird's
aide give him the latest.
"He's not even here," went the conservation.
"Who?"
"Banzai."
"Where the hell is he?"
"At the hotpsial in El paso."
"What? Why weren't' we informed? What's wrong with him?"
%
```

SUMMARY   As you can tell, the vi editor is quite powerful, and it has a plethora of commands. Just moving about and inserting text, you have learned 24 commands, as summarized in Table 10.1.

TABLE 10.1   Summary of vi Motion and Insertion Commands

Command	Meaning
0	Move to the beginning of the line.
$	Move to the end of the line.
a	Append text—enter into insert mode after the current character.
^b	Back up one screen of text.
B	Back up one space-delimited word.

TABLE 10.1   continued

Command	Meaning
b	Back up one word.
Backspace	Move left one character.
^d	Move down half a page.
Escape	Leave insert mode, and return to command mode.
^f	Move forward one screen of text.
h	Move left one character.
i	Insert text—enter into insert mode before the current character.
j	Move down one line.
k	Move up one line.
l	Move right one character.
O	Open a new line for inserting text above the current line.
o	Open a new line for inserting text below the current line.
Return	Move to the beginning of the next line.
^u	Move up half a page.
W	Move forward one space-delimited word.
w	Move forward one word.
:w	Write the file to disk.
:q	Quit vi and return to the Unix system prompt.
:q!	Quit vi and return to the Unix system prompt, throwing away any changes made to the file.

In this table, I use the simple shorthand notation introduced in Hour 7, "Looking into Files." Unix users often use a caret (^) followed by a character instead of the awkward Control-c notation. Therefore, ^f has the same meaning as Control-f. Expressing this operation as ^f does not change the way it's performed: You still press and hold down the Control key, and then type f. It's just a shorter notation.

You've already learned quite a few commands, but you have barely scratched the surface of the powerful vi command!

Task 10.5: Deleting Text

DESCRIPTION You now have many of the pieces you need to work efficiently with the vi editor, to zip to any point in the file, and to add text wherever you'd like. Now you need to learn how to delete characters, words, and lines.

The simplest form of the delete command is the x command, which functions as though you were writing an *X* over a letter you don't want on a printed page: It deletes the character under the cursor. Type x five times, and you delete five characters. Deleting a line of text this way can be quite tedious, so vi has some alternative commands. (Are you surprised?) One command that many vi users don't know about is the D (for "delete through the end of the line") command. Wherever you are on a line, if you type D, you immediately will delete everything after the cursor to the end of that line of text.

If there's an uppercase D command, you can bet there's a lowercase d command too. The d delete command is the first of a set of more sophisticated vi commands which you follow with a second command that indicates a range. You already know that w and W move you forward a word in the file; they're known as *addressing commands* in vi. You can follow d with one of these addressing commands to specify what you want to delete. For example, to delete a word, simply type dw.

> Sometimes you might get a bit overzealous and delete more than you antici-
> pated. That's not a problem—well, not too much of a problem—because vi
> remembers the state of the file prior to the most recent action taken. To
> undo a deletion (or insertion, for that matter), use the u command. To undo
> a line of changes, use the U command. Be aware that once you've moved off
> the line in question, the U command is unable to restore it!

ACTION

1. Start vi again with the big.output file you used earlier:

```
leungtc  ttyrV   Dec  1 18:27   (magenta)
tuyinhwa ttyrX   Dec  3 22:38   (expert)
hollenst ttyrZ   Dec  3 22:14   (dov)
brandt   ttyrb   Nov 28 23:03   (age)
holmes   ttyrj   Dec  3 21:59   (age)
yuxi     ttyrn   Dec  1 14:19   (pc)
frodo    ttyro   Dec  3 22:01   (mentor)
labeck   ttyrt   Dec  3 22:02   (dov)
chenlx2  ttyru   Dec  3 21:53   (mentor)
leungtc  ttys0   Nov 28 15:11   (gold)
chinese  ttys2   Dec  3 22:53   (excalibur)
cdemmert ttys5   Dec  3 23:00   (mentor)
yuenca   ttys6   Dec  3 23:00   (mentor)
janitor  ttys7   Dec  3 18:18   (age)
mathisbp ttys8   Dec  3 23:17   (dov)
janitor  ttys9   Dec  3 18:18   (age)
cs541    ttysC   Dec  2 15:16   (solaria)
yansong  ttysL   Dec  1 14:44   (math)
mdps     ttysO   Nov 30 19:39   (localhost)
md       ttysU   Dec  2 08:45   (muller)
jac      ttysa   Dec  3 18:18   (localhost)
eichsted ttysb   Dec  3 23:21   (pc1)
sweett   ttysc   Dec  3 22:40   (dov)
"big.output" 40 lines, 1659 characters
```

10

Type x a few times to delete a few characters from the beginning of the file:

```
gtc ttyrV   Dec  1 18:27   (magenta)
tuyinhwa ttyrX   Dec  3 22:38   (expert)
hollenst ttyrZ   Dec  3 22:14   (dov)
brandt   ttyrb   Nov 28 23:03   (age)
holmes   ttyrj   Dec  3 21:59   (age)
```

Now type u to undo the last deletion:

```
ngtc ttyrV   Dec  1 18:27   (magenta)
tuyinhwa ttyrX   Dec  3 22:38   (expert)
hollenst ttyrZ   Dec  3 22:14   (dov)
brandt   ttyrb   Nov 28 23:03   (age)
holmes   ttyrj   Dec  3 21:59   (age)
```

If you type u again, what do you think will happen?

```
gtc  ttyrV   Dec  1 18:27   (magenta)
tuyinhwa ttyrX   Dec  3 22:38   (expert)
hollenst ttyrZ   Dec  3 22:14   (dov)
brandt   ttyrb   Nov 28 23:03   (age)
holmes   ttyrj   Dec  3 21:59   (age)
```

The undo command alternates between the last command having happened or not having happened. To explain it a bit better, the undo command is an action unto itself, so the second time you type u, you're undoing the undo command that you just requested. Type u a few more times to convince yourself that this is the case.

Some versions of vi have a considerably more sophisticated undo capability and the u key goes back, and back, and back until you're looking at an empty file. If you have that version of vi, you'll want to use the :redo command (type in the colon first) to go "forward in time" if you undo too far.

2. It's time to make some bigger changes to the file. Type dw twice to delete the current word and the next word in the file. It should look something like this after using the first dw:

```
ttyrV  Dec  1 18:27   (magenta)
tuyinhwa ttyrX   Dec  3 22:38   (expert)
hollenst ttyrZ   Dec  3 22:14   (dov)
brandt   ttyrb   Nov 28 23:03   (age)
holmes   ttyrj   Dec  3 21:59   (age)
```

Then it should look like this after using the second dw:

```
Dec  1 18:27   (magenta)
tuyinhwa ttyrX   Dec  3 22:38   (expert)
hollenst ttyrZ   Dec  3 22:14   (dov)
brandt   ttyrb   Nov 28 23:03   (age)
holmes   ttyrj   Dec  3 21:59   (age)
```

Type u. You see that you can undo only the most recent command. At this point, though, because I haven't moved from the line I'm editing, the U, or restore-this-line command will restore the line to its original splendor:

```
leungtc  ttyrV   Dec  1 18:27  (magenta)
tuyinhwa ttyrX   Dec  3 22:38  (expert)
hollenst ttyrZ   Dec  3 22:14  (dov)
brandt   ttyrb   Nov 28 23:03  (age)
holmes   ttyrj   Dec  3 21:59  (age)
```

3. Well, in the end, I really don't want to see some of these folk. Fortunately, I can change the contents of this file using the dd command to delete lines. When you're using one of these two-letter commands, repeating the letter means to apply the command to the entire line. What if I want to delete the entries for chinese and janitor, both of which are visible on this screen?

   The first step is to use the cursor keys to move down to any place on the line for the chinese account, about halfway down the screen:

```
chenlx2  ttyru   Dec  3 21:53  (mentor)
leungtc  ttys0   Nov 28 15:11  (gold)
chinese  ttys2   Dec  3 22:53  (excalibur)
cdemmert ttys5   Dec  3 23:00  (mentor)
yuenca   ttys6   Dec  3 23:00  (mentor)
janitor  ttys7   Dec  3 18:18  (age)
mathisbp ttys8   Dec  3 23:17  (dov)
```

   If your cursor isn't somewhere in the middle of this line, move it so that you too are not at an edge.

   I had planned to remove this line completely, but perhaps I'd rather just remove the date, time, and name of the system (in parentheses) instead. To accomplish this, I don't need to type dw many times, or even x many times, but rather D to delete through the end of the line:

```
chenlx2  ttyru   Dec  3 21:53  (mentor)
leungtc  ttys0   Nov 28 15:11  (gold)
chinese  ttys2   _
cdemmert ttys5   Dec  3 23:00  (mentor)
yuenca   ttys6   Dec  3 23:00  (mentor)
janitor  ttys7   Dec  3 18:18  (age)
mathisbp ttys8   Dec  3 23:17  (dov)
```

10

Oh, that's not quite what I wanted to do. No problem, the undo command can fix it. Simply typing u restores the text I deleted:

```
chenlx2  ttyru   Dec  3 21:53   (mentor)
leungtc  ttys0   Nov 28 15:11   (gold)
chinese  ttys2   Dec  3 22:53   (excalibur)
cdemmert ttys5   Dec  3 23:00   (mentor)
yuenca   ttys6   Dec  3 23:00   (mentor)
janitor  ttys7   Dec  3 18:18   (age)
mathisbp ttys8   Dec  3 23:17   (dov)
```

4. The problem is that I wanted to delete the two entries chinese and janitor from the file, but I used the wrong command. Instead of using the D command, I should use dd. Typing dd once has these results:

```
Dec  1 18:27    (magenta)
tuyinhwa ttyrX   Dec  3 22:38   (expert)
hollenst ttyrZ   Dec  3 22:14   (dov)
brandt   ttyrb   Nov 28 23:03   (age)
holmes   ttyrj   Dec  3 21:59   (age)
yuxi     ttyrn   Dec  1 14:19   (pc)
frodo    ttyro   Dec  3 22:01   (mentor)
labeck   ttyrt   Dec  3 22:02   (dov)
chenlx2  ttyru   Dec  3 21:53   (mentor)
leungtc  ttys0   Nov 28 15:11   (gold)
cdemmert ttys5   Dec  3 23:00   (mentor)
yuenca   ttys6   Dec  3 23:00   (mentor)
janitor  ttys7   Dec  3 18:18   (age)
mathisbp ttys8   Dec  3 23:17   (dov)
janitor  ttys9   Dec  3 18:18   (age)
cs541    ttysC   Dec  2 15:16   (solaria)
yansong  ttysL   Dec  1 14:44   (math)
mdps     ttysO   Nov 30 19:39   (localhost)
md       ttysU   Dec  2 08:45   (muller)
jac      ttysa   Dec  3 18:18   (localhost)
eichsted ttysb   Dec  3 23:21   (pc1)
sweett   ttysc   Dec  3 22:40   (dov)
wellman  ttysd   Dec  3 23:01   (dov)
```

Notice that a new line of information has been pulled onto the screen at the bottom to replace the blank line you removed.

If you try using the u command now, what happens?

I'm almost finished. A few presses of the Return key and I'm down to the entry for the janitor account. Using dd removes that line too:

```
Dec  1 18:27     (magenta)
tuyinhwa ttyrX   Dec  3 22:38    (expert)
hollenst ttyrZ   Dec  3 22:14    (dov)
brandt   ttyrb   Nov 28 23:03    (age)
holmes   ttyrj   Dec  3 21:59    (age)
yuxi     ttyrn   Dec  1 14:19    (pc)
frodo    ttyro   Dec  3 22:01    (mentor)
labeck   ttyrt   Dec  3 22:02    (dov)
chenlx2  ttyru   Dec  3 21:53    (mentor)
leungtc  ttys0   Nov 28 15:11    (gold)
cdemmert ttys5   Dec  3 23:00    (mentor)
yuenca   ttys6   Dec  3 23:00    (mentor)
mathisbp ttys8   Dec  3 23:17    (dov)
janitor  ttys9   Dec  3 18:18    (age)
cs541    ttysC   Dec  2 15:16    (solaria)
yansong  ttysL   Dec  1 14:44    (math)
mdps     ttysO   Nov 30 19:39    (localhost)
md       ttysU   Dec  2 08:45    (muller)
jac      ttysa   Dec  3 18:18    (localhost)
eichsted ttysb   Dec  3 23:21    (pc1)
sweett   ttysc   Dec  3 22:40    (dov)
wellman  ttysd   Dec  3 23:01    (dov)
tuttleno ttyse   Dec  3 23:03    (indyvax)
```

Each line below the one deleted moves up a line to fill in the blank space, and a new line, for tuttleno, moves up from the following screen.

5. Now I want to return to the buckaroo file to remedy some of the horrendous typographical errors! I don't really care whether I save the changes I've just made to the file, so I'm going to use :q! to quit, discarding these changes to the big.output file. Entering vi buckaroo starts vi again:

```
I found myself stealing a peek at my own watch and overheard
General Catbird's
aide give him the latest.
"He's not even here," went the conservation.
"Who?"
"Banzai."
"Where the hell is he?"
"At the hotpsial in El paso."
"What? Why weren't' we informed? What's wrong with him?"
~
~
~
~
~
~
~
~
~
~
~
~
~
"buckaroo" 9 lines, 277 characters
```

You can make a couple of fixes in short order. The first is to change conservation to conversation on the third line. To move there, press the Return key twice, and then use W to zip forward until the cursor is at the first letter of the word you're editing:

```
I found myself stealing a peek at my own watch and overheard
General Catbird's
aide give him the latest.
"He's not even here," went the conservation.
"Who?"
"Banzai."
"Where the hell is he?"
```

Then use the dw command:

```
I found myself stealing a peek at my own watch and overheard
General Catbird's
aide give him the latest.
"He's not even here," went the .
"Who?"
"Banzai."
"Where the hell is he?"
```

Now enter insert mode by typing i, type the correct spelling of the word conversation, and then press Escape:

```
I found myself stealing a peek at my own watch and overheard
General Catbird's
aide give him the latest.
"He's not even here," went the conversation.
"Who?"
"Banzai."
"Where the hell is he?"
```

6. That's one fix. Now move down a couple of lines to fix the atrocious misspelling of hospital:

```
"Banzai."
"Where the hell is he?"
"At the hotpsial in El paso."
"What? Why weren't' we informed? What's wrong with him?"
~
```

Again, use dw to delete the word, type i to enter insert mode, type hospital, and then press Escape. Now all is well on the line:

```
"Banzai."
"Where the hell is he?"
"At the hospital in El paso."
"What? Why weren't' we informed? What's wrong with him?"
~
```

Well, almost all is well. The first letter of `Paso` needs to be capitalized. Move to it by typing `w` to move forward a few words:

```
"Banzai."
"Where the hell is he?"
"At the hospital in El paso."
"What? Why weren't' we informed? What's wrong with him?"
~
```

7. It's time for a secret `vi` expert command! Instead of typing `x` to delete the letter, `i` to enter insert mode, `P` as the correct letter, and then Escape to return to command mode, you can use a much faster method to *transpose case*: the ~ (tilde) command. Type ~ once, and here's what happens:

```
"Banzai."
"Where the hell is he?"
"At the hospital in El Paso."
"What? Why weren't' we informed? What's wrong with him?"
~
```

Cool, isn't it? Back up to the beginning of the word again, using the `h` command, and type ~ a few times to see what happens. Notice that each time you type ~, the character's case switches—transposes—and the cursor moves to the next character. Type ~ four times, and you should end up with this:

```
"Banzai."
"Where the hell is he?"
"At the hospital in El pASO."
"What? Why weren't' we informed? What's wrong with him?"
~
```

Return to the beginning of the word, and type ~ until the word is correct.

8. One more slight change, and the file is fixed! Move to the last line of the file, to the extra apostrophe in the word `weren't'`, and type `x` to delete the offending character. The screen should now look like this:

```
      I found myself stealing a peek at my own watch and overheard
      General Catbird's
      aide give him the latest.
      "He's not even here," went the conversation.
      "Who?"
      "Banzai."
      "Where the hell is he?"
      "At the hospital in El Paso."
      "What? Why weren't we informed? What's wrong with him?"
      ~
      ~
      ~
      ~
      ~
      ~
      ~
      ~
      ~
      ~
      ~
      ~
      ~
      ~
```

That looks great! It's time to save it for posterity. Use :wq, a shortcut that has vi
write out the changes and immediately quit the program:

```
      ~
      ~
      ~
      "buckaroo" 9 lines, 276 characters
      %
```

SUMMARY   Not only have you learned about the variety of deletion options in vi, but you
also have learned a few simple shortcut commands: ~ to transpose case, and :wq
to write out the changes and quit the program all in one step.

You should feel pleased; you're now a productive and knowledgeable vi user, and you
can modify files, making easy or tough changes. Go back to your system and experiment
further, modifying some of the other files. Be careful, though, not to make changes in
any of your dot files (for example, .profile) lest you cause trouble that would be difficult to fix!

Summary

Table 10.2 summarizes the basic vi commands you learned in this hour.

TABLE 10.2 Basic vi Commands

Command	Meaning
0	Move to the beginning of the line.
$	Move to the end of the line.
a	Append text—enter into insert mode after the current character.
^b	Back up one screen of text.
B	Back up one space-delimited word.
b	Back up one word.
Backspace	Move left one character.
^d	Move down half a page.
D	Delete through the end of the line.
d	Delete —dw = delete word, dd = delete line.
Escape	Leave insert mode and return to command mode.
^f	Move forward one screen of text.
G	Go to the last line of the file.
nG	Go to the nth line of the file.
h	Move left one character.
i	Insert text—enter into insert mode before the current character.
j	Move down one line.
k	Move up one line.
l	Move right one character.
n	Repeat last search.
O	Open new line for inserting text above the current line.
o	Open new line for inserting text below the current line.
Return	Move to the beginning of the next line.
^u	Move up half a page.
U	Undo —restore current line if changed.
u	Undo the last change made to the file.
W	Move forward one space-delimited word.
w	Move forward one word.
X	Delete a single character.

Workshop

The Workshop summarizes the key terms you learned and poses some questions about the topics presented in this chapter. It also provides you with a preview of what you will learn in the next hour.

Key Terms

addressing commands   The set of vi commands that enable you to specify what type of object you want to work with. The d commands serve as an example: dw means delete word, and db means delete the preceding word.

command mode   The mode in which you can manage your document; this includes the capability to change text, rearrange it, and delete it.

insert mode   The vi mode that allows you to enter text directly into a file. The i command starts the insert mode, and Escape exits it.

modal   A modal program has multiple environments, or modes, that offer different capabilities. In a modal program, the Return key, for example, might do different things, depending on which mode you are in.

modeless   A modeless program always interprets a key the same way, regardless of what the user is doing.

transpose case   To switch uppercase letters to lowercase, or lowercase to uppercase.

Exercises

1. What happens if you try to quit vi by using :qw? Before you try it, do you expect it to work?

2. If you're familiar with word processing programs in the Mac or Windows environments, would you describe them as modal or modeless?

3. The d command is an example of a command that understands addressing commands. You know of quite a few. Test them to see whether they will all work following d. Make sure you see whether you can figure out the command that has the opposite action to the D command.

4. Do all the following three commands give the same result?
   ```
   D
   d$
   dG
   ```

10

5. Imagine you're in command mode in the middle of a line that's in the middle of the screen. Describe what would happen if you were to type each of the following:

```
Badluck
Window
blad$
```

Preview of the Next Hour

The next hour expands your knowledge of the vi editor. It introduces you to the sophisticated search and replace capability, explores the useful colon commands, and details the command-line options you'll want to know.

Hour **11**

Advanced vi Tricks, Tools, and Techniques

In the preceding hour, you learned what probably seems like a ton of vi commands that enable you to easily move about in files, insert text, delete other text, search for specific patterns, and move from file to file without leaving the program. This hour expands your expertise by showing you some more powerful vi commands. Before you begin this hour, I strongly recommend that you use vi to work with a few files. Make sure you're comfortable with the different modes of the program.

Goals for This Hour

In this hour, you will learn

- How to search within a file
- How to search and replace
- How to have vi start correctly
- The key colon commands in vi

- The change and replace commands
- How to use the `:!` command to access Unix commands

This might seem like a small list, but there's a lot packed into it. I'll be totally honest: You can do fine in vi without ever reading this hour. You already know how to insert and delete text, and save or quit without saving, and you can search for particular patterns, too—even from the command line as you start vi for the first time! On the other hand, vi is like any other complex topic: The more you're willing to study and learn, the more the program will bow to your needs. This means you can accomplish a wider variety of daily tasks.

Advanced Editing with vi

The preceding hour focused on the basics of inserting and deleting text and moving around within a file. This hour adds a critical capability: searching and replacing text within a file.

Task 11.1: Searching Within a File

DESCRIPTION With the addition of two more capabilities, you'll be ready to face down any vi expert, demonstrating your skill and knowledge of the editor, and, much more importantly, you will be able to really fly through files, moving immediately to the information you desire.

The two new capabilities we're going to explore in this chapter are for finding specific words or phrases in a file and for moving to specific lines in a file. Similar to searching for patterns in more, the */pattern* command searches forward in the file for a specified pattern, and *?pattern* searches backward for the specified pattern. To repeat the preceding search, use the n command to tell vi to search again, in the same direction, for the next instance of the same pattern.

You can move easily to any specific line in a file by using the G, or go-to-line, command. If you type a number before you type G, the cursor will move to that line in the file. If you type G without a line number, the cursor will zip you to the last line of the file (by default).

ACTION

1. Start vi again with the big.output file:

```
leungtc   ttyrV   Dec  1 18:27   (magenta)
tuyinhwa  ttyrX   Dec  3 22:38   (expert)
hollenst  ttyrZ   Dec  3 22:14   (dov)
brandt    ttyrb   Nov 28 23:03   (age)
holmes    ttyrj   Dec  3 21:59   (age)
yuxi      ttyrn   Dec  1 14:19   (pc)
frodo     ttyro   Dec  3 22:01   (mentor)
labeck    ttyrt   Dec  3 22:02   (dov)
chenlx2   ttyru   Dec  3 21:53   (mentor)
leungtc   ttys0   Nov 28 15:11   (gold)
chinese   ttys2   Dec  3 22:53   (excalibur)
cdemmert  ttys5   Dec  3 23:00   (mentor)
yuenca    ttys6   Dec  3 23:00   (mentor)
janitor   ttys7   Dec  3 18:18   (age)
mathisbp  ttys8   Dec  3 23:17   (dov)
janitor   ttys9   Dec  3 18:18   (age)
cs541     ttysC   Dec  2 15:16   (solaria)
yansong   ttysL   Dec  1 14:44   (math)
mdps      ttysO   Nov 30 19:39   (localhost)
md        ttysU   Dec  2 08:45   (muller)
jac       ttysa   Dec  3 18:18   (localhost)
eichsted  ttysb   Dec  3 23:21   (pc1)
sweett    ttysc   Dec  3 22:40   (dov)
"big.output" 40 lines, 1659 characters
```

Remember that I used :q! to quit earlier, so my changes were not retained.

To move to the last line of the file, I type G once, and I see this:

```
cdemmert  ttysk   Dec  3 22:37   (xsun)
jrlee     ttysn   Dec  3 22:53   (mac1)
fitzgejs  ttyso   Dec  3 23:18   (dov)
doerrhb   ttysp   Dec  3 23:20   (dov)
cdemmert  ttysq   Dec  3 23:00   (xsun)
frazierw  ttysr   Dec  3 23:01   (dov)
buckeye   ttyss   Dec  3 23:20   (mac2)
mtaylor   ttyst   Dec  3 23:22   (dov)
look      ttysu   Dec  3 23:12   (age)
```

continues

11

```
janitor   ttysw    Dec  3 18:29    (age)
ajones    ttysx    Dec  3 23:23    (rassilon)
~
    ~
    ~
    ~
    ~
    ~
    ~
    ~
    ~
    ~
```

To move to the third line of the file, I type 3 followed by G:

```
leungtc   ttyrV    Dec  1 18:27    (magenta)
tuyinhwa  ttyrX    Dec  3 22:38    (expert)
hollenst  ttyrZ    Dec  3 22:14    (dov)
brandt    ttyrb    Nov 28 23:03    (age)
holmes    ttyrj    Dec  3 21:59    (age)
yuxi      ttyrn    Dec  1 14:19    (pc)
frodo     ttyro    Dec  3 22:01    (mentor)
labeck    ttyrt    Dec  3 22:02    (dov)
chenlx2   ttyru    Dec  3 21:53    (mentor)
leungtc   ttys0    Nov 28 15:11    (gold)
chinese   ttys2    Dec  3 22:53    (excalibur)
cdemmert  ttys5    Dec  3 23:00    (mentor)
yuenca    ttys6    Dec  3 23:00    (mentor)
janitor   ttys7    Dec  3 18:18    (age)
mathisbp  ttys8    Dec  3 23:17    (dov)
janitor   ttys9    Dec  3 18:18    (age)
cs541     ttysC    Dec  2 15:16    (solaria)
yansong   ttysL    Dec  1 14:44    (math)
mdps      ttysO    Nov 30 19:39    (localhost)
md        ttysU    Dec  2 08:45    (muller)
jac       ttysa    Dec  3 18:18    (localhost)
eichsted  ttysb    Dec  3 23:21    (pc1)
sweett    ttysc    Dec  3 22:40    (dov)
```

Notice that the cursor is on the third line of the file.

2. Now it's time to search. From my previous travels in this file, I know that the very last line is for the account `ajones`, but instead of using `G` to move there directly, I can search for the specified pattern by using the `/` search command.

Typing `/` immediately moves the cursor to the bottom of the screen:

```
md        ttysU   Dec  2 08:45   (mueller)
jac       ttysa   Dec  3 18:18   (localhost)
eichsted ttysb    Dec  3 23:21   (pc1)
sweett    ttysc   Dec  3 22:40   (dov)
/_
```

Now I can type in the pattern `ajones`:

```
md        ttysU   Dec  2 08:45   (mueller)
jac       ttysa   Dec  3 18:18   (localhost)
eichsted ttysb    Dec  3 23:21   (pc1)
sweett    ttysc   Dec  3 22:40   (dov)
/ajones_
```

When I press Return, `vi` spins through the file and moves me to the first line following the line that the cursor was sitting on that contains the specified pattern:

```
cdemmert ttysk   Dec  3 22:37   (xsun)
jrlee     ttysn   Dec  3 22:53   (mac1)
fitzgejs ttyso    Dec  3 23:18   (dov)
doerrhb  ttysp    Dec  3 23:20   (dov)
cdemmert ttysq   Dec  3 23:00   (xsun)
frazierw ttysr    Dec  3 23:01   (dov)
buckeye  ttyss    Dec  3 23:20   (mac2)
mtaylor  ttyst    Dec  3 23:22   (dov)
look      ttysu   Dec  3 23:12   (age)
janitor  ttysw    Dec  3 18:29   (age)
ajones    ttysx   Dec  3 23:23   (rassilon)
~
~
~
~
~
~
```

continues

~
~
~
~
~
~

3. If I type n to search for this pattern again, a slash appears at the bottom line to show that vi understood my request. But the cursor stays exactly where it is, which indicates that this is the only occurrence of the pattern in this file.

4. Looking at this file, I noticed that the account janitor has all sorts of sessions running. To search backward for occurrences of the account, I can use the ? command:

```
~
~
?janitor_
```

The first search moves the cursor up one line, which leaves the screen looking almost the same:

```
cdemmert ttysk   Dec  3 22:37   (xsun)
jrlee    ttysn   Dec  3 22:53   (mac1)
fitzgejs ttyso   Dec  3 23:18   (dov)
doerrhb  ttysp   Dec  3 23:20   (dov)
cdemmert ttysq   Dec  3 23:00   (xsun)
frazierw ttysr   Dec  3 23:01   (dov)
buckeye  ttyss   Dec  3 23:20   (mac2)
mtaylor  ttyst   Dec  3 23:22   (dov)
look     ttysu   Dec  3 23:12   (age)
janitor  ttysw   Dec  3 18:29   (age)
ajones   ttysx   Dec  3 23:23   (rassilon)
~
~
~
~
~
~
~
```

continues

```
~
~
~
~
?janitor
```

Here's where the n, or next search, can come in handy. If I type n this time and another occurrence of the pattern is in the file, vi moves me directly to the match:

```
yuxi      ttyrn    Dec  1 14:19   (pc)
frodo     ttyro    Dec  3 22:01   (mentor)
labeck    ttyrt    Dec  3 22:02   (dov)
chenlx2   ttyru    Dec  3 21:53   (mentor)
leungtc   ttys0    Nov 28 15:11   (gold)
chinese   ttys2    Dec  3 22:53   (excalibur)
cdemmert  ttys5    Dec  3 23:00   (mentor)
yuenca    ttys6    Dec  3 23:00   (mentor)
janitor   ttys7    Dec  3 18:18   (age)
mathisbp  ttys8    Dec  3 23:17   (dov)
janitor   ttys9    Dec  3 18:18   (age)
cs541     ttysC    Dec  2 15:16   (solaria)
yansong   ttysL    Dec  1 14:44   (math)
mdps      ttysO    Nov 30 19:39   (localhost)
md        ttysU    Dec  2 08:45   (muller)
jac       ttysa    Dec  3 18:18   (localhost)
eichsted  ttysb    Dec  3 23:21   (pc1)
sweett    ttysc    Dec  3 22:40   (dov)
wellman   ttysd    Dec  3 23:01   (dov)
tuttleno  ttyse    Dec  3 23:03   (indyvax)
wu        ttysf    Dec  3 23:10   (term01)
daurismj  ttysg    Dec  3 23:10   (dov)
cs414     ttysh    Dec  3 23:12   (xds)
```

11

When you're done, quit vi by using :q.

Not dozens, but hundreds of commands are in vi. Rather than overwhelm you with all of them, even in a table, I have opted to work with the most basic and important commands. By the time you're done with this hour, your knowledge of vi commands will be substantial, and you will be able to use the editor with little difficulty. The rest of this hour will expand your knowledge with more shortcuts and efficiency commands.

SUMMARY This task focused on searching for patterns, which is a common requirement and helpful feature of any editor. In addition, you learned how to move to the top of the file (1G) and to the bottom of the file (G), as well as anywhere in between.

Task 11.2: The Colon Commands in `vi`

DESCRIPTION Without too much explanation, you have learned a couple of colon commands, commands that have a colon as the first character. The colon immediately zooms the cursor to the bottom of the screen for further input. These commands are actually a subset of quite a large range of commands, all part of the `ex` editor on which `vi` is based.

The colon commands that are most helpful are as listed here:

Command	Function
`:e` *filename*	Stop editing the current file, and edit the specified file.
`:n`	Stop editing the current file, and edit the next file specified on the command line.
`:q`	Quit the editor.
`:q!`	Quit regardless of whether any changes have occurred.
`:r` *filename*	Include the contents of the specified file at this position in the file that is currently being edited.
`:w`	Save the file to disk.
`:w` *filename*	Save the file to disk with the specified filename.

ACTION

1. Start `vi` again, this time specifying more than one file on the command line; `vi` quickly indicates that you want to edit more than one file:

   ```
   % vi buckaroo big.output
   2 files to edit.
   ```

   Then it clears the screen and shows you the first file:

```
I found myself stealing a peek at my own watch and overheard
General Catbird's
aide give him the latest.
"He's not even here," went the conversation.
"Who?"
"Banzai."
"Where the hell is he?"
"At the hospital in El Paso."
"What? Why weren't we informed? What's wrong with him?"
~
~
~
~
~
~
~
~
~
~
~
~
~
~
~
"buckaroo" 9 lines, 276 characters
```

11

Using :w results in this:

```
~
~
~
"buckaroo" 9 lines, 276 characters
```

2. Instead, try writing to a different file, using :w newfile:

```
~
~
:w newfile_
```

When you press Return, you see this:

```
~
~
"newfile" [New file] 9 lines, 276 characters
```

3. Now pay attention to where the cursor is in the file. The :r, or read-file, command
   always includes the contents of the file below the current line. Just before I press
   Return, then, here's what my screen looks like:

```
I found myself stealing a peek at my own watch and overheard
General Catbird's
aide give him the latest.
"He's not even here," went the conversation.
"Who?"
"Banzai."
"Where the hell is he?"
"At the hospital in El Paso."
"What? Why weren't we informed? What's wrong with him?"
~
~
~
~
~
~
~
~
~
~
~
~
~
~
:r newfile_
```

Pressing Return yields this:

```
I found myself stealing a peek at my own watch and overheard
General Catbird's
I found myself stealing a peek at my own watch and overheard
General Catbird's
aide give him the latest.
"He's not even here," went the conversation.
"Who?"
"Banzai."
"Where the hell is he?"
"At the hospital in El Paso."
"What? Why weren't we informed? What's wrong with him?"

aide give him the latest.
"He's not even here," went the conversation.
"Who?"
"Banzai."
"Where the hell is he?"
"At the hospital in El Paso."
"What? Why weren't we informed? What's wrong with him?"
~
~
~
~
~
~
```

11

This can be a helpful way to include files within one another, or to build a file that contains lots of other files.

4. Now that I've garbled the file, I want to save it to a new file, buckaroo.confused:

```
~
~
:w buckaroo.confused_
```

When I press Return, I see this:

```
~
~
"buckaroo.confused" [New file] 17 lines, 546 characters
```

5. Now it's time to move to the second file in the list of files given to vi at startup. To do this, I use the :n, or next-file, command:

```
~
~
:n_
```

Pressing Return results in the next file being brought into the editor to replace the first:

```
leungtc  ttyrV   Dec  1 18:27   (magenta)
tuyinhwa ttyrX   Dec  3 22:38   (expert)
hollenst ttyrZ   Dec  3 22:14   (dov)
brandt   ttyrb   Nov 28 23:03   (age)
holmes   ttyrj   Dec  3 21:59   (age)
yuxi     ttyrn   Dec  1 14:19   (pc)
frodo    ttyro   Dec  3 22:01   (mentor)
labeck   ttyrt   Dec  3 22:02   (dov)
chenlx2  ttyru   Dec  3 21:53   (mentor)
leungtc  ttys0   Nov 28 15:11   (gold)
chinese  ttys2   Dec  3 22:53   (excalibur)
cdemmert ttys5   Dec  3 23:00   (mentor)
yuenca   ttys6   Dec  3 23:00   (mentor)
janitor  ttys7   Dec  3 18:18   (age)
mathisbp ttys8   Dec  3 23:17   (dov)
janitor  ttys9   Dec  3 18:18   (age)
cs541    ttysC   Dec  2 15:16   (solaria)
yansong  ttysL   Dec  1 14:44   (math)
mdps     ttysO   Nov 30 19:39   (localhost)
md       ttysU   Dec  2 08:45   (muller)
jac      ttysa   Dec  3 18:18   (localhost)
eichsted ttysb   Dec  3 23:21   (pc1)
sweett   ttysc   Dec  3 22:40   (dov)
"big.output" 40 lines, 1659 characters
```

6. In the middle of working on this, I suddenly realize that I need to make a slight change to the recently saved buckaroo.confused file. That's where the :e command comes in handy. Using it, I can edit any other file:

```
~
~
:e buckaroo.confused_
```

I press Return and see this:

```
I found myself stealing a peek at my own watch and overheard
General Catbird's
I found myself stealing a peek at my own watch and overheard
General Catbird's
aide give him the latest.
"He's not even here," went the conversation.
"Who?"
"Banzai."
"Where the hell is he?"
"At the hospital in El Paso."
"What? Why weren't we informed? What's wrong with him?"

aide give him the latest.
"He's not even here," went the conversation.
"Who?"
"Banzai."
"Where the hell is he?"
"At the hospital in El Paso."
"What? Why weren'l we informed? What's wrong with him?"
~
~
~
~
~
~
~
"buckaroo.confused" 17 lines, 546 characters
```

SUMMARY That's it! You now know a considerable amount about one of the most important, and certainly most used, commands in Unix. There's more to learn (isn't there always?), but you now can edit your files with aplomb!

Task 11.3: How to Start vi Correctly

DESCRIPTION The vi command wouldn't be part of Unix if it didn't have some startup options available, but there really are only two options worth mentioning. The -R flag sets up vi as a read-only file, to ensure that you don't accidentally modify a file. The second option doesn't start with a dash, but with a plus sign: Any command following the plus sign is used as an initial command to the program. This is more useful than it might sound. The command vi +$ sample, for example, starts the editor at the bottom of the file sample, and vi +17 sample starts the editor on the 17th line of sample.

ACTION

1. First, this is the read-only format:

   `% vi -R buckaroo`

   ```
   I found myself stealing a peek at my own watch and overheard
   General Catbird's
   aide give him the latest.
   "He's not even here," went the conversation.
   "Who?"
   "Banzai."
   "Where the hell is he?"
   "At the hospital in El Paso."
   "What? Why weren't we informed? What's wrong with him?"
   ~
   ~
   ~
   ~
   ~
   ~
   ~
   ~
   ~
   ~
   ~
   ~
   "buckaroo" [Read only] 9 lines, 276 characters
   ```

   Notice the addition of the [Read only] message on the status line. You can edit the file, but if you try to save the edits with :w, you will see this:

   ```
   ~
   ~
   "buckaroo" File is read only
   ```

   Quit vi with :q!.

2. Next, recall that janitor occurs in many places in the big.output file. I'll start vi on the file line that contains the pattern janitor in the file:

   `% vi +/janitor big.output`

```
brandt    ttyrb   Nov 28 23:03   (age)
holmes    ttyrj   Dec  3 21:59   (age)
yuxi      ttyrn   Dec  1 14:19   (pc)
frodo     ttyro   Dec  3 22:01   (mentor)
labeck    ttyrt   Dec  3 22:02   (dov)
chenlx2   ttyru   Dec  3 21:53   (mentor)
leungtc   ttys0   Nov 28 15:11   (gold)
chinese   ttys2   Dec  3 22:53   (excalibur)
cdemmert  ttys5   Dec  3 23:00   (mentor)
yuenca    ttys6   Dec  3 23:00   (mentor)
janitor   ttys7   Dec  3 18:18   (age)
mathisbp  ttys8   Dec  3 23:17   (dov)
janitor   ttys9   Dec  3 18:18   (age)
cs541     ttysC   Dec  2 15:16   (solaria)
yansong   ttysL   Dec  1 14:44   (math)
mdps      ttysO   Nov 30 19:39   (localhost)
md        ttysU   Dec  2 08:45   (muller)
jac       ttysa   Dec  3 18:18   (localhost)
eichsted  ttysb   Dec  3 23:21   (pc1)
sweett    ttysc   Dec  3 22:40   (dov)
wellman   ttysd   Dec  3 23:01   (dov)
tuttleno  ttyse   Dec  3 23:03   (indyvax)
wu        ttysf   Dec  3 23:10   (term01)
"big.output" 40 lines, 1659 characters
```

This time, notice where the cursor is sitting.

3. Finally, launch vi with the cursor on the third line of the file buckaroo:

```
% vi +3 buckaroo
```

```
I found myself stealing a peek at my own watch and overheard
General Catbird's
aide give him the latest.
"He's not even here," went the conversation.
"Who?"
"Banzai."
"Where the hell is he?"
"At the hospital in El Paso."
"What? Why weren't we informed? What's wrong with him?"
~
~
~
~
~
~
```

continues

```
~
~
~
~
~
~
~
~
"buckaroo" 9 lines, 276 characters
```

Again, notice where the cursor rests.

SUMMARY It can be helpful to know these two starting options. In particular, I often use
+/*pattern* to start the editor at a specific pattern, but you can use vi for years
without ever knowing more than just the name of the command itself.

Task 11.4: Search and Replace

DESCRIPTION Though most of vi is easy to learn and use, one command that always causes
great trouble for users is the search-and-replace command. The key to understanding this command is to remember that vi is built on the line editor (ex). Instead of
trying to figure out some arcane vi command, it's easiest to just drop to the line editor
and use a simple colon command to replace an old pattern with a new one. To replace an
existing word on the current line with a new word (the simplest case), use :s/*old*/*new*/.
If you want to have all occurrences on the current line matched, you need to add the g
(global) suffix: :s/*old*/*new*/g.

To change all occurrences of one word or phrase to another across the entire file, the
command is identical to the preceding command, except that you must prefix an indication of the range of lines affected. Recall that $ is the last line in the file, and that ranges
are specified by two numbers separated by a comma. It should be no surprise that the
command is :1,$ s/*old*/*new*/g.

ACTION

1. Start vi again with the buckaroo file, add the additional text on the first and last
   lines using the existing vi commands you know, and then use 1G to jump to the top
   of the file.

```
Excerpt from "Buckaroo Banzai" by Earl MacRauch
I found myself stealing a peek at my own watch and overheard
General Catbird's
aide give him the latest.
"He's not even here," went the conversation.
"Who?"
"Banzai."
"Where the hell is he?"
"At the hospital in El Paso."
"What? Why weren't we informed? What's wrong with him?"

Go Team Banzai! Go Team Banzai! Go Team Banzai!

~
~
~
~
~
~
~
~
~
~
~
~
~
```

The cursor is on the first line. I'm going to rename Earl. I type :, the cursor immediately moves to the bottom, and then I type s/Earl/Duke/. Pressing Return produces this:

```
Excerpt from "Buckaroo Banzai" by Duke MacRauch
I found myself stealing a peek at my own watch and overheard
General Catbird's aide
give him the latest.
"He's not even here," went the conversation.
```

As you can see, this maneuver was simple and effective.

2. I've decided that development psychology is my bag. Now, instead of having this Banzai character, I want my fictional character to be called Bandura. I could use the preceding command to change the occurrence on the current line, but I really want to change all occurrences within the file.

This is no problem. I type :1,$ s/Banzai/Bandura/ and press Return. Here's the result:

```
Excerpt from "Buckaroo Bandura" by Duke MacRauch
I found myself stealing a peek at my own watch and overheard
General Catbird's
aide give him the latest.
"He's not even here," went the conversation.
"Who?"
"Bandura."
"Where the hell is he?"
"At the hospital in El Paso."
"What? Why weren't we informed? What's wrong with him?"

Go Team Bandura! Go Team Banzai! Go Team Banzai!

~
~
~
~
~
~
~
~
~
~
~
```

The result is not quite right. Because I forgot the trailing g in the substitute command, vi changed only the very first occurrence on each line, leaving the "go team" exhortation rather confusing.

To try again, I type :1,$ s/Banzai/Bandura/g and press Return, and the screen changes as desired:

```
Excerpt from "Buckaroo Bandura" by Duke MacRauch
I found myself stealing a peek at my own watch and overheard
General Catbird's
aide give him the latest.
"He's not even here," went the conversation.
"Who?"
```

continues

```
"Bandura."
"Where the hell is he?"
"At the hospital in El Paso."
"What? Why weren't we informed? What's wrong with him?"

Go Team Bandura! Go Team Bandura! Go Team Bandura!

~
~
~
~
~
~
~
~
~
~
7 substitutions
```

Notice that vi also indicates the total number of substitutions in this case.

3. I'll press u to undo the last change.

SUMMARY Search and replace is one area where a windowing system like that of a Macintosh or PC running Windows comes in handy. A windowing system offers different boxes for the old and new patterns; it shows each change and a dialog box asking, "Should I change this one?" Alas, this is Unix, and it's still designed to run on ASCII terminals.

Task 11.5: The Change and Replace Commands

DESCRIPTION In the preceding section, you saw me fix various problems by deleting words and then replacing them with new words. There is, in fact, a much smarter way to do this, and that is by using either the change or the replace command.

Each command has a lowercase version and an uppercase version, and each is quite different from the other. The r command replaces the character that the cursor is sitting on with the next character you type, whereas the R command puts you into *replace mode* so that anything you type overwrites whatever is already on the line until you stop typing. By contrast, C replaces everything on the line with whatever you type. (It's a subtle difference—but I demonstrate it, so don't fear.) The c command is the most powerful of them all. The change command, c, works just like the d command did, as described in

the preceding hour. You can use the c command with any address command, and it will
enable you to change text through to that address, whether it's a word, a line, or even the
rest of the document.

ACTION

1. Start vi with the buckaroo.confused file.

```
I found myself stealing a peek at my own watch and overheard
General Catbird's
I found myself stealing a peek at my own watch and overheard
General Catbird's
aide give him the latest.
"He's not even here," went the conversation.
"Who?"
"Banzai."
"Where the hell is he?"
"At the hospital in El Paso."
"What? Why weren't we informed? What's wrong with him?"

aide give him the latest.
"He's not even here," went the conversation.
"Who?"
"Banzai."
"Where the hell is he?"
"At the hospital in El Paso."
"What? Why weren't we informed? What's wrong with him?"


~
~
~
~
~
~
~
"buckaroo.confused" 17 lines, 546 characters
```

Without moving the cursor at all, type R. Nothing happens, or so it seems. Now
type the words Excerpt from "Buckaroo Banzai", and watch what happens:

```
Excerpt from "Buckaroo Banzai"at my own watch and overheard
General Catbird's
I found myself stealing a peek at my own watch and overheard
General Catbird's
aide give him the latest.
"He's not even here," went the conversation.
```

Now press Escape and notice that what you see on the screen is exactly what's in the file.

2. This isn't, however, quite what I want. I could use either D or d$ to delete through the end of the line, but that's a bit awkward. Instead, I'll use 0 to move back to the beginning of the line. You do so, too:

```
Excerpt from "Buckaroo Banzai" at my own watch and overheard
General Catbird's
I found myself stealing a peek at my own watch and overheard
General Catbird's
aide give him the latest.
"He's not even here," went the conversation.
```

This time, type C to change the contents of the line. Before you even type a single character of the new text, notice what the line now looks like:

```
Excerpt from "Buckaroo Banzai" at my own watch and overheard
General Catbird'$
I found myself stealing a peek at my own watch and overheard
General Catbird's
aide give him the latest.
"He's not even here," went the conversation.
```

Here's where a subtle difference comes into play. Look at the last character on the current line. Where the s had been, when you pressed C, the program placed a $ instead to show the range of the text to be changed by the command. Press the Tab key once, and then type Excerpt from "Buckaroo Bansai" by Earl MacRauch.

```
Excerpt from "Buckaroo Bansai" by Earl MacRauchheard General Catbird'$
I found myself stealing a peek at my own watch and overheard
General Catbird's
aide give him the latest.
"He's not even here," went the conversation.
```

This time, watch what happens when I press Escape:

```
Excerpt from "Buckaroo Bansai" by Earl MacRauch
I found myself stealing a peek at my own watch and overheard
General Catbird's
aide give him the latest.
"He's not even here," went the conversation.
```

3. I think I made another mistake. The actual title of the book is *Buckaroo Banzai* with a *z*, but I've spelled it with an *s* instead. This is a chance to try the new r command.

   Use cursor control keys to move the cursor to the offending letter. I'll use b to back up words and then h a few times to move into the middle of the word. My screen now looks like this:

```
Excerpt from "Buckaroo Bansai" by Earl MacRauch
I found myself stealing a peek at my own watch and overheard
General Catbird's
aide give him the latest.
"He's not even here," went the conversation.
```

Now type r. Again, nothing happens; the cursor doesn't move. Type r again to make sure it worked:

```
Excerpt from "Buckaroo Banrai" by Earl MacRauch
I found myself stealing a peek at my own watch and overheard
General Catbird's
aide give him the latest.
"He's not even here," went the conversation.
```

That's no good. It replaced the s with an r, which definitely isn't correct. Type rz, and you should have the following:

```
Excerpt from "Buckaroo Banzai" by Earl MacRauch
I found myself stealing a peek at my own watch and overheard
General Catbird's
aide give him the latest.
"He's not even here," went the conversation.
```

4. Okay, those are the easy ones. Now it's time to see what the c command can do for you. In fact, it's incredibly powerful. You can change just about any range of information from the current point in the file in either direction!

To start, move to the middle of the file, where the second copy of the passage is located:

```
Excerpt from "Buckaroo Banzai" by Earl MacRauch
I found myself stealing a peek at my own watch and overheard
General Catbird's
aide give him the latest.
"He's not even here," went the conversation.
"Who?"
"Banzai."
"Where the hell is he?"
"At the hospital in El Paso."
"What? Why weren't we informed? What's wrong with him?"

aide give him the latest.
"He's not even here," went the conversation.
"Who?"
"Banzai."
"Where the hell is he?"
"At the hospital in El Paso."
"What? Why weren't we informed? What's wrong with him?"


~
~
~
~
~
~
~
"buckaroo.confused" 17 lines, 546 characters
```

11

I think I'll just change the word `aide` that the cursor is sitting on to `The tall beige wall clock opted` to instead. First, I type `c` and note that, as with many other commands in `vi`, nothing happens. Now I type `w` because I want to change just the first word. The screen should look like this:

```
"At the hospital in El Paso."
"What? Why weren't we informed? What's wrong with him?"

aid$ give him the latest.
"He's not even here," went the conversation.
"Who?"
"Banzai."
```

Again, the program has replaced the last character in the range of the change to a `$` so that I can eyeball the situation. Now I type `The tall beige wall clock opted to`. Once I reach the `$`, the editor stops overwriting characters and starts inserting them instead; the screen now looks like this:

```
"At the hospital in El Paso."
"What? Why weren't we informed? What's wrong with him?"

The tall beige wall clock opted to_give him the latest.
"He's not even here," went the conversation.
"Who?"
"Banzai."
```

Press Escape and you're done (though you can undo the change with the `u` or `U` commands, of course).

5. Tall and beige or not, this section makes no sense now, so change this entire line by using the `$` motion command you learned in the preceding hour. First, use `0` to move to the beginning of the line, and then type `c$`:

```
"At the hospital in El Paso."
"What? Why weren't we informed? What's wrong with him?"

The tall beige wall clock opted to give him the latest$
"He's not even here," went the conversation.
"Who?"
"Banzai."
```

This is working. The last character changed to $. Press Escape, and the entire line is deleted:

```
"At the hospital in El Paso."
"What? Why weren't we informed? What's wrong with him?"


_
"He's not even here," went the conversation.
"Who?"
"Banzai."
```

6. Six lines are still below the current line. I could delete them and then type the information I want, but that's primitive. Instead, the c command comes to the rescue. Move down one line, type c6, and press Return. Watch what happens:

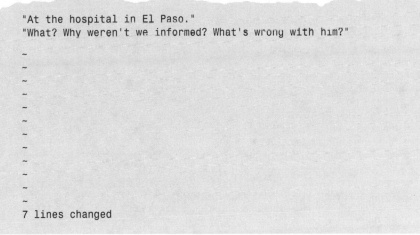

```
"At the hospital in El Paso."
"What? Why weren't we informed? What's wrong with him?"
~
~
~
~
~
~
~
~
~
~
7 lines changed
```

In general, you always can change the current and next line by using c followed by a Return (because the Return key is a motion key, too, remember). By prefacing the command with a number, I changed the range from two lines to six.

You might be asking, "Why two lines?" The answer is subtle. In essence, whenever you use the c command, you change the current line plus any additional lines that might be touched by the command. Pressing Return moves the cursor to the following line; therefore, the current line (starting at the cursor location) through the following lines are changed. The command probably should change just to the beginning of the following line, but that's beyond even my control!

Now press Tab four times, type `(page 8)`, and then press the Escape key. The screen should look like this:

```
"Where the hell is he?"
"At the hospital in El Paso."
"What? Why weren't we informed? What's wrong with him?"


                                    (page 8)

~
~
~
```

7. What if I change my mind? That's where the u command comes in handy. Typing u once undoes the last command:

```
Excerpt from "Buckaroo Banzai" by Earl MacRauch
I found myself stealing a peek at my own watch and overheard
General Catbird's
aide give him the latest.
"He's not even here," went the conversation.
"Who?"
"Banzai."
"Where the hell is he?"
"At the hospital in El Paso."
"What? Why weren't we informed? What's wrong with him?"


"He's not even here," went the conversation.
"Who?"
"Banzai."
"Where the hell is he?"
"At the hospital in El Paso."
"What? Why weren't we informed? What's wrong with him?"

~
~
~
~
~
~
6 more lines
```

SUMMARY The combination of replace and change commands adds a level of sophistication to an editor that you might have suspected could only insert or delete. There's more to cover in this hour, so don't stop now!

Task 11.6: Accessing Unix with !

DESCRIPTION This final task on vi introduces you to one of the most powerful, and least-known, commands in the editor: the ! escape-to-Unix command. When prefaced with a colon (:!, for example), it enables you to run Unix commands without leaving the editor. More powerfully, the ! command in vi itself, just like d and c, accepts address specifications, feeds that portion of text to the command, and replaces that portion with the results of having run that command on the text.

Let's have a look.

ACTION

1. Let's leave Buckaroo Banzai alone for a bit to switch to a classic, Charles Dickens's *A Tale of Two Cities*. I've created a file called dickens.note for this exercise, and you can either type it yourself or grab a copy of the file on our Web site, http://www.intuitive.com/tyu24/. The file is shown here:

```
% cat dickens.note

                A Tale of Two Cities
                      Preface

    When I was acting, with my children and friends, in Mr Wilkie
➥Collins's
    drama of The Frozen Deep, I first conceived the main idea of this
    story. A strong desire was upon me then, to
    embody it in my own person;
    and I traced out in my fancy, the state of mind of which it would
    necessitate the presentation
    to an observant spectator, with particular
    care and interest.

    As the idea became familiar to me, it gradually shaped itself into
➥its
    present form. Throughout its execution, it has had complete
➥possession
    of me; I have so far verified what
    is done and suffered on these pages,
    as that I have certainly done and suffered it all myself.

    Whenever any reference (however slight) is made here to the
➥condition
```

11

```
of the French people before or during the Revolution, it is truly
➥made,
on the faith of the most trustworthy
witnesses. It has been one of my hopes to add
something to the popular and picturesque means of
understanding that terrible time, though no one can
hope to add anything to the philosophy of Mr Carlyle's wonderful
➥book.

Tavistock House
November 1859
```

With this file on my system, I'll start by invoking vi with the file name, then use a command escape to double-check what files I have in my home directory. To do this, I type : !, which moves the cursor to the bottom line:

```
of the French people before or during the Revolution, it is truly
➥made,
on the faith of the most trustworthy
witnesses.  It has been one of my hopes to add
something to the popular and picturesque means of
:!_
```

I simply type ls -F and press Return, as if I were at the % prompt in the command line:

```
of the French people before or during the Revolution, it is truly
➥made,
on the faith of the most trustworthy
witnesses.  It has been one of my hopes to add
something to the popular and picturesque means of
:!ls -F
Archives/           big.output          dickens.note        src/
InfoWorld/          bigfiles            keylime.pie         temp/
Mail/               bin/                newfile             tetme
News/               buckaroo            owl.c
OWL/                buckaroo.confused   sample
awkscript           demo                sample2
[Hit any key to continue] _
```

If I press Return, I'm back in the editor, and I have quickly checked what files I have in my home directory.

2. Now for some real fun, move to the beginning of the first paragraph and add the text Chuck, here are my current files:. Press Return twice before using the Escape key to return to command mode. My screen now looks like this:

```
                        A Tale of Two Cities
                            Preface

Chuck, here are my current files:

_

When I was acting, with my children and friends, in Mr Wilkie
➡Collins's
drama of The Frozen Deep, I first conceived the main idea of this
story.  A strong desire was upon me then, to
```

Notice that the cursor was moved up a line. (Caveat: some Unix implementations have a version of vi that leaves you at the original insertion point.) I'm now on a blank line, and the line following is also blank.

To feed the current line to the Unix system and replace it with the output of the command, vi offers an easy shortcut: !!. When I type the second ! (or, more precisely, after vi figures out the desired range specified for this command), the cursor moves to the bottom of the screen and prompts with a single ! character:

```
of the French people before or during the Revolution, it is truly
➡made,
on the faith of the most trustworthy
witnesses. It has been one of my hopes to add
something to the popular and picturesque means of
:!_
```

To list all the files in my directory, I can type ls -F and press Return. After a second, vi adds the output of that command to the file:

```
                        A Tale of Two Cities
                            Preface

Chuck, here are my current files:
Archives/               bigfiles            newfile
InfoWorld/              bin/                owl.c
```

continues

```
Mail/                  buckaroo               sample
News/                  buckaroo.confused      sample2
OWL/                   demo                   src/
awkscript              dickens.note           temp/
big.output             keylime.pie            tetme

When I was acting, with my children and friends, in Mr Wilkie
➡Collins's
drama of The Frozen Deep, I first conceived the main idea of this
story.  A strong desire was upon me then, to
embody it in my own person;
and I traced out in my fancy, the state of mind of which it would
necessitate the presentation
to an observant spectator, with particular
care and interest.

As the idea became familiar to me, it gradually shaped itself into
➡its
present form.  Throughout its execution, it has had complete
➡possession
6 more lines
```

Notice that this time the status on the bottom indicates how many lines were added to the file.

Type u to undo this change. Notice that the vi status indicator on the bottom line says there are now six fewer lines.

3. Move back to the W in When. You are now ready to learn one of the commands I like most in vi. This command enables you to hand a paragraph of text to an arbitrary Unix command.

This time I'm going to use the Unix stream editor "sed" to perform a neat trick: prefacing each selected line with >. The actual command I'll use is sed 's/^/> /'. Ready? This is where the } command comes in handy, too. To accomplish this trick, I type !}, moving the cursor to the bottom of the screen, and then type the sed command as you saw earlier: sed 's/^/> /'. Pressing Return feeds the lines to sed. The sed command makes the change indicated and replaces those lines with the output of the sed command. Voila! The screen now looks as shown next.

The sed editor is one of your best friends in Unix because you can use it in any command pipe to modify the data as it passes through. A quick read of the sed man page will be time well spent.

```
                      A Tale of Two Cities
                          Preface

Chuck, here are my current files:


> When I was acting, with my children and friends, in Mr Wilkie
⮕Collins's
> drama of The Frozen Deep, I first conceived the main idea of this
> story.  A strong desire was upon me then, to
> embody it in my own person;
> and I traced out in my fancy, the state of mind of which it would
> necessitate the presentation
> to an observant spectator, with particular
> care and interest.

As the idea became familiar to me, it gradually shaped itself into
⮕its
present form.  Throughout its execution, it has had complete
⮕possession
of me; I have so far verified what
is done and suffered in these pages,
as that I have certainly done and suffered it all myself.

Whenever any reference (however slight) is made here to the condition
of the French people before or during the Revolution, it is truly
⮕made,
!sed 's/^/> /'
```

4. I hope you're excited to see this command in action! It's a powerful way to interact with Unix while within vi.

I'll provide a few more examples of ways to interact with Unix while within vi. First, I don't really want the prefix to each line, so I'm going to type u to undo the change.

Instead, I would rather have the system actually tighten up the lines, ensuring that a reasonable number of words occur on each line and that no lines are too long. On most systems, there is a command called either fmt or adjust to accomplish this. To figure out which works on your system, simply use the :! command, and feed a word or two to the fmt command to see what happens:

```
Whenever any reference (however slight) is made here to the condition
of the French people before or during the Revolution, it is truly
➥made,
:!echo hi | fmt
[No write since last change]
hi
[Hit any key to continue] _
```

In this case, fmt did what I hoped, so I can be sure that the command exists on my system. If your response was command unknown, adjust is a likely alternative. If neither exists, complain to your vendor!

Armed with this new command, you can try another variant of !}, this time by feeding the entire paragraph to the fmt command. I'm still at the beginning of the word When in the text. So when I type the command !}fmt, the paragraph is cleaned up, and the screen changes to this:

```
                           A Tale of Two Cities
                                Preface

Chuck, here are my current files:


When I was acting, with my children and friends, in Mr Wilkie
➥Collins's
drama of The Frozen Deep, I first conceived the main idea of this
story.  A strong desire was upon me then, to embody it in my own
person; and I traced out in my fancy, the state of mind of which it
would necessitate the presentation to an observant spectator, with
particular care and interest.

As the idea became familiar to me, it gradually shaped itself into
➥its
present form.  Throughout its execution, it has had complete
➥possession
of me; I have so far verified what
is done and suffered in these pages,
as that I have certainly done and suffered it all myself.

Whenever any reference (however slight) is made here to the condition
of the French people before or during the Revolution, it is truly
➥made,
on the faith of the most trustworthy
witnesses.  It has been one of my hopes to add
2 fewer lines
```

Again, vi tells us that the number of lines in the file has changed as a result of the command. In this situation, tightening up the paragraph actually reduced it by two display lines.

This command is so helpful that I often have it bound to a specific key with the map command. A typical way to do this in an .exrc might be this:

```
:map ^P !}fmt^M
```

The ^M is what vi uses to record a Return. (Recall that you need to use the ^v beforehand.) With this defined in my .exrc, I can press ^p to format the current paragraph.

SUMMARY   Clearly, the ! command opens up vi to work with the rest of the Unix system. There's almost nothing you can't somehow manage to do within the editor, whether it's add or remove prefixes, clean up text, or even show what happens when you try to run a command or reformat a passage within the current file.

Summary of vi Commands

A summary of the commands you learned in this hour is shown in Table 11.1.

TABLE 11.1   Advanced vi Commands

Command	Meaning
!!command	Replace the current line with the output of the specified Unix command.
!}command	Replace the current paragraph with the results of piping it through the specified Unix command or commands.
(	Move backward one sentence.
)	Move forward one sentence.
C	Change text from the point of the cursor through the end of the line.
c	Change text in the specified range—cw changes the following word, whereas c} changes the next paragraph.
e	Move to the end of the current word.
^g	Show the current line number and other information about the file.
R	Replace text from the point of the cursor until Escape is pressed.
r	Replace the current character with the next pressed.
^v	Prevent vi from interpreting the next character.
{	Move backward one paragraph.
}	Move forward one paragraph.

11

TABLE 11.1   continued

Command	Meaning
`:!`*command*	Invoke the specified Unix command.
`:ab` *a* *bcd*	Define abbreviation *a* for phrase *bcd*.
`:ab`	Show current abbreviations, if any.
`:map` *a* *bcd*	Map key *a* to the `vi` commands *bcd*.
`:map`	Show current key mappings, if any.
`:s/`*old*`/`*new*`/`	Substitute *new* for the first instance of *old* on the current line.
`:s/`*old*`/`*new*`/g`	Substitute *new* for all occurrences of *old* on the current line.
`:set nonumber`	Turn off line numbering.
`:set number`	Turn on line numbering.

Summary

Clearly, `vi` is a very complex and sophisticated tool that enables you not only to modify your text files, but also to customize the editor for your keyboard. Just as important, you can access all the power of Unix while within `vi`.

Workshop

The Workshop summarizes the key terms you learned and poses some questions about the topics presented in this chapter. It also provides you with a preview of what you will learn in the next hour.

Key Terms

colon commands   The `vi` commands that begin with a colon, usually used for file manipulation.

escape sequence   An unprintable sequence of characters that usually specifies that your terminal take a specific action, such as clearing the screen.

replace mode   A mode of `vi` in which any characters you type replace those already in the file.

Exercises

1. What does the following command do?

   ```
   :1,5 s/kitten/puppy
   ```

2. What do these commands do?

   ```
   15i?ESCh
   i15?ESCh
   i?ESC15h
   ```

3. What would happen if you were to use the following startup flags?

   ```
   vi +0 test
   vi +/joe/ names
   vi +hhjjhh
   vi +:q testme
   ```

4. Try ^g on the first and last lines of a file. Explain why the percentage indicator might not be what you expected.

5. What's the difference between the following four strings?

   ```
   rr
   RrESC
   cwrESC
   CrESC
   ```

6. What key mappings do you have in your version of vi? Do you have labeled keys on your keyboard that could be helpful in vi but aren't defined? If so, define them in your .exrc file using the :map command.

7. What do you think the following command will do? Try it and see whether you're right.

   ```
   !}ls
   ```

Preview of the Next Hour

With this hour and the preceding one, you now know more about vi than the vast majority of people using Unix today. There's a second popular editor, however, one that is modeless and offers its own interesting possibilities for working with files and the Unix system. It's called emacs, and if you have it on your system, it's definitely worth a look. In the next hour, you learn about this editor and some of the basics of using it.

11

Hour 12

An Overview of the emacs Editor

The only screen-oriented editor that's guaranteed to be included with the Unix system is vi, but that doesn't mean that it's the only good editor available in Unix! An alternative editor that has become quite popular in the past decade (remember that Unix is over 25 years old) is called emacs. This hour teaches you the fundamentals of this very different and quite powerful editing environment.

Goals for This Hour

In this hour, you will learn how to

- Launch emacs and insert text
- Move around in a file
- Delete characters and words
- Search and replace in emacs

- Use the emacs tutorial and help system
- Work with other files

Remember what I said in the preceding hour when I mentioned the emacs editor: emacs is modeless, so be prepared for an editor that is quite unlike vi. And because it's modeless, there's no insert or command mode. The result is that you have ample opportunity to use the Control key.

> Over the years, I have tried to become an emacs enthusiast, once even forcing myself to use it for an entire month. I had crib sheets of commands taped up all over my office. At the end of the month, I had attained an editing speed that was about half of my speed in vi, an editor I've used thousands of times in the past 20+ years I've worked in Unix. I think emacs has a lot going for it, and generally I think that modeless software is better than modal software. The main obstacle I see for emacs, however, is that it's begging for pull-down menus like a Mac or Windows program has. Using Control, Meta, Shift-Meta, and other weird key combinations just isn't as easy to use for me. On the other hand, your approach to editing might be different, and you might not have years of vi experience affecting your choice of editing environments. I encourage you to give emacs a fair shake by working through all the examples I have included. You might find that it matches your working style better than vi.

The Other Popular Editor: emacs

The vi editor is a full, feature-rich editing package, but there's an alternative that's worth exploring, too, before you settle on the editor you'll use within the Unix environment. The alternative is the brilliant, if complex, emacs editor.

Task 12.1: Launching emacs and Inserting Text

DESCRIPTION Starting emacs is as simple as starting any other Unix program. Type the name of the program, followed by any file or files you'd like to work with. The puzzle with emacs is figuring out what it's actually called on your system, if you have it. You can use a couple of ways to try to identify emacs; I'll demonstrate these methods in the "Action 2" section for this task.

When you are in emacs, it's important to take a look at your computer keyboard. emacs requires you to use not just the Control key, but another key known as the *Meta key*, a sort of alternative Control key. If you have a key labeled Meta or Alt (for Alternative) on your keyboard, that's the one. If, like me, you don't, simply press Escape every time a Meta key is indicated.

Because both Control and Meta keys are in emacs, the notation for indicating commands is slightly different. Throughout this book, a control-key sequence has been shown either as Control-f or as ^f. emacs people write this differently, to allow for the difference between Control and Meta keys. In emacs notation, ^f is shown as C-f, where C- always means Control. Similarly, M-x is the Meta key plus the character specified by x. If you don't have a Meta key, the sequence is Escape, followed by x. Finally, some arcane commands involve both the Control and the Meta keys being pressed (simultaneously with the other key involved). This notation is C-M-x and indicates that you need either to press and hold down both the Control and the Meta keys while typing x, or, if you don't have a Meta (or Alt) key, to press Escape, followed by C-x.

With this notation in mind, you leave emacs by pressing C-x C-h C-h C-h (Control-x, followed by Control-c).

ACTION

1. First, see whether your system has emacs available. The easiest way to find out is to type emacs at the command line and see what happens:

```
% emacs
emacs: Command not found.
%
```

This is a good indication that emacs isn't available. If your command worked and you now are in the emacs editor, move down to step 2 in this task.

A popular version of emacs is from the Free Software Foundation, and it's called GNU emacs. To see whether you have this version, type gnuemacs or gnumacs at the command line.

2. Rather than start with a blank screen, quit the program (C-x C-h C-h C-h), and restart emacs with one of the earlier test files, dickens.note:

```
% gnuemacs dickens.note
```

12

```
                   _              A Tale of Two Cities
                                       Preface

      When I was acting, with my children and friends, in Mr Wilkie
      Collins's drama of The Frozen Deep, I first conceived the main idea of
      this story. A strong desire was upon me then, to
      embody it in my own person;
      and I traced out in my fancy, the state of mind of which it would
      necessitate the presentation

                                                              continues
```

```
to an observant spectator, with particular
care and interest.

As the idea became familiar to me, it gradually shaped itself into
its present form. Throughout its execution, it has had complete
possession of me; I have so far verified what
is done and suffered in these pages,
as that I have certainly done and suffered it all myself.

Whenever any reference (however slight) is made here to the condition
of the French people before or during the Revolution, it is truly
made, on the faith of the most trustworthy
witnesses. It has been one of my hopes to add
-----Emacs: dickens.note              (Fundamental)----Top-------------
```

As you can see, it's quite different from the display shown when vi starts up. The status line at the bottom of the display offers useful information as you edit the file at different points, and it also reminds you at all times of the name of the file, a feature that can be surprisingly helpful. emacs can work with different kinds of files, and here you see by the word Fundamental in the status line that emacs is prepared for a regular text file. If you're programming, emacs can offer special features customized for your particular language.

3. Quit emacs by using the C-x C-h C-h C-h sequence, but let a few seconds pass after you press C-x to watch what happens. When I press C-x, the bottom of the screen suddenly changes to this:

```
on the faith of the most trustworthy
witnesses. It has been one of my hopes to add
-----Emacs: dickens.note              (Fundamental)----Top-------------
C-x-
```

Confusingly, the cursor remains at the top of the file, but emacs reminds me that I've pressed C-x and that I need to enter a second command after I've decided what to do. I now press C-h C-h C-h and immediately exit emacs.

SUMMARY Already you can see some dramatic differences between emacs and vi. If you're comfortable with multiple key sequences such as C-x C-h C-h C-h to quit, I think you're going to enjoy learning emacs. If not, stick with it anyway. Even if you never use emacs, it's good to know a little bit about it.

Why learn about a tool you're not going to use? In this case, the answer is that Unix people tend to be polarized around the question of which editor is better. Indeed, the debate between vi and emacs is referred to as a "religious war" because of the high levels of heat and low levels of actual sensibility of the participants. My position is that different users will find that different tools work best for them. If emacs is closer to how you edit files, that's wonderful, and it's great that Unix offers emacs as an alternative to vi. Ultimately, the question isn't whether one is better than the other, but whether you can edit your files more quickly and easily in one or the other.

Task 12.2: How to Move Around in a File

DESCRIPTION Files are composed of characters, words, lines, sentences, and paragraphs, and emacs has commands to help you move about. Most systems have the arrow keys enabled, which helps you avoid worrying about some of the key sequences, but it's best to know them all anyway.

The most basic motions are C-f and C-b, which are used to move the cursor forward and backward one character, respectively. Switch those to the Meta command equivalents, and the cursor will move by words: M-f moves the cursor forward a word, and M-b moves it back a word. Pressing C-n moves the cursor to the next line, C-p to the previous line, C-a to the beginning of the line, and C-e to the end of the line. (The vi equivalents for all of these are l, h, w, and b for moving forward and backward a character or word; j and k for moving up or down a line; and 0 or $ to move to the beginning or end of the current line. Which makes more sense to you?)

To move forward a sentence, you can use M-e, which actually moves the cursor to the end of the sentence. Pressing M-a moves it to the beginning of a sentence. Notice the parallels between Control and Meta commands: C-a moves the cursor to the beginning of the line, and M-a moves it to the beginning of the sentence.

To scroll within the document, you use C-v to move forward a screen and M-v to move back a screen. To move forward an actual page (usually 60 lines of text; this is based on a printed page of information), you can use either C-x] or C-x [for forward motion or backward motion, respectively.

Finally, to move to the top of the file, use M-<, and to move to the bottom, use the M-> command.

12

ACTION

1. Go back into emacs and locate the cursor. It should be at the top of the screen:

```
    _                        A Tale of Two Cities
                                  Preface

When I was acting, with my children and friends, in Mr Wilkie Collins's
drama of The Frozen Deep, I first conceived the main idea of this
story. A strong desire was upon me then, to
embody it in my own person;
and I traced out in my fancy, the state of mind of which it would
necessitate the presentation
to an observant spectator, with particular
care and interest.

As the idea became familiar to me, it gradually shaped itself into
its present form. Throughout its execution, it has had complete
possession of me; I have so far verified what
is done and suffered in these pages,
as that I have certainly done and suffered it all myself.

Whenever any reference (however slight) is made here to the condition
of the French people before or during the Revolution, it is truly
made, on the faith of the most trustworthy
witnesses. It has been one of my hopes to add
-----Emacs: dickens.note            (Fundamental)----Top-------------
```

Move down four lines by using C-n four times. Your cursor should now be sitting on the d of drama:

```
Preface

When I was acting, with my children and friends, in Mr Wilkie Collins's
drama of The Frozen Deep, I first conceived the main idea of this
story. A strong desire was upon me then, to
embody it in my own person;
and I traced out in my fancy, the state of mind of which it would
```

2. Next, move to the end of this sentence by using the M-e command (emacs expects two spaces to separate sentences):

```
When I was acting, with my children and friends, in Mr Wilkie Collins's
drama of The Frozen Deep, I first conceived the main idea of this
story._ A strong desire was upon me then, to
embody it in my own person;
and I traced out in my fancy, the state of mind of which it would
```

Now type the following text: I fought the impulse to write this novel vociferously, but, dear reader, I felt the injustice of the situation too strongly in my breast to deny. Don't press Return or Escape when you're done. The screen should now look similar to this:

```
drama of The Frozen Deep, I first conceived the main idea of this
story. I fought the impulse to write this novel vociferously, but, dear
reader,\
 I felt
the injustice of the situation too strongly in my breast to deny_  A strong
des\
ire was upon me then, to
embody it in my own person;
and I traced out in my fancy, the state of mind of which it would
necessitate the presentation
```

You can see that emacs wrapped the line when the line became too long (between the words felt and the), and because the lines are still too long to display, a few of them end with a backslash. The backslash isn't actually a part of the file; with it, emacs is telling me that those lines are longer than can be displayed.

3. Now try to move back a few characters by pressing Backspace.

Uh oh! If your system is like mine, the Backspace key doesn't move the cursor back up a character at all. Instead it starts the emacs help system, where you're suddenly confronted with a screen that looks like this:

```
You have typed C-h, the help character. Type a Help option:

A  command-apropos.  Give a substring, and see a list of commands
                (functions interactively callable) that contain
                    that substring. See also the  apropos  command.
B  describe-bindings. Display table of all key bindings.
```

continues

12

```
C  describe-key-briefly. Type a command key sequence;
              it prints the function name that sequence runs.
F  describe-function. Type a function name and get documentation of it.
I  info. The  info  documentation reader.
K  describe-key. Type a command key sequence;
              it displays the full documentation.
L  view-lossage. Shows last 100 characters you typed.
M  describe-mode. Print documentation of current major mode,
              which describes the commands peculiar to it.
N  view-emacs-news. Shows emacs news file.
S  describe-syntax. Display contents of syntax table, plus explanations
T  help-with-tutorial. Select the Emacs learn-by-doing tutorial.
V  describe-variable. Type name of a variable;
              it displays the variable's documentation and value.
W  where-is. Type command name; it prints which keystrokes
              invoke that command.
--**-Emacs: *Help*                 (Fundamental)----Top-------------
A B C F I K L M N S T V W C-h C-h C-h C-d C-n C-w or Space to scroll: _
```

To escape the help screen (you'll learn more about it later in this hour), press
Escape, and your screen should be restored. The status line shows what file you're
viewing, but you aren't always viewing the file you want to work with.

The correct key to move the cursor back a few characters is C-b. Use that to back
up, and then use C-f to move forward again to the original cursor location.

4. Check that the last few lines of the file haven't changed by using the emacs move-
   to-end-of-file command, M->. (Think of file redirection to remember the file
   motion commands.) Now the screen looks like this:

```
Whenever any reference (however slight) is made here to the condition
of the French people before or during the Revolution, it is truly
made, on the faith of the most trustworthy
witnesses. It has been one of my hopes to add
something to the popular and picturesque means of
understanding that terrible time, though no one can hope
to add anything to the philosophy of Mr Carlyle's wonderful book.

Tavistock House
November 1859

_
```

continues

```
    --**-Emacs: dickens.note              (Fundamental)----Bot-------------
```

5. Changing the words of Charles Dickens was fun, so save these changes and quit. If you try to quit the program with C-x C-h C-h C-h, emacs reminds you that there are unsaved changes:

```
    --**-Emacs: dickens.note              (Fundamental)----Bot-------------
    Save file /users/taylor/dickens.note? (y or n)  _
```

Typing y saves the changes; n quits without saving the changes; and if you instead decide to return to the edit session, Escape will cancel the action entirely. Typing n reminds you a second time that the changes will be lost if you don't save them.

```
    --**-Emacs: dickens.note              (Fundamental)----Bot-------------
    Modified buffers exist; exit anyway? (yes or no)  _
```

This time type y and, finally, you're back on the command line.

Entering text in emacs is incredibly easy. It's as though the editor is always in insert mode. The price you pay for this, however, is that just about anything else you do requires Control or Meta sequences. Even the Backspace key did something other than what you wanted.

The motion commands are summarized in Table 12.1.

TABLE 12.1   emacs Motion Commands

Command	Meaning
M->	Move to the end of the file.
M-<	Move to the beginning of the file.
C-v	Move forward a screen.

12

TABLE 12.1 continued

Command	Meaning
M-v	Move backward a screen.
C-x]	Move forward a page.
C-x [	Move backward a page.
C-n	Move to the next line.
C-p	Move to the previous line.
C-a	Move to the beginning of the line.
C-e	Move to the end of the line.
M-e	Move to the end of the sentence.
M-a	Move to the beginning of the sentence.
C-f	Move forward a character.
C-b	Move backward a character.
M-f	Move forward a word.
M-b	Move backward a word.

Task 12.3: How to Delete Characters and Words

DESCRIPTION Inserting text into an emacs buffer is simple, and after you get the hang of it, moving about in the file isn't too bad, either. How about deleting text? The series of Control and Meta commands that enable you to insert text are a precursor to all commands in emacs, and it should come as no surprise that C-d deletes the current character, M-d deletes the next word, M-k deletes the rest of the current sentence, and C-k deletes the rest of the current line. If you have a key on your keyboard labeled DEL, RUBOUT, or Delete, you're in luck because Delete deletes the previous character, M-Delete deletes the previous word, and C-x Delete deletes the previous sentence.

Unfortunately, although I have a Delete key, it's tied to the Backspace function on my system, so every time I press it, it actually sends a C-h sequence to the system, not the DEL sequence. The result is that I cannot use any of these backward deletion commands.

Actually, VersaTerm Pro, the terminal emulation package I use on my Macintosh to connect to the various Unix systems, is smarter than that. I can tell it whether pressing the Delete key should send a C-h or a DEL function in the keyboard configuration screen. One flip of a toggle, and I'm fully functional in emacs. Unfortunately, it's not always this easy to switch from Backspace to DEL.

ACTION

1. Restart emacs with the dickens.note file, and move the cursor to the middle of the fifth line (remember, C-n moves to the next line, and C-f moves forward a character). It should look like this:

```
Preface

When I was acting, with my children and friends, in Mr Wilkie Collins's
drama of The Frozen Deep, I first conceived the main idea of this
story. A strong desire was upon me then, to
embody it in my own person;
and I traced out in my fancy, the state of mind of which it would
necessitate the presentation
to an observant spectator, with particular
```

Notice that my cursor is on the w in was on the fifth line here.

2. Press C-d C-d C-d to remove the word was. Now type came to revise the sentence slightly. The screen should now look like this:

```
Preface

When I was acting, with my children and friends, in Mr Wilkie Collins's
drama of The Frozen Deep, I first conceived the main idea of this
story. A strong desire came_ upon me then, to
embody it in my own person;
and I traced out in my fancy, the state of mind of which it would
necessitate the presentation
to an observant spectator, with particular
```

Now press Delete once to remove the last letter of the new word, and then type e to reinsert it. Instead of backing up a character at a time, I am instead going to use M-Delete to delete the word just added. The word is deleted, but the spaces on either side of the word are retained:

12

```
Preface

When I was acting, with my children and friends, in Mr Wilkie Collins's
drama of The Frozen Deep, I first conceived the main idea of this
story. A strong desire _upon me then, to
embody it in my own person;
and I traced out in my fancy, the state of mind of which it would
necessitate the presentation
to an observant spectator, with particular
```

I'll try another word to see whether I can get this sentence to sound the way I'd prefer. Type `crept` to see how it reads.

3. On the other hand, it's probably not good to revise classic stories such as *A Tale of Two Cities*, so the best move is for me to delete this entire sentence. If I press C-x Delete, which is an example of a *multikeystroke command* in emacs, will it do the right thing? Recall that C-x Delete deletes the previous sentence. I press C-x Delete, and the results are helpful, if not completely what I want to accomplish.

> emacs also requires some multikeystroke commands, where you might press a control sequence and follow it with a second keystroke. Although this allows you to have many commands to control your text, it also means you need to know many commands.

```
Preface

When I was acting, with my children and friends, in Mr Wilkie Collins's
drama of The Frozen Deep, I first conceived the main idea of this
story. _upon me then, to
embody it in my own person;
and I traced out in my fancy, the state of mind of which it would
necessitate the presentation
to an observant spectator, with particular
```

That's okay. Now I can delete the second part of the sentence by using the M-k command. Now the screen looks like what I want:

```
When I was acting, with my children and friends, in Mr Wilkie Collins's
drama of The Frozen Deep, I first conceived the main idea of this
story. _

As the idea became familiar to me, it gradually shaped itself into its
present form. Throughout its execution, it has had complete possession
of me; I have so far verified what
```

4. Here's a great feature of emacs! I just realized that deleting sentences is just as wildly inappropriate as changing words, so I want to undo the last two changes. If I were using vi, I'd be stuck because vi remembers only the last change; but emacs has that beat. With emacs, you can back up as many changes as you'd like, usually until you restore the original file. To step backward, use C-x u.

The first time I press C-x u, the screen changes to this:

```
When I was acting, with my children and friends, in Mr Wilkie Collins's
drama of The Frozen Deep, I first conceived the main idea of this
story. _upon me then, to
embody it in my own person;
and I traced out in my fancy, the state of mind of which it would
necessitate the presentation
to an observant spectator, with particular
care and interest.

As the idea became familiar to me, it gradually shaped itself into its
present form. Throughout its execution, it has had complete possession
```

The second time I press it, the screen goes even further back in my revision history:

```
When I was acting, with my children and friends, in Mr Wilkie Collins's
drama of The Frozen Deep, I first conceived the main idea of this
story. A strong desire crept_upon me then, to
embody it in my own person;
and I traced out in my fancy, the state of mind of which it would
necessitate the presentation
to an observant spectator, with particular
care and interest.

As the idea became familiar to me, it gradually shaped itself into its
present form. Throughout its execution, it has had complete possession
```

12

Finally, using C-x u three more times causes the original text to be restored:

```
                        A Tale of Two Cities
                              Preface

When I was acting, with my children and friends, in Mr Wilkie Collins's
drama of The Frozen Deep, I first conceived the main idea of this
story. A strong desire came upon me then, to
embody it in my own person;
and I traced out in my fancy, the state of mind of which it would
necessitate the presentation
to an observant spectator, with particular
care and interest.

As the idea became familiar to me, it gradually shaped itself into its
present form. Throughout its execution, it has had complete possession
of me; I have so far verified what
is done and suffered in these pages,
as that I have certainly done and suffered it all myself.

Whenever any reference (however slight) is made here to the condition
of the French people before or during the Revolution, it is truly made,
on the faith of the most trustworthy
witnesses. It has been one of my hopes to add
--**-Emacs: dickens.note           (Fundamental)----Top-------------
Undo!
```

SUMMARY If you don't have a Delete key, some of the deletion commands will be unavailable to you, regrettably. Generally, though, emacs has as many ways to delete text as vi has, if not more. The best feature, however, is that, unlike vi, emacs remembers edit changes from the beginning of your editing session. You can always back up as far as you want by using the C-x u undo request.

The deletion commands are summarized in Table 12.2.

TABLE 12.2   Deletion Commands in emacs

Command	Meaning
Delete	Delete the previous character.
C-d	Delete the current character.
M-Delete	Delete the previous word.
M-d	Delete the next word.
C-x Delete	Delete the previous sentence.

TABLE 12.2   continued

Command	Meaning
M-k	Delete the rest of the current sentence.
C-k	Delete the rest of the current line.
C-x u	Undo the last edit change.

Task 12.4: Search and Replace in emacs

DESCRIPTION   Because emacs reserves the last line of the screen for its own system prompts, searching and replacing are easier than in vi. Moreover, the system prompts for the fields and asks, for each occurrence, whether to change it. On the other hand, this command isn't a simple keystroke or two, but rather it is an example of a *named* emacs command. A named emacs command is a command that requires you to type its name, such as query-replace, rather than a command key or two.

Searching forward for a pattern is done by pressing C-s, and searching backward is done with C-r (the mnemonics are search forward and reverse search). To leave the search when you've found what you want, press Escape, and to cancel the search and return to your starting point, use C-g.

> Unfortunately, you might find that pressing C-s does very strange things to your system. In fact, ^s and ^q are often used as *flow control* on a terminal, and by pressing the C-s key, you're actually telling the terminal emulator to stop sending information until it sees a C-q. Flow control is the protocol used by your computer and terminal to make sure that neither outpaces the other during data transmission. If this happens to you, you need to try to turn off XON/XOFF flow control. Ask your system administrator for help.

12

Query and replace is really a whole new feature within emacs. To start a query and replace, use M-x query-replace. emacs will prompt for what to do next. When a match is shown, you can type various commands to affect what happens: y makes the change; n leaves it as is but moves to the next match; Escape or q quits replace mode; and ! automatically replaces all occurrences of the pattern without further prompting.

ACTION

1. I'm still looking at the `dickens.note` file, and I have moved the cursor to the upper-left corner by using M-<. Somewhere in the file is the word `Revolution`, but I'm not sure where. Worse, every time I press C-s, the terminal freezes up until I press C-q because of flow control problems. Instead of searching forward, I'll search backward by first moving the cursor to the bottom of the file with M-> and then pressing C-r.

```
-----Emacs: dickens.note          (Fundamental)----Bot-------------
I-search backward:
```

As I type each character of the pattern `Revolution`, the cursor dances backward, matching the pattern as it grows longer and longer, until emacs finds the word I seek:

```
Whenever any reference (however slight) is made here to the condition
of the French people before or during the Revolution, it is truly
made, on the faith of the most trustworthy
witnesses. It has been one of my hopes to add
something to the popular and picturesque means of
understanding that terrible time, though no one can hope
to add anything to the philosophy of Mr Carlyle's wonderful book.

Tavistock House
November 1859




-----Emacs: dickens.note          (Fundamental)----Bot-------------
I-search backward: Revol
```

2. Now to try the `query-replace` feature. To begin, I move to the top of the file with M-< and then press M-x, which causes the notation to show up on the bottom status line:

```
of the French people before or during the Revolution, it is truly made,
on the faith of the most trustworthy
witnesses. It has been one of my hopes to add
--**-Emacs: dickens.note           (Fundamental)----Top--------------
M-x _
```

I then type the words query-replace and press Return. emacs understands that I want to find all occurrences of a pattern and replace them with another. emacs changes the prompt to this:

```
of the French people before or during the Revolution, it is
truly made, on the faith of the most trustworthy
witnesses. It has been one of my hopes to add
--**-Emacs: dickens.note           (Fundamental)----Top--------------
Query replace: _
```

Now I type the word I want to replace. To cause confusion in the file, I think I'll change French to Danish, because maybe *A Tale of Two Cities* really takes place in London and Copenhagen! To do this, I type French and press Return. The prompt again changes to this:

```
of the French people before or during the Revolution, it is truly made,
on the faith of the most trustworthy
witnesses. It has been one of my hopes to add
--**-Emacs: dickens.note           (Fundamental)----Top--------------
Query replace French with: _
```

I type Danish and again press Return.

```
as that I have certainly done and suffered it all myself.

Whenever any reference (however slight) is made here to the condition
of the French_people before or during the Revolution, it is truly
made, on the faith of the most trustworthy
witnesses. It has been one of my hopes to add
--**-Emacs: dickens.note           (Fundamental)----Top--------------
Query replacing French with Danish:
```

It might not be completely obvious, but emacs has found a match (immediately before the cursor) and is prompting me for what to do next. The choices here are summarized in Table 12.3.

TABLE 12.3   Options During Query and Replace

Command	Meaning
y	Change this occurrence of the pattern.
n	Don't change this occurrence, but look for another.
q	Don't change this occurrence. Leave query-replace completely (you can also use Escape for this function).
!	Change this occurrence and all others in the file.

I opt to make this, and all other possible changes in the file, by pressing !, and the screen changes to tell me that there were no more occurrences:

```
Whenever any reference (however slight) is made here to the condition
of the Danish_people before or during the Revolution, it is truly
made, on the faith of the most trustworthy
witnesses. It has been one of my hopes to add
--**-Emacs: dickens.note          (Fundamental)----Top-------------
Done
```

SUMMARY   Searching in emacs is awkward, particularly because of the flow control problems you may incur because of your terminal. However, searching and replacing with the query-replace command is fantastic, much better, and more powerful than the vi alternative. As I said earlier, your assessment of emacs all depends on what features you prefer.

Task 12.5: Using the emacs Tutorial and Help System

DESCRIPTION   Unlike vi and, indeed, unlike most of Unix, emacs includes its own extensive built-in documentation and a tutorial to help you learn how to use the program. As I noted earlier, you access the entire help system by pressing C-h. Pressing C-h three times brings up the general help menu screen. There is also an information browser called info (accessed with C-h i) and a tutorial system you can start by pressing C-h t.

emacs enthusiasts insist that the editor is modeless, but in fact it does have modes of its own. You used one just now, the query-replace mode. To obtain help on the current mode you're working in, you can use C-h m.

ACTION

1. Boldly, I opted to press C-h C-h C-h, and the entire screen is replaced with this:

```
You have typed C-h, the help character. Type a Help option:

A  command-apropos.  Give a substring, and see a list of commands
              (functions interactively callable) that contain
              that substring. See also the  apropos  command.
B  describe-bindings. Display table of all key bindings.
C  describe-key-briefly. Type a command key sequence;
              it prints the function name that sequence runs.
F  describe-function. Type a function name and get documentation of it.
I  info. The  info  documentation reader.
K  describe-key. Type a command key sequence;
              it displays the full documentation.
L  view-lossage. Shows last 100 characters you typed.
M  describe-mode. Print documentation of current major mode,
              which describes the commands peculiar to it.
N  view-emacs-news. Shows emacs news file.
S  describe-syntax. Display contents of syntax table, plus explanations
T  help-with-tutorial. Select the Emacs learn-by-doing tutorial.
V  describe-variable. Type name of a variable;
              it displays the variable's documentation and value.
W  where-is. Type command name; it prints which keystrokes
              invoke that command.
--**-Emacs: *Help*                (Fundamental)----Top-------------
A B C F I K L M N S T V W C-x  b C-d C-n C-w or Space to scroll: _
```

What to do now? Seventeen options are possible from this point, as shown in Table 12.4.

TABLE 12.4   emacs Help System Command Options

Command	Meaning
A	List all commands matching the specified word.
B	List all key mappings.
C	Describe any key sequence pressed, instead of doing it.
F	Describe the specified function.
I	Start the info browser.
K	Fully describe the result of a particular key sequence.
L	Show the last 100 characters you typed.
M	Describe the current mode you're in.

12

Command	Meaning
N	Show emacs news file.
S	List a command syntax table.
T	Start the emacs tutorial.
V	Define and describe the specified variable.
W	Indicate what keystroke invokes a particular function.
C-x b	Display emacs copyright and distribution information.
C-d	Display emacs ordering information.
C-n	Display recent emacs changes.
C-w	Display emacs warranty.

2. I choose K and then press M-< to see what that command really does. The first
   thing that happens after I type K is that the table of help information vanishes, to
   be replaced by my original text, and then the prompt appears along the bottom:

```
of the Danish_people before or during the Revolution, it is truly
made, on the faith of the most trustworthy
witnesses. It has been one of my hopes to add
--**-Emacs: dickens.note          (Fundamental)----Top-------------
Describe key:-
```

Pressing M-< brings up the desired information:

```
                    A Tale of Two Cities
                         Preface


When I was acting, with my children and friends, in Mr Wilkie
Collins's drama of The Frozen Deep, I first conceived the main idea
of this story. A strong desire came upon me then, to
embody it in my own person;
and I traced out in my fancy, the state of mind of which it would
necessitate the presentation
to an observant spectator, with particular
-----Emacs: dickens.note~          (Fundamental)----Top-------------
beginning-of-buffer:
Move point to the beginning of the buffer; leave mark at previous
position.
With arg N, put point N/10 of the way from the true beginning.
```

continues

```
      Don't use this in Lisp programs!
      (goto-char (point-min)) is faster and does not set the mark.




-----Emacs: *Help*              (Fundamental)----All-------------
Type C-x 1 to remove help window.
```

A quick C-x 1 removes the help information when I'm done with it.

SUMMARY A considerable amount of help is available in the emacs editor. If you're interested in learning more about this editor, the online tutorial is a great place to start. Try C-h t to start it, and go from there.

Task 12.6: Working with Other Files

DESCRIPTION By this point, it should be no surprise to you that about a million commands are available within the emacs editor, even though it can be a bit tricky to get to them. There are many file-related commands too, but I'm going to focus on just a few essential commands so that you can get around in the program. The emacs help system can offer lots more. (Try using C-h a *file* to find out what functions are offered in your version of the program.)

To add the contents of a file to the current edit buffer, use the command C-x i. It will prompt for a filename. Pressing C-x C-w prompts for a file to write the buffer into, rather than the default file. To save to the default file, use C-x C-s (that is, if you can; the C-s might again hang you up, just as it did when you tried to use it for searching). If that doesn't work, you always can use the alternative, C-x s, which also works. To move to another file, use C-x C-f (emacs users never specify more than one filename on the command line; they use C-x C-f to move between files instead). What's nice is that when you use the C-x C-f command, you load the contents of that file into another buffer, so you can zip quickly between files by using the C-x b command to switch buffers. emacs allows you to edit several files at once using different areas of the screen; these areas are called buffers.

12

ACTION

1. Without leaving emacs, I press C-x C-f to read another file into the buffer. The system then prompts me as follows:

```
of the Danish people before or during the Revolution, it is truly
made, on the faith of the most trustworthy
witnesses. It has been one of my hopes to add
-----Emacs: dickens.note          (Fundamental)----Top-------------
Find file: ~/ _
```

I type buckaroo, and the editor opens a new buffer, moving me to that file:

```
I found myself stealing a peek at my own watch and overheard
General Catbird's
aide give him the latest.
"He's not even here," went the conversation.
"Who?"
"Banzai."
"Where the hell is he?"
"At the hospital in El Paso."
"What? Why weren't we informed? What's wrong with him?"




-----Emacs: buckaroo             (Fundamental)----All-------------
```

2. Now I'll flip back to the other buffer with C-x b. When I enter that command, however, it doesn't automatically move me there. Instead, it offers this prompt:

```
--**-Emacs: buckaroo              (Fundamental)----All-------------
Switch to buffer: (default dickens.note) _
```

When I type ?, I receive a split screen indicating what the possible answers are here:

```
I found myself stealing a peek at my own watch and overheard
General Catbird's
aide give him the latest.
"He's not even here," went the conversation.
"Who?"
"Banzai."
"Where the hell is he?"
"At the hospital in El Paso."
"What? Why weren't we informed? What's wrong with him?"



--**-Emacs: buckaroo              (Fundamental)----All-------------
Possible completions are:
*Buffer List*                      *Help*
*scratch*                          buckaroo
dickens.note




-----Emacs: *Completions*          (Fundamental)----All-------------
Switch to buffer: (default dickens.note) _
```

The default is okay, so I press Return. Voila! I'm back in the Dickens file. One more C-x b; this time the default is buckaroo, so I again press Return to move back.

3. I'm in the buckaroo file, and I want to see what happens if I read dickens.note into this file. This is done easily. I move the cursor to the end of the file with M->, press C-x i, and answer dickens.note to the prompt: Insert file: ~/. Pressing Return yields the following screen display:

12

```
I found myself stealing a peek at my own watch and overheard
General Catbird's
aide give him the latest.
"He's not even here," went the conversation.
"Who?"
"Banzai."
"Where the hell is he?"
"At the hospital in El Paso."
"What? Why weren't we informed? What's wrong with him?"

                        A Tale of Two Cities
                              Preface

When I was acting, with my children and friends, in Mr Wilkie
Collins's drama of The Frozen Deep, I first conceived the main idea
of this story. A strong desire came upon me then, to
embody it in my own person;
and I traced out in my fancy, the state of mind of which it would
necessitate the presentation
to an observant spectator, with particular
care and interest.

As the idea became familiar to me, it gradually shaped itself into
its present form. Throughout its execution, it has had complete possession
--**-Emacs: buckaroo                 (Fundamental)----Top-------------
```

4. It's time to quit and split. To do this, I press C-x s and wait for an emacs prompt or two. The first one displayed is this:

```
As the idea became familiar to me, it gradually shaped itself into
its present form. Throughout its execution, it has had complete possession
--**-Emacs: buckaroo                 (Fundamental)----Top-------------
Save file /users/taylor/buckaroo? (y or n) _
```

I answer y to save this muddled file. I'm returned to the top of the file, and a quick C-x C-c drops me back to the system prompt.

SUMMARY   One of the more useful facets of emacs you have learned about is the capability to work with multiple files.

Summary

You have now learned quite a bit about the emacs editor. Some capabilities exceed those of the vi editor, and some are considerably more confusing. Which of these editors you choose is up to you, and your choice should be based on your own preferences for working on files. You should spend some time working with the editor you prefer, making sure that you can create simple files and modify them without any problems.

Workshop

The Workshop summarizes the key terms you learned and poses some questions about the topics presented in this chapter. It also provides you with a preview of what you will learn in the next hour.

Key Terms

buffer   An area of the screen used to edit a file in emacs.

flow control   The protocol used by your computer and terminal to make sure that neither outpaces the other during data transmission.

key bindings   The emacs term for key mapping.

Meta key   Analogous to a Control key, this is labeled either Meta or Alt on your keyboard.

named emacs command   A command in emacs that requires you to type its name, such as query-replace, rather than a command key or two.

XON/XOFF   A particular type of flow control. The receiving end can send an XON (delay transmission) character until it's ready for more information, when it sends an XOFF (resume transmission).

Exercises

1. How do you get to the emacs help system?
2. Check your keyboard. If you don't have a Meta or Alt key, what alternative strategy can you use to enter commands such as M-x?
3. What's the command sequence for leaving emacs when you're done?
4. What was the problem I had with the Delete key? How did I solve the problem? What's the alternative delete command if Delete isn't available?

12

5. How do you do global search-and-replace in emacs, and what key do you press to stop the global search-and-replace when you are prompted for confirmation at the first match?

6. Use the emacs help system to list the emacs copyright information. What's your reaction?

Preview of the Next Hour

The next hour is an in-depth look at the different shells available in Unix, how to configure them, and how to choose which you'd like to use. You will also learn about the contents of the default configuration files for both csh and sh, the two most common shells in Unix.

HOUR **13**

Introduction to Command Shells

Welcome to your 13th hour of learning Unix. You should take a moment to pat yourself on the back. You've come a long way, and you're already quite a sophisticated user. In the past few hours, I've occasionally touched on the differences between the shells, but I haven't really stopped to explain what shells are available, how they differ from one another, and which is the best for your style of interaction. That's what this hour is all about.

Shells, you'll recall, are the command-line interface programs through which you tell the computer what to do. All Unix systems include C shell (csh) and its predecessor, the Bourne shell (sh). All modern Unix systems also include some nifty newer shells, notably Korn shell (ksh) and a new rewrite of sh humorously called the Bourne Again shell (bash). It's the bash shell that I'm going to focus on for all our shell-specific discussion in this book because, although it isn't the most popular shell at this time, it's moving up very fast. By the time you read this chapter, it will be number one or number two! In any case, it's so powerful and flexible—it includes all the cool features of both csh and sh and adds tons of additional stuff—that it's a great place to start.

Goals for This Hour

In this hour, you will learn

- What shells are available and how they differ from one another
- How to identify which shell you're running
- How to choose a new shell
- More about the environment of your shell
- How to explore bash configuration files

Various shells are available in Unix, but two are guaranteed to be included in just about all Unix versions: the Bourne shell (sh) and the C shell (csh). Primarily, however, you'll learn about bash and Korn shell in this lesson.

The (Command) Shell Game

You can't get very far with Unix on most systems without having a command-line interpreter. This lesson gets you up and running with the bash command shell quickly.

Task 13.1: What Shells Are Available?

DESCRIPTION If I asked an expert how many command interpreters are available for the PC, the immediate answer would be "one, of course." After a few minutes of reflection, however, the answer might be expanded to include The Norton Desktop, Windows 95, Windows 98, Windows Me, and others. This expanded answer reflects the reality that whenever different people use a computer, different styles of interacting with the machine and different products to meet these needs will evolve. Similarly, the Macintosh has several command interpreters. If you decide that you don't like the standard interface, perhaps you will find that MachTen, At Ease, or Square One works better.

From the very beginning, Unix has been a programmer's operating system, designed to allow programmers to extend the system easily and gracefully. It should come as no surprise, then, that quite a few shells are available. Not only that, but any program can serve as a command shell, so you could even start right in emacs if you wanted and then use escapes to Unix for actual commands. (Don't laugh—I know people who've done it.)

The original shell was written by Ken Thompson, back in the early Unix's laboratory days, as part of his design of the Unix file system. Somewhere along the way, Steven Bourne, also at AT&T, got ahold of the shell and started expanding it. By the time Unix began to be widely distributed, sh was known as the Bourne shell. Characterized by speed and simplicity, it was the default shell for writing shell scripts, but is rarely used as a command shell for users any more.

The next shell was designed by the productive Bill Joy, author of vi. Entranced by the design and features of the C programming language, Joy decided to create a command shell that shared much of the C language structure and that would make it easier to write sophisticated shell scripts: the C shell, or csh. He also expanded the shell concept to add command aliases, command history, and job control. *Command aliases* enable users to rename and reconfigure commands easily. *Command history* ensures that users never have to enter commands a second time. *Job control* enables users to run multiple programs at once. Before bash appeared on the scene, the C shell was the shell I had used since I first logged in to a BSD Unix system in 1980.

A *command alias* is a shortcut for a command, allowing you to enter a shorter string for the entire command. The *command history* is a mechanism by which the shell remembers commands you have typed and allows you to repeat the command without retyping the whole command. *Job control* is a mechanism that allows you to start, stop, and suspend commands.

In the 1990s, another AT&T Labs (now Lucent) software wizard, David Korn, built an eponymous shell. The Korn shell, also known as ksh, is designed to be a superset of the Bourne shell, sharing its configuration files (.profile) and command syntax, but including many of the more powerful features of the C shell, too, including command aliases (albeit in a slightly different format), command history, and job control. This shell is becoming more popular, but it isn't yet widely distributed. You might not have it on your version of Unix.

The shell we focus on in this book, however, was written as part of the extensive GNU Project by a large group of programmers known as the Free Software Foundation. The original goal of the GNU Project was to create a version of Unix that was free of any licensing or intellectual property restrictions. System V and BSD both shared core code from earlier AT&T release and weren't available for free distribution. Although much of what the Foundation released was a re-implementation of the exact same commands that were already part of Unix, in a few areas they pushed the envelope and innovated, sometimes spectacularly.

In my eyes, the three best pieces of the GNU Project were the terrific compiler system they developed (a compiler so good that it then was incorporated into many commercial versions of Unix because it produced better code than the commercial alternative!), the extensively hacked GNU emacs, and the humorously named "Bourne Again Shell" (remember Steve Bourne wrote the original Unix shell), known as bash.

13

What makes bash such a standout is that the designers included a remarkable set of features and capabilities that enable sh, csh, and ksh users to switch with minimal, if any, changes to their existing keystroke sequences. It's nice to innovate, but forcing users to learn something completely new is a tough road to travel, and they avoided that mistake. In addition, bash sports some remarkable features and capabilities all its own.

Other shells exist in special niches. A modified version of the C shell, tcsh, a version that incorporates the slick history-editing features of the Korn shell, has appeared. Maintained by some engineers at Cornell University, it is 95% csh and 5% new features. The most important tcsh additions to the C shell are these:

- emacs-style command-line editing
- Visual perusal of the command history list
- Interactive command, file, and identifying files with the first few unique characters
- Spelling correction of command, file, and usernames
- Automatic logout after an extended idle period
- The capability to monitor logins, users, or terminals
- New pre-initialized environment variables $HOST and $HOSTTYPE.
- Support for a meaningful and helpful system status line

Another shell you might bump into is called the MH shell, or msh, and it's designed around the MH electronic mail program, originally designed at the Rand Corporation. In essence, the MH shell provides you with instant access to any electronic mail you might encounter. For sites that have security considerations, a restricted version of the Bourne shell is also available, called rsh (ingeniously, it's called the restricted sh shell). Persistent rumors of security problems with rsh suggest that you should double-check before you trust dubious users on your system with rsh as their login shell (the shell you use, by default, when you log in to the system).

Another variant of the Bourne shell is worth mentioning: jsh is a version of the Bourne shell that includes C shell-style job control features.

 Licensing restrictions and intellectual property laws occasionally have stymied the growth of Unix. Although Unix is unquestionably popular with programmers, these same programmers have a burning desire to see what's inside, to learn about how Unix works by examining Unix itself. Unix is owned by AT&T. Few people are able to view the source legally. Those who do look into Unix are "tainted": Anything they write in the future might be inspired by proprietary code of AT&T. The situation is fuzzy in many ways,

> and that's where the Free Software Foundation comes in. The brainchild of
> Richard Stallman, the FSF is slowly rewriting all the major Unix utilities and
> then distributing them with the source as part of the ambitious GNU pro-
> ject. GNU emacs is one example; the Bourne Again shell is another; and
> Linux, a great free Unix implementation, is a third.

ACTION

1. The easiest way to ascertain what shells are available on your system is to look for
   `*sh` in the /bin directory. I'll do this most easily with an ls wildcard:

   ```
   $ ls -F /bin/*sh
   /bin/csh*   /bin/ksh*   /bin/rksh*  /bin/sh*
   ```

2. Where's bash? Well, different systems have "non-Posix"—which is to say, non-
   standard—shells in other places. A smart place to figure out where other shells
   might be located is to look at your PATH environment variable:

   ```
   $ echo $PATH
   /usr/bin:/bin:/usr/sbin:/sbin:/usr/X11R6/bin:/usr/local/bin:/home/taylor/
   ➥bin:/home/taylor/bin:/home/taylor/bin:/home/taylor/bin:/home/taylor/bin:/
   ➥home/taylor/bin
   ```

   A lot is in this PATH, but I'm looking for other bin directories. I can list them all
   one by one (for example, ls /sbin/*sh) but I'm going to use a different strategy:
   I'm going to explicitly look for the Bourne Again Shell:

   ```
   $ which bash
   /usr/local/bin/bash
   ```

   Now I know where the system has bash, let's see if there are any other shells in
   this directory:

   ```
   % ls -F /usr/local/bin/*sh
   /usr/local/bin/bash*
   ```

3. Ah well, that's the only shell in that particular directory.

SUMMARY As you can see, this particular version of Unix offers five different login shells:
csh, ksh, rksh, sh, and bash. I've opted to use bash for my interaction with the
Unix system.

13

Task 13.2: Identifying Your Shell

DESCRIPTION   You can use many different approaches to identify which shell you're using. The
easiest, however, is to type echo $SHELL or, if that fails, swoop into the
/etc/passwd file to see what your account lists. It's helpful to know some alternatives
because searching the /etc/passwd file isn't always an option (some systems hide the
/etc/passwd file in the interest of security).

ACTION

1. One simple technique to identify your shell is to check your prompt. If your
   prompt contains a %, you probably are using the C shell or modified C shell (tcsh).
   If your prompt contains $, you could be using the Bourne shell, the Korn shell,
   bash, or a variant thereof.

2. Another easy way is to check the value of your SHELL environment variable with
   the echo command.

   ```
   $ echo SHELL
   SHELL
   ```

   Oops! Let's try again, remembering the $ to indicate that we're asking for the
   value of the variable named SHELL, not the word itself!

   ```
   $ echo $SHELL
   /usr/local/bin/bash
   ```

   (On your system, it might well be /bin/bash instead).

3. A cool way to ascertain which shell you're using is to ask the operating system
   what program you're currently running. The shell variable $$ identifies the process
   ID of the shell. You can use the helpful ps (*processor status*) command with its -p
   process flag to see what shell you have. Here's what happens when I try it:

   ```
   $ ps -p $$
     PID TT   STAT      TIME COMMAND
    9503 p0   Ss     0:00.12 -bash (bash)
   ```

   You can see that I'm running bash. There is a leading dash on the indication of
   what shell I'm running because that's how the system denotes that this particular
   shell process is my login shell.

4. Another way to find out what shell I'm running is to peek into the /etc/passwd
   file, which you can do with grep:

   ```
   % grep taylor /etc/passwd
   taylor:*:1001:999:Dave Taylor,,,:/home/taylor:/usr/local/bin/bash
   taylorsu:*:0:0:Dave as Root:/home/taylorsu:/bin/csh
   ```

Helpful results, but I ended up with two matches: both the taylor account (which is my current login account) and the taylorsu account, which I don't want to see.

5. Remembering what was covered in Lesson 9, "Wildcards and Regular Expressions," here's the fancy regular expression way to ensure that I match only my current account:

```
$ grep '^taylor:' /etc/passwd
taylor:*:1001:999:Dave Taylor,,,:/home/taylor:/usr/local/bin/bash

grep $LOGNAME /etc/passwd
```

That's what I want! In the /etc/passwd file, fields of information are separated by colons, and the last field is the login shell. As expected, you can see that it's /usr/local/bin/bash.

One more refinement: Let's use the cut command to slice out just the login shell, rather than seeing all the stuff in the /etc/passwd file.

```
$ grep '^taylor:' /etc/passwd | cut -d: -f7
/usr/local/bin/bash
```

In a nutshell, we tell cut to use the : as a field delimiter and then show us just the seventh field (which is the login shell—count it for yourself).

6. For fun, I used the preceding cut command as the basis of a command sequence on a busy system to see what shells people were using. The program extracts the last field of each line in the password file, and then sorts and counts matches, showing the number of occurrences of the shell and the shell, one per line. Ready?

```
$ cut -d: -f7 /etc/passwd | sort | uniq -c
   1 /abuse
  30 /bin/bash
 475 /bin/csh
  23 /bin/ksh
 259 /bin/tcsh
   2 /bin/zsh
 382 /noshell
   3 /usr/local/bin/bash
   6 /usr/local/bin/tcsh
```

As you can see, many people have been disabled with the noshell option, and, on this system, csh is the most popular. Also note that apparently two versions of bash and tcsh are on this system.

The cut command is a great one to remember when you want to slice a column out of a data file like /etc/passwd. Take a minute and learn more about it with man cut on your system.

13

SUMMARY When you've identified your shell, you can contemplate choosing a different one. I suggest you try bash if you aren't using it already because it enables you to try all the examples in the next few lessons for yourself.

Task 13.3: How to Choose a New Shell

DESCRIPTION In the past, the only way to switch login shells on many systems was to ask the system administrator to edit the /etc/passwd file directly. This usually meant waiting until the sysadmin had time, which could be hours, or even days. The good news is that a simple program (on almost all Unix systems) now exists to change login shells—it's chsh, or change shell. It has no starting flags or options, does not require that any files be specified, and can be used regardless of your location in the file system. Type chsh and press Return.

ACTION

1. To change my login shell to any of the alternative shells, or even to verify what shell I'm running, I can use the chsh command.

   The original implementation of chsh had the system prompt for a new shell on the command line:

   ```
   % chsh
   Changing login shell for taylor.
   Old shell: /bin/csh
   New shell: _
   ```

   At this point, the program shows me that I currently have /bin/csh as my login shell and asks me to specify an alternative shell. I'll try to confuse it by requesting that emacs become my login shell:

   ```
   % chsh
   Changing login shell for taylor.
   Old shell: /bin/csh
   New shell: /usr/local/bin/gnuemacs
   /usr/local/bin/gnuemacs is unacceptable as a new shell.
   ```

2. The program has some knowledge of valid shell names, and it requires you to specify one. Unfortunately, it doesn't divulge that information, so typing ? to find what's available results in the program complaining that ? is unacceptable as a new shell.

   You can, however, peek into the file that this version of chsh uses to confirm which programs are valid shells, if this is what you're seeing as you try this command. The data file is called /etc/shells and it looks like this:

```
% cat /etc/shells# List of acceptable shells for chpass(1).
# Ftpd will not allow users to connect who are not using
# one of these shells.

/bin/sh
/bin/csh
/bin/tcsh
/bin/bash
/bin/zsh
/bin/ksh
/usr/local/bin/ksh
/usr/local/bin/tcsh
/usr/local/bin/bash
```

I'll leave my shell alone by pressing Enter. If you'd like to change yours, type in
the new name:

```
% chsh
Changing login shell for taylor
Old shell: /bin/csh
New shell: /usr/local/bin/bash
```

Notice that, in typical Unix style, you do not see any actual confirmation that anything was done. I conclude that, because I did not get any error messages, the program worked. Fortunately, I can check easily by either using chsh again or redoing
the awk program with a C shell history command:

```
% !grep
grep '^taylor:' /etc/passwd | cut -d: -f7
/usr/local/bin/bash
```

In the next hour, you learn more about the powerful bash command-history mechanism, but here just notice that I only had to type the first few letters of the previous command to have it automatically run. Quite a timesaver!

13

> Because of the growing popularity of the bash shell, the next few hours
> focus on the bash shell. To get the most out of those hours, I strongly recom-
> mend that you use the bash shell.

> If you can't change your login shell, perhaps because of not having chsh,
> you always can enter bash after you log in by typing bash.

SUMMARY It's easy to change your login shell. You can try different shells until you find the one that best suits your style of interaction. For the most part, though, shells all have the same basic syntax and use the same commands: `ls  -l` does the same thing in any shell. The differences, then, really come into play when you use the more sophisticated capabilities, including programming the shell (with shell scripts), customizing its features through command aliases, and saving on keystrokes by using a history mechanism. That's where `bash` has an edge, and why it's becoming so popular. It is easy, straightforward, and has powerful aliasing, history, and job-control capabilities, as you learn in the next hour.

Task 13.4: Learning the Shell Environment

DESCRIPTION Earlier in this book, you used the `env` or `printenv` command to learn the various characteristics of your working environment. Now it's time to use this command again to look more closely at the shell environment and define each of the variables therein.

ACTION

1. To start out, I enter `env` to list the various aspects of my working environment. Do the same on your system, and although your environment will not be identical to mine, you should see considerable similarity between the two.

```
% env | cat -n
     1  PWD=/home/taylor
     2  HOSTNAME=staging
     3  USER=taylor
     4  MACHTYPE=i386-pc-openbsd2.8
     5  MAIL=/var/mail/taylor
     6  EDITOR=/usr/bin/vi
     7  LOGNAME=taylor
     8  SHLVL=1
     9  SHELL=/usr/local/bin/bash
    10  HOSTTYPE=i386
    11  OSTYPE=openbsd2.8
    12  HOME=/home/taylor
    13  TERM=vt100
    14  PATH=.:/home/taylor/bin:/usr/bin:/bin:/usr/sbin:
/sbin:/usr/X11R6/bin:/usr/local/bin
    15  SSH_TTY=/dev/ttyp0
    16  EXINIT=:set ignorecase
    17      =/usr/bin/env
```

This probably seems pretty overwhelming. What are all these things, and why on earth should they matter? They matter because it's important for you to learn exactly how your own environment is set up so that you can change things if you desire. As you soon will be able to recognize, I have modified much of my system's environment so that the shell does what I want it to do, rather than what its default would tell it to do.

2. When I log in to the system, the system defines some environment variables, indicating where my home directory is located, what shell I'm running, and so on. These variables are listed in Table 13.1.

TABLE 13.1   Default Variables Set by Unix on Login

Variable	Description
HOME	This is my home directory, obtained from the fourth field of the password file. Try the command `grep $LOGNAME /etc/passwd | cut -d: -f6` to see what your home directory is set to, or just use `echo $HOME`. This is not only the directory that I start in, but also the directory that `cd` moves me back to when I don't specify a different directory. My HOME variable is `/home/taylor`.
SHELL	When Unix programs such as `vi` process the `!` command to execute Unix commands, they check this variable to see which shell I'm using. If I were to type `:!` followed by Return in `vi`, the program would create a new `bash` shell for me. If I had `SHELL=/bin/sh`, `vi` would start a Bourne shell. My SHELL variable is set to `/bin/bash`.
TERM	By default, your terminal is defined by the value of this environment variable, which starts out as `unknown`. (Recall that when you first were learning about `vi`, the program would complain `unknown: terminal not known`.) Many sites know what kind of terminals are using which lines, however, so this variable is often set to the correct value before you even see it. If it isn't set, you can define it to the appropriate value within your `.profile` or `.bash_profile` file. (You will learn to do this later in the hour.) My TERM is set to `vt100`, for a Digital Equipment Corporation Visual Terminal model 100, which is probably the most commonly emulated terminal in communications packages.
USER	Programs can quickly look up your user ID and match it with an account name. However, predefining your account name as an environment setting saves time. That's exactly what USER, and its companion LOGNAME, are—timesavers. My USER is set to `taylor`.

13

TABLE 13.1   continued

Variable	Description
PATH	Earlier, you learned that the Unix shell finds a command by searching from directory to directory until it finds a match. The environment variable that defines which directories to search and the order in which to search them is the PATH variable. Rather than keep the default settings, I've added some directories to my search path, which is now as follows:

`.:/home/taylor/bin:/usr/bin:/bin:/usr/sbin:/sbin:/usr/X11R6/`
`bin:/usr/local/bin`

I have told the shell always to look first for commands in the current directory (.), and then in my `bin` directory (`/home/taylor/bin`), and after that in the standard system directories (`/usr/bin`, `/bin`, `/usr/sbin`, `/sbin`). If the commands are not found in any of those areas, the shell should try looking in some unusual directories (`/usr/X11R6/bin`, `/usr/local/bin`).

> I admit it: Using . as the first entry in the PATH variable is a security hazard. Why? Imagine this: A devious chap has written a program that will do bad things to my directory when I invoke that bad program. But how will he make me invoke it? The easiest way is to give the bad program the same name as a standard Unix utility, such as ls, and leave it in a commonly accessed directory, such as /tmp. So what happens? Imagine that the . (current directory) is the first entry in my PATH, and I change directories to /tmp to check something. While I'm in /tmp, I enter ls without thinking, and voila! I've run the bad program without knowing it. Having the . at the end of the search path would avoid all this because then the default ls command is the correct version. I have it because I often do want to override the standard commands with new ones that I'm working on (an admittedly lazy practice).

Variable	Description
MAIL	One of the most exciting and enjoyable aspects of Unix is its powerful and incredibly well-connected electronic mail capability. Various programs can be used to check for new mail, read mail, and send mail messages. All of these programs need to know where my default incoming mailbox is located, which is what the MAIL environment variable defines. My MAIL is set to `/var/mail/taylor`.
LOGNAME	LOGNAME is a synonym for USER. My LOGNAME is set to `taylor`.

> Having both LOGNAME and USER defined in my environment demonstrates how far Unix has progressed since the competition and jostling between the Berkeley and AT&T versions (BSD and SVR3, respectively) of Unix. When I started working with Unix, if I was on a BSD system, the account name would be defined as LOGNAME, and if I used an SVR3 system, the account name would be defined as USER. Programs had to check for both, which was frustrating. Over time, each system has begun to use both terms (instead of using the solution that you and I might think is most obvious, which is to agree on a single word).

3. A glance back at the output of the env command reveals that more variables are in my environment than are listed in Table 13.1. That's because you can define anything you want in the environment. Certain programs can read many environment variables that customize their behavior.

Many Unix programs allow you to enter text directly, and then they spin off into an editor, if needed. Others start your favorite editor for entering information. Both types of programs use the EDITOR environment variable to identify which editor to use. I have mine set to /usr/bin/vi.

You learned earlier that vi can have default information stored in the .exrc file, but the program also can read configuration information from the environment variable EXINIT. To make all my pattern searches *not case sensitive* (meaning that a search for precision will match Precision), I set the appropriate vi variable in the EXINIT. Mine is set to :set ignorecase. If you want line numbers to show up always, you could easily have your EXINIT set to :set number.

The bash shell sets some internal variables too, most notably SHLVL (shell level), which tracks how many levels of subshell you're within. It also gives easy access to some system-level information: MACHTYPE is the type of machine I'm running (i386-pc-openbsd2.8), HOSTTYPE is the type of hardware I have (i386-based architecture) and OSTYPE is the exact version of the operating system on this particular computer (here it's openbsd2.8).

SUMMARY You can define many possible environment variables for yourself. Most large Unix programs have environment variables of their own, enabling you to tailor the program's behavior to your needs and preferences. Unix itself has quite a few environment variables, too. Until you're an expert, however, I recommend that you stick with viewing these variables and ensuring that they have reasonable values, rather than changing them. Particularly focus on the set of variables defined in Table 13.1. If they're wrong, you could have trouble, whereas if other environment variables are wrong, you're probably not going to have too much trouble.

13

Task 13.5: Exploring bash Configuration Files

DESCRIPTION The bash shell uses two files to configure itself, and although neither of them needs to be present, both probably can be found in your home directory: .profile (or .bash_profile) and .bashrc. The difference between them is subtle but very important. The .profile file is read only once, when you log in, and the .bashrc file is read every time a shell is started. As a result, if you're working in vi and you enter :!ls, vi carries out the command by starting a new shell and then feeding the command to that shell. Therefore, new bash shells started from within programs such as vi won't see any shell-local configuration changes that are in your .profile.

This split between two configuration files isn't too bad, actually, because most modifications to the environment are automatically included in all subshells (a shell other than the login shell) invoked. To be specific, all environment variables are pervasive, but shell command aliases are lost and, therefore, must be defined in the .bashrc file to be available within all occurrences of bash. You learn more about command aliases in the next hour, "Advanced Shell Interaction."

ACTION

1. To begin, I use cat to list the contents of my .profile file. Remember that any line beginning with a # is a comment and is ignored.

```
$ cat .profile
# .profile

# Read in my aliases before going any further
. ~/.bashrc

# Tweak my environment variables to reflect my favorites

# Note that I'm adding '.' to the beginning of my PATH. This is
# very dangerous and you should read - and think about - the
# note about this in the book before doing it yourself.

PATH=.:$HOME/bin:$PATH

SHELL=/usr/local/bin/bash
EDITOR="/usr/bin/vi"
EXINIT=":set ignorecase"

export PATH SHELL EDITOR EXINIT
```

```
# now set the prompt to the current directory (base name) and
# the current command number (for "!n" escapes)

PS1='\W \!: '

# I'd like 'vi' style command-line editing, don't want to log
# out when I accidentally type "^D" at the command line, and
# don't want to accidentally delete files if I attempt to
# blindly overwrite them:

set -o vi ignoreeof noclobber

# Finally, I'd like to have the default file permission be
# 755 (rwxr-xr-x) on files/directories, hence this umask

umask 022

newmail
mesg y
```

This is pretty straightforward, after you remove all the comments. Environmental variables are set with the NAME=value lines, and then I ensure that they're available to the current shell (in addition to any subshells) with the export command. To allow me to use any .bashrc aliases or functions within my .profile, I start by having the shell read in the file (that's what . means at the beginning of the first non-comment line). You can see that some of the variables shown in the previous unit are defined in my .profile file.

By setting the PS1 variable, I create a custom prompt rather than the default bash prompt of the shell name and a dollar sign (it looks like this: bash2.3$ and isn't very friendly in my opinion!). Instead, I have the prompt set to the base name of the current directory, the command number (in the history list) and a colon. It looks like this: bin 343: showing me that I'm in the bin directory and that this is the 343rd command in my history list. In the next lesson you'll learn some of the many nifty things you can place in your command prompt.

Finally, the set commands are configuration options for the shell. I have told the shell to ignore ^D sequences at the command line so I don't accidentally log myself out (instead, I'll need to use exit or logout), and warn me before it overwrites existing files with file redirection (noclobber).

The three commands at the end of the .profile file are invoked as though I'd entered them on the command line. Umask sets my default file creation mask, the newmail variable watches for new electronic mail (in the mailbox defined by the environment variable MAIL, in fact) and tells me when it arrives. The mesg y variable makes sure that I have my terminal configured so that other folks can beep me or say hello using talk, a communication tool discussed in Hour 21, "Communicating with E-mail."

13

2. How about the other file—the one that's read by the shell each time a shell is
    started?

```
$ cat .bashrc
# .bashrc
# This contains all user specific aliases and functions

# If there are shared global definitions, read them in

if [ -f /etc/bashrc ]; then
   . /etc/bashrc
fi

# now some useful aliases

alias ls="ls -F"
alias who="who | sort"

alias cp="/bin/cp -i"
alias rm="/bin/rm -i"

# Note that these aliases for 'cp' and 'rm' are redundant
# because of the 'set -o noclobber' in my .bash_profile
# file. They're here to show you that there's more than one
# way to minimize the risk of accidentally stepping on and
# deleting files with these commands.
```

Again, any line that begins with a # is considered a comment. There are, therefore,
very few commands in this file: one that reads a systemwide .bashrc if it exists in
the /etc directory and the other that sets a couple of useful command aliases that I
prefer.

You learn all about aliases in the next hour, but for now you should know that the
format is alias *word=command* (or *commands*) to execute. When I enter ls, for
example, you can see that the shell has that aliased to ls -F, which saves me from
having to type the -F flag each time.

The shell also has conditional statements and various other commands to indicate
what commands to run. Here I'm using if [*expression*]; then to execute a
command only if the file it wants to access exists on the system. The condition
-f /etc/bashrc is true if the file exists. If not, the condition is false, and the shell
zips to the fi before resuming execution of the commands.

SUMMARY   If you're thinking that there are various ways to configure your shell, you are
              correct. You can have an incredibly diverse set of commands in both your
.profile and your .bashrc files, enabling you to customize many aspects of the shell
and the Unix environment. If you use the C shell or the tcsh shell, the configuration
information is kept in a similar file called .login.

Summary

Armed with the information learned in this hour about shells and shell environments, explore your own environment; examine your `.profile` and `.bashrc` files also.

Workshop

The Workshop summarizes the key terms you learned and poses some questions about the topics presented in this chapter. It also provides you with a preview of what you will learn in the next hour.

Key Terms

command alias A shorthand command mapping, with which you can define new command names that are aliases of other commands or sequences of commands. This is helpful for renaming commands so that you can remember them, or for having certain flags added by default.

command history A mechanism the shell uses to remember what commands you have entered already, and to allow you to repeat them without having to type the entire command again.

job control A mechanism for managing the various programs that are running. Job control enables you to push programs into the background and pull them back into the foreground as desired.

login shell The shell you use, by default, when you log in to the system.

subshell A shell other than the login shell.

Exercises

1. Draw lines to connect the original shells with their newer variants:

    sh

    ksh

    tcsh

    csh

    bash

2. What does `chsh` do?

3. What shell are you running? What shells are your friends on the system running?

13

4. What's the difference between the `.profile` and the `.bashrc` files?

5. What's the `csh` equivalent of the `bash` `.profile` file?

6. What aliases do you think could prove helpful for your daily Unix interaction?

Preview of the Next Hour

I hope this hour has whetted your appetite for learning more about the shell! In the next hour, you learn how to really customize the shell and make your interaction with Unix quite a bit easier. Topics include how to create command aliases, how to use the history mechanism and how to edit your previously edited commands interactively.

HOUR 14

Advanced Shell Interaction

The preceding hour gave you an overview of the different shells available in Unix. In this hour, you learn all about the bash shell and how to use it to your best advantage. You also learn valuable tips about working with the immediate predecessor to bash, the Korn shell, a popular alternative shell. The goal is for you to be able to customize your Unix environment to fit your working style.

Goals for This Hour

In this hour, you will learn

- How to turn on the bash and Korn shell history mechanism
- How to use bash history and ksh history to cut down on typing
- About command aliases in the bash and Korn shells
- Some power aliases for bash
- How to set custom prompts

This hour focuses on two key facets of the bash and Korn shells: the history mechanism and the command alias capability. I guarantee that within a few minutes of learning about these two functions, you will be certain that you couldn't have survived as happily in Unix without them. There are three ways to ensure that you don't enter commands more than once: Shell history enables you to repeat previous commands without re-entering them, an alias enables you to name one command as another, and shell scripts enable you to toss many commands into a file to be used as a single command. The last of these three, shell scripts, is covered in depth in the next lesson, "Shell Programming Overview."

One of the fun parts of Unix is that you can customize the prompt that greets you each time you use the system. There's no need to be trapped with a boring $ prompt anymore!

Which Shell Is Which?

Let's dig in and find some of the key additional capabilities of the most popular Unix command shells.

Task 14.1: The Shell History Mechanisms

DESCRIPTION If you went through school in the United States, you doubtless have heard the aphorism "Those who do not study history are doomed to repeat it." Unix stands this concept on its head. For Unix, the aphorism is best stated "Those who are aware of their history can easily repeat it."

Both bash and the Korn shell build a table of commands as you enter them and assign them each a command number. Each time you log in, the first command you enter is command #1, and the command number is incremented for each subsequent command you enter. You can review or repeat any previous command easily with just a few keystrokes.

Unlike earlier command shells such as C Shell, both bash and ksh have a default history list of 128 or more commands, plenty for anyone. To review your history in bash or ksh, you can use the history command. Actually, though, it's an alias, and the real command for both shells is the more cryptic fc -l.

ACTION

1. Log in to your system so that you have a shell prompt. If you're currently in the C Shell or a shell other than bash, this would be a great time to use chsh to change shells (see the preceding lesson, "Introduction to Command Shells," for more details on how to change your login shell).

```
% history 10
  270   more /etc/shells
  271   exit
  272   ls
  273
  274   grep '^taylor:' /etc/passwd
  275   grep '^taylor:' /etc/passwd | cut -d: -f7
  276   env
  277   printenv
  278   alias
  279   exit
  280   history 10
$
```

I just logged in. Where'd all this come from?

Notice command #279: exit. That's giving you the clue. The shell remembers
commands across different invocations, so the commands I see on this list are from
the last time I logged in! (In fact, #271 is exit too, so command #270 is actually
from two logins ago).

2. You can change whether or not your history is remembered across login sessions,
   and you can also change the size of the history list. Both of these are done with
   environment variables. Let's see if any of them are set. First:

   ```
   % echo $HISTSIZE $HISTFILESIZE500  500
   ```

   This indicates that bash is keeping track of the 500 most recent commands I've
   typed in, and will also store 500 commands in my history file so that they'll be
   automatically available next time I log in.

3. If 500 seems too large, this is easily set to a different value, ideally in the
   .bash_profile or .profile files:

   ```
   set HISTSIZE=200 ; export HISTSIZE
   ```

   If for any strange reason you don't seem to have any history (the default value is
   500, so having it explicitly set to zero would be a bit weird) then you can turn the
   feature on by specifying a HISTSIZE as shown above.

You shouldn't end up having to do anything to get your history mechanism enabled for
your shell, but now you know how, if it's necessary.

SUMMARY One final note: C Shell requires most people to fiddle with the environment variables too: Look for set history=200 or set savehist=200 in the .cshrc
(though a better alternative is to simply switch to bash instead!).

14

Task 14.2: Using History to Cut Down on Typing

DESCRIPTION There are three main mechanisms for working with the history list. You can specify a previous command by its command number, by the first word of the command, or, if you've set your command editing parameters, interactively on the command line.

Non-interactive history commands begin with an exclamation point. If the 33rd command you entered was the who command, for example, you can execute it by referring to its command number: Enter !33 at the command line. You can execute it also by entering one or more characters of the command: !w, !wh, or !who. Be careful though: The most recent match is executed without you seeing it, so if you typed who, but afterward typed an alias called w, it would be the latter that would match the !w sequence, but the former with !wh or !who.

A very useful shorthand is !!, which repeats the most recently executed command. Two other history references are valuable to know: !$ expands to the last word of the preceding command (which makes sense because $ always refers to the end of something, whether it be a line, the file, or, in this case, a command), and !* expands to all the words in the preceding command except the first word. So, for example, if I entered the command ls /usr /etc /dev and then immediately entered echo !*, it would be expanded automatically to echo /usr /etc /dev.

Korn shell offers a similar, though slightly more awkward, history repeat mechanism. You can repeat commands by number by specifying r*n*, where *n* is the command number (for example, r 33, but make sure you include the space). You can also repeat by name with r*name*, as in rwho to repeat the most recent who command. Without any arguments, r will repeat the preceding command.

ACTION

1. First, I need to spend a few minutes building up a history list by running various commands:

```
$ cat buckaroo
I found myself stealing a peek at my own watch and overhead
General Catbird's
aide give him the latest.
"He's not even here," went the conversation.
"Who?"
"Banzai."
"Where the hell is he?"
"At the hospital in El Paso."
```

```
"What? Why weren't we informed? What's wrong with him?"
$ who
taylor    ttyp0    Feb  1 11:50  (198.76.82.151)
$ date
Thu Feb  1 14:09:08 PST 2001
$ echo $HISTSIZE $HOME
500 /home/taylor$
```

2. Now I will check my history list to see what commands are squirreled away for later:

```
% history 10
  310  echo $HISTFILESIZE
  311  who
  312  ls
  313  vi buckaroo
  314  cat buckaroo
  315  who
  316  date
  317  echo $HISTSIZE $HOME
  318  history 10
```

3. To repeat the date command, I can specify its command number:

```
% !316
date
Thu Feb  1 14:11:36 PST2001
```

Notice that the shell shows the command I've entered as command number 316 (date) and then executes it. The ksh equivalent here would be r 316.

4. A second way to accomplish this repeat, a way that is much easier, is to specify the first letter of the command:

```
% !w
who
taylor    ttyp0    Feb  1 11:50  (198.76.82.151)
```

5. Now glance at the history list:

```
% history 10
  314  cat buckaroo
  315  who
  316  date
  317  echo $HISTSIZE $HOME
  318  history 10
  319  cat buckaroo
  320  date
  321  who
  322  history 10
```

14

Commands expanded by the history mechanism are stored as the expanded command, not as the history repeat sequence that was actually entered. Thus, this is an exception to the earlier rule that the history mechanism always shows what was previously entered. It's an eminently helpful exception, however!

History commands are quite helpful for people working on a software program. The most common cycle for programmers to repeat is edit-compile-run, over and over again. The commands Unix programmers use most often probably will look something like vi test.c, cc -o test test.c, and ./test, to edit, compile, and run the program, respectively. Using the shell history mechanism, a programmer easily can enter !v to edit the file, !c to compile it, and then !. to test it. As your commands become longer and more complex, this function proves more and more helpful.

6. It's time to experiment a bit with file wildcards:

```
% ls
Archives          awkscript          dickens.note     src
InfoWorld         bin                keylime.pie      temp
Mail              buckaroo           owl.c
News              buckaroo.confused  sample
OWL               cshrc              sample2x
```

Oops! I meant to specify the -F flag to ls. I can use !! to repeat the command; then I can add the flag:

```
% !! -F
ls -F
Archives/         awkscript          dickens.note     src/
InfoWorld/        bin/               keylime.pie      temp/
Mail/             buckaroo           owl.c
News/             buckaroo.confused  sample
OWL/              cshrc              sample2
```

The general idea of all these history mechanisms is that you specify a pattern that is replaced by the appropriate command in the history list. So you could enter echo !! to have the system echo the last command, and it would end up echoing twice. Try it.

Korn shell users will find that echo !! produces !! and that the ksh repeat-last-command of r also will fail. If your last command was echo r, the result will be r. Alas, there is no analogous shorthand to the convenient !! -F in csh. On the other hand, if FCEDIT is set to vi or EMACS, you can pop into the editor to change the command by typing fc.

I want to figure out a pattern or two that will let me specify both buckaroo files, the dickens file, and sample2, but not sample. This is a fine example of where the echo command can be helpful:

```
% echo b* d* s*
bin buckaroo buckaroo.confused dickens.note sample sample2 src
```

That's not quite it. I'll try again:

```
% echo bu* d* sa*
buckaroo buckaroo.confused dickens.note sample sample2
```

That's closer. Now I just need to remove the sample file:

```
% echo bu* d* sa*2
buckaroo buckaroo.confused dickens.note sample2
```

That's it. Now I want to compute the number of lines in each of these files. If I use the csh history mechanism, I can avoid having to enter the filenames again:

```
% wc -l !*
wc -l bu* d* sa*2
      36 buckaroo
      11 buckaroo.confused
      28 dickens.note
       4 sample2
      79 total
```

Notice that the !* expanded to the entire preceding command *except the very first word*.

7. What happens if I use !$ instead?

```
% wc -l !$
wc -l sa*2
       4 sample2
```

8. If you are using bash, here's where it truly shines! Make sure that the environment variable EDITOR is set to your preferred editor (use echo $EDITOR) and then set the editor preference within the shell to either vi or emacs. I prefer the former, so I use:

```
$ set -o vi
$
```

Now, any time you're entering a command, you can press the Escape key and be in bash history-edit command mode. The usual vi commands work, including h and l to move left and right; i and Escape to enter and leave insert mode; w, W, b, and B to zip about by words; and 0 and $ to move to the beginning or end of the line.

Much more useful are k and j, which replace the current command with the preceding or next, enabling you to zip through the history list.

14

If I'd just entered who and then ls, to append | wc -l to the who command, I could press the Escape key:

$_.

Now each time I type k, I will see the preceding command. Typing k one time reveals this:

$ls

Typing k a second time reveals this:

$who

That's the right command, so $ moves the cursor to the end of the line:

$who

Typing a appends, at which point I can add | wc -l like this:

$who **| wc -l**

Pressing Return results in ksh actually executing the command:

```
$ who | wc -l
       1
$_
```

SUMMARY The history mechanisms of the shells are wonderful time savers when you're working with files. I find myself using the bash !! and !*word* mechanisms daily either to build up complex commands (such as the preceding example, in which I built up a very complex command, step by step) or to repeat the most recently used edit commands. Table 14.1 summarizes the available bash history mechanisms. I encourage you to learn and use them. They will become second nature and save you lots of typing.

TABLE 14.1 Bash History Commands

Command	Function
!!	Repeat the preceding command.
!$	Repeat the last word of the preceding command.
!*	Repeat all but the first word of the preceding command.
^a^b	Replace a with b in the preceding command.
!n	Repeat command n from the history list.

Task 14.3: Command Aliases

DESCRIPTION If you think the history mechanism has the potential to save you typing, you'll be glad to learn about the command-alias mechanism in the bash and Korn shells. Using aliases, you can easily define new commands that do whatever you'd like, or even redefine existing commands to work differently, have different default flags, or more!

The general format for using the alias mechanism in both shells is alias
word=commands. If you enter alias without any specified words, the output shows a list
of aliases you have defined. If you enter alias *word*, the output lists the current alias, if
there is one, for the specified word.

ACTION

1. One of the most helpful aliases you can create specifies certain flags to ls so that
   each time you enter ls, the output will look as though you used the flags with the
   command. I like to have the -F flag set.

```
% ls
Archives           awkscript          dickens.note       src
InfoWorld          bin                keylime.pie        temp
Mail               buckaroo           owl.c
News               buckaroo.confused  sample
OWL                cshrc              sample2
```

Now I'll create a bash alias and try it again:

```
% alias ls='ls -CF'
% ls
Archives/          awkscript          dickens.note       src/
InfoWorld/         bin/               keylime.pie        temp/
Mail/              buckaroo           owl.c
News/              buckaroo.confused  sample
OWL/               cshrc              sample2
```

This is very helpful!

2. If you're coming from the DOS world, you might have found some of the Unix file
   commands confusing. In DOS, for example, you use DIR to list directories, REN to
   rename files, COPY to copy them, and so on. With aliases, you can re-create all
   those commands, mapping them to specific Unix equivalents:

```
% alias DIR 'ls -lF'
% alias REN 'mv'
% alias COPY 'cp -I'
% alias DEL 'rm -I'
% DIR
total 33
drwx------  2 taylor        512 Nov 21 10:39 Archives/
drwx------  3 taylor        512 Dec  3 02:03 InfoWorld/
drwx------  2 taylor       1024 Dec  3 01:43 Mail/
drwx------  2 taylor        512 Oct  6 09:36 News/
drwx------  4 taylor        532 Dec  6 18:31 OWL/
-rw-rw----  1 taylor        126 Dec  3 16:34 awkscript
drwx------  2 taylor        512 Oct 13 10:45 bin/
-rw-rw----  1 taylor       1393 Dec  5 18:48 buckaroo
```

14

```
-rw-rw----  1 taylor       458 Dec  4 23:22 buckaroo.confused
-rw-------  1 taylor      1339 Dec  2 10:30 cshrc
-rw-rw----  1 taylor      1123 Dec  5 18:16 dickens.note
-rw-rw----  1 taylor     12556 Nov 16 09:49 keylime.pie
-rw-rw----  1 taylor      8729 Dec  2 21:19 owl.c
-rw-rw----  1 taylor       199 Dec  3 16:11 sample
-rw-rw----  1 taylor       207 Dec  3 16:11 sample2
drwx------  2 taylor       512 Oct 13 10:45 src/
drwxrwx---  2 taylor       512 Nov  8 22:20 temp/
% COPY sample newsample
%
```

3. To see what aliases have been defined, use the `alias` command:

```
% alias
alias COPY='cp -i'
alias DEL='rm -i'
alias DIR='ls -1F'
alias REN='mv'alias ls='ls -F'
```

4. You could improve the alias for DIR by having the output of `ls` fed directly into the `more` program so that a directory listing with a lot of output will automatically pause at the end of each page. To redefine an alias, just define it again:

```
% alias DIR= 'ls -1F | more'
```

To confirm that the alias is set as you desire, try this:

```
% alias DIR
alias DIR='ls -1F | more'
```

> If you're defining just one command with an alias, you don't really need to use the quotation marks around the command argument. But what would happen if you entered `alias DIR ls -1F | more`? The alias would be set to `ls -1F`, and the output of the `alias` command would be fed to the `more` program, which is quite different from what you desired. Therefore, it's just good form to use the quotation marks and a good habit to get into.

SUMMARY Aliases are a great addition to any command shell, and with the arcane Unix commands, they also can be used to define full-word commands as synonyms. For example, if you decide you'd like the simplicity of remembering only the command `move` to move a file somewhere else, you could add the new alias `alias move='mv'` to your `.bashrc`, and the shell would include a new command.

Task 14.4: Some Power Aliases

DESCRIPTION Because I have used the C shell for many years, I have created various aliases to help me work efficiently. A few of the best are shown in this section.

ACTION

1. To see what aliases I have defined, I can use the same command I used earlier:

```
% alias
alias diff='/usr/bin/diff -c -w'
alias from='frm -n'
alias info='ssinfo'
alias ls='/bin/ls -F'
alias mail='Mail'
alias mailq='/usr/lib/sendmail -bp'
alias netcom='echo Netcom login: taylor;rlogin netcom.com'
alias newaliases='echo you mean newalias...'
alias rn='/usr/local/bin/rn -d$HOME -L -M -m -e -S -/'
alias ssinfo='echo "connecting..." ; rlogin oasis'
alias sunworld='echo SunWorld login: taylor;rlogin sunworld.com'
```

Recall that each of these aliases started out in my .bashrc file:

```
% grep alias .bashrc
alias   diff='/usr/bin/diff -c -w'
alias   from='frm -n'
alias   ll='ls -l'
alias   ls='/bin/ls -F'
alias   mail=Mail
alias   mailq='/usr/lib/sendmail -bp'
alias   netcom='echo Netcom login: taylor;rlogin netcom.com'
alias   sunworld='echo SunWorld login: taylor;rlogin sunworld.com'
alias   newaliases='echo you mean newalias...'
alias   rn='/usr/local/bin/rn -d$HOME -L -M -m -e -S -/'
# special aliases:
alias info='ssinfo'
alias ssinfo='echo "connecting..." ; rlogin oasis'
```

Also notice that the shell always keeps an alphabetically sorted list of aliases, regardless of the order in which they were defined.

2. Most of these aliases are easy to understand. For example, the first alias, diff, ensures that the command diff always has the default flags -c and -w. If I enter from, I want the system to invoke frm -n; if I enter ll, I want the system to invoke ls -l; and so on.

14

Some commands can cause trouble if entered, so creating an alias for each of those commands is a good way to stay out of trouble. For example, I have an alias for newaliases; if I accidentally enter that command, the system gently reminds me that I probably meant to use the newalias command:

```
% newaliases
you mean newalias...
```

3. I have created aliases for connecting to accounts on other systems. I like to name each alias after the system to which I'm connecting (for example, netcom, sunworld):

```
% alias netcom
alias netcom='echo Netcom login: taylor;rlogin netcom.com'
% alias sunworld
alias sunworld='echo SunWorld login: taylor;rlogin sunworld.com'
```

You can't enter alias netcom sunworld to list the netcom and sunworld aliases because that command means to replace the alias for netcom with the command sunworld.

Separating commands with a semicolon is the Unix way of having multiple commands on a single line, so when I enter the alias netcom, for example, it's as if I'd entered all these commands one after another:

```
echo Netcom login: taylor
rlogin netcom.com
```

SUMMARY Aliases make the shell such a great command interface. I can, and do, easily customize the set of commands and the default flags (look at all the options I set as default values for the r n command). I even turn off some commands that I don't want to enter accidentally. Let your imagination run wild with aliases. If you decide you really like one and you're using bash, add the alias to your .bashrc so that it's permanent (you can also put these into your .profile if you prefer). If you want to turn off an alias, you can use the unalias command, and it's gone until you log in again. For example, unalias netcom would temporarily remove from the shell the netcom alias shown earlier.

Task 14.5: Setting Custom Prompts

DESCRIPTION Up to this point, the command prompt I've seen is a boring $. It turns out that bash lets you set your prompt to just about any possible value, with PS1="value". Note that PS1 must be all uppercase for this to work.

ACTION

1. I'm getting tired of Unix being so inhospitable. Fortunately, I easily can change how it responds to me:

   ```
   % PS1="Yes, master? "
   Yes, master?
   ```

   That's more fun!

2. There are a lot of things you can tuck away in your prompt that can be of great help, and they all take the form of \X. The first useful variable is \w, which holds the current working directory:

   ```
   Yes, master? PS1="In \w, oh master: "
   In /users/taylor, oh master:
   ```

   What happens if I change directories?

   ```
   In /users/taylor, oh master: cd /
   In /, oh master:
   ```

   Cool, eh?

3. There are a ton of different variables you can add, the most useful of which are shown in Table 14.2.

TABLE 14.2   Special Values for the System Prompt

Value	Expands to
\d	The date in Weekday Month Day format (example: Thu Feb 1).
\H	The full system hostname (ex: limbo.intuitive.com)
\h	The system name (ex: limbo)
\n	Carriage return sequence (yes, you can have a two-line prompt, if you want!)
\s	The name of the shell (ex: bash2.4)
\T	Current time in HH:MM:SS format (ex: 04:23:28)
\t	Same as \T, but in 24 hour format (ex: 16:23:28)
\@	Current time in am/pm format (ex: 04:23pm)
\u	Username of current user (ex: taylor)
\w	Current working directory (ex: /home/taylor/bin)
\W	Base name of current directory (ex: bin)

14

Remember earlier how you learned about using the command numbers to repeat commands (like !37 to repeat command #37)? It turns out that there's an environment variable HISTCMD that contains the current command number. It can prove quite valuable with prompts:

```
In /, oh master: PS1="(\$HISTCMD) $ "
(132) $
```

The ksh equivalent is PS1="(\!) $ ".

The number in parentheses is the command number, as used by the shell history mechanism:

```
(132) $ echo hi
hi
(133) $ ls News
mailing.lists.usenet   usenet.1              usenet.alt
(134) $ !132
echo hi
hi
(135) $
```

Here's another example that you might find valuable:

```
(135) % PS1="\h (\$HISTCMD) % "
limbo (136) $
```

This is close to what I use myself, but I like to include the *basename* of the current directory. Basename means the closest directory name, so the basename of /home/taylor is taylor, for example. Also, I replace the dollar sign with a colon, which is a bit easier to read.

```
limbo (136) $ PS1="\h (\W) \$HISTCMD : "
limbo (taylor) 137 :
```

SUMMARY Experiment and find a set of variables that can help you customize your Unix prompt. I strongly recommend that you use command numbers to familiarize yourself with the history mechanism.

The command-alias capability is a helpful way to cut down on entering short commands time and again, but what if you have a series of 5 or 10 commands you often enter in sequence? That's where shell scripts can help.

Summary

This hour introduced you to many of the most powerful aspects of Unix command shells. Practice creating aliases and working with the history list to minimize your typing. Also, find a prompt you like and set it in your .bashrc or .profile so that it will be your default.

Workshop

The Workshop summarizes the key terms you learned and poses some questions about the topics presented in this chapter. It also provides you with a preview of what you will learn in the next hour.

Key Terms

basename   The closest directory name. For example, the basename of /usr/home/ taylor is taylor.

command number   The unique number by which the shell indexes all commands. You can place this number in your prompt by using \$HISTCMD and use it with the history mechanism as !command-number.

Exercises

1. How do you tell bash that you want it to remember the last 30 commands during a session, and to remember the last 10 commands across login sessions?

2. Assume that you get the following output from entering history:

   ```
   1    ls -CF
   2    who | grep andrews
   3    wc -l < test
   4    cat test
   5    history
   ```

   What would be the result of entering each of the following history commands?

   ```
   !2    !w    !wh    echo !1
   ```

3. Some Unix systems won't enable you to do the following. What danger do you see lurking in this alias?

   ```
   alias who    who -a
   ```

4. Which of the following aliases do you think would be useful?

   ```
   alias alias='who'
   alias ls='cp'
   alias copy='cp -'
   alias logout='vi'
   alias vi='logout'
   alias bye='logout'
   ```

14

5. Set your prompt to the following value. Remember that 33 should be replaced with the appropriate command number each time.

   `#33 - I know lots about Unix. For example:`

6. Find and examine two shell scripts that are found in either the `/bin` or the `/usr/bin` directories on your system. Remember, any line beginning with a # is a comment.

Preview of the Next Hour

In the next hour, you learn how to get even more out of your shell. You learn about shell programming and how to create shell programs on-the-fly.

HOUR 15

Shell Programming Overview

In the preceding hour, you learned about a few of the options available to you when you use a command shell. Using these shells enables you to enter commands for Unix. What most people don't realize when they first start using Unix is that these shells are also programming environments and that you can write your own shell programs.

Goals for This Hour

In this hour, you will learn all about

- Shell variables
- Shell arithmetic
- Comparison functions
- Conditional expressions
- Looping expressions
- bash functions

Because shells are really just interpreted languages, any sequence of commands you want to run can be placed in a file and run regularly. This is a shell program. Originally, Unix experts wrote their shell scripts for the Bourne shell (/bin/sh) because that shell was standard on every Unix platform. More recently, the extra flexibility and capabilities of the bash shell have made it a popular alternative, and that's what I use in this chapter.

> I strongly urge you to look at the shells you have available. The best shell to use is the one that makes you the most productive.

Build Your Own Commands

Unix is remarkably capable and includes hundreds of different commands, but sometimes that's not sufficient. When it becomes time to create your own unique commands, a simple shell script often suffices.

Task 15.1: Shell Variables

DESCRIPTION   Programming languages usually include variables, and the shell naturally does too. Variables are just tags to identify values that can change as a program is used. In the shell, these variables can take a single value and are always interpreted as strings. Even numeric values are strings to the shell.

You can use any string-manipulation command, such as sed or cut, to change a shell variable.

ACTION

1. Here is an example of setting the value of a shell variable:

   ```
   $ color=blue
   ```

   This sets the variable color to the string blue. One can output the value of any variable with the echo command:

   ```
   $ echo $color
   blue
   ```

   This also indicates how to reference a shell variable: It must be preceded by the dollar sign ($). This can cause some problems.

2. If you are using a shell variable as a prefix, and you want to append text immediately, you might think that this would work:

   ```
   $ leaning='anti-'
   $ echo Joe is basically $leaningtaxes
   ```

15

The output here is just Joe is basically. The shell does not know to differentiate between the variables $leaning and what appears to be a new variable, $leaningtaxes. Because no value is assigned to $leaningtaxes, the output is a NULL string. To solve this problem, enclose the variable in curly braces.

```
$ echo Joe is basically ${leaning}taxes
Joe is basically anti-taxes
```

If leaning is undefined, the output might not make sense. It would be Joe is basically taxes. Fortunately, the shell provides a means to have a default value if a variable is undefined:

```
$ echo Joe is basically ${leaning:-pro }taxes
Joe is basically pro taxes
```

3. If leaning is undefined, the : - syntax tells the shell to use the following string, including the space character, instead of leaving the output blank. This does not assign a new value to the variable. If you need to use the variable repeatedly, you might want to assign a new value to it, if it is undefined. The := character does this:

```
$ echo Joe is basically ${leaning:=pro }taxes and ${leaning}spending.
Joe is basically pro taxes and pro spending.
```

The first interpretation of the variable finds it undefined, so the shell assigns "pro " (pro with a trailing space) to the variable and outputs that. The second time the variable is interpreted, it has the value "pro ."

4. Variables often are assigned by the read command. This assigns an individual word to a specified variable, with the last variable in the list being assigned the remaining words.

```
$ read city state message
CapeMay, New Jersey Hi Mom!
$ echo $city is city
CapeMay, is city
$ echo $state is state
New is state
$ echo $message is message
Jersey Hi Mom! is message
```

As you can see, only New is assigned to state. The best way around this is to escape the space (make sure that the space isn't interpreted as separating variable values) with a backslash:

```
$ read city state message
CapeMay, New\ Jersey Hi Mom!
$ echo $city is city
CapeMay, is city
$ echo $state is state
```

```
New Jersey is state
$ echo $message is message
Hi Mom! is message
```

This can be a bit tricky at first.

5. The third common way to assign variables is from command-line arguments. The shell has built-in variables to access the command line. If you've written a script to copy files and named it copy-files, you might want to list all the files on the command line:

```
$ copy-files file1 file2 file3
```

The program would access these arguments as $1, $2, and $3:

```
cp $1 destination
cp $2 destination
cp $3 destination
```

The $0 variable is a special case for looking at the command name, and $* lists all the command-line variables.

SUMMARY   The standard data in any shell program is the variable. These variables can be assigned in several ways: directly assigned, read in from a user's typing, or assigned from the command line. The shell also provides means to provide some default manipulation of variables.

Task 15.2: Shell Arithmetic

DESCRIPTION   Although the shell treats variables as strings, methods are available for performing some basic mathematics on shell variables.

ACTION

1. If a variable is assigned a numeric value, you can perform some basic arithmetic on the value by using the command expr. This command takes several arguments to perform arithmetic:

```
$ expr 1 + 1
2
```

Arguments must be separated by spaces, and must be present, for the expr command to work. If a variable is undefined or does not have a value assigned to it (sometimes called *zero length*), the result is a syntax error. Here is where the : - syntax is particularly helpful:

```
$ echo $noval

$ expr $noval + 1
expr: syntax error
$ expr ${noval:-0} + 1
1
```

expr also supports subtraction, multiplication, integer division, and remainders. These are illustrated here:

```
$ expr 11 - 5
6
$ expr 11 \* 5
55
$ expr 11 / 5
2
$ expr 11 % 5
1
```

Note that I had to escape the asterisk with a backslash. If I didn't do that, the shell would expand it to be the list of files in the current directory, and the expr program wouldn't understand that.

2. You can assign the results of the arithmetic to other variables by enclosing the command in backquotes:

```
$ newvalue=`expr ${oldvalue:-0} + 1`
```

If *oldvalue* is assigned, it is incremented by 1. If not, *newvalue* is set to 1. This is useful when looping through data for a number of iterations.

3. The expr command also can work with complex arithmetic. You can write an expression to add two numbers and then multiply by a third number. Normally, you would need to worry about operator precedence, but expr is not that sophisticated:

```
$ expr 11 + 5 \* 6
41
```

Instead, you just group the operations in parentheses:

```
$ expr \( 11 + 5 \) \* 6
96
```

This command first adds 11 and 5, and then multiplies the result by 6. Because the parentheses are important shell characters, I need to escape them with backslashes.

SUMMARY The expr command is a very useful command for performing arithmetic in any shell. Strings must be numbers, or errors will occur; the results of the expr command can be assigned to other variables.

> The expr command is much more powerful than described here; it includes the capability to perform logical operations and perform operations on strings. For more information, check the man page.

Task 15.3: Comparison Functions

DESCRIPTION   Often, when writing a program, you may want the actions taken to be dependent on certain values. A simple example is the rm -i command, where the -i flag tells rm to prompt you before deleting a file. Type y, and a file is deleted. Type n, and it remains. The shell also has similar options. These next two tasks cover how to use those options.

Just as expr is a powerful program for solving arithmetic expressions and performing operations on strings, the test command can be used to perform comparisons. test will perform comparisons on strings, as well as numeric values. test will always return zero if the condition is true, and non-zero if it is false. It is standard for Unix shells to use these values as true and false.

test is used for three types of operations: numeric comparisons, string comparisons, and status tests for the file system. First up are the numeric comparisons.

ACTION

1. Because the shell treats the less-than and greater-than symbols as redirection characters, they can't be used within the test command. Instead, I have a series of two-letter flags, as described in Table 15.1. These flags are always placed between the two arguments:

   test 3 -eq 4

   This example would return non-zero because 3 and 4 are not equal.

TABLE 15.1   Test Operators

Comparison Flag	Meaning
-eq	True if the numbers are equal
-ne	True if the numbers are not equal
-lt	True if the first number is less than the second number
-le	True if the first number is less than or equal to the second number
-gt	True if the first number is greater than the second number
-ge	True if the first number is greater than or equal to the second number

15

2. You can use the result of `expr`, or any other command that returns a numeric value, in `test`. There is also a special expression in test, `-l` *string*, which returns the length of a string. So you can write the following tests, after setting a couple of useful variables:

```
value=3 ; string="my horse Horace"
test $value -eq -l $string
test `wc -l filename` -ge 10000
```

The first test determines whether `$value` is the same as the length of `$string`. The second takes a count of the number of lines in a file, and it is `true` if 10,000 or more lines are present.

3. The second type of comparison is on strings. The first two are unary, which means they apply to only one string:

```
test -z $string
test -n $string
```

The first test is true if the string is of zero length or undefined. The second is true if the string has some content.

4. The next two tests compare strings with each other. The simple exclamation point and equals sign (commonly used to mean "not!" in Unix) are used for these comparisons:

```
test alphabet = Alphabet
test alphabet != Alphabet
```

The first is false; the second is true.

> When comparing string variables, you might see something like this:
>
> ```
> test X$string1 = X$string2
> ```
>
> The presence of the X prevents a null string from confusing test. If string1 is null, and string2 is string, you'd expand to this:
>
> ```
> test X = Xstring
> ```
>
> Without the X, the test would be expanded to this:
>
> ```
> test = string
> ```
>
> This is a syntax error. The other option is to enclose the string in quotation marks:
>
> ```
> test "$string1" = "$string2"
> ```
>
> That expands to this:
>
> ```
> test "" = "string"
> ```

5. The final test operators work on the file system. They are single flags, as listed in Table 15.2, followed by a path.

TABLE 15.2   The Most Useful File System Flags

Option	Meaning
-L	True if the file exists and points to another file (symbolic link)
-d	True if the file is a directory
-e	True if the file exists
-f	True if the file exists and is a regular file
-g	True if the file exists and runs in a specific group
-r	True if the file exists and is readable
-s	True if the file exists and has data
-w	True if the file exists and is writable
-x	True if the file exists and is executable

Here's a sample test:

```
test -d $HOME/bin
```

This checks to see whether you have a directory named `bin` in your home directory. The most common flags you see in shell programs are the `-f` flag and the `-d` flag. The others are used only in unusual situations.

6. The file system also has three binary comparisons. The `-ef` test determines whether the two files are the same. (When you create a link between files, this is true.) The `-nt` flag is true if the first file is newer than the second, and the `-ot` flag is true if the first file is older than the second. You might see a test in a looping statement like this:

```
test file1 -ot file2
```

This test compares the two files, and it is true if *file1* is older than *file2*. If you are waiting for data to appear in *file1*, you might use this test to cause a shell program to wait for the first file to appear.

7. Test commands can be negated with the exclamation point, or combined with `-a` for *and*, and `-o` for *or*. You can make arbitrarily long conditions, at the cost of readability:

```
test $var -eq 0 -a ! -e file
```

This checks to see whether the value of `$var` is zero, and whether *file* exists.

8. test also has a second form. Instead of explicitly calling test, you can surround the condition by square brackets:

```
[ -f file ]
```

Doing this makes shell programs considerably more readable. Indeed, you'll rarely see test as shown here.

SUMMARY One of the most used commands in shell programming is the test command. It is essential to understanding the next two tasks, conditional expressions and loops.

Task 15.4: Conditional Expressions

DESCRIPTION Sometimes, when writing a program, you want to perform an action only when another action returns the value true. Shell programming provides you with this capability by way of the if command, the case command, and two special command separators.

ACTION

1. The if command is the most commonly seen conditional command. It takes the following form:

```
if
    command-block
then
    command-block
fi
```

A *command-block* is a sequence of one or more shell commands. The first command-block is always executed. The return value of the last statement executed is used to determine whether the second block is executed. The most commonly used command at the end of the first command-block is the test command in its [ ] notation:

```
if
    [ -f $file ]
then
    echo $file is a regular file
fi
```

This if statement notifies the user that a file is a regular file. If the file is not a regular file (such as a directory), you don't see output.

2. Sometimes, you might want output regardless of the situation. In the preceding case, you might be interested in the status of the file even if it is not a regular file. The `if` command can expand with the `else` keyword to provide that second option:

```
if
    [ -f $file ]
then
    echo $file is a regular file
else
    echo $file is not a regular file
fi
```

This statement provides output regardless of the status of the file.

3. For these simple tests and output, the shell provides a second, quicker means of executing the `if` statement. If the two commands are joined by `&&`, the second command is executed if the first command is evaluated as true. If the commands are joined by `||`, the second command is executed if the first is false. The preceding command would, therefore, look like:

```
[ -f $file ] && echo $file is a regular file
[ -f $file ] || echo $file is not a regular file
```

This shorthand is very useful but can be confusing for a novice. If you accidentally place a space between the characters, you have a wildly different command; the `&` will run the first command at the same time as the `echo`, and the `|` will pipe the output of the test (none) to the `echo`.

4. If you want even more information, your `if` statement can have more than two options. You need multiple tests and the `elif` keyword:

```
if
    [ -f $file ]
then
    echo $file is a regular file
elif
    [ -d $file ]
then
    echo $file is a directory
else
    echo $file is not a regular file or a directory.
fi
```

This command first tests to see whether the file is a regular file; if not, it checks to see whether it is a directory; if it is neither, it gives output. You can expand any `if` statement with an unlimited number of `elif` branches.

One nice thing is that you can indent your code to make things easier to understand, and you can also compress the statements themselves, so the preceding listing could be more compactly written as:

15

```
if [ -f $file ] ; then
  echo $file is a regular file
elif [ -d $file ] ; then
  echo $file is a directory
else
  echo $file is not a regular file or a directory
fi
```

Note that the then should appear on a second line, so the semicolon after the expression is necessary (indeed, many shell programmers leave the then on its own line, even though it's not quite as space efficient).

5. At some point, if-then-else code can become confusing. When you have many possible branches, you should use the case command. The syntax is more complicated than that for if:

```
case string in
pattern) command-block ;;
pattern) command-block ;;
...
esac
```

If you were looking for possible values for a variable, you could use case:

```
echo What do you want:
read var remainder
case $var in
house)    echo The price must be very high;;
car)      echo The price must be high;;
popsicle) echo The price must be low;;
*)        echo I do not know the price;;
esac
```

This case statement follows an input request and gives the user a rough idea of the price. A case list can contain any number of items.

Here's another example, a mini file command:

```
case $filename in
  *.gif) echo Graphics Interchange Format ;;
  *.jpg) echo Joint Photographic Experts Group ;;
  *.png) echo Progressive Networking Group ;;
  *.tif) echo Tagged Interchange Format ;;
  *.scx) echo Screen Capture format ;;
  *)     echo unknown format ${filename#*.}
esac
```

In both of the previous examples, the pattern-matching algorithms used are for wildcards. Also note the bash variable trick to extract the filename suffix in the last conditional with the #*. modifier to the filename variable reference. To extract the other side (just the filename without the suffix) you could use:

```
${filename%.*}
```

6. Here's a simple sample shell script where the `read` command and `if` statements could be useful together:

```
echo "Delete which file? "
read filename
if [ ! -f $filename ] ; then
  echo Can\'t delete $filename since it doesn't exist
else
  echo Deleting file $filename
  /bin/rm $filename
fi
```

It prompts for the filename, and `then` tests to see whether the file exists before it tries to delete it with the `/bin/rm` invocation.

There are two basic conditional expressions, and a third shortcut. You can test a condition and perform alternative actions by using `if` statements and their shortcuts. Or you can compare strings and perform any number of actions by using the `case` statement.

Task 15.5: Looping Expressions

DESCRIPTION   If you want to run the same set of commands many times, instead of writing them once for each time, you are better off using looping commands. There are two types of loops: the determinate loop and the indeterminate loop.

A *determinate* loop is one where you know exactly how many times you want to execute the commands before you enter the loop. Stepping through a list of files is a good example; you might not know the exact number of files, but when you do, you can start the loop for those files.

An *indeterminate* loop is one where you need to keep executing a command-block until a condition is no longer `true`. You might be either waiting for something or performing a series of modifications to reach a goal.

ACTION

1. The usual command for a determinate loop is the `for` command. It has the following syntax:

```
for var in list
do
     command-block
done
```

You can build any list you like. It could be a sequence of numbers or the output of a command. Earlier, I mentioned looping through a list of files. This is performed with the following loop:

15

```
for var in `ls`
do
    if
        [ -f $var ]
    then
        echo $var is a regular file
    fi
done
```

This steps through all the files listed in the `ls` output, showing only regular files.

A modification to the preceding code is that because you're in a shell script, you can use shell expansion to accomplish some things too. Instead of using ls, how about the following?

```
for var in * ; do
    if [ -f $var ] ; then
    echo $var is a regular file
 fi
done
```

You can also see in this example how reformatting the script can make it considerably more readable too!

2. A nice trick that can be performed in a shell program is to step through the list of command-line arguments. The for loop provides a neat mechanism: If the in *list* part is omitted from the command, the for loop steps through the list of command-line arguments.

```
j=0
for i
do
    j=`expr $j + 1`
     echo $i is argument $j
done
```

This snippet steps through the command-line arguments and identifies where they are in the order of arguments.

In both cases, when you enter the for loop, you know how many times you need to run the loop. If you look at the case where you are waiting for something to happen, though, you need to use a different loop. The while loop is the solution for this problem.

3. In Task 15.3, I mentioned the case where you might want to wait on the arrival of a file. This echoes a real-world situation I recently faced. We were processing a program log file, but we did not know exactly when it would be placed in our directory. We tried to set up the job to run after the file arrived, but this approach still ran into problems.

Using the while loop, we solved the problem. At the end of the execution of our script, we created a checkpoint file. At the beginning, if the checkpoint file were newer than the log file, we would wait. Programmatically, that is:

```
while
    [ checkpoint -nt logfile ]
do
    sleep 60
done
```

This program would wait one minute between checks. If the new logfile had not been written, the program would go back to sleep for a minute.

4. while loops also can be used in a determinate manner. In the case where you are not concerned with a variable's value, but know a count of times to run a command-block, you can use a counter to increment through the number:

```
i=0
while
    [ $i -lt 100 ]
do
    i=`expr "$i" + 1`
    commands
done
```

This is certainly easier than listing 100 items in a list!

SUMMARY The shell provides two convenient mechanisms for running a group of commands repeatedly. These loop commands are useful from both the command line and a program.

Task 15.6: bash Functions

DESCRIPTION Much of what's been covered in this chapter has been what I characterize as *flow control*: ways to specify what command to execute in what set of conditions. What's interesting about using bash as a programmatic shell is that you can actually create your own functions and use them throughout your scripting, as if you were in a more formal (powerful) programming environment.

The greatest value of functions is that they give you the ability to specify and access parameters.

Let's get our feet wet and see how they can significantly help you develop powerful shell scripts!

ACTION

1. Functions are defined as follows:

```
function functionname
{
    shell commands
}
```

In some sense, all command aliases, as discussed earlier in the book, are really simple functions. Here's an example:

```
$ alias ls
alias ls='ls -F'
```

This can be rewritten as the function

```
function ls
{
    /bin/ls -F
}
```

and it would work in almost exactly the same way. The biggest difference is that there's no way to specify any other arguments to the ls command with the function, as written.

2. To add parameters, I simply add $* after the -F flag:

```
function ls {
/bin/ls -F $*
}
```

Now a command like ls /tmp will work as desired!

3. Of course, the real value of using functions rather than aliases is that you can dramatically increase the level of sophistication of your new command.

As an example, I'd like to have a command that expands on the earlier snippet which told you the file type based on filename suffix. In the new version, I'd like to actually output some HTML fragments if the graphic can be viewed in a Web browser (that is, if it's a GIF or JPG image). The new version would also offer clickable links to HTML files found and would enable users to click to step into directories as they browse the system.

Here's my first stab at the problem, pre-functions:

```
#!/usr/local/bin/bash
# A Web-friendly directory browser that knows
# how to show graphic images:
```

```
directory=${QUERY_STRING:-$HOME}
iamcalled="browse.cgi"
webroot="/web"

echo "Content-type: text/html"
echo ""

echo "<H2>Directory $directory</H2><UL>"

cd $webroot/$directory

for filename in *
do
  case $filename in
    *.gif ) echo "<LI><IMG SRC=$directory/$filename>"
            echo "<BR><TT>$filename</TT></LI>" ;;
    *.jpg ) echo "<LI><IMG SRC=$directory/$filename>"
            echo "<BR><TT>$filename</TT></LI>" ;;
    *.htm ) echo "<LI><A HREF=$filename>$filename</A></LI>" ;;
    *.html) echo "<LI><A HREF=$filename>$filename</A></LI>" ;;
    *)      if [ -d $filename ] ; then
              echo "<LI><TT><A "
                        echo "HREF=$iamcalled?$directory/$filename>"
              echo "[$filename]</A></TT></LI>"
            else
              echo "<LI><TT>$filename</TT></LI>"
            fi
            ;;
  esac
done

echo "</UL>"

exit 0
```

This works well, but there's much duplication of individual lines in the script, which is a perfect use for a function or two.

The first one I'll define is showname:

```
function showname
{
  echo "<TT><B>$1</B></TT></LI>"
}
```

That's simple enough, but now we have the statement in one spot, rather than three, making it easier to maintain and expand the script.

4. One more refinement: Case conditionals can have multiple conditions, which can
make this considerably simpler:

```bash
#!/usr/local/bin/bash
# A Web-friendly directory browser that knows
# how to show graphic images:

directory=${QUERY_STRING:-$HOME}
iamcalled="browse.cgi"
webroot="/web"

function showname
{
  echo "<TT><B>$1</B></TT></LI>"
}

echo "Content-type: text/html"
echo ""

echo "<H2>Directory $directory</H2><UL>"

cd $webroot/$directory

for filename in *
do
  case $filename in
    *.gif|*.jpg )
            echo "<LI><IMG SRC=$directory/$filename><BR>"
            showname $filename
            ;;
    *.htm|*.html )
            echo "<LI><A HREF=$filename>$filename</A></LI>" ;;
    *)      if [ -d $filename ] ; then
              echo \
            "<LI><TT><A HREF=$iamcalled?$directory/$filename>"
              echo "[$filename]</A></TT></LI>"
            else
              echo "<LI>"
              showname $filename
            fi
            ;;
  esac
done

echo "</UL>"

exit 0
```

15

5. Of course, the entire conditional and such could be poured into the function and then the code becomes even cleaner. In fact, the main routine is just the following:

```
echo "Content-type: text/html"
echo ""

echo "<H2>Directory $directory</H2><UL>"

showdirectory $directory

echo "</UL>"
```

That's not too bad. All the complex case statement conditionals are tucked neatly into the showdirectory function:

```
function showdirectory
{
  if [ ! -d $webroot/$1 ] ; then
    echo "Error: no directory $1 found"
    exit 0
  fi

  cd $webroot/$1

  for filename in *
  do
    case $filename in
      *.gif|*.jpg )
            echo "<LI><IMG SRC=$directory/$filename><BR>"
            showname $filename
            ;;
      *.htm|*.html )
            echo "<LI><A HREF=$filename>$filename</A></LI>" ;;
      *)      if [ -d $filename ] ; then
              echo \
            "<LI><TT><A HREF=$iamcalled?$directory/$filename>"
              echo "[$filename]</A></TT></LI>"
            else
              echo "<LI>"
              showname $filename
            fi
            ;;
    esac
done
}
```

You can see that it's now easy to add error checking in the function (the -d test to see whether it's a directory before moving there with the cd command).

SUMMARY   Functions can be quite complex, but even simple functions can help you get the most out of your shell interaction.

Summary

In this hour, you just skimmed the basics of shell programming. You were introduced to the control structures of the shell and to two important commands. You can learn much more about shell programming; *Sams Teach Yourself Shell Programming in 24 Hours* is one place you can look.

15

Workshop

The Workshop summarizes the key terms you learned and poses some questions about the topics presented in this chapter. It also provides you with a preview of what you will learn in the next hour.

Key Terms

command block   A list of one or more shell commands that are grouped in a conditional or looping statement.

conditional expression   This is an expression that returns either `true` or `false`.

determinate loop   A loop where the number of times the loop is run is known before the loop is started.

expression   This is a command that returns a value.

indeterminate loop   A loop where the number of times the loop is run is not known before the loop is started.

loop   This is a sequence of commands that are repeatedly executed while a condition is true.

variables   These are names to label data that can change during the execution of a program.

zero-length variable   A variable that does not have a value assigned to it.

Exercises

1. How would you read in an address in a shell program? How would you read in a name?

2. If you read in the number of people who read a newspaper, and the number of people who subscribe to a particular paper, how would you determine the ratio of subscribers to readers?

3. How do you know whether a file has data?

4. How do you wait for data to be placed in a file?

Preview of the Next Hour

In the next hour, you are introduced to two great Unix commands that are critical additions to any shell programmer toolkit: awk and sed.

Hour **16**

Slicing and Dicing Command-Pipe Data

By this point, you've learned enough about Unix to be able to build quite sophisticated command-line pipes, sequences of standard commands that offer flexibility and power. You need to add a couple of key tools to your toolkit, however, and they're the focus of this lesson.

The first and most powerful of the tools is awk, a programming system build specifically to work with data streams. You can build very complex processing systems in awk, but in fact the most common awk programs are typically just a line or two long.

Adding to the explanation of awk will be three additional pipeline commands that you will doubtless find essential for your toolbox: sed, a stream editor; tr, a character mapping facility; and cut, a utility that makes it remarkably easy to slice individual columns of data out of a pipeline of information.

Goals for This Hour

In this hour, you will

- Learn about the awk programming pystem
- Explore how to use cut in pipes
- Compare sed and tr for in-line transformations

There's one interesting characteristic of awk that's worth mentioning before we go further: It's a powerful programming language, and you can use it to duplicate many of the actual utilities that are an essential part of the Unix operating system. In a moment, I'll show you how to duplicate the wc command with a few lines of awk.

Later in the book, we'll explore the Perl programming language and how it's integrated into modern Unix systems. Like awk, Perl has the ability to duplicate many of the most common Unix commands. Indeed, Perl is considerably more powerful and sophisticated than awk.

I don't recommend rewriting existing commands, but it's good to know which of the tools in the Unix toolbox are actually all-purpose utilities rather than focused on a single, specific task.

The awk Programming System

Whether it's C, Pascal, BASIC, Java, or even Fortran, all programming languages have their forte, the area where they really shine. If it's BASIC, it's simple introductory programming. If it's Java, it's platform-independent software. awk is a hybrid, living somewhere in the middle between simple shell scripts and these sophisticated languages. It doesn't have many features and characteristics of a formal programming environment, but in its own way it's tremendously powerful and ideal for in-line data processing.

Task 16.1: Learning to Use awk

DESCRIPTION The foundation of awk is that all awk programs contain a pattern followed by a command. If you skip the pattern, it applies to all lines in the data stream. If you skip the command, all matching lines are printed (sent to the output data stream).

As a very simple example, the program NF == 3 (yep, that's all you'd need for this program!) will print all lines of input that have exactly three fields. The program $1 > 3 { print $1 } will print the first field of all lines where that field has a numeric value greater than three.

Let's take a closer look.

ACTION

1. I want to figure out the average size of all the e-mail files on a new system I've been building. To accomplish this, I'll start with `ls` to get the file sizes:

```
$ ls -l
total 8474
-rw-r--r--  1 taylor  taylor     3111 Dec 14 16:09 baby-responses
-rw-r--r--  1 taylor  taylor    19930 Dec 14 16:09 barbara
-rw-r--r--  1 taylor  taylor   298719 Dec 14 16:09 dunlap
-rw-r--r--  1 taylor  taylor     5758 Dec 14 16:09 evan
-rw-r--r--  1 taylor  taylor    14577 Dec 14 16:09 glee
-rw-r--r--  1 taylor  taylor     1610 Dec 14 16:09 hbrayman
-rw-r--r--  1 taylor  taylor    10788 Dec 14 16:09 jkindred
-rw-r--r--  1 taylor  taylor  2746614 Dec 14 16:09 mail.sent
-rw-r--r--  1 taylor  taylor    18106 Dec 14 16:09 mbeaudoin
-rw-r--r--  1 taylor  taylor     6753 Dec 14 16:09 pennyln
-rw-r--r--  1 taylor  taylor   128815 Dec 14 16:09 permission
-rw-r--r--  1 taylor  taylor  1011092 Dec 14 16:09 taylor
-rw-r--r--  1 taylor  taylor    17549 Dec 14 16:09 wellnitz
$
```

As you can see, the lines of output from `ls` are very consistent, and if you assume that "one or more spaces without any other characters between them" is the separator between fields, the 5th field is the size of the file.

2. Now, let's use awk to extract the fifth field:

```
$ ls -l | awk '{print $5}'

3111
19930
298719
5758
14577
1610
10788
2746614
18106
6753
128815
1011092
17549
$
```

Pretty simple, isn't it?

It's not quite what I want, however, because the very first line of output from `ls` is a summary of the blocks taken up by the entire directory (the "Total 8474" line), and the awk script sees that and counts it as a line, even though it doesn't have a fifth field. If we leave this as-is, the eventual average mailbox size will be wrong because it'll be taking "n+1" records into account.

3. The standard Unix way to solve this would be to drop something else into the pipeline that'll extract that line, or filter just the lines of valid data. That might look like this:

```
$ ls -l | grep taylor | awk '{print $5}'
3111
19930
298719
5758
14577
1610
10788
2746614
18106
6753
128815
1011092
17549
$
```

This works, but it's not very elegant, particularly because awk can do the job.

4. The awk solution would be to apply a pattern that uses the special NF (number of fields) variable:

```
$ ls -l | awk 'NF > 2 { print $5 }'
3111
19930
298719
5758
14577
1610
10788
2746614
18106
6753
128815
1011092
17549
$
```

Great. Here you can see a pattern (NF > 2) and a statement (print $5) combined to make a very powerful and very simple addition to our pipeline.

5. Now let's make our script a bit more sophisticated. It needs to total all the sizes and count how many files it counted too. Those statements are added within the curly brackets, but before I get to that point, I'm going to simplify things by putting the longer awk script in its own file.

Here's how it looks once I've added the two counting variables:

```
$ cat average.awk
NF > 2 { count += 1
         totalsize += $5
       }
$
```

There's no point in running this yet, because there isn't any output. Try it yourself, you'll see what I mean.

16

> The += notation is a shorthand way of saying "add the following value to the current value of the variable," and it saves having to type count = count + 1 and totalsize = totalsize + 1.

6. To add output, I need to add an END block. END is a special pattern that is matched once after every line of input is processed:

```
$ cat average.awk
NF > 2 { count += 1
         totalsize += $5
       }

END { print "Counted " count " mailboxes"
      print "average size = " totalsize/count
    }
$
```

That's all that's needed to compute the average file size. It's invoked with the -f flag to awk:

```
$ ls -l | awk -f average.awk
Counted 14 mailboxes
average size = 305969
$
```

Where there's an END, there's also a BEGIN statement, if you need to initialize variables prior to the script being run.

This demonstrates a very typical use of the awk command and also shows how most sophisticated pipelines are built one step at a time.

7. Now let's look at some of the common one-liner programs for which you'll find awk particularly useful.

One quick note first: You've already seen two special variables in this simple awk script: NF is the number of fields in a line of input, and $5 is the fifth field in each line. It turns out that there's also a NR, which contains the current record number, and, in the END block, the total number of records (lines) encountered.

The $5 variable is also an instance of a general naming scheme: $n will give you the *n*th field, and $0 is the entire line.

8. How many lines are in the input stream?

   ```
   'END {print NR}'
   ```

9. Print the 8th line of input only?

   ```
   'NR == 8'
   ```

10. Print just the last field of each line?

    ```
    '{ print $NF }'
    ```

    (That last one requires a wee bit of explanation. Because NF is the number of fields, the reference $NF is evaluated as the last field. If the input line has 5 fields, NF=5 and $NF is the contents of the fifth field.)

11. Print the maximum number of fields in any line?

    ```
    'NF > maxnf { maxnf = NF }  END { print maxnf }'
    ```

    (Again, notice that you can compress scripts onto a single line if it's easier to type.)

12. One more example: You should have tried the wc (word count) command, and you know that it returns the number of characters, words, and lines in its input stream. It turns out that duplicating this with an awk script is remarkably easy:

    ```
    $ cat wc.awk
    { chars += length($0) + 1    # 1 for the carriage return
      words += NF;
    }

    END {
      print chars " characters, " words " words, and " NR " lines."
    }
    $
    ```

    It can be used just as we used the earlier script:

    ```
    $ ls -l | awk -f wc.awk
    908 characters, 137 words, and 16 lines.
    ```

    To make sure that the results are accurate, here's the same ls output run through the official wc command:

    ```
    $ ls -l | wc
          16     137     908
    ```

    They are indeed the same!

SUMMARY With a programming environment as sophisticated as awk we can only scratch the surface in this book. What's frustrating is that there are remarkably few resources that let you learn more about the helpful awk programming language. About the only one I can recommend is the dry *The AWK Programming Language*, written by the authors of the program, Alfred Aho, Brian Kernighan, and Peter Weinberger (Addison-Wesley Longman; ISBN: 020107981X).

Whether you choose to get a copy of that book or simply explore and poke around by yourself, my experience suggests that a good grasp of awk is a valuable addition.

Alternatively, you'll find many Perl fanatics tell you that it can do absolutely everything that awk can do, and much, much more. They're right, but the price is complexity: I find awk to be much more simple and straightforward for tasks like those shown above. You'll need to decide for yourself whether you want to stick with Perl for all programmatic tasks or explore the other tools in your Unix toolbox.

16

How to Use cut in Pipes

While awk is a general purpose tool that you can bend to your needs (sort of like a geeky Swiss army knife!), there are specific tasks where other Unix tools are better suited.

Earlier you saw the simple '{print $5}' to extract the fifth column of the data stream, but in fact there's a faster way to do that, with the simple cut command.

Action 16.2: Slicing and Dicing with cut

DESCRIPTION In the example earlier, the fields were all neatly separated by *white space*. What happens if you need to get a specific set of characters regardless of spaces, however? That's one great example of where cut can be your friend.

More typically, however, you're working with a database-like file and there's a specific *delimiter* that separates each of the fields.

ACTION

1. An interesting data file to explore is the /etc/passwd file, which contains account record information for each login account on the system.

   Here's the tail of one on a busy system I use:

   ```
   $ tail /etc/passwd
   djk:*:23678:100:Doug King:/home/djk:/ bin/csh
   voxroom:*:24108:100:Gregory Smith:/home/voxroom:/bin/csh
   allied:*:24138:100:Gordon Wilkinson:/home/allied:/ bin/csh
   rottn1:*:24173:100:The Rott'n One:/home/rottn1:/bin/tcsh
   effugas:*:24263:100:Dan Kaminsky:/home/effugas:/bin/tcsh
   stinkbug:*:24331:100:Edward Fuller:/home/stinkbug:/ bin/bash
   ```

```
hrweb:*:24434:100:Human Rights Web:/home/hrweb:/ bin/tcsh
lcamag:*:24522:100:David Heller:/home/lcamag:/bin/csh
kodachen:*:24547:100:Jaimie Mc Curry:home/kodachen:/bin/tcsh
nobody:*:65534:65534:Unprivileged user:/nonexistent:/nonexistent
```

If we isolate one line, it's a bit less overwhelming:

```
$ grep 'taylor:' /etc/passwd
taylor:*:101:99:Dave Taylor:/home/taylor:/bin/bash
```

Without going into exhaustive detail, the first field is the account name, the fifth field is the username, the sixth their home directory, and the seventh is the login shell.

Now, let's see how cut can make our analysis of this file a bit more interesting. An important flag to know: -d lets you specify the field delimiter (the default is a tab)

2. First, let's get a list of usernames:

```
$ cut -d: -f5 /etc/passwd
Charlie &
Bourne-again Superuser
Owner of many system processes
Administrative Sandbox
Binaries Commands and Source
Administrative Sandbox

lots and lots of output removed

Edward Fuller
Human Rights Web
David Heller
Jaimie Mc Curry
Unprivileged user
$
```

3. Instead, we'll make a quick analysis of what shells people are using by pulling out the seventh field with cut and then piping it to sort and uniq with the important -c flag to show a count of matching results:

```
$ cut -d: -f7 /etc/passwd | sort | uniq -c
  51 /bin/bash
 857 /bin/csh
  40 /bin/ksh
   1 /bin/sh
 382 /bin/tcsh
   9 /bin/zsh
   8 /noshell
   5 /usr/local/bin/bash
   7 /usr/local/bin/tcsh
$
```

> If you want to have the output sorted from most popular to least popular, you could use another sort on the end of the pipe: sort -rn will sort in reverse numerical order.

4. One more interesting example of cut before we go: If you've been paying attention, you'll notice that the first character of the ls-1 output is a d when it's a directory, and a - when it's just a regular file.

Here's a relatively complex pipe that summarizes how many of each suffix are found in a given directory:

```
$ ls -l | awk 'NF > 2' | cut -c1 | sort | uniq -c
  15 -
  12 d
$
```

The awk weeds out all lines that don't have at least three fields (remember the "Total" line?) then cut slices just the first character of output, and then we simply sort and uniq it and voilà! 12 directories and 15 plain files in the test directory.

SUMMARY The cut command has a very narrow set of capabilities, but when you're extracting specific columns of information, it's a winner.

Inline Editing with sed and tr

Before we leave the topic of pipeline power tools in Unix, you need to learn a bit about two programs that are designed to change information as it goes through a stream of data. The sed command is the more common of the two and is used primarily to substitute one pattern for another as information goes past. The tr command is even more limited: It translates one set of characters to another.

Action 16.3: Inline Editing with sed and tr

DESCRIPTION To more fully understand how each of these commands work, it's useful to see them in action.

ACTION

1. A common task for a pipeline is to change all uppercase letters into lowercase, or vice versa. There are doubtless a number of ways to accomplish this within the Unix world, but the tr command makes it very easy:

```
$ cut -d: -f5 /etc/passwd | tr '[a-z]' '[A-Z]' | tail
GREGORY SMITH
GORDON WILKINSON
THE ROTT'N ONE
DAN KAMINSKY
EDWARD FULLER
HUMAN RIGHTS WEB
DAVID HELLER
JAIMIE MC CURRY
UNPRIVILEGED USER
$
```

The tr command does a 1:1 matching of what's specified in the first argument
with what's specified in the second argument. In this case, you can see two ranges
specified: all lowercase letters, and then all uppercase letters.

2. To translate all vowels into a dash, you can again use tr to accomplish the task:

```
$ cut -d: -f5 /etc/passwd | tr 'aeiou' '-----' | tail
Gr-g-ry Sm-th
G-rd-n W-lk-ns-n
Th- R-tt'n On-
D-n K-m-nsky
Edw-rd F-ll-r
H-m-n R-ghts W-b
D-v-d H-ll-r
J--m-- Mc C-rry
Unpr-v-l-g-d -s-r
$
```

Looks like some sort of code, doesn't it?

3. A more common use of tr is to do a simple rotation cipher for encryption. If
you've read any Usenet groups, you might have bumped into a common one:
ROT13, which is a simple rotation by thirteen characters of the text. This means that
a becomes *n*, *b* becomes *o*, and so on.

Sound complex? It's very easy with tr on the job:

```
$ cat badjoke | tr '[a-zA-Z]' '[n-za-mN-ZA-M]'
Jul qvq gur puvpxra pebff gur ebnq?
Gb purpx uvf rznvy!
$
```

The reverse translation can be most easily done by switching the second and third
arguments to the tr command:

```
$ cat badjoke.rot13 | tr '[n-za-mN-ZA-M]' '[a-zA-Z]'
Why did the chicken cross the road?
To check his email!
$
```

4. This would be a perfect place for a shell alias, something like

```
alias rot13="tr '[a-zA-Z]' '[n-za-mN-ZA-M]'"
alias unrot13="tr '[n-za-mN-ZA-M]' '[a-zA-Z]'"
```

and then you can encode things with rot13 *filename* and decode things with *unrot13 filename.*

5. The sed command is considerably more powerful, and it doesn't need any sort of 1:1 matching on the patterns specified. For example, here's a smarter way to translate all vowels into dashes:

```
$ cat badjoke | sed 's/[aeiouAEIOU]/-/g'
Why d-d th- ch-ck-n cr-ss th- r--d?
T- ch-ck h-s -m--l!
$
```

6. Unlike the earlier version with tr, this works with upper- and lowercase vowels.

7. A more common usage would be to change words, rather than letters, however. Perhaps I'd like to change the punch line a wee bit:

```
$ cat badjoke | sed 's/email/portfolio/'
Why did the chicken cross the road?
To check his portfolio!
$
```

8. sed is actually a powerful programming environment in its own right, even though we've only looked at the *substitute* capability. The general form of sed commands is

```
{address{,address}}command{arguments}
```

where the {} denote optional information. The previous use of sed had s as the command, and the old and new patterns as the argument.

Table 16.1 shows a summary of some of the many capabilities of sed:

TABLE 16.1 The Most Useful sed Commands

Command	Example	Explanation
d	4,8d	Delete the fourth through eighth line
p	11p	Print the 11th line
s	s/old/new/	Replace all occurrences of *old* with *new*

9. Addresses can be individual numbers, as shown in Table 16.1, or $ to match the last line in the stream, but they can also be regular expressions. Want to delete all the lines that contain the word *road*? You can use /road/d for the task.

16

10. Regular expressions can have special characters too: ^ is the beginning of the line, and $ is the end of the line, for example. Want to quickly preface all lines with a > sequence to indicate quoting? Use s/^/> / to do the job.

SUMMARY As with awk I've only scratched the surface of the sed command in this chapter. If your interest is piqued, I strongly encourage you to learn more about it, either by reading the man page or seeking out some useful online resources that can expand your knowledge.

Summary

The more you learn about the tools in Unix, the more you realize that there's really almost nothing you can't do with a combination of two or three commands. That's what I really like about Unix, frankly. In your own power toolkit, awk and sed are two well worth a special spot.

Workshop

The Workshop poses some questions about the topics presented in this chapter.

Exercises

1. How did awk get its name?

2. The -F flag in awk lets you change field delimiters. How would you use awk to extract all the home directories out of the /etc/passwd file?

3. ROT13 is useful, but ROT7 could be even better. How would you write aliases for both encoding and decoding a ROT7 system?

4. The output of ls-l has the file permission shown as a character sequence: rwx, r-x, and so on. Can you come up with a combination of cut and grep to identify whether you have any files that only have write or execute permission?

Next Lesson

In the next hour you'll learn about how Unix handles jobs and how you can manipulate them. Commands you will learn include jobs and ps, to see what processes are running; fg and bg, to move jobs back and forth between the foreground and background; and kill, to terminate jobs you no longer want around.

HOUR **17**

Job Control

In this hour you will learn about how Unix handles jobs and how you can manipulate them. Commands you will learn include jobs and ps, to see what processes are running; fg and bg, to move jobs back and forth between the foreground and background; and kill, to terminate jobs you no longer want around.

Goals for This Hour

In this hour, you will learn

- About job control in the shell: stopping jobs
- How to put jobs in the background and bring them back to the foreground
- How to find out what tasks are running by using jobs and ps
- How to terminate errant processes by using kill

Throughout this book, I've indicated that my focus is on the most important and valuable flags and options for the commands covered. That's all well and good, but how do you find out about the alternatives that might actually work better for your use?

This hour presents an explanation of a Unix philosophical puzzle: What is a running program? To learn the answer, you are introduced to ps and jobs, for controlling processes; fg and bg, to move your own processes back and forth between the foreground and background; and the quasi-omnipotent kill command, for stopping programs in their proverbial tracks.

Wrestling with Your Jobs

Every program you run is a job according to the Unix system, and although it might not be obvious, you have the ability to start and stop them at any time, and more.

Task 17.1: Job Control in the Shell: Stopping Jobs

DESCRIPTION Whether you're requesting a man page, listing files with ls, starting vi, or running just about any Unix command, you're starting one or more processes. In Unix, any program that's running is a *process*. You can have multiple processes running at once. The pipeline ls -l | sort | more invokes three processes: ls, sort, and more. Processes in both the C and Korn shells are also known as *jobs*, and the program you're running is known as the *current job*.

Any job or process can have various states, with "running" being the most typical state. In both shells, you can stop a job by pressing ^z. To restart it, enter fg when you are ready.

ACTION

1. Earlier I was perusing the man page entry for sort. I had reached the bottom of the first screen:

```
$ man sort

SORT(1)              DYNIX Programmer's Manual              SORT(1)

NAME
     sort - sort or merge files

SYNOPSIS
     sort [ -mubdfinrtx ] [ +pos1 [ -pos2 ] ] ... [ -o name ] [
```
continues

```
       -T directory ] [ name ] ...

DESCRIPTION
       Sort sorts lines of all the named files together and writes
       the result on the standard output.  The name `-' means the
       standard input.  If no input files are named, the standard
       input is sorted.

       The default sort key is an entire line.  Default ordering is
       lexicographic by bytes in machine collating sequence.  The
       ordering is affected globally by the following options, one
       or more of which may appear.

       b    Ignore leading blanks (spaces and tabs) in field com-
--More-- _
```

I'd like to try using the -b flag mentioned at the bottom of this screen, but I want to read the rest of the man page, too. Instead of typing q to quit and then restarting the man program later, I can stop the program. I press ^z and see this:

```
       ordering is affected globally by the following options, one
 or more of which may appear.

       b    Ignore leading blanks (spaces and tabs) in field com-
--More--
Stopped
$
```

At this point, I can do whatever I'd like:

```
$ ls -sF | sort -b | head -4
   1 Archives/
   1 InfoWorld/
   1 Mail/
   1 News/
   1 OWL/
```

2. I can resume at any time. I enter fg, the program reminds me where I was, and man
   (which is actually the more program invoked by man) returns to its prompt:

```
$ fg
man sort
--More-- _
$
```

3. Screen-oriented programs are even smarter about stopping and starting jobs. For example, vi refreshes the entire screen when you return from it having been stopped. If I were in vi working on the dickens.note file, the screen would look like this:

```
                        A Tale of Two Cities
                             Preface

When I was acting, with my children and friends, in Mr Wilkie
Collins's drama of The Frozen Deep, I first conceived the main idea
 of this story.  A strong desire came upon me then, to
embody it in my own person;
and I traced out in my fancy, the state of mind of which it would
necessitate the presentation
to an observant spectator, with particular
care and interest.

As the idea became familiar to me, it gradually shaped itself into its
present form.  Throughout its execution, it has had complete possession of
me;
 I have so far verified what
is done and suffered in these pages,
as that I have certainly done and suffered it all myself.

Whenever any reference (however slight) is made here to the condition
of the Danish people before or during the Revolution, it is truly made,
 on the faith of the most trustworthy
witnesses.  It has been one of my hopes to add
something to the popular and picturesque means of
"dickens.note" 28 lines, 1123 characters
```

Pressing ^z would result in this:

```
witnesses.  It has been one of my hopes to add
something to the popular and picturesque means of
"dickens.note" 28 lines, 1123 characters

Stopped
$ _
```

I can check to see whether someone is logged in and then return to vi with the fg command.

```
$ who | grep marv
$ fg
```

```
                           A Tale of Two Cities
                                 Preface

      When I was acting, with my children and friends, in Mr Wilkie
      Collins's drama of The Frozen Deep, I first conceived the main idea of this
      story.  A strong desire came upon me then, to
      embody it in my own person;
      and I traced out in my fancy, the state of mind of which it would
      necessitate the presentation
      to an observant spectator, with particular
      care and interest.

      As the idea became familiar to me, it gradually shaped itself
      into its present form.  Throughout its execution, it has had complete
       possession of me; I have so far verified what
      is done and suffered in these pages,
      as that I have certainly done and suffered it all myself.

      Whenever any reference (however slight) is made here to the condition
      of the Danish people before or during the Revolution, it is truly made,
      on the faith of the most trustworthy
      witnesses.  It has been one of my hopes to add
      something to the popular and picturesque means of
      "dickens.note" 28 lines, 1123 characters
```

SUMMARY Processes and jobs in Unix have many aspects, particularly regarding the level of control offered by the shell. The rest of this hour explains how to exploit these capabilities to make your work easier and faster.

Task 17.2: Foreground/Background and Unix Programs

DESCRIPTION Now that you know how to suspend programs in their tracks, it's time to learn how to have them keep running in the background (by using the bg command) while you're doing something else, and how to have programs instantly go into the background (by using the & notation).

In the first hour, you learned that one of the distinguishing characteristics of Unix is that it's a true multitasking operating system. It is capable of running hundreds of programs at the same time. The best part is that you're not limited to just one process! If you want to save a couple of man pages to a file, for example, you can run those processes in the background while you are working on something else.

Once a job is stopped, you can enter fg to restart it as the program you're working with. (The fg command takes its name from *foreground*, which refers to the program that your display and keyboard are working with.) If the process will continue without any output

17

to the screen and without any requirement for input, you can use bg to move it into the *background*, where it runs until it is done. If the program needs to write to the screen or read from the keyboard, the system will stop its execution automatically and inform you. You then can use fg to bring the program into the foreground to continue running.

If you find that background jobs are just writing information to your screen, try the stty tostop command to fix the problem.

You can also use job control to start a couple of programs and then use the fg command, with the job ID as an argument, to start the job you want to work with. Not entering the job ID will bring the most recently stopped job back to the foreground. If your system takes a long time to start big applications (such as emacs or vi), this could save you lots of time.

Although a job can be stopped, it still consumes resources, so you should be careful not to have too many stopped programs around, in deference to the other users of your machine. To free resources, kill or terminate the jobs instead.

A different strategy is to start a program in the background, letting Unix manage it. If the program needs some input or output, it stops, just like processes you've put into the background with bg after they've already started running. To have a program (or pipeline!) automatically start in the background, simply type an & at the end of the command line.

ACTION

1. Here's an example of a very complex awk command that processes files without needing any input or offering any output:

```
$ awk -F: '{print $1" = "$5}' < /etc/passwd | \
awk -F, '{print $1}'| \
awk '{ if (NF > 2) print $0 }' | \
sort > who.is.who
```

After about 20 seconds, the $ prompt returns; it takes that long to feed the password file through the three-part awk filter, sort the entire output, and save it to the file who.is.who.

When you're working with long commands, it's useful to know that you always can move to the next line—even in the middle of entering something—by ending the current line with a single backslash. Note that the backslash must be the *very last character* on the line.

With this new file, I easily can look up an account to see the full name of that user:

```
$ alias lookup='grep -i \!* who.is.who'
$ who | head
root       console Dec  6 18:02
maritanj ttyAa   Dec  8 21:20
efb        ttyAb   Dec  8 12:12
wifey     ttyAc   Dec  8 19:41
phamtu   ttyAe   Dec  8 21:14
curts     ttyAf   Dec  8 21:14
seifert   ttyAg   Dec  8 21:11
taylor    ttyAh   Dec  8 21:09
halcyon  ttyAi   Dec  8 18:34
jamilrr   ttyAj   Dec  8 20:25
Broken pipe
$ lookup maritanj
maritanj = Jorge Maritan
$ lookup efb
efb = Edward F. Billiard
$
```

2. To have the build process run in the background, I can stop the process immediately after I start it, by using ^z:

```
$ !awk
awk -F: '{print $1" = "$5}' < /etc/passwd | awk -F, '{print $1}'
➥| awk '{ if (NF > 2) print $0 }' | sort > who.is.who
Stopped
$
```

Notice that the command I repeated using the history mechanism was listed as being all on a single line.

At this point, bg will continue the program, running it in the background:

```
$ bg
[1]     awk -F: {print $1" = "$5} < /etc/passwd | awk -F, {print $1}
➥| awk { if (NF > 2) print $0 } | sort > who.is.who &
$
```

The number in square brackets is this job's *control number* in the shell. In a moment, you learn why this is a handy number to note.

On some systems a completed background job will notify you immediately that it's done, but on most systems, after a completed background job has finished running, it waits until you press Return to get a new system prompt before it lets you know. After about 30 or 40 seconds, I press Return and see this:

```
$
[1]    Done                        awk -F:
{print $1" = "$5} < /etc/passwd | awk -F,
{print $1} | awk { if (NF > 2) print $0 } | sort > who.is.who
$
```

3. Alternatively, a better strategy for moving a program into the background is to move the process to the background automatically by adding a & to the end:

```
$ !awk &
awk -F: '{print $1" = "$5}' < /etc/passwd | awk -F, '{print $1}'
➡| awk '{ if (NF > 2) print $0 }' | sort > ! who.is.who &
[1] 27556 27557 27558 27559
$
```

This is more interesting. This command is shown with a control number of 1, but the four numbers listed after it are the actual process ID numbers of each piece of the pipeline: 27556 is the first awk process, 27557 is the second awk process, 27558 is the third awk process, and 27559 is the sort program.

Again, when it's complete, pressing Return lets me know:

```
$
[1]    Done                      awk -F: {print $1" = "$5} < /etc/passwd |
➡awk -F, {print $1} | awk { if (NF > 2) print $0 } | _
➡ sort > who.is.who
$
```

4. What happens if I try to automatically move to the background a program that has input or output?

```
$ vi &
[1] 28258
$
```

This looks fine. Pressing Return indicates otherwise, though:

```
$
[1]   + Stopped (tty output) vi
$
```

You can see that this program has stopped because of some information (output) it wants to display. If the program expected input, the message would be Stopped (tty input) *program name*.

I can use fg to bring this program into the foreground and work with it, or even just to quit vi.

SUMMARY Because so much of the Unix design focuses on running streams of data through filters and saving the output to a file, you could be running various commands in the background, freeing you up to do other work in the meantime. Remember also that you can put in the background jobs that take a fair amount of processing time and then display information on the screen. When it's time to write something to the screen, the program will stop automatically until you enter fg to pull it into the foreground again.

Task 17.3: Finding Out What Tasks Are Running

DESCRIPTION There are two ways to keep tabs on what programs are flying around in the Unix operating system. The easier way, jobs, shows what processes you've stopped and moved into the background in the shell. Enter jobs, and it tells you what programs, if any, are stopped or running.

The alternative is a complex command called ps, which shows the processor status for the entire computer. The processor is another name for the computer itself. Fortunately, without any arguments, it shows the active or stopped programs associated with your terminal only. The ps program actually has more flags than even ls, I think. The vast majority of them, however, are never going to be of value to you or any normal Unix user. Worse, the flags are very different between BSD systems and System V. Table 17.1 summarizes the flags that are most helpful.

TABLE 17.1 Useful Flags to the ps Command, BSD-Style

Flag	Meaning
-a	Shows all processes associated with terminals attached to the system.
-g	Shows all interesting processes on the system (that is, all processes other than those required by the operating system).
-l	Gives the long listing format for each line.
-t *xx*	Lists only processes associated with the specified tty*xx*.
-u	Produces user-oriented output.
-w	Uses wide output format. If repeated (-ww), it will show as much of each command as possible.
-x	Shows all processes in the system.

17

The -a, -g, and -x flags all affect how much information is displayed by ps. To use either the -g or the -x command, you also must use the -a command. On most machines, -ax yields considerably more output than -ag. The most commonly used flags (and flag combinations) are -u, to have only your processes listed in a friendly format; -aux, to see everything on the machine (you almost always want to pipe this to grep or more, lest you be overrun with hundreds of lines of information); and -wtxx, to show all the processes associated with ttyxx, in wide format.

> The ps program varies from System V to Berkeley Unix more than any other command. Fortunately, the two or three most common flags are similar across the two systems. To explore more about the ps command on your system, you should start by reading the man page.

ACTION

1. To begin, I'm going to start vi in the background:

```
$ vi dickens.note &
[1] 4352
$
```

I'll start that awk job again too:

```
$ !awk
awk -F: '{print $1" = "$5}' < /etc/passwd | awk -F, '{print $1}'
➡| awk '{ if (NF > 2) print $0 }' | sort > ! who.is.who &
[2] 4532 4534 4536 4537
$
```

The jobs command will show what processes I have running:

```
$ jobs
[1]  + Stopped (tty output) vi dickens.note
[2]  - Running              awk -F: {print $1" = "$5} < /etc/passwd
➡| awk -F,
{print $1} | awk { if (NF > 2) print $0 } | sort > who.is.who
$
```

2. Now that you know the job numbers (the numbers in square brackets here), you can easily move specific jobs into the foreground or the background by specifying the job number prefixed by %. To show what I mean, I'll put a couple more vi jobs in the background:

```
$ vi buckaroo.confused &
[2] 13056
$ vi awkscript csh.man cheryl mbox &
[3] 13144
$
```

Now I'll use the jobs command to see what's running:

```
$ jobs
[1]    Stopped (tty output) vi dickens.note
[2]  - Stopped (tty output) vi buckaroo.confused
[3]  + Stopped (tty output) vi awkscript csh.man cheryl mbox
$
```

Notice that the awk job finished.

To edit the buckaroo.confused note, I need only to enter fg %2 to pull the file into the foreground. To terminate these processes (something you learn more about later in this hour), I can use the kill command:

```
$ kill %2 %3
$
```

Nothing happened. Or did it? Pressing Return reveals what occurred in the operating system:

```
$
[3]  - Done                 vi awkscript csh.man cheryl mbox
[2]  - Done                 vi buckaroo.confused
$
```

3. Restart the awk command with !awk. Contrast the output of jobs with the output of the Berkeley (BSD) ps command:

```
$ ps
  PID TT STAT   TIME COMMAND
 4352 Ah T      0:00 vi dickens.note
 4532 Ah R      0:03 awk - : {print $1"
 4534 Ah R      0:02 awk - , {print $1}
 4536 Ah S      0:01 - k { if (NF > 2) print $0 } (awk)
 4537 Ah S      0:00 sort
 4579 Ah R      0:00 ps
$
```

You can see here that four unique processes are really running for that pipeline: three awk processes and one sort process. In addition, vi and ps are listed as running. Note that my login shell (bash) isn't in this listing.

Figure 17.1 explains each field, and Table 17.2 lists possible values for the STAT program status column.

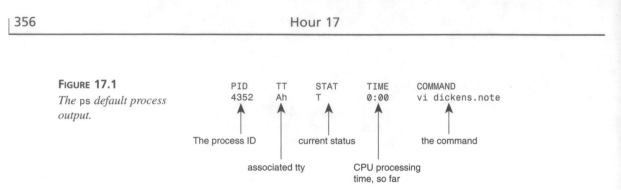

FIGURE 17.1

The ps *default process output.*

TABLE 17.2 Possible Process Status Values

Value	Meaning
R	Running
S	Sleeping (20 seconds or less)
I	Idle (sleeping more than 20 seconds)
T	Stopped
Z	Zombie process

Other process states exist, but they rarely show up for most users. A *zombie process* is one that has ended but hasn't freed up its resources. Usually, it takes a second or two for the system to completely recover all memory used by a program. Sometimes, zombies are stuck in the process table for one reason or other. Unix folk refer to this as a *wedged process,* which stays around until the system is rebooted. Sometimes it's listed as <defunct> in process listings. Any process that is preceded by a sleep command is noted as sleeping.

4. Adding some flags can change the output of ps quite dramatically:

```
$ ps -x
  PID TT STAT   TIME COMMAND
 4352 Ah T      0:00 vi dickens.note
 6171 Ah R      0:02 awk - : {print $1"
 6172 Ah R      0:01 awk - , {print $1}
 6173 Ah S      0:01 - k { if (NF > 2) print $0 } (awk)
 6174 Ah S      0:00 sort
 6177 Ah R      0:00 ps -x
19189 Ah S      0:06 -bash (bash)
19649 Ah I      0:02 newmail
$
```

Two new processes show up here: -bash (the shell), which is, finally, my login shell; and newmail, a program that automatically starts in the background when I log in to the system (it's located at the end of my .login).

> The shell process is shown with a leading dash to indicate that it's a login shell. Any other copies of bash that I run won't have that leading dash. That's one way the shell knows not to read through the .login file every time it's run.

5. To see more about what's happening, I add yet another flag, -u, to expand the output on the display:

```
$ ps -xu
USER       PID  %CPU %MEM   SZ  RSS TT STAT ENG    TIME COMMAND
taylor    7011  10.4  0.2  184  100 Ah R      6   0:02 awk - : " "
➥{print $1"
taylor    7012   6.3  0.1  160   92 Ah S          0:01 awk - , "
➥{print $1}
taylor    7013   5.9  0.1  160   92 Ah R      3   0:01 - k
➥{ if (NF > 2) print
taylor   19189   1.1  0.2  256  148 Ah S          0:07 -bash (bash)
taylor    7014   1.0  0.1  316   64 Ah S          0:00 sort
taylor    7022   0.1  0.2  180  116 Ah R      0   0:00 ps -xu
taylor    4352   0.0  0.3  452  168 Ah T          0:00 vi
➥dickens.note
taylor   19649   0.0  0.1  124   60 Ah I          0:02 newmail
$
```

Figure 17.2 explains these fields.

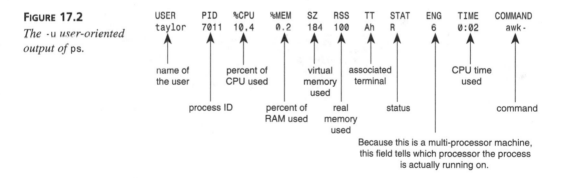

FIGURE 17.2
The -u *user-oriented output of* ps.

6. I won't show the output from the -aux flags, but you should look at the number of lines produced by the -ag and -ax flags:

```
$ ps -ag | wc -l
     377
$ ps -ag | head
  PID TT STAT  TIME COMMAND
 1403 co IW   0:01 -csh (csh)
```

17

```
 2200 p3 IW     0:18 server
 6076 p6 I      0:13 rlogin sage -l hirschna
 6082 p6 I      0:11 rlogin sage -l hirschna
25341 p8 IW     0:06 -tcsh (tcsh)
  681 pa IW     0:05 -tcsh (tcsh)
10994 pa IW     2:10 ghostview pop5.ps
11794 pa IW     0:12 pwlookup
13861 pa I      0:56 gs
Broken pipe
$
```

You can see here that each process is owned by a specific terminal but that these processes are all idle (that is, they've been sleeping for more than 20 seconds). This probably means that these users have turned away for a little while. Look back at the output generated by ps -xu, and you will see that newmail is also idle. That's because the program runs in a loop: It sleeps for five minutes, checks for new mail, goes back to sleep again, and so on. Processes that have the W after the I in the status column are processes that have been moved out of main memory and are swapped out to disk. This is not a problem, and the users might not even realize that anything has happened; the only symptom of this is that when the users wake up their programs, the programs will take an additional fraction of a second to return.

What is the output from ps -ax?

```
$ ps -ax | wc -l
    765
$ ps -ax | head
  PID TT STAT   TIME COMMAND
    0 ?  D      8:58 swapper
    1 ?  S     14:45 (init)
    2 ?  D     20:43 pagedaemon
   27 ?  I      0:00 rpc.rquotad
   59 ?  S      6:36 /etc/syslogd -m480
   70 ?  I      0:02 /etc/portmap
   74 ?  IW     0:00 (biod)
   75 ?  IW     0:00 (biod)
   76 ?  IW     0:00 (biod)
Broken pipe
$
```

These are some of the "guts" of the Unix operating system. Notice that none of these processes is actually associated with a terminal. Also notice that some of these processes have incredibly low process ID numbers! Any one-digit process ID is a program that is a part of the core Unix system and must be running for Unix to be alive. Any two-digit process is also started by the system itself but is probably optional. The D status for some of these processes indicates that they're waiting for disk resources of some sort. Finally, note how much time these processes have taken. I venture that you will never have a process that takes 20 minutes of CPU time—ever!

7. On a Sun workstation, the output of the ps commands is a bit different:

```
$ ps
  PID TT STAT  TIME COMMAND
 8172 qb S     0:00 -bash (bash)
 8182 qb T     0:00 vi
 8186 qb R     0:00 ps
$
```

In many ways, though, these different workstations have very similar output from the ps commands. For example, compare this Sequent output from ps -xu to the ps -xu output on the Sun that I already showed:

```
$ ps -xu
USER      PID %CPU %MEM   SZ  RSS TT STAT START  TIME COMMAND
taylor   8191  7.7  0.4  284  536 qb R   19:16  0:00 ps -xu
taylor   8182  0.0  0.4  140  432 qb T   19:16  0:00 vi
taylor   8172  0.0  0.3   68  400 qb S   19:16  0:00 -bash (bash)
taylor   8180  0.0  0.1   52  144 qb S   19:16  0:00 newmail
$
```

The ENG column of the previous examples is replaced by a START column on the Sun workstation. The numbers in the START column indicate the exact time when the processes were started on the computer.

SUMMARY Unix works with processes. Your login shell, the edit session you run, and even the ls program listing your files are all processes in the operating system. This means that you can work with processes. You can stop programs temporarily to do something else, restart them as you choose, and even look at all the programs you're running at any time, including otherwise hidden processes such as your login shell itself.

Task 17.4: Terminating Processes with kill

DESCRIPTION Now that you know how to create multiple processes, tuck some into the background, and find stray processes, you need some way to permanently stop them from running, as needed. The command to accomplish this in Unix is kill. For the most part, to use kill, you specify the process ID numbers of those programs you want to terminate. Both the C shell and the Korn shell have a convenient shorthand you've already seen: the percent–job-number notation.

The kill command can send various signals to a process. To specify a job control action, you need to specify to kill one of the various signals. Table 17.3 lists signals you can use with kill.

TABLE 17.3   Some Signals to Use with `kill`

Number	Name	Meaning
1	SIGHUP	Hang up
2	SIGINT	Interrupt
9	SIGKILL	`kill` (cannot be caught or ignored)
15	SIGTERM	Software termination signal from `kill`

Unix knows about more than 30 signals, but Table 17.3 lists the ones that are most helpful. The SIGHUP signal is sent to every process you are running just before you hang up (log out of the system). SIGINT is the signal sent when you press ^c; many programs respond in specific ways when this signal is received. SIGKILL is the "Terminator" of the Unix signals: Programs cannot ignore it and cannot process it. The process is terminated immediately, without even a chance to clean up after itself. SIGTERM is the more graceful alternative: It requests an immediate termination of the program, but it allows the program to remove temporary files it might have created.

By default, `kill` sends a SIGTERM to the processes specified. You can specify other signals, however, by using either the number or the name of the signal (minus the SIG prefix, that is). On many systems, you also can specify the `-l` flag to `kill` to see what signals are available.

> The `kill` command should be used with caution. It can get you into a lot of trouble. For example, do you want to log out rather suddenly? To do that, find the process ID of your login shell and terminate it. Learn to use `kill`, but learn to use it cautiously.

ACTION

1. The simplest way to use the `kill` command is from the shell. First, start a job in the background:

```
$ vi &
[1] 6016
$
```

I can terminate this process now by using either `kill %1` or `kill 6016`, but if I try both of them, the second command will fail because the first already will have terminated the process:

```
$ kill %1
$ kill 6016
6016: No such process
[1]    Done                    vi
$
```

Just as if I had dropped a process into the background and it instantly stopped because it needed to produce output, the kill process also had no feedback and took a second or two to occur. In the interim, I entered the second kill command, which then output the error message No such process. Following that, I get an indication from the shell itself that the job ended.

2. Using the ps command, I can find that pesky newmail program that's always running in the background:

```
$ ps -ux | grep newmail
taylor   6899   0.1  0.1   52   28 Av S        0:00 grep newmail
taylor   25817  0.0  0.1   124  60 Av I        0:01 newmail
$
```

I want to send that process a hang-up signal (SIGHUP):

```
$ kill -HUP 25817
$ !ps
ps -ux | grep newmail
taylor   7220   0.0  0.1   52   28 Av S        0:00 grep newmail
$
```

Because the newmail program isn't in this listing, I can conclude that the SIGHUP signal stopped newmail.

> Because kill tells you whether a process cannot be found, the typical Unix solution to finding out whether the command worked is to enter !! immediately to repeat the kill command a second time. If kill worked, you see No such process.

3. Some processes are pesky and can resist the less powerful signals SIGTERM and SIGHUP. (In Unix, this is called "catching" a signal. In some processes, you need to send and catch signals to perform certain actions.) That's when you need to use what I call the "Big Guns," or SIGKILL. You see this referred to sometimes as the terminate-with-extreme-prejudice command; the format is kill -9 *processID*, and it's not for the faint of heart!

I strongly recommend that you just let kill send the SIGTERM signal and see whether that does the job. If it doesn't, try SIGHUP, and if that also fails, use SIGKILL as a last resort.

4. What happens if you try to use `kill` on jobs that aren't yours? Fortunately, it doesn't work:

```
$ ps -aux | head -5
USER       PID  %CPU %MEM   SZ  RSS TT STAT ENG   TIME COMMAND
news      7460  97.7  0.4  336  252 ?  R N    4  4:33 sort -u
→ /tmp/nnsubj6735a
phaedrus  8693  18.1  1.1 1260  720 rm S          0:03 nn
root      8741  14.4  0.4  416  252 ?  R      9  0:03 nntpd
root      8696  13.9  0.4  416  252 ?  S          0:03 nntpd
Broken pipe
$ kill 7460
7460: Not owner
$
```

5. Finally, if you forget and leave stopped jobs in the background and try to log out, here's what happens:

```
$ logout
There are stopped jobs.
$
```

You must either use `fg` to bring each job into the foreground and terminate each normally, or use `kill` to terminate each of the jobs and then log out.

 In this task, you have been introduced to the `kill` command and some of the signals associated with it.

Summary

Although the file is the underlying unit in the Unix file system, including all directories, the most fundamental piece of Unix is the process. In this hour, you learned how to have background processes, how to stop and restart processes, and how to use `kill` to quit any errant program—running or not.

Workshop

The Workshop summarizes the key terms you learned and poses some questions about the topics presented in this chapter. It also provides you with a preview of what you will learn in the next hour.

Key Terms

control number   A unique number that the C shell assigns to each background job for easy reference and for using with other commands, such as `fg` and `kill`.

current job   The job that is currently running on the terminal and keyboard (it's the program you're actually running and working within).

errant process   A process that is not performing the job you expected it to perform.

foreground job   A synonym for current job.

job   A synonym for process.

kill   Terminate a process.

login shell   The shell process that started when you logged in to the system. This is usually where you're working when you're logged in to Unix.

process   A program stopped or running within the Unix operating system. Also known as a job.

signals   Special messages that can be sent to stopped or running processes.

stop a job   Stop the running program without terminating it.

wedged process   A process that is stuck in memory and can't free up its resources even though it has ceased running. This is rare, but annoying.

zombie   A terminated process that has not been cleaned up by the parent process.

Exercises

1. Start a program, such as vi, and use ^z to stop it. Now terminate the process by using kill.
2. Start vi again, stop it, and put it in the background. Work on something else, and then return vi to the foreground.
3. Use ps to check the status of processes to see what processes you have running that aren't shown on jobs. Why might ps and jobs list different processes?

Preview of the Next Hour

The next hour focuses on the many facets of printing and generating hard copy on the Unix system. It's not as easy as you might think, so stay tuned!

HOUR 18

Printing in the Unix Environment

Printing is one of the greatest shortcomings of Unix. Generating printouts is a sufficiently common task that it should be fairly easy to accomplish. However, in this one area of Unix, continual conflict exists between the System V and BSD groups, to the detriment of all.

This hour focuses on some of the most common Unix commands for working with printers. It is a primer on learning what printers are hooked up to your system, how to send output to a printer, how to check that your print requests are in the queue for printing, and how to remove your print requests from the queue if you decide not to print.

Goals for This Hour

In this hour, you will learn how to

- Find local printers with `printers`
- Send a print job to a printer with `lpr` or `lp`

- Format print jobs with `pr` and `col`
- Work with the print queue by using `lpq`, `lprm`

Various techniques can minimize the complexity of printing in Unix, the best of which is to create an alias called `print` that has all the default configuration information you want. If you define `PRINTER` as an environment variable, most of the Unix print utilities will default to the printer you specify as the value of the `PRINTER` environment variable, for example, when searching print queues for jobs. The queue, or list, is where all print jobs are placed for processing by the specific printer.

> The differing "philosophies" of BSD and System V have caused problems in the area of printing. In a nutshell, because Unix systems are almost always networked (that is, hooked together with high-speed data-communications lines), the most valuable feature of a printing tool would be allowing the user to choose to print on any of the many printers attached. For this to work, each machine with an attached printer must be listening for requests from other machines. The root of the BSD versus System V problem is that the two listen for different requests. A System V machine can't send a print job to a printer attached to a BSD machine, and vice versa.

Making a Printed Copy

It's one thing to create wonderful material in your Unix account, and another entirely to have it printed. That's what this lesson is all about.

Task 18.1: Find Local Printers with `printers`

DESCRIPTION Of the many problems with printing in Unix, none is more grievous than trying to figure out the names of all the different printers available, what kinds of printers they are, and where they're located. A complicated configuration file—`/etc/printcap`—contains all this information, but it's definitely not easy to read. So what do you do?

> Some systems have an `lpstat` command, which lists printers available on the system. I find the output of this command difficult to read, hence my inclusion of the `printers` script here. If you find the output acceptable (see the next task in this hour for a sample), you can skip this first unit, although you still might want to spend a few minutes looking at the `printers` script anyway.

I will present a simple 20-line shell script, `printers`, that reads through the `/etc/printcap` file and creates an attractive and easily read listing of all printers configured on your system. This hour presents the script and shows it at work on a few different computer systems. I encourage you to enter this script and place it in your own `bin` directory (`$HOME/bin` should be in your `PATH` for this to work).

You can also get your own copy of this script by popping over to the official Web site of this book, at `http://www.intuitive.com/tyu24/`.

ACTION

1. To start, take a quick look at the contents of the `/etc/printcap` file:

```
$ head -23 /etc/printcap
# $Header: /usr/msrc/usr/etc/printcap/RCS/printcap,v 1.235 93/11/04
➥10:55:21 mm
Exp Locker: mm $
aglw\ag\Iway:\
        :dr=/usr/local/lib/lp/lpmq:\
        :gc=cc:\
        :lf=/usr/spool/lpr/aglw/logfile:\
        :lo=/usr/spool/lpr/aglw/lock:lp=/dev/null:\
        :mj#25:mx#3000:nd=/usr/local/lib/lp/lpnc:\
        :pf=gnpt:\
        :rm=server.utech.edu:rw:sd=/usr/spool/lpr/aglw:sh:\
        :gf=/usr/local/bin/psplot:\
        :nf=/usr/local/lib/devps/devps:\
        :qo=age:mq=aglw1,aglw2,aglw3,aglw4:mu:\
        :wi=AG 23:wk=multiple Apple LaserWriter IINT:
aglw1:\
        :dr=/usr/local/lib/lp/lwp.sh:\
        :gc=cc:\
        :lf=/usr/spool/lpr/aglw1/logfile:\
        :lo=/usr/spool/lpr/aglw1/lock:lp=/dev/null:\
        :mj#25:mx#3000:nd=/usr/local/lib/lp/lpnc:\
        :pf=gnpt:\
        :rm=server.utech.edu:rw:sd=/usr/spool/lpr/aglw1:sh:\
        :gf=/usr/local/bin/psplot:\
        :nf=/usr/local/lib/devps/devps:\
        :wi=AG 23:wk=Apple LaserWriter IINT:
```

Don't panic! I won't go into exhaustive detail about the meaning of each field in this listing. It suffices to say that the first line in each entry lists the name of the printer, a | character, and any other possible names for the printer. Each field following the printer name is surrounded by colons and has a two-letter field name (for example, `dr`, `nf`), followed by the value of that particular field or setting. The fields of interest are the printer name; the `wi` field, which indicates the location of the printer; and the `wk` field, which indicates the type of printer.

18

2. There are no commonly available Unix utilities to keep you from having to slog
   through this configuration file. I have written a short yet powerful shell script
   called `printers` to list the desired information in a readable format:

```
$ cat bin/printers
# printers - create a simple list of printers from the /etc/printcap
#            file on the system.
#
# From
# Teach Yourself Unix in 24 Hours

printcap=/etc/printcap
awkscript=/tmp/awkscript.$$

/bin/rm -f $awkscript

cat << 'EOF' > $awkscript
NF == 2 { split($1, words, "|""");
          prname=words[1]
        }
NF > 2  { printf(""%-10s %s\n"", prname, $0) }
'EOF'

egrep '(^[a-zA-Z]|:wi)' $printcap | \
  sed 's/:/ /g' | \
  awk -f $awkscript | \
  sed 's/wi=//;s/wk=/(/;s/ $/)/' | \
  more

/bin/rm -f $awkscript

exit 0
```

Some of this script is beyond what you have learned in this book about commands
and scripts. In particular, the `awk` script, although only four lines long, shows some
of the more powerful features of the program. Enter this as shown, and be careful
to match the quotes and slash characters. Also, `sed`, the Unix stream editor, plays
an invaluable role in stripping out the more cryptic and mysterious parts of the
printer definition database.

3. After you've entered this script, enter the following:

```
$ chmod +x bin/printers
```

That will ensure that it's an executable script. Now you can try your new shell
script:

```
$$ printers | head -15
aglw           AG 23 (multiple Apple LaserWriter IINT)
aglw1          AG 23 (Apple LaserWriter IINT)
aglw2          AG 23 (Apple LaserWriter IINT)
```

```
aglw3           AG 23 (Apple LaserWriter IINT)
aglw4           AG 23 (Apple LaserWriter IINT)
alpslw          LIB 111 (Apple LaserWriter IINTX)
bio             COM B117 (DataPrinter (self-service))
cary            CQuad (NE-B7) (IBM 4019 Laser Printer)
cslw            CS 2249 (Apple LaserWriter IIg)
cs115lw         CS 115 (IBM 4019 LaserPrinter (for CS180))
cs115lw2        CS 115 (IBM 4019 LaserPrinter (for CS180))
csg40lw         CS G040 (IBM 4019 LaserPrinter )
csg50lw         CS G050 (IBM 4019 LaserPrinter )
cslp1           CS G73 (C.Itoh, white paper (self-service))
eng130ci        ENG 130 (C.Itoh, white paper (self-service))
Broken pipe
```

You can use this script also to find printers of a certain type or in a specific location, if the descriptions in your /etc/printcap file are configured in the correct manner:

```
$ printers | grep -i plotter
knoxhp          KNOX 316A (Hewlett Packard 7550+ Plotter)
ccp             MATH G109 (CALCOMP 1073 Plotter)
cvp             MATH G109 (VERSATEC V-80 Plotter)
$ printers | grep -i math
lwg186          MATH G186 (Apple LaserWriter IINT(private))
mathci          MATH R9 (C.Itoh, white paper (self-service))
mathlw          MATH 734 (multiple Apple LaserWriter IINT)
mathlw1         MATH 734 (Apple LaserWriter IINT)
mathlw2         MATH 734 (Apple LaserWriter IINT)
mathlw3         MATH 734 (Apple LaserWriter IINT)
cci             MATH G109 (C.Itoh, 3 hole white paper)
ccp             MATH G109 (CALCOMP 1073 Plotter)
cil             MATH G109 (IBM 4019 Laser Printer)
cvp             MATH G109 (VERSATEC V-80 Plotter)
```

4. You now should be able to choose a printer that's most convenient for your location. Set the environment variable PRINTER to that value. You also might want to tuck that into the last line of your .profile file so that next time you log in, the system will remember your printer selection.

```
$ PRINTER=mathlw
$ vi .profile

NAME="Dave Taylor"
BIN="889"

newmail

mesg y
PRINTER=mathlw; export PRINTER
~
~
```

18

> If your printer is not responding to what you set the PRINTER variable to, try using the LPDEST variable, especially on System V.

SUMMARY The first, and perhaps biggest, hurdle for printing on Unix has been solved: figuring out what the system calls the printer you're interested in using. Not only do you now have a new command, printers, for your Unix system, but you also can see how you can customize Unix to meet your needs by creating aliases and shell scripts.

Task 18.2: Printing Files with lpr or lp

DESCRIPTION Now that you have identified the name of the printer to use, how about sending information to the printer? If you are on a BSD system, the command to do this is lpr. You can print the results of a pipe command by adding lpr at the end of the pipeline, or you can print files directly by specifying them to the program. You can even use < to redirect input.

If you're using a System V version of Unix, you will need to use the lp command instead. As you read through this hour, you will see the differences between lpr and lp indicated. Note how the philosophies of the two vary.

The flags available for lpr and lp are numerous, and the most valuable ones are listed in Table 18.1 and Table 18.2. Notice the different meanings of the -P flag in the two commands.

TABLE 18.1 Useful Flags for LPR

Flag	Meaning
-h	Do not print the header page.
-i	Indent the entire file eight spaces before printing.
-L	Print in landscape (sideways) mode, if the printer is capable of doing so.
-P*pr*	Send the print job to printer *pr*.
-R	Print pages in reverse order.

TABLE 18.2 Useful Flags for LP

Flag	Meaning
-d*ptr*	Send the print job to the printer named *ptr*.
-P*n*	Print only page *n*.
-t*title*	Use *title* as the cover page title, where *title* is any string.

ACTION

1. Here's a demonstration of what happens if you try to use lp or lpr without specifying a printer and without having the PRINTER environment variable set. First,
   remove the environment variable definition for PRINTER by setting it to an empty
   string:

   ```
   $ PRINTER=""
   $ who | lpr
   lpr: No printer specified
   Broken pipe
   ```

   Some systems default to a printer named lp in this situation, so if you don't get an
   error message, that's what happened. If you have lpstat (a command for checking
   the status of a printer), the -d flag will result in lpstat listing your default printer.

   To specify a printer, use the -P flag with lpr or the -d flag with lp, followed
   immediately by the name of the printer:

   ```
   $ who | lpr -Pmathlw
   ```

   Specifying a printer with the -P flag (or -d with lp) will always override the environment variable specified in PRINTER; therefore, you can specify the default
   printer with PRINTER and specify other printers as needed without any danger.

   Notice that I printed the output of the who command but received absolutely no
   information from the lpr command regarding what printer it was sent to, the print
   job number, or any other information.

   To make life easier, I'm going to redefine PRINTER:

   ```
   $ PRINTER=mathlw
   ```

2. To find out what's in the print queue, I can use lpstat -pprinter on System V or
   the lpq -Pprinter command:

   ```
   $ lpq -Pmathlw

   mathlw@server.utech.edu:   driver not active
           Printing is disabled.

   Pos  User       Bin    Size  Jobname
   ...  ....       ....   ....  ........
     1  KOSHIHWE   0104   008   KOSHIHWE0104a
     2  KOSHIHWE   0104   008   KOSHIHWE0104b
     3  KOSHIHWE   0104   008   KOSHIHWE0104c
     4  kleimanj   0317   032   kleimanj0317a
     5  zeta       0042   008   zeta0042a
     6  jharger    0167   008   jharger0167a
     7  jharger    0167   008   jharger0167b
     8  ssinfo     0353   000   ssinfo0353a
   ```

18

```
 9  fuelling  0216  024  fuelling0216a
10  zeta      0042  152  zeta0042b
11  tkjared   0142  012  tkjared0142a
12  SUJATHA   0043  016  SUJATHA0043a
13  SUJATHA   0043  024  SUJATHA0043b
14  SUJATHA   0043  044  SUJATHA0043c
15  bee       0785  012  bee0785a
16  bee       0785  056  bee0785b
17  bee       0785  028  bee0785c
18  ssinfo    0353  004  ssinfo0353b
19  ssinfo    0353  000  ssinfo0353c
20  ssinfo    0353  000  ssinfo0353d
21  ssinfo    0353  004  ssinfo0353e
22  stacysm2  0321  000  stacysm20321a
23  ssinfo    0353  000  ssinfo0353f
24  taylor    0889  000  taylor0889a
```

```
mathlw: waiting to be transmitted to server.utech.edu
```

```
The queue is empty.
```

Quite a few print jobs are waiting to be sent, but it's not obvious why the printer is disabled. The output of the `lpq` and `lpstat` commands is explained in detail later in this hour.

3. To print the file `dickens.note` in landscape mode, without a header page, indented eight spaces, and in reverse order, I can use the following flags:

```
$ lpr -hiLR < dickens.note
```

If I did this often, a shell alias could be helpful:

```
$ alias lpr='lpr -hiLR'
```

On a System V machine, you also could create the alias `lpr='lp'`, though none of these particular options is available with `lp`.

If you find yourself printing to a couple of different printers quite often, you easily can define a few shell aliases to create printer-specific `print` commands:

```
$ alias mathprint='lpr -Pmathlw'
$ alias libprint='lpr -Plibrary'
$ alias edprint='lpr -Pedlw'
```

On System V machines, the aliases would be this:

```
$ alias mathprint='lp -dmathlw'
$ alias libprint='lp -dlibrary'
$ alias edprint='lp -dedlw'
```

4. Some systems have a command `lpinfo` that also offers information about printers:

```
$ lpinfo mathlw
mathlw: server.utech.edu; MATH 734; multiple Apple LaserWriter IINT
```

To find out more information about the printer, you can specify the -v flag:

```
$ lpinfo -v mathlw
mathlw description:
        driver: /usr/local/lib/lp/lpmq
        printer control group: cc
        graphic filter: /usr/local/bin/psplot
        log file: /usr/spool/lpr/mathlw/logfile
        lock file: /usr/spool/lpr/mathlw/lock
        hardware line: /dev/null
        maximum job count per user = 25
        subqueue list: mathlw1,mathlw2,mathlw3
        maximum print file blocks = 3000
        make unique via bin change
        network driver: /usr/local/lib/lp/lpnc
        ditroff filter: /usr/local/lib/devps/devps
        print formats: graphics, ditroff, use pr, troff
        queue ordering: age
        host attachment: server.utech.edu
        spooling directory: /usr/spool/lpr/mathlw
        location: MATH 734
        description: multiple Apple LaserWriter IINT
```

5. The lpinfo command also can show you a list of what printers are available, but I find the output format considerably more difficult to understand than lpstat:

```
$ lpinfo -a | head -15
aglw:    server.utech.edu; AG 23; multiple Apple LaserWriter IINT
aglw1:       server.utech.edu; AG 23; Apple LaserWriter IINT
aglw2:       server.utech.edu; AG 23; Apple LaserWriter IINT
aglw3:       server.utech.edu; AG 23; Apple LaserWriter IINT
aglw4:       server.utech.edu; AG 23; Apple LaserWriter IINT
alpslw: sentinel.utech.edu; LIB 111; Apple LaserWriter IINTX
bio:     ace.utech.edu; COM B117; DataPrinter (self-service)
cary:    franklin.utech.edu; CQuad (NE-B7); IBM 4019 Laser Printer
cslw: server.utech.edu; CS 2249; Apple LaserWriter IIg
cs115lw:     expert.utech.edu; CS 115; IBM 4019 LaserPrinter (for CS180)
cs115lw2:    expert.utech.edu; CS 115; IBM 4019 LaserPrinter (for CS180)
csg40lw:     franklin.utech.edu; CS G040; IBM 4019 LaserPrinter
csg50lw:     franklin.utech.edu; CS G050; IBM 4019 LaserPrinter
cslp1: expert.utech.edu; CS G73; C.Itoh, white paper (self-service)
eng130ci:    age.utech.edu; ENG 130; C.Itoh, white paper (self-service)
Broken pipe
```

If you find this output readable, you're undoubtedly becoming a real Unix expert!

SUMMARY The output of the printers command specifies the location of the printer that printed the file. I need to go to another building to pick up my hard copy. (The location is specified in the output of the printers command.)

18

Task 18.3: Formatting Print Jobs with `pr` and `col`

DESCRIPTION The printout I generated looked good, but boring. I would like to have a running header on each page that specifies the name of the file and the page number. I'd also like to have a bit more control over some other formatting characteristics. This is exactly where the `pr` command comes in handy. Not intended just for printing, `pr` is a general pagination and formatting command that can be used to display information on the screen. Even better, `pr` is available on both BSD and System V Unix.

The `pr` program is loaded with options, most of which are quite useful at times. For example, `-2` makes the output two columns, which is useful for printing results of the `who` command in landscape mode. The most useful options are presented in Table 18.3.

TABLE 18.3 Useful Flags in `PR`

Flag	Meaning
-n	Produce n-column output per page.
+n	Begin printing on the nth page.
-f	Don't print the page header and footer information.
-hhdr	Use hdr as the head of each page.
-wn	Set the page width to n characters (for landscape mode).
-m	Print all files at once, one per column.

ACTION

1. My printout of the `who` command showed me that my choice of paper was poor. In a 128-character-wide landscape printout, I actually used only the first 30 characters or so of each line. Instead, I can use `pr` to print in two-column mode:

> On some Unix systems, the `-f` flag to `pr` causes the program to put form feeds at the bottom of each printed page. To suppress the header and footer, use `-t`.

```
$ who | pr -2 | more

Dec  9 13:48 2000   Page 1
```

```
root      console Dec 6 18:02    ab       ttypk   Dec 9 07:57  (nova)
princess  ttyaV   Dec 9 13:44    dutch    ttypl   Dec 8 13:36  (dov)
tempus    ttyaW   Dec 9 13:43    malman   ttypm   Dec 9 13:07  (dov)
enatsuex  ttyaY   Dec 9 13:41    bakasmg  ttypq   Dec 9 13:09  (age)
coxt      ttyaZ   Dec 9 13:35    dodsondt ttyps   Dec 8 11:37  (age)
scfarley  ttyAa   Dec 9 13:36    md       ttypv   Dec 8 08:23  (kraft)
nancy     ttyAb   Dec 9 13:12    rothenba ttypw   Dec 9 13:15  (trinetra)
rick      ttyAc   Dec 9 13:12    xuxiufan ttypy   Dec 9 13:16  (ector)
fitzte    ttyAd   Dec 9 13:47    nashrm   ttyq3   Dec 9 13:04  (pc115)
maluong   ttyAe   Dec 9 13:46    dls      ttyq5   Dec 9 13:06  (dialup01)
af5       ttyAg   Dec 9 09:12    myounce  ttyq8   Dec 9 02:14  (limbo)
zjin      ttyAh   Dec 9 13:44    liyan    ttyq9   Dec 9 13:11  (volt)
herbert1  ttyAi   Dec 9 13:29    daffnelr ttyqA   Dec 9 13:36  (localhost)
ebranson  ttyAj   Dec 9 13:44    mm       ttyqB   Dec 9 10:32  (mm)
billiam   ttyAk   Dec 9 13:36    jlapham  ttyqC   Dec 9 12:46  (mac18)
linet2    ttyAm   Dec 9 11:04    chuicc   ttyqE   Dec 9 13:38  (icarus)
--More-- _
```

Notice that the pr program not only made this a two-column listing, but also added
a page header that indicates the current date and page number.

2. The header still doesn't contain any information about the command name, which
is what would really be helpful. Fortunately, I easily can add the header information I want by using pr:

```
$ who | pr -h "(output of the who command)" -2 | more
```

```
Dec  9 13:50 2000  (output of the who command) Page 1
```

```
root      console Dec 6 18:02    ab       ttypk   Dec 9 07:57  (nova)
princess  ttyaV   Dec 9 13:44    dutch    ttypl   Dec 8 13:36  (dov)
tempus    ttyaW   Dec 9 13:43    malman   ttypm   Dec 9 13:07  (dov)
enatsuex  ttyaY   Dec 9 13:41    bakasmg  ttypq   Dec 9 13:09  (age)
coxt      ttyaZ   Dec 9 13:35    dodsondt ttyps   Dec 8 11:37  (age)
scfarley  ttyAa   Dec 9 13:36    md       ttypv   Dec 8 08:23  (kraft)
nancy     ttyAb   Dec 9 13:12    rothenba ttypw   Dec 9 13:15  (trinetra)
rick      ttyAc   Dec 9 13:12    xuxiufan ttypy   Dec 9 13:16  (ector)
fitzte    ttyAd   Dec 9 13:47    dls      ttyq5   Dec 9 13:06  (dialup01)
maluong   ttyAe   Dec 9 13:46    myounce  ttyq8   Dec 9 02:14  (limbo)
maritanj  ttyAf   Dec 9 13:49    liyan    ttyq9   Dec 9 13:11  (volt)
af5       ttyAg   Dec 9 09:12    daffnelr ttyqA   Dec 9 13:36  (localhost)
zjin      ttyAh   Dec 9 13:48    mm       ttyqB   Dec 9 10:32  (mm)
herbert1  ttyAi   Dec 9 13:29    jlapham  ttyqC   Dec 9 12:46  (mac18)
ebranson  ttyAj   Dec 9 13:44    chuicc   ttyqE   Dec 9 13:38  (icarus)
--More-- _
```

That's much better.

18

3. I might want to compare the contents of two different directories. The -1 flag to ls forces the ls program to list the output one filename per line, so I can create a couple of files in this format easily:

```
$ ls -1 src > src.listing
$ ls -1 /tmp > tmp.listing
```

These files look like this:

```
$ head src.listing tmp.listing
==> src.listing <==
calc-help
calc.c
fixit.c
info.c
info.o


==> tmp.listing <==
Erik/
GIri/
Garry/
MmIsAlive
Re01759
Re13201
Sting/
VR001187
VR002540
VR002678
```

Now I will use pr to build a two-column output:

```
$$ pr -m src.listing tmp.listing | head -15


Dec  9 13:53 2000    Page 1


calc-help                      Erik/
calc.c                         GIri/
fixit.c                        Garry/
info.c                         MmIsAlive
info.o                         Re01759
massage.c                      Re13201
                               Sting/
                               VR001187
                               VR002540
Broken pipe
```

4. This would be more helpful if I could turn off the blank lines automatically included at the top of each listing page, which is a job for the -f flag (or -t, if your version of pr is -f for form feeds):

```
$ pr -f -m src.listing tmp.listing | head -15
Dec  9 13:56 2000   Page 1


calc-help                      Erik/
calc.c                         GIri/
fixit.c                        Garry/
info.c                         MmIsAlive
info.o                         Re01759
massage.c                      Re13201
                               Sting/
                               VR001187
                               VR002540
                               VR002678
                               VR002982
                               VR004477

Broken pipe
```

5. It looks good. Now it's time to print by piping the output of the pr command to the lpr command:

```
$ !pr | lpr
pr -f -m src.listing tmp.listing | lpr
```

6. As you proceed with printing tasks in Unix, you might find sporadically that you get output of the form "H^HH^HH^Hhe^He^He^Hel^Hl^Hl^Hll^Hl^Hl^Hlo^Ho^Ho^Hlo". Many versions of the man command output bold in just this fashion: What you're seeing is a letter followed by a backspace, the letter, a backspace, the letter, and a backspace, and the letter one last time. The above is "Hello" in this manner.

> The backspace-for-emphasis format is from old daisy-wheel and dot-matrix printers (remember those? I do!) and makes no sense with modern printing equipment. If you see this, you'll want to know about the useful col command, and its -b flag, which strips out all the backspace sequences. You'd simply add it to your pipe:
>
> ```
> $ pr -f -m src.listing tmp.listing | col -b | lpr
> ```

SUMMARY The pr command can be used to ensure that your printouts are always clean and readable. Again, it's a perfect place to create an alias: `alias print='pr | lpr'` or `alias print='pr | lp'`. Even without any flags, pr automatically adds page numbers to the top of each page.

Task 18.4: Working with the Print Queue

DESCRIPTION On a personal computer, you might be used to having your printer directly connected to your system, so anything you print using File -> Print (on Windows
and the Mac) instantly prints. Unfortunately, Unix doesn't grant you the luxury of using
your own personal printer. Instead, it handles print requests in a print queue, a managed
list of files to print. When you send a file to a printer with lpr or lp, the request is added
to a queue of files waiting to print. Your request goes to the bottom of the list, and any
subsequent print requests are added below yours. Your print request gradually moves up
to the top of the list and prints, without interrupting the print requests of those folks
ahead of you.

Sometimes it can be frustrating to wait for a printout. However, a queuing system has
some advantages over simply allowing users to share a single printer. The greatest is that
you can use the lprm command to change your mind and remove print requests from the
queue before they waste paper. The lprm command works with the *print job name*,
which you can learn by checking the print queue using lpq. Both lprm and lpq can
either use the default PRINTER setting or can have printers specified with -P*printer*. The
lpq command also can limit output to just your jobs by adding your account name to the
command.

If your system doesn't have lprm, use the cancel command to remove entries from the
print queue. The lpstat command is also the System V replacement for the lpq command, though many sites alias lpq = lpstat to make life a bit easier.

To use cancel, you need to specify the name of the printer and the job ID, as shown in
the lpstat output. If I had print request ID 37 on printer hardcopy, I could cancel the
print request with the command cancel hardcopy -37.

ACTION

1. A glance at the mathlw queue shows that many files are waiting to print:

   ```
   $ lpq

   mathlw@server.utech.edu:   driver not active
            Printing is disabled.

   Pos  User      Bin   Size  Jobname
   ---  ----      ----  ----  -------
     1  KOSHIHWE  0104  008   KOSHIHWE0104a
     2  KOSHIHWE  0104  008   KOSHIHWE0104b
     3  KOSHIHWE  0104  008   KOSHIHWE0104c
     4  kleimanj  0317  032   kleimanj0317a
     5  zeta      0042  008   zeta0042a
   ```

```
 6   jharger    0167   008   jharger0167a
 7   jharger    0167   008   jharger0167b
 8   ssinfo     0353   000   ssinfo0353a
 9   fuelling   0216   024   fuelling0216a
10   zeta       0042   152   zeta0042b
11   tkjared    0142   012   tkjared0142a
12   SUJATHA    0043   016   SUJATHA0043a
13   SUJATHA    0043   024   SUJATHA0043b
14   SUJATHA    0043   044   SUJATHA0043c
15   bee        0785   012   bee0785a
16   bee        0785   056   bee0785b
17   bee        0785   028   bee0785c
18   info       0353   004   info0353b
19   info       0353   000   info0353c
20   info       0353   000   info0353d
21   info       0353   004   info0353e
22   stacysm2   0321   000   stacysm20321a
23   info       0353   000   info0353f
24   taylor     0889   000   taylor0889a
```

```
mathlw: waiting to be transmitted to server.utech.edu
```

```
The queue is empty.
```

My print job is job number 24, with the print job name `taylor0889a`. Figure 18.1 explains the different fields in the queue listing.

FIGURE 18.1

The `lpq` *output format explained.*

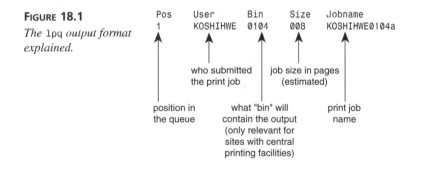

The printer is also turned off. You can see at the top of the `lpq` output the telltale message `driver not active, printing is disabled`. Obviously, if the printer is disabled, it's rather futile to wait for a printout.

2. To limit the output to just those print jobs that are mine, I specify my account name:

18

```
$ lpq taylor
mathlw@server.utech.edu:    driver not active
        Printing is disabled.

Pos  User      Bin   Size  Jobname
---  ----      ----  ----  -------
  1  taylor    0889  004   taylor0889a

mathlw: waiting to be transmitted to server.utech.edu

The queue is empty.
```

3. To check the status of another printer, I can specify the printer with the `-P` flag:

```
$ lpq -Pb280il

b280il@franklin.utech.edu:       driver not active

The queue is empty.

b280il:    waiting to be transmitted to franklin.utech.edu

The queue is empty.
```

That's better. The queue is empty.

4. To remove my print job from the `mathlw` print queue, I simply specify the print job name from the `lpq` output:

```
$ lprm taylor0889a
```

Unix carries out my command without giving me confirmation that it has done so, but a quick check with `lpq` shows me that it worked:

```
$ lpq taylor
mathlw@server.utech.edu:    driver not active
        Printing is disabled.

The queue is empty.

mathlw: waiting to be transmitted to server.utech.edu

The queue is empty.
```

I wish that the default for the `lpq` command would show only print jobs that I have in the queue, and I could use the `-a` flag to show all print jobs queued. Furthermore, instead of incorrectly saying `The queue is empty`, `lpq` should report something more useful, such as `there are 23 other print jobs in the queue`.

5. Now I resubmit the print job request, this time to the b280il printer:

```
$ !pr -Pb280il
pr -f -m src.listing tmp.listing | head -15 | lpr -Pb280il
```

Uh oh! I don't want that head -15 cutting off the information in the printout.

```
$ lpq -Pb280il
b280il@franklin.utech.edu:      driver active; no job printing

Pos  User      Bin   Size  Jobname
---  ----      ----  ----  -------
  1  nfsuser   0058  268   nfsuser0058a
  2  nfsuser   0054  012   nfsuser0054a
  3  taylor    0889  000   taylor0889a

b280il:    waiting to be transmitted to franklin.utech.edu

The queue is empty.
```

To remove my print request, I use lprm:

```
$ lprm taylor0889a
"taylor0889a" not located.
```

I've made a second mistake! I need to specify the printer:

```
$ lprm -Pb280il taylor0889a
```

Now I can fix the original command and print the files correctly:

```
$ pr -f -m src.listing tmp.listing | lpr -Pb280il
```

SUMMARY Unix offers some printing capabilities you might not be accustomed to working with, particularly the capability to change your mind and stop a print job before it touches paper. You can see that it's a good idea to set the PRINTER environment variable to your favorite printer so that you can save yourself from struggling to enter weird printer names each time you print a file.

Summary

A few judiciously defined aliases can save you a lot of frustration down the road. Choose your favorite printer, define the PRINTER environment variable to point to that printer, and give yourself an alias such as print to include all the default options you like for your printouts. You might consider creating an alias pq to show your own print requests queued for your favorite printer. (This is easy to do. Use alias pq='lpq $LOGNAME' or alias pq='lpstat -u $LOGNAME'.) You also could show only your print requests, if any, by tucking a grep into the command: alias pq='lpq | grep $LOGNAME'.

Workshop

The Workshop summarizes the key terms you learned and poses some questions about the topics presented in this chapter. It also provides you with a preview of what you will learn in the next hour.

Key Terms

print job name   The unique name assigned to a print job by the `lpr` or `lp` command.

print queue   The queue, or list, in which all print jobs are placed for processing by the specific printer.

Exercises

1. Use the `lpinfo -a` or `printers` command to find out what printers are available on your system. Which command is easier to use? How many printers are available?

2. Is your `PRINTER` variable already set to a printer? Is it the printer you would choose?

3. Use `man -k` to see what commands you have on your system that work with the printers and print queues. Use `man` to peruse them.

4. Show three ways to print the file `dickens.note` with `lpr`.

5. Add a print job to the queue and then remove it with `lprm`. What happened?

6. How would you use `pr` to add `A Tale of Two Cities` as a running title across each printout page of the file `dickens.note`? How would you start the printout on the second page of the file?

Preview of the Next Hour

In the next hour, you learn about the `find` command with its unique command flags and its partner `xargs`. This command enables you to search the Unix file system for files that meet specific criteria, and `xargs` enables you to perform actions on those files.

HOUR 19

Searching for Information and Files

One of the greatest challenges in Unix is to find the files you want, when you want them. Even the best organization in the world, with mnemonic subdirectories and carefully named files, can break down and leave you saying to yourself, "I know it's somewhere, and I remember that it contains a bid for Acme Acres Construction to get that contract; but for the life of me, I just can't remember where it is!"

Goals for This Hour

In this hour, you will learn about

- The `find` command and its weird options
- How to use `find` with `xargs`

In this hour, you learn sophisticated ways to find specific information on the Unix system. The powerful `find` command and its partner, `xargs`, are the contents of this hour.

Finding What's Where

The more you use Unix, the more likely you'll end up losing track of where some of your files are. In Unix, however, there's a cool tool to help you find them again.

Task 19.1: The `find` Command and Its Weird Options

DESCRIPTION   The `grep` family can help you find files by their content. There are many other ways to look for things in Unix, and that's where the `find` command can help. This command has a notation that is completely different from all other Unix commands: It has full-word options rather than single-letter options. Instead of `-n` *pattern* to match filenames, for example, `find` uses `-name` *pattern*.

The general format for this command is to specify the starting point for a search through the file system, followed by any actions desired. The list of possible options, or flags, is shown in Table 19.1.

TABLE 19.1   Useful Options for the `find` Command

Option	Meaning
`-atime` *n*	True if the file was accessed *n* days ago.
`-ctime` *n*	True if the file was created *n* days ago.
`-exec` *command*	Execute *command*.
`-mtime` *n*	True if the file was modified *n* days ago.
`-name` *pattern*	True if the filename matches *pattern*.
`-print`	Print names of the files matched.
`-type` *c*	True if the file is of type *c* (as shown in Table 19.2).
`-user` *name*	True if the file is owned by user *name*.

The `find` command checks the specified options, going from left to right, once for each file or directory encountered. Further, `find` with any of the time-oriented commands can search for files more recent than, older than, or exactly the same age as a specified date, with the specifications *-n*, *+n*, and *n*, respectively. Some examples will make this clear.

ACTION

1. At its simplest, `find` can be used to create a list of all files and directories below the current directory:

   ```
   $ find . -print
   .
   ./OWL
   ```

```
./OWL/owl.h
./OWL/owl
./OWL/owl.c
./OWL/simple.editor.c
./OWL/ask.c
./OWL/simple.editor.o
./OWL/owl.o
```

lots and lots of output removed

```
./dead.letter
./who.is.who
./src.listing
./tmp.listing
./.wrongwords
./papert.article
```

2. To limit the output to just those files that are C source files (those that have a .c suffix), I can use the -name option before the -print option:

```
$ find . -name "*.c" -print
./OWL/owl.c
./OWL/simple.editor.c
./OWL/ask.c
./OWL/handout.c
./OWL/WordMap/msw-to-txt.c
./OWL/WordMap/newtest.c
./OWL/feedback.c
./OWL/define.c
./OWL/spell.c
./OWL/submit.c
./OWL/utils.c
./OWL/parse.c
./OWL/sendmail.c
./owl.c
./src/calc.c
./src/info.c
./src/fixit.c
./src/massage.c
```

Using the -name option before the -print option can be very handy.

3. To find just those files that have been modified in the past seven days, I can use -mtime with the argument -7 (include the hyphen):

```
$ find . -mtime -7 -name "*.c" -print
./OWL/owl.c
./OWL/simple.editor.c
./OWL/ask.c
./OWL/utils.c
./OWL/sendmail.c
```

19

If I use just the number 7 (without a hyphen), I will match only those files that were modified exactly seven days ago:

```
$ find . -mtime 7 -name "*.c" -print
$
```

To find those C source files that I haven't touched for at least 30 days, I use +30:

```
$ find . -mtime +30 -name "*.c" -print
./OWL/WordMap/msw-to-txt.c
./OWL/WordMap/newtest.c
./src/calc.c
./src/info.c
./src/fixit.c
./src/massage.c
```

4. With find, I now have a tool for looking across vast portions of the file system for specific file types, filenames, and so on.

To look across the /bin and /usr directory trees for filenames that contain the pattern cp, I can use the following command:

```
$ find /bin /usr -name "*cp*" -print
/usr/diag/sysdcp
/usr/spool/news/alt/bbs/pcbuucp
/usr/spool/news/alt/sys/amiga/uucp
/usr/spool/news/comp/mail/uucp
/usr/spool/news/comp/os/cpm
/usr/spool/news/comp/protocols/tcp-ip
/usr/man/man4/tcp.4p
/usr/man/man8/tcpd.8l
/usr/man/cat3f/%unitcp.3f.Z
/usr/man/cat3f/unitcp.3f.Z
/usr/unsup/bin/cpio
/usr/unsup/gnu/man/man1/cccp.1
/usr/news/cpulimits
/usr/doc/local/form/cp
/usr/doc/local/form/cpio
/usr/doc/local/form/rcp
/usr/doc/uucp
```

> This type of search can take a long time on a busy system. When I ran this command on my system, it took almost an hour to complete!

5. To find a list of the directories I've created in my home directory, I can use the -type specifier with one of the values shown in Table 19.2. Here's one example:

```
$ find . -type d -print
.
./OWL
```

```
./OWL/Doc
./OWL/WordMap
./.elm
./Archives
./InfoWorld
./InfoWorld/PIMS
./Mail
./News
./bin
./src
./temp
$
```

TABLE 19.2   Helpful find -type File Types

Letter	Meaning
d	Directory
f	File
l	Link

6. To find more information about each of these directories, I can use the -exec option to find. Unfortunately, I cannot simply enter the command; the exec option must be used with {}, which will be replaced by the matched filename, and \; at the end of the command. (If the \ is left out, the shell will interpret the ; as the end of the find command.) You also must ensure that there is a space between the {} and the \; characters.

```
$ find . -type d -exec ls -ld {} \;
drwx------ 11 taylor      1024 Dec 10 14:13 .
drwx------  4 taylor       532 Dec  6 18:31 ./OWL
drwxrwx---  2 taylor       512 Dec  2 21:18 ./OWL/Doc
drwxrwx---  2 taylor       512 Nov  7 11:52 ./OWL/WordMap
drwx------  2 taylor       512 Dec 10 13:30 ./.elm
drwx------  2 taylor       512 Nov 21 10:39 ./Archives
drwx------  3 taylor       512 Dec  3 02:03 ./InfoWorld
drwx------  2 taylor       512 Sep 30 10:38 ./InfoWorld/PIMS
drwx------  2 taylor      1024 Dec  9 11:42 ./Mail
drwx------  2 taylor       512 Oct  6 09:36 ./News
drwx------  2 taylor       512 Dec 10 13:58 ./bin
drwx------  2 taylor       512 Oct 13 10:45 ./src
drwxrwx---  2 taylor       512 Nov  8 22:20 ./temp
```

7. The find command is commonly used to remove core files that are more than a few days old. These core files are copies of the actual memory image of a running program when the program dies unexpectedly.

19

```
$ find . -name core -ctime +4 -print
./Archives/core
./bin/core
$
```

These core files can be huge, so occasionally trimming them is wise. It's just a small step from the preceding find command, which shows matching core files:

```
$ find . -name core -ctime +4 -exec /bin/rm -f {} \;
$
```

There's no output from this command because I didn't use the -print at the end of the command. What it does is find all files called core that have a creation time that's more than four days ago and remove them.

SUMMARY The find command is a powerful command in Unix and one of my favorites. It helps you find files by owner, type, filename, and just about any other attributes. The most awkward part of the command is the required elements of the -exec option, and that's where the xargs command helps immensely.

Task 19.2: Using find with xargs

DESCRIPTION You can use find to search for files, and you can use grep to search within files, but what if you want to search a combination? That's where xargs is helpful.

ACTION

1. A few days ago, I was working on a file that was computing character mappings of files. I'd like to find it again, but I don't remember either the filename or where the file is located.

   First, what happens if I use find and have the -exec argument call grep to find files containing a specific pattern?

```
$ find . -type f -exec grep -i mapping {} \;
typedef struct mappings {
map-entry character-mapping[] = {
int        long-mappings = FALSE;
        case 'l': long-mappings = TRUE;
            if (long-mappings)
        /** do a short mapping **/
        /** do a long mapping **/
        /** Look up the specified character in the mapping database
➥ **/
        while ((character-mapping[pointer].key < ch) &&
            (character-mapping[pointer].key > 0))
        if (character-mapping[pointer].key == ch)
          return ( (map-entry *) &character-mapping[pointer]);
```

```
# map,uucp-map     = The UUCP Mapping Project = nca-maps@apple.com
grep -i "character*mapping" * */* */*/*
to print PostScript files produced by a mapping application that
➥runs on the
bionet.genome.chromosomes          Mapping and sequencing of
➥eucaryote chromosomes.
./bin/my.new.cmd: Permission denied
typedef struct mappings {
map-entry character-mapping[] = {
int         long-mappings = FALSE;
        case '1': long-mappings = TRUE;
           if (long-mappings)
       /** do a short mapping **/
       /** do a long mapping **/
       /** Look up the specified character in the mapping database
➥**/
           while ((character-mapping[pointer].key < ch) &&
              (character-mapping[pointer].key > 0))
           if (character-mapping[pointer].key == ch)
             return ( (map-entry *) &character-mapping[pointer]);
or lower case values. The table mapping upper to
```

The output is interesting and somewhat overwhelming, but it doesn't contain any filenames, so there's no way to know from which files these lines were extracted.

2. A second, smarter strategy would be to use the -l flag to grep so that grep specifies only the matched filename:

```
$ find . -type f -exec grep -l -i mapping {} \;
./OWL/WordMap/msw-to-txt.c
./.elm/aliases.text
./Mail/mark
./News/usenet.alt
./bin/my.new.cmd: Permission denied
./src/fixit.c
./temp/attach.msg
$
```

19

3. That's a step in the right direction, but the problem with this approach is that each time find matches a file, it invokes grep, which is a very resource-intensive strategy. Instead, you use the xargs to read the output of find and build calls to grep (remember that each time a file is seen, the grep program will check through it) that specify a lot of files at once. This way, grep is called only four or five times even though it might check through 200 or 300 files. By default, xargs always tacks the list of filenames to the end of the specified command, so using it is easy:

```
$ find . -type f -print | xargs grep -l -i mapping
./OWL/WordMap/msw-to-txt.c
./.elm/aliases.text
./Mail/mark
```

```
./News/usenet.alt
./bin/my.new.cmd: Permission denied
./src/fixit.c
./temp/attach.msg
```

This gave the same output, but it was quite a bit faster.

4. What's nice about this approach to working with find is that because grep is getting multiple filenames, it will automatically include the filename of any file that contains a match when grep shows the matching line. Removing the -l flag results in exactly what I want:

```
$ find . -type f -print | xargs grep -i mapping
./OWL/WordMap/msw-to-txt.c:typedef struct mappings {
./OWL/WordMap/msw-to-txt.c:map-entry character-mapping[] = {
./OWL/WordMap/msw-to-txt.c:int          long-mappings = FALSE;
./OWL/WordMap/msw-to-txt.c:        case 'l': long-mappings = TRUE;
./OWL/WordMap/msw-to-txt.c:        if (long-mappings)
./OWL/WordMap/msw-to-txt.c:        /** do a short mapping **/
./OWL/WordMap/msw-to-txt.c:        /** do a long mapping **/
./OWL/WordMap/msw-to-txt.c:        /** Look up the specified character
➥in the mapping database **/
./OWL/WordMap/msw-to-txt.c:        while ((character-
➥mapping[pointer].key
./src/fixit.c:  /** do a long mapping **/
./src/fixit.c:  /** Look up the specified character in the
➥mapping database **/
./src/fixit.c:  while ((character-mapping[pointer].key < ch) &&
./src/fixit.c:          (character-mapping[pointer].key > 0))
./src/fixit.c:  if (character-mapping[pointer].key == ch)
./src/fixit.c:    return ( (map-entry *) &character-
➥mapping[pointer]);
./temp/attach.msg:or lower case values. The table mapping upper to
```

SUMMARY When used in combination, find, grep, and xargs are a potent team to help find files lost or misplaced anywhere in the Unix file system. I encourage you to experiment further with these important commands to find ways they can help you work with Unix.

Summary

The find command is one of the more potent commands in Unix. It has many esoteric options, and to get the full power from find, xargs, and grep, you need to experiment.

Workshop

This Workshop poses some questions about the topics presented in this chapter. It also provides you with a preview of what you will learn in the next hour.

Exercises

1. Use `find` and `wc -l` to count how many files you have. Be sure to include the `-type f` option so that you don't include directories in the count.

2. Use the necessary commands to list the following:
   - All filenames that contain abc
   - All files that contain abc

Preview of the Next Hour

The next hour introduces you to the various Unix tools available to communicate with other users, whether interactively character-by-character or with one of the many e-mail utilities.

19

HOUR **20**

Archives and Backups

It's your worst nightmare: You wake up, log in to your newly customized Unix account, and find that everything is gone. All your aliases, shell scripts, mail files, and HTML documents…missing. You e-mail the administrator—a panicked e-mail—and she responds, "Oh, yeah, sorry."

To avoid this sort of horrible mishap you need a solid archival and backup strategy, and that's what this lesson is going to focus on. In particular, we will explore the `tar` command as a simple tool for making single-file backup images of large amounts of information, and we will examine the `compress` command to shrink the resultant archive as small as possible.

A number of ways are possible to write your backup data to a tape unit, CD-RW, or network backup device. Most of those work with the `cpio` or `tcio` commands, so they'll be examined too, but after twenty-plus years of Unix, `tar` has really always been the cornerstone of my own backup strategy.

Goals for This Hour

In this hour, you will

- Learn about the `tar` tape archive utility
- Explore `compress` to shrink down large files
- Learn about `cpio` and `tcio`
- Examine a common personal backup scheme

Regardless of which of these backup strategies you choose, I highly recommend that you do *something* to ensure the survival of your data. Even if the administrator of the server you use insists that she does regular backups, it's dangerous to rely on someone else to protect your precious data!

Indeed, I have personal experience with the danger of relying on backups. It was mid-December, 1999 when I noticed a hacker had broken into our Unix system and was destroying files (I used `ps` to see what he was doing). I tried to stop him, but it was too late. We lost everything. Fortunately, we had backup tapes...until we tried to use them. Then we found the unpleasant truth: The backups hadn't been working for weeks and weeks, but the failed backups kept overwriting the tape data. The result was that we lost over a month of work, which was not a pretty sight.

The `tar` Tape Archive Utility

It's not glamorous, but `tar` has been around forever on Unix and has helped create millions of backups. What most people don't realize is that `tar` can be just as useful for regular folk who don't need to learn how to write to a tape device or otherwise administer the computer.

Task 20.1: Learning to use `tar`

DESCRIPTION Even though you can give about twenty different flags to `tar`, fundamentally the program has three modes of operating: building an archive, showing the contents of an archive, or extracting files from an archive. They are `tar -c` (for creation), `tar -t` (for a table of contents of an archive), and `tar -x` (to extract data). `tar` commands look like `tar [flags] file or directory names`.

Let's take a look.

ACTION

1. To start out, I'd like to create a quick archival snapshot of all the files and folders in my home directory. To do this, I'll create an output file in /tmp:

```
$ tar -cf /tmp/backup.tar *
$
```

There was no output, but it took about 10 seconds to execute, so I assume something happened. The -c flag tells tar to create an archive, remember, and -f *file* indicates the name of the output file. *, of course, indicates that all files and folders in the current directory should be matched.

> Be careful with * expansion and tar. In this first example, the backup didn't include any of my dot files, including my .profile and .bashrc files. Instead, use . as the starting directory for the archive to ensure that you get absolutely everything.

A quick peek with ls tells the surprising story:

```
$ ls -l /tmp/backup.tar
-rw-r--r--  1 taylor  wheel  15360000 Feb  8 02:52 /tmp/backup.tar
$
```

Wow! That's a big output file. 15.3 Megabytes, to be exact.

2. To get more output and have a better idea what's going on, I'll add the -v (verbose) flag:

```
$ tar -cvf /tmp/backup.tar .
.
./.cshrc
./.login
./.mailrc
./.profile
./.rhosts
./.bash_history
./Talks
./Talks/Writeups
./Talks/Writeups/biz-and-the-net
./Talks/Writeups/html-half.1
./Talks/Writeups/html-half.2
./Talks/Writeups/instant-homepage
./Talks/Writeups/intro-to-the-net

lots and lots of output removed
```

20

```
./pict.pict
./browse.sh
./test.html
./Exchange
./Exchange/build-exchrate
./Exchange/exchange.pl
./Exchange/exchange.db
./etcpasswd
./badjoke
./badjoke.rot13
$
```

Pretty simple, isn't it?

3. To have a peek at what's inside a `tar` archive file, I'll use the `-t` flag instead of `-c`:

```
$ tar -tf /tmp/backup.tar | head
.
././.cshrc
././.login
././.mailrc
././.profile
././.rhosts
././.bash_history
./Talks
./Talks/Writeups
./Talks/Writeups/biz-and-the-net
$
```

Notice that I piped the output to `head` so that I'd only see the top ten lines.

You can get more information about the archival files by combining `-t` with the `-v` verbose flag:

```
$ tar -tvf /tmp/backup.tar | head
drwxr-xr-x  2 taylor    taylor       0 Feb  7 14:41 .
-rw-r--r--  1 taylor    taylor     817 Dec 14 16:09 ././.cshrc
-rw-r--r--  1 taylor    taylor     581 Dec 14 16:09 ././.login
-rw-r--r--  1 taylor    taylor     105 Dec 10 04:04 ././.mailrc
-rw-r--r--  1 taylor    taylor     201 Dec 10 04:04 ././.profile
-rw-------  1 taylor    taylor      65 Dec 10 04:04 ././.rhosts
-rw-------  1 taylor    taylor    7545 Feb  7 15:30 ././.bash_history
drwxrwxr-x  2 taylor    taylor       0 Dec 14 16:09 ./Talks
drwxrwxr-x  2 taylor    taylor       0 Dec 14 16:09 ./Talks/Writeups
-rw-r--r--  1 taylor    taylor    1832 Dec 14 16:09 ./Talks/Writeups/biz-and-
➥the-net
$
```

4. Now that I have a basic archival file, what can I do with it? Well, the easiest thing is to change the output from a file to a Unix tape device, enabling me to make a quick backup:

```
$ tar cf /dev/rst0 .
$
```

This took about 20 minutes to write to a backup tape, but now I can eject the tape, drop it in my pocket, and have my own personal copy of all the data files without worrying about whether the computer might crash in 15 minutes!

5. In addition to writing backups to tape and creating snapshots of files and folders for safety purposes, tar turns out to be a great way to transfer many files from one computer to another.

ftp is the file transfer program that lets you easily send files between two computers. It's covered in depth in Lesson 22, "Using telnet, ssh, and ftp." If you want to, flip forward and read about it. Otherwise, just remember that it's basically a login-transfer file-logout system.

With the /tmp/backup.tar file created, all I'd have to do is use ftp to transfer it to another computer, and then tar on that computer to unpack it and replicate all of my files and folders:

```
$ ftp shell3.ba.best.com
Connected to shell3.ba.best.com.
220 shell3.ba.best.com FTP server (Version wu-2.6.1(1)
➥ Mon Oct 2 14:46:30 PDT 2000) ready.
Name (shell3.ba.best.com:taylor): taylor
331 Password required for taylor.
Password:
230 User taylor logged in.
Remote system type is UNIX.
Using binary mode to transfer files.
ftp> put /tmp/backup.tar backup.tar
local: /tmp/backup.tar remote: backup.tar
500 'EPSV': command not understood.
227 Entering Passive Mode (206,184,139,134,121,43)
150 Opening BINARY mode data connection for backup.tar.
226 Transfer complete.
15800320 bytes sent in 171.45 seconds (90.00 KB/s)
ftp> quit
221-You have transferred 15800320 bytes in 1 files.
221-Total traffic for this session was 15800805 bytes in 1 transfers.
221-Thank you for using the FTP service on shell3.ba.best.com.
221 Goodbye.
$
```

After the archive file has been transferred to the remote system, it's just a matter of unpacking things:

```
$ ls
$ tar -xf backup.tar
$ ls -F
```

20

```
CraigsList/      Shuttle/        buckaroo            pict.pict
Exchange/        Src/            etcpasswd           test.html
Gator/           Stuff/          getmodemdriver.sh*  test.sh*
Lists/           Talks/          getstocks.sh*       testfile
Lynx.trace       badjoke         gettermsheet.sh*    tif.tif
Mail/            badjoke.rot13   gif.gif
News/            bin/            jpg.jpg
Old/             browse.sh*      niftylister.tar
$
```

Quickly and easily done.

6. If you'd wanted to get output from the tar extraction as it went along, you could add the -v flag:

```
$ tar -xvf backup.tar
.
./.cshrc
./.login
./.mailrc
./.profile
./.rhosts
./.bash_history
./Talks
./Talks/Writeups
./Talks/Writeups/biz-and-the-net
./Talks/Writeups/html-half.1
./Talks/Writeups/html-half.2
./Talks/Writeups/instant-homepage
./Talks/Writeups/intro-to-the-net

lots and lots of output removed

./pict.pict
./browse.sh
./test.html
./Exchange
./Exchange/build-exchrate
./Exchange/exchange.pl
./Exchange/exchange.db
./etcpasswd
./badjoke
./badjoke.rot13
$
```

7. One important capability of tar worth showing here is that you can extract specific files and folders from an archive based on a pattern given to the program:

```
$ tar -xvf backup.tar Exchange
tar: WARNING! These patterns were not matched:
Exchange
$
```

8. Oops! Patterns have to be left-rooted. Let's try again:

```
$ tar -xvf backup.tar ./Exchange
./Exchange
./Exchange/build-exchrate
./Exchange/exchange.pl
./Exchange/exchange.db
$
```

The tar command has a ton of options; the most useful are summarized in Table 20.1.

TABLE 20.1 Useful Options to tar

Option	Meaning
-c	Create an archive
-f	Use the specified output filename
-h	Follow symbolic links as if they were normal files or directories
-H	Follow symbolic links on the command line only
-m	Do not preserve file modification times
-p	Preserve user and group ID as well as file mode information.
-t	Show the table of contents of an archive
-v	Verbose mode: more explanatory output
-x	Extract files from archive
-Z	Compress archive using compress
-z	Compress archive using gzip

SUMMARY One great use of tar if you have a remote Unix account and a local PC or Macintosh is to occasionally build an archival snapshot of all your files and then FTP them to your local computer. That's what we'll talk about more in the last part of this lesson.

20

Shrinking Your Files with compress

The first thing you'll notice about the tar command is that it can generate remarkably large files. In fact, although disk space is relatively cheap nowadays, a single tar file can easily put you over quota on your system or at least make you unpopular with the other users.

The good news is that there's a solution called compress. In fact, there are two solutions because the same Free Software Foundation folk who gave us GNUEMACS and the terrific gcc compiler also wrote a version of the popular PC utility ZIP for Unix, called gzip.

Action 20.2: Shrinking Large Files on Unix

DESCRIPTION The compress command is available on all versions of Unix, though gzip is becoming a popular addition too. Both fundamentally do the same thing: They use different compression algorithms to minimize the size of the file or files given.

ACTION

1. First, let's see what compress can do with the huge backup.tar file we created earlier.

```
$ ls -l backup.tar
-rw-r--r--  1 taylor  wheel  15800320 Feb  8 02:58 backup.tar
$ compress backup.tar
$ ls -l backup.tar
ls: backup.tar: No such file or directory
```

Uh oh! No need to panic, though: The compress program automatically renames the compressed file to have a .Z filename suffix, so you know it's compressed:

```
$ ls -l backup.tar.Z
-rw-r--r--  1 taylor  wheel  7807489 Feb  8 02:58 backup.tar.Z
```

Not too bad: It's gone down from 15.8MB to 7.8MB.

2. To uncompress the file and have it return to its original state, use uncompress:

```
$ uncompress backup.tar.Z
$ ls -l backup.tar
-rw-r--r--  1 taylor  wheel  15800320 Feb  8 02:58 backup.tar
```

3. It turns out that there's a useful flag to compress that lets you see how much it's compressed things. Let's do it one more time to see:

```
$ compress -v backup.tar
backup.tar:    49.4% OK
```

A quick turn with a calculator will confirm that it's just about 50% smaller in size. Before we're done, let's uncompress it again:

```
$ uncompress -v backup.tar.Z
backup.tar.Z:   202.3% OK
```

4. For comparison, let's have a quick look at the gzip command, which offers very similar capabilities:

```
$ ls -l backup.tar
-rw-r--r--  1 taylor  wheel  15800320 Feb  8 02:58 backup.tar
$ gzip backup.tar
$ ls -l backup.tar.Z
ls: backup.tar.Z: No such file or directory
```

Again, don't panic. gzip uses a different filename suffix to indicate that the file has been compressed: .gz.

```
$ ls -l backup.tar.gz
-rw-r--r--  1 taylor  wheel  5584285 Feb  8 02:58 backup.tar.gz
$
```

You can see that it did a better job of compressing this particular file than compress did: It's only 5.5MB, instead of 7.8MB. Different files will have different compress/gzip results, and some rare files won't be any smaller when compressed, for reasons known only to the folk who invented the compression algorithms.

5. To uncompress (expand) the file, use gunzip:

```
$ gunzip backup.tar.gz
$
```

All back to normal!

6. Just like compress, gzip also has a -v flag that gives you some interesting information about the compression as it transpires:

```
$ gzip -v backup.tar
backup.tar:              64.6% -- replaced with backup.tar.gz
```

 SUMMARY Most of the files you have are doubtless too small to worry about compressing them to save space. But if you are building large archival files or if you're planning on transferring large files through FTP, compress or gzip can be your new best friend, saving you minutes, if not hours, of transfer time.

 For example, let's say that a 56K modem connection can transfer roughly 25Kbps of actual data, so the 15MB uncompressed tar archive would take approximately 10 minutes to transfer. Compress that with gzip to 5.5MB, and you'll finish up the data transfer in a speedier 3.6 minutes.

20

Exploring the Unix Tape Command: cpio

It shouldn't surprise you that the Unix system has general purpose backup programs that optionally can write to a tape device unit. It's very consistent with the overall philosophy of Unix.

In fact, even the program written specifically for backups, cpio, has other more general-purpose applications for users.

Action 20.3: A Quick Exploration of cpio

DESCRIPTION   To more fully understand how this command works, it's necessary to see it in action.

ACTION

1. The most important difference between cpio and tar is that cpio expects to read the list of files needing backup from standard input, rather than as a directory specifier on the command line.

   This doesn't seem like a big deal, but it really is, particularly when you combine cpio with the find command. Here's a typical usage:

   ```
   $ find . -name "*.c" -print | cpio -oO sourcefiles.cpio
   $
   ```

   This invocation (-o indicates I want to create an output archive, and -O lets me specify the output filename) makes an archive called sourcefiles.cpio that comprises all the *.c source files in the current directory and below. This would be essentially impossible to accomplish with tar.

2. To examine the contents of the archive:

   ```
   $ cpio -itI sourcefiles.cpio
   ./bin/fixit.c
   ./Src/Embot/embot.c
   ./Src/Embot/error.c
   ./Src/Embot/interact.c
   ./Src/Embot/log.c
   ./Src/Embot/mail_utils.c
   ./Src/Embot/savemsg.c
   ./Src/Embot/sendfile.c
   ./Src/Embot/utils.c
   ./Src/Misc/usage_summary.c
   ./Src/Misc/fixit.c
   ./Src/Misc/info.c
   ./Src/Misc/isnew.c
   ./Src/Misc/mydate.c
   ./Src/Misc/showmatches.c
   ./Src/Misc/change.c
   ./Src/change.c
   ./Src/cleanup.c
   ./Src/cribbage.c
   ./Src/expandurl.c
   ```

```
./Src/extract-mail.c
./Src/futuredate.c
./Src/import.c
./Src/assemble.c
./Src/make-html.c
./Src/old-import.c
./Src/process-data.c
./Src/showmatches.c
./Src/sum-up.c
./Src/text-counter.c
./Src/login.c
./Src/calc.c
$
```

In this case, the -i flag indicates that I want to have it read an existing archive, -t indicates that I only want a listing of the files, not to have them extracted, and -I lets me specify the input filename.

3. To actually extract a file, the easiest way is to specify the pattern that should be compared. Notice in this case that I'm going to feed the archive into cpio as standard input. It's much more common:

```
$ cpio -i cribbage < *cpio
cpio: WARNING! These patterns were not matched:
cribbage
$
```

Nope. The pattern *cribbage* didn't work. In fact, it wasn't a regular expression, so cpio helpfully indicated there weren't any matches. An improved attempt:

```
$ cpio -i '*cribbage*' < *cpio
cpio: Unable to create ./Src/cribbage.c <No such
file or directory>
$
```

4. Almost, but there's still a problem, though the cpio error message isn't too explanatory. The problem is that there is no Src directory and the program can't create subdirectories without a new flag -d being added. While I'm at it, I'll also add -v to ensure some output:

```
$ cpio -ivd '*cribbage*' < *cpio
./Src/cribbage.c
30 blocks
$
```

Got it. Hurray!

Table 20.2 summarizes the most useful cpio flags.

20

TABLE 20.2 Useful cpio Starting Flags

Flag	Description
-A	Appends specified files to an existing archive
-a	Resets access times of input files after copying
-d	Creates directories as required
-E	Lets you specify a file containing all the filenames to be added to the archive
-i	Extracts files from a cpio archive
-I	Lets you specify an input archive file
-L	Follows symbolic links
-o	Creates an output archive
-O	Specifies the output filename (the default is to send the information to standard output)
-R	Sets owner of extracted files to specified user ID
-t	Prints a table of contents (used with -i flag)
-v	Verbose output format

SUMMARY The examples here might not make the value of cpio obvious, but the reason that system administrators love this program is because it can read standard input for a list of files to add to an archive. As you'll see in the next section, this makes a very sophisticated level of archival behavior a breeze.

Personal Backup Solutions

Before we leave this discussion of backup and archive solutions, I'd like to talk a bit about a couple of ways that you can use these commands to improve the reliability and safety of your own interaction with Unix.

There are two basic ways that I use these tools myself: to create "snapshots," automatically dated archives of the files I'm currently creating, and to create "last changed" files that I can write to a tape device.

Action 20.4: A Personal Backup Scheme

DESCRIPTION It's a good thing that you paid attention during the shell scripting lesson (Lesson 15, "Shell Programming Overview,") because the snapshot solution is a shell script that uses tar to build instant archives.

ACTION

1. The first step in this script building process is to figure out a solution for creating filenames that automatically have the date and time included. This is done with a backquote invocation of the `date` command, but an invocation that exploits the format string option:

```
$ date +%m.%d.%Y.%H:%M
02.08.2001.14:34
$
```

The date is *month.day.year.hour:minute*.

2. Now to create a snapshot filename with this suffix:

```
snapdir="$HOME/Snapshots"
thedate="`date +%m.%d.%Y.%H:%M`"
outfile="$snapdir/snapshot.$thedate.tar.gz"
```

This saves the date/time format as variable `thedate`, and then creates an `outfile` filename for use later in the script that is prefaced with the name of the snapshot directory. On my system, `outfile` ends up looking like

```
/home/taylor/Snapshots/snapshot.02.08.2001.14:40.tar.gz
```

which is just what we want.

3. There isn't much more to the script, just the actual invocation to the `tar` command itself. To make it a bit more sophisticated, the script will use the first argument, if present, as the directory to back up. Otherwise, it'll use the current directory as the default. Also notice the use of the `-z` flag to automatically `gzip` the resultant output (which is why the `.gz` was added to the `outfile` variable above, too).

Here's the entire script, short and sweet:

```
$ cat snapshot.sh
#!/usr/local/bin/bash

snapdir="$HOME/Snapshots"
thedate="`date +%m.%d.%Y.%H:%M`"
outfile="$snapdir/snapshot.$thedate.tar.gz"

if [ $# -gt 0 ] ; then
  dirs=$1
else
  dirs="."
fi

echo "Backing up $dirs to $outfile"
```

20

```
tar -czf $outfile $dirs

echo "done."

exit 0
$
```

4. And, in use:
```
$ alias snapshot="$HOME/bin/snapshot.sh"
$ snapshot
Backing up . to /home/taylor/Snapshots/snapshot.02.08.2001.14:50.tar
done.
$
```

With this in your toolkit, you can easily save a current copy of your work at any time prior to major edits, or at any historic time in the history of your project.

5. In a similar way, backup scripts usually use a *marker* file that saves the last-backed-up time and date for comparison purposes. It relies on the -cnewer *marker-file* option to find, which then compares the last-modified date of all files encountered against the marker file, only listing those that are newer.

It'd be used as part of a pipeline:
```
find $HOME -cnewer $HOME/.marker -print | cpio -o /dev/rst0
touch $HOME/.marker
```

Amazingly, that's all that is needed to have an incremental backup written to /dev/rst0 (usually your tape device on your Unix system) where the only files added are those that you've changed more recently than the previous backup.

SUMMARY   The combination of tar, cpio, the compress utilities and a bit of imagination regarding how to put them all together can yield remarkably valuable results and expand your toolkit a great deal.

Perhaps just as importantly, the last action of the find pipe to cpio demonstrates the fundamental elegance of Unix: an entire backup regimen in two lines of script. Pretty cool, eh?

Summary

Whether it's to assuage your anxiety about unstable servers, to avoid possible problems with poor backups and inattentive administrators, or simply to help you package up and move large sets of files around, tar and its partner programs are a great help. Every time I have to move from one system to another, I invariably use tar, compress, and ftp as a power trio.

Workshop

The Workshop poses some questions about the topics presented in this chapter.

Exercises

1. What's the key difference between `tar` and `cpio`?

   What's wrong with this command?

   ```
   tar cvf OUTPUT.tar *
   ```

3. Try both `compress` and `gzip` on a few large files to see which produces better results. Try `gzip` on a very small file too, and see what happens.

Next Lesson

In the next hour you'll learn about what's probably the single most exciting aspect of the operating system: the ability to communicate with other users on your computer, both interactively and through electronically transmitted mail, e-mail.

20

HOUR 21

Communicating with E-mail

It's time to learn about what's probably the single most exciting aspect of the operating system: the ability to communicate with other users on your computer, both interactively and through electronically transmitted mail, e-mail.

Goals for This Hour

In this hour, you will learn about

- Enabling messages using `mesg`
- Writing to other users
- Reading electronic mail with `mailx`
- Sending electronic mail with `mailx`
- Internet e-mail addresses
- The smarter alternative for sending mail, `elm`
- A peek at Pine

Of all the places in Unix where there is variety, most of it surely is found in electronic mail, or *e-mail*. At least 15 programs are available from various vendors to accomplish two tasks: to read mail from and send mail to other folks. In this hour, you learn about the standard electronic mail system, Berkeley Mail. I also take a little time to whet your appetite by showing you the Elm Mail System, a full-screen alternative mail program that's widely distributed.

 You'd have to be sleeping under a pretty big rock not to know that there's a much bigger world than just your own machine, a world called the Internet. You'll learn more about how Unix enables you to be a power participant on the network in subsequent chapters.

Interacting with the World

Much of what you've learned in this book has been about how you can exploit Unix to be more productive. Now it's time to learn how to communicate with others, to learn about what I consider the "killer app" of Unix: electronic mail.

Task 21.1: Enabling Messages Using `mesg`

DESCRIPTION Earlier you learned that all peripherals hooked up to Unix are controlled by device drivers and that each device driver has an associated /dev file. If you want to talk with other users on the system, you need to ensure that they can communicate with you too. (This pertains only to `talk`, however; e-mail works regardless of the `mesg` setting.)

ACTION

1. To find out through what device I'm connected to the system, I can use the Unix command `tty`:

```
$ tty
/dev/ttyAo
```

The `tty` device is just another Unix file, so I can look at it as I'd look at any other file:

```
$ ls -l /dev/ttyAo
crw---x--- 1 taylor    21,  71 Dec  8 10:34 /dev/ttyAo
```

Notice that I own the file and that I have write permission, but others do not.

2. To enable other users to communicate with me directly, I need to ensure that they can run programs that can write to my terminal. That is, I need to give them write permission to my tty device. Instead of using the chmod command—tracking down what line I'm on and all that—I use a simple alternative, mesg. To turn messages on—enabling other users to communicate with me—I specify the y flag to mesg:

```
$ mesg y
$ ls -l `tty`
crw-rwx--- 1 taylor     21,  71 Dec  8 10:33 /dev/ttyAo
```

To disable messages (perhaps if I'm busy and don't want to be bothered), I can use the n flag, which says that no, I don't want messages:

```
$ mesg n
$ ls -l `tty`
crw---x--- 1 taylor     21,  71 Dec  8 10:34 /dev/ttyAo
```

3. At any point, you can double-check your current terminal write permission by entering mesg without any flags. The output is succinct, but it tells you what you want to know:

```
$ mesg
is n
```

To see the settings of your tty, use the backquotes with the tty command, as shown in the preceding examples.

SUMMARY Don't tell anyone this secret. After you have write permission to someone else's terminal, you can redirect the output of commands to their tty device as easily as to any other file in Unix. In fact, that's how the write command works: It opens the other person's tty device for writing, and each line you enter is also written to the other person's screen. I note this simply so that you can see why the permissions of your /dev/tty line are so important, not so that you can go wild and start tormenting your fellow Unix users!

Task 21.2: Writing to Other Users

DESCRIPTION Now that you can allow others to write to your terminal as well as prevent them from writing to it, it's time to find out how to chat with them using the talk command. talk is quite slick because it splits your screen into two windows: The top window shows what you're saying to the other party, and the bottom window shows what they're typing. Unlike with many online discussion and "chat" systems, however, both people can type simultaneously, which can be quite fun!

21

talk is the Unix precursor to Instant Messaging, if you've ever used America Online, Yahoo! IM, or similar.

What's even more valuable about the talk command is that you can actually interact directly with users on other, remote computers too!

You don't need to guess whether they're online; to see who is logged in to a remote system you can use a command called finger, which by default will show you a summary of who is on the local machine. Add a username to the command, and it will show information about the specified account. Specify a user on a remote system, and you can find out whether that user is logged in. Specify just the remote site, and it shows you who is logged in at the current moment. To check on a local account, use finger *accountname*. To make it a remote system, append the hostname: finger *account@host.domain*. To check all users on a remote site, use finger *@host.domain*.

ACTION

1. A quick glance at the output of who shows that many people are currently logged in to the local system:

```
$ finger
Login        Name                 TTY Idle    When     Location
root     root                     *co 1:13 Mon 18:02
taylor   Dave Taylor              aV       Mon 16:49
kippje   Jeff Kip                 Ab       Mon 16:41
adamr    Adam Coy                 *Ae      Mon 18:36
daffnelr Lawrence Daff            sK       Mon 12:45    (dov27)
tsa      Earl the Unctuous Aardva sL    42 Mon 12:48    (expert)
daffnelr Lawrence Daff            *sM      Mon 12:49    (localhost)
ben      Ben Moon                 sN 8:42 Mon 09:16     (corona)
ben      Ben Moon                 sR 8:47 Mon 09:22     (corona)
marteldr David Martel             *sY   7d Mon 18:41    (limbo)
gerlema  David Geman              sb       Mon 18:38    (mac19)
mk       Michael Kenzie           *sc 2:48 Mon 08:07    (mk)
mzabel   Mary Zabeliski           *sf      Mon 18:45    (sun1)
fritzg   Geoff Fritzen            sh     9 Mon 18:45    (pc43)
brynta   Bryan Ayerson            *si      Mon 18:46    (limbo)
deckersl Sharon Deck              sk     3 Mon 18:51    (xds31)
```

2. To learn more about the account mk, I can specify that account name to the finger program:

```
$ finger mk
```

```
Login name: mk          (messages off) Real name: Michael Kenzie
Office: Math 204                        Home phone:
```

```
Directory: /users/mk                    Shell: /bin/ksh
Universe: universe(ucb)
Member of groups: utech root actadmin source
On since Dec 13 08:07:12 on ttysc from mk
2 hours 50 minutes Idle Time
No unread mail on this host.
Plan:
```

You can see that this is full of information. Notice that Michael is currently logged in to the system (the output says On since Dec 13 08:07:12 on ttysc).

3. To see who is logged in to the USENIX Association main computer in Berkeley, California, I can use this:

```
$ finger @usenix.org
[usenix.org]
Login      Name                TTY Idle    When      Where
pmui       Peter Mui           co    2d Tue 10:10
ah         Alain Henon        Z5       Mon 15:58    remote # 5408955 Dia
toni       Toni Veglia         p1    3d Thu 17:09    exec
diane      Diane DeMartini     p3     9 Mon 08:41    mac2.usenix.ORG
mis        Mark Seiden         p4    3d Thu 21:46    seiden.com
mis        Mark Seiden         p5    2d Fri 15:18    msbnext.internex
scott      Scott Seebass       p6    3d Tue 14:54    biohazard
lilia      Lilia Carol Scott   p7  1:12 Mon 08:39    thing1
mis        Mark Seiden         p8    3d Thu 22:09    seiden.com
toni       Toni Veglia         pa    3d Mon 10:38    exec
ellie      Ellie Young         q1  1:00 Mon 10:33    boss:0.0
scott      Scott Seebass       q2   18: Wed 15:36    biohazard
ellie      Ellie Young         q3  1:01 Mon 10:33    boss:0.0
mis        Mark Seiden         q6    1d Fri 11:28    seiden.com
```

Here you can see that many folks are logged in but almost everyone has a lot of idle time. A d suffix indicates the number of days idle. So you can see that Peter Mui's account has been idle for two days.

> To find out what the weather is like in the greater San Francisco area, try finger weather@rogue.llnl.gov, which will connect you to the Lawrence Livermore National Laboratories in Walnut Creek, California.

4. To talk with someone on a remote system, use finger to verify that the person is logged in, not off doing something else (which is what a high idle time usually suggests), and then use talk:

```
$ finger marv@netcom.com
Login name: marv                        In real life: Marvin Raab
Directory: /u1/marv                     Shell: /bin/csh
```

21

```
Logged in since Mon Dec  6 15:22 on ttys8
5 seconds idle time
Mail last read Mon Dec 13 15:22:22 1993
No Plan.
$ talk marv@netcom.com
```

```
[Waiting for your party to respond]




.................................................................
```

On the remote system, here's what Marvin sees:

```
Message for marv(ttyaV) from Talk_Daemon@limbo.utech.edu at 18:55 ...
talk: connection requested by taylor@limbo.utech.edu.
talk: respond with: "talk taylor@limbo.utech.edu"
```

After he responds, the screen looks like this:

```
[Connected]
Hello Marv!  Have you seen the latest news on CNN?
=




.................................................................
Hi Dave! What's going on?
```

Notice that the cursor is in the top pane. Anything I enter will, character by character, be sent along to Marvin, so we can interactively chat and even type at the same time without our words getting jumbled. When I'm done, I simply press ^C to quit the program.

SUMMARY The `finger` program offers further information about users on your own and remote systems, and using it is an essential first step in talking with your friends on the Internet through `talk`. Try entering taylor@intuitive.com, and if I'm logged in, what the heck! Try using `talk` to say hi interactively.

> `talk` is a great tool for interacting with others, but because a couple of different versions of the program are usually incompatible with each other, using it can be frustrating. You'll know that things aren't working correctly when you see "waiting for permission" messages over and over again. A lower-tech alternative for talking with people on your own system is the more primitive write command. Try man write to learn more about how to use it.

Task 21.3: Reading Electronic Mail with `mailx`

DESCRIPTION The `write` command is helpful for those situations when your friend or colleague is logged in to the computer at the same time you are, but what do you do if the person is not logged in and you want to leave a note? What if you want a friend to receive a copy of a note you're sending to, say, your boss?

That's where electronic mail moves into the spotlight. Of all the capabilities of Unix, one of the most popular is undoubtedly this capability to send electronic mail to another user—even on another computer system—with a few keystrokes. In this section, you learn how to work with other users on your own computer, and later in this hour you learn how to send mail to folks who are on different computers, even in different countries.

Various programs for reading mail can be used on Unix systems, but the two most common are `mail` and `Mail`. (The latter is also often called `mailx` on SVR4 systems.) Because of the similarity of the names, the former is known as "mail" and the latter as either "cap mail" ("cap" for the uppercase, or capital *M*) or "Berkeley Mail." I refer to "Mail" either as Berkeley Mail or as its AT&T name, `mailx`. You should never use `mail` to read or write mail if Berkeley Mail is available to you because Berkeley Mail is much easier to use. I will focus on using Berkeley Mail.

To envision electronic mail, imagine that you have a butler who is friendly with the local post office. You can hand him mail with only the name of the recipient written on the envelope, and the butler will make sure that it's delivered. If new mail arrives, the butler discreetly lets you know about it, so you can then display the messages, one by one, and read them. Furthermore, your butler organizes your old mail in a big filing cabinet, filing each message by any criteria you request.

21

That's almost exactly how Berkeley Mail works. To send mail, you simply state on the command line the account name of the recipient, indicate a subject, enter the message itself, and poof! Your message is sent through the system and arrives at the recipient's terminal posthaste. When mail arrives for you, the shell or one of various utilities, such as `biff` or `newmail`, can notify you. Each time you log in, the system checks for electronic mail, and if you have any, the system will say `You have mail` or `You have new mail`. You can save mail in files called *mail folders*.

Berkeley Mail has many command options, both flags that you can specify when you invoke the program from the command line, and commands used within the program. Fortunately, you can always request help while you're in the program to review these options. The most noteworthy flags are `-s` *subject*, which enables you to specify the subject of the message on the command line, and `-f` *mailfolder*, which enables you to specify a mail folder to read rather than the default (which is your incoming mailbox).

The most valuable commands to use within the program are summarized in Table 21.1.

TABLE 21.1   Berkeley Mail Command Summary

Command	Meaning
delete *msgs*	Mark the specified messages for deletion.
headers	Display the current page of *headers* (the cryptic lines of information at the top of an *e-mail* message; I explain them a bit later in this lesson). Add a + to see the next page, or a - to see the preceding page.
help	Display a summary of Berkeley Mail commands.
mail *address*	Send mail to the specified address.
print *msgs*	Show the specified message or messages.
quit	Leave the Berkeley Mail program.
reply	Respond to the current message.
save *folder*	Save the current message to the specified mail folder.
undelete *msgs*	Undelete the messages you've specified for deletion using the delete command.

ACTION

1. I have lots of electronic mail in my mailbox. When I logged in to the system today, the shell indicated that I had new mail. To find out what the new messages are, I use `mailx` (though I also could have typed `Mail` because they're synonymous on my machine):

```
$ mailx
Mail version 5.2 6/21/85.  Type ? for help.
"/usr/spool/mail/taylor": 9 messages 5 new
     1 disserli Mon Nov 22 19:40  54/2749 "Re: Are you out there"
>N   2 Laura.Ramsey Tue Nov 30 16:47  46/1705 "I've got an idea..."
 N   3 ljw      Fri Dec  3 22:57  130/2712 "Re: Attachments"
 N   4 sartin   Sun Dec  5 15:15  15/341 "I need your address"
 N   5 rustle   Tue Dec  7 15:43  29/955 "flash cards"
     6 harrism  Tue Dec  7 16:13  58/2756 "Re: Writing Lab OWL proj"
     7 CBUTCHER Tue Dec  7 17:00  19/575 "Computer Based GRE's"
     8 harrism  Tue Dec  7 21:46  210/10636 "writing  environments"
 N   9 v892127  Wed Dec  8 07:09  38/1558 "Re: Have you picked up"
& _
```

I have lots of information here. On the first line, the program identifies itself as Mail version 5.2, built June 21, 1985. Somewhat tucked away in that top corner is the reminder that I can type ? at any point to get help on the commands.

The second line tells me what mailbox I'm reading. In this case, I'm looking at the default mailbox for my incoming mail, which is /usr/spool/mail/taylor. On your system, you might find your mailbox in this directory, or you might find it in a directory similarly named /usr/mail. Either way, you don't have to worry about where it's located because Berkeley Mail can find it automatically.

The 3rd through 11th lines list mail messages I have received from various people. The format is N in the first column if I haven't seen the piece of mail before, a unique index number (the first item in each listing is one), the account that sent the message, the date and time the message was sent, the number of lines and characters in the message, and the subject of the message, if known. Figure 21.1 illustrates this more clearly.

FIGURE 21.1
Understanding the message display in mailx.

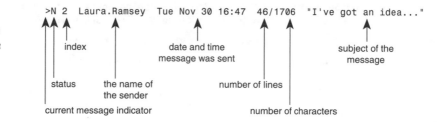

2. To read a specific message, I need enter only the index number of that message:

```
& 7
Message  7:
From: CBUTCHER Tue Dec  7 17:00:28 2000
From: Cheryl <CBUTCHER>
```

21

```
Subject:     Computer Based GRE's
To: Dave Taylor <TAYLOR>

I've scheduled to take the computer based GRE's in Indy on Jan. 6th.
Call me crazy but someone's got to do it.  I'll let you know how it goes.

Do you know anyone else that has taken the GRE's this way?  I figure
there's a paper in it somewhere.......

If you have that handout from seminar in a file, could you please send it
to me?

Thanks.

& =
```

This message is from my friend Cheryl Butcher. Collectively, the first set of lines in the message—each a single word, a colon, and some information or other—is the *header* of the message, or the electronic equivalent of the postmark and envelope. The header always will include From:, Subject:, and To:, specifying the name and electronic address of the sender, the subject of the message, and the list of recipients.

3. To respond to this message, I enter reply:

```
& reply
To: CBUTCHER
Subject: RE: Computer Based GRE's

=
```

Anything I now enter will be sent back to Cheryl:

```
Hi. I am very interested in hearing about your reaction to the
computer-based GRE test. I'm sure you're correct that there is
a paper there, but wouldn't it be best to work with ETS on the
project?

I'll dig around and find those handouts soonest.

Happy holidays!

Dave
```

To end the message, I either press ^d on its own line, or use the shorthand . by itself:

```
.
Cc: =
```

Berkeley Mail is now asking me to specify any other people I might like to have receive *carbon copies* of this message. Entering an account name or two here will allow the designated people to see a copy of this message to Cheryl. Because I don't want anyone else to read this message, I press Return, which sends the message and returns me to the & prompt:

```
& _
```

4. I now can use the `headers` command to see what is the current message (the one I just read). It's the message indicated by the >. (Refer to Figure 21.1 if you're having trouble finding it.)

```
& headers
      1 disserli Mon Nov 22 19:40  54/2749 "Re: Are you out there"
      2 Laura.Ramsey Tue Nov 30 16:47  46/1705 "I've got an idea..."
  N   3 ljw      Fri Dec  3 22:57  130/2712 "Re: Attachments"
  N   4 sartin   Sun Dec  5 15:15  15/341 "I need your address"
  N   5 rustle   Tue Dec  7 15:43  29/955 "flash cards"
      6 harrism  Tue Dec  7 16:13  58/2756 "Re: Writing Lab OWL proj"
  >   7 CBUTCHER Tue Dec  7 17:00  19/575 "Computer Based GRE's"
      8 harrism  Tue Dec  7 21:46  210/10636 "writing environments"
  N   9 v892127  Wed Dec  8 07:09  38/1558 "Re: Have you picked up"
& _
```

To save Cheryl's message in a folder called "cherylmail," I use the `save` command:

```
& save cherylmail
"cherylmail" [New file] 19/575
& _
```

5. Now that I'm done with this message, I can mark it for deletion with the `delete` command:

```
& delete 7
&
```

Notice that after I enter `headers`, Cheryl's message vanishes from the list:

```
& headers
      1 disserli Mon Nov 22 19:40  54/2749 "Re: Are you out there"
      2 Laura.Ramsey Tue Nov 30 16:47  46/1705 "I've got an idea..."
  N   3 ljw      Fri Dec  3 22:57  130/2712 "Re: Attachments"
  N   4 sartin   Sun Dec  5 15:15  15/341 "I need your address"
  N   5 rustle   Tue Dec  7 15:43  29/955 "flash cards"
      6 harrism  Tue Dec  7 16:13  58/2756 "Re: Writing Lab OWL proj"
  >   8 harrism  Tue Dec  7 21:46  210/10636 "writing environments"
  N   9 v892127  Wed Dec  8 07:09  38/1558 "Re: Have you picked up"
&
```

Look closely at the list, and you will see that it hasn't completely forgotten the message; the program hides message 7 from this list. I could still read the message by using `print 7`, and I could use `undelete 7` to pull it off the deletion list.

> Deleted messages in Berkeley Mail are actually marked for future deletion and aren't removed until you quit the program. When you quit, however, there's no going back. A deleted message is gone. While you're within the program, you can delete and undelete to your heart's content.

6. Now I want to delete both of the messages from harrism (numbers 6 and 8):

```
& delete 6 8
```

Now the list of messages in my mailbox is starting to look pretty short:

```
& h
     1 disserli Mon Nov 22 19:40  54/2749 "Re: Are you out there"
     2 Laura.Ramsey Tue Nov 30 16:47  46/1705 "I've got an idea..."
 N   3 ljw      Fri Dec  3 22:57  130/2712 "Re: Attachments"
 N   4 sartin   Sun Dec  5 15:15  15/341 "I need your address"
 N   5 rustle   Tue Dec  7 15:43  29/955 "flash cards"
>N   9 v892127  Wed Dec  8 07:09  38/1558 "Re: Have you picked up"
&
```

> Most commands in Berkeley Mail can be abbreviated to just their first letter, which cuts down on typing.

7. You can save a group of messages to a file by specifying the numbers between the save command and the folder name:

```
& save 6 8 harris
6: Inappropriate message
```

Oops. I had deleted messages 6 and 8. I must undelete them before I can proceed:

```
& undelete 6 8
& save 6 8 harrismail
"harrismail" [New file] 268/13392
```

8. Use the quit command to get out of this program:

```
& quit
Saved 1 message in mbox
Held 6 messages in /usr/spool/mail/taylor
$
```

The messages that I viewed and didn't delete are moved out of my incoming mailbox to the file mbox. The messages I saved and the messages I marked for deletion are silently removed, and all remaining messages are retained in /usr/spool/mail/taylor.

The biggest complaint I have with Berkeley Mail is that it does all this activity silently. I don't like the fact that saved messages are deleted automatically from the incoming mailbox when I quit and that—more importantly—messages I've read are tossed automatically into another folder. To ensure that messages you've read aren't moved into mbox when you quit, you can use the preserve command, which you can use with a list of numbers, the same way you can use other Berkeley Mail commands. Any message with which you use preserve will remain in your incoming mailbox.

SUMMARY After you get the hang of it, Berkeley Mail offers quite a lot of power, enabling you to read through your electronic mail, save it, and respond as needed with ease. The program has considerably more commands than are shown here, so further study is helpful.

Task 21.4: Sending Mail with `mailx`

DESCRIPTION Now you know how to read your electronic mail using Berkeley Mail (`mailx`), and you know how to send mail from within the program. How do you send messages and files to people from the command line? It's quite simple. You even can specify the message subject with the `-s` starting flag.

ACTION

1. To send a message to someone, enter the name of the command followed by the recipient's account name:

```
$ mail marv
Subject: Interested in lunch tomorrow?
```

I now can enter as many lines of information as I want, ending, as within the Berkeley Mail program itself, with either ^d or .:

```
I'm going to be in town tomorrow and would like to
rustle up some Chinese food. What's your schedule
look like?

Dave
.
Cc:
```

Again, I'm offered the option of copying someone else, but—again—I opt not to do so. Pressing Return sends the message.

21

2. To send a file to someone, combine file redirection with the use of the -s flag:

```
$ mail -s "here's the contents of sample.file" marv < sample.file
```

The file was sent without any fuss.

3. Even though Berkeley Mail gives you no indication, several commands are available for use while you're entering the text of a message, and all can be listed with ~?:

```
$ mail dunlap
Subject: Good morning!
~?
-------------------------------------------------------------
The following ~ escapes are defined:
~~                Quote a single tilde
~b users          Add users to "blind" cc list
~c users          Add users to cc list
~d                Read in dead.letter
~e                Edit the message buffer
~h                Prompt for to list, subject and cc list
~m messages       Read in messages, right shifted by a tab
~p                Print the message buffer
~r file           Read a file into the message buffer
~s subject        Set subject
~t users          Add users to to list
~v                Invoke display editor on message
~w file           Write message onto file.
~?                Print this message
~!command         Invoke the shell
~|command         Pipe the message through the command
-------------------------------------------------------------
=
```

The ones most important to remember are ~v, to start vi in the message; ~r, to read in a file; ~h, to edit the message headers; ~! , to invoke a shell command; and ~p, to show the message that's been entered so far:

```
    I wanted to wish you a cheery good morning!  You asked about
the contents of that one file, so here it is:
~!ls
Archives/       bin/                deleteme        sample
InfoWorld/      buckaroo            dickens.note    sample2
Mail/           buckaroo.confused   keylime.pie     src/
News/           cheryl              mbox            temp/
OWL/            csh.man             newsample
awkscript       dead.letter         owl.c
!
```

The output of the command isn't included in the message, as is shown if you use the ~p command:

```
~p
-------
Message contains:
To: dunlap
Subject: Good morning!


    I wanted to wish you a cheery good morning!  You asked about
the contents of that one file, so here it is:
(continue)
_
```

4. To read in a file, use the ~r command:

```
~r dickens.note
"dickens.note" 28/1123
```

Here, the contents of the file are included in the note, but mailx didn't list the contents to the screen. Again, using ~p will list the current message:

```
-------
Message contains:
To: dunlap
Subject: Good morning!


    I wanted to wish you a cheery good morning!  You asked about
the contents of that one file, so here it is:

                        A Tale of Two Cities
                              Preface

When I was acting, with my children and friends, in Mr Wilkie Collins's
drama of The Frozen Deep, I first conceived the main idea of this
story.  A strong desire came upon me then, to
embody it in my own person;
and I traced out in my fancy, the state of mind of which it would
necessitate the presentation
to an observant spectator, with particular
care and interest.

As the idea became familiar to me, it gradually shaped itself into its
present form.  Throughout its execution, it has had complete possession
of me; I have so far verified what
is done and suffered in these pages,
as that I have certainly done and suffered it all myself.

Whenever any reference (however slight) is made here to the condition
of the Danish people before or during the Revolution, it is truly made,
```

21

```
on the faith of the most trustworthy
witnesses.  It has been one of my hopes to add
something to the popular and picturesque means of
understanding that terrible time, though no one can hope
to add anything to the philosophy of Mr Carlyle's wonderful book.

Tavistock House
November.1859
(continue)
```

5. I can fine-tune the headers using the ~h command:

   ~h
   ```
   To: dunlap_
   ```

   Pressing Return leaves it as is, and pressing Backspace lets me change it as desired. A Return moves to the next header in the list:

   ```
   Subject: Good morning!
   ```

   Pressing Return a few more times gives me the opportunity to change other headers in the message:

   ```
   Cc:
   Bcc:
   (continue)
   ```

   The `Cc:` header allows me to specify other people to receive this message. The `Bcc:` is what's known as a *blind carbon copy*, an invisible copy of the message. If I send a message to `dunlap` and a carbon copy to `cbutcher`, each can see that the other received a copy because the message will have `To: dunlap` as a header and also will list the other's name after `Cc:`. If I want to send a copy to someone without any of the other parties knowing about it, that's where a blind carbon copy can be helpful. Specifying someone on the `Bcc:` list means that that person receives a copy of the message, but his or her name doesn't show up on any header in the message itself.

6. Finally, I use `^d` to end the message.

   ^d
   ```
   Cc:
   $
   ```

SUMMARY All so-called *tilde commands* (so named because they all begin with the ~, or tilde, character) are available when you send mail from the command line. They also are available when you send mail while within the Berkeley Mail program.

Task 21.5: Internet E-mail Addresses

DESCRIPTION   The most common use of the Internet is probably to send electronic mail between individuals and to mailing lists. What's really a boon is that everyone, from New York to Los Angeles, Japan to Germany, South Africa to India, has an address that's very similar, and you've already seen it shown here. The notation is *user@host.domain*, where *user* is the account name or full name, *host* is the name of the user's machine, and *domain* is the user's location in the world.

By reading the host and domain information from right to left (from the outside in, really), you can decode information about someone by looking at the person's e-mail address. My address at a system called Netcom, for example, is taylor@netcom2.netcom.com, which, reading right to left, tells you that I'm at a commercial site (com) with a company by the name of Netcom (netcom), and the name of the computer I'm using is netcom2. My account on Netcom is taylor.

There are lots of top-level domains; the most common are shown in Table 22.1.

TABLE 22.1   Common Top-Level Internet Domains

Domain	Type of Site or Network
edu	Educational sites
com	Commercial businesses
mil	Military or defense systems
net	Alternative networks accessible via Internet
org	Nonprofit organizations
us	United States systems not otherwise classified

ACTION

1. To send mail to someone on the Internet is easy. If you'd like to send me a message, for example, you could use this:

```
$ mailx taylor@intuitive.com
Subject: _
```

Enter the message and end with a ^d as you would in any e-mail message. It is immediately sent to me.

21

> I encourage you to drop me a note if you're so inclined, letting me know
> how you're enjoying this book, any problems you might have encountered,
> and any commands you were puzzled by that might be easier with a bit
> more explanation. If nothing else, just say hi!

2. Although electronic mail addresses always follow the same format, they can vary quite a bit. To give you an idea of the variation, I used `grep` to extract the `From:` addresses of some mail I've recently received:

```
$ grep '^From:' /usr/spool/mail/taylor
From: Steve Frampton <frampton@vicuna.ocunix.on.ca>
From: Joanna Tsang <tsang@futon.SFSU.EDU>
From: "Debra Isserlis" <disserli@us.oracle.com>
From: "Jay Munro [PC Mag]" <72241.554@CompuServe.COM>
From: ljw@ras.amdahl.com (Linda Wei)
From: Cheryl <CBUTCHER@VM.CC.PURDUE.EDU>
From: harrism@mace.utech.edu (Mickey Harris)
From: v892127@nooteboom.si.hhs.nl
From: "ean houts" <ean_houts@ccgate.infoworld.com>
From: harrism@mace.utech.edu (Mickey Harris)
From: "Barbara Maxwell" <maxwell@sales.synergy.com>
From: steve@xalt.com (Steve Mansour)
From: abhasin@itsmail1.hamilton.edu (Aditya Bhasin)
From: gopher@scorpio.kent.edu
From: marv@netcom.com (Marvin Raab)
```

The notational convention for the `From:` line in electronic mail clearly varies. You see three basic notations in this list: just an address, such as the one from `gopher@scorpio.kent.edu`; an address with the name in parentheses, such as the message from Linda Wei about one-third way down the list; and a line with the person's name followed by his or her e-mail address in angle brackets, such as the first listed line.

Notice the various sites from which I've received electronic mail in the past few days: `SFSU.EDU` is San Francisco State University, `oracle.com` is Oracle Corporation in California, `PURDUE.EDU` is Purdue University, `CompuServe.COM` is the CompuServe network, `ccgate.infoworld.com` is *InfoWorld* magazine's Macintosh network running Cc:Mail, `xalt.com` is from XALT Corporation, and `kent.edu` is Kent State University. The message from `v892127@nooteboom.si.hhs.nl` is from an educational institution in The Netherlands!

SUMMARY Sending electronic mail back and forth with users throughout the world is one of the most exciting and fun parts of learning Unix. I often read magazine articles, for example, in which the author lists an electronic mail address. It's a simple task to zip out a message if I have questions or kudos on the piece. Many magazines, from the *Utne Reader* to *MacWorld*, even list electronic mail addresses for the editorial staff. Even reporters from the *Wall Street Journal* and the *New York Times* are on the Internet.

Task 21.6: The Smarter Electronic Mail Alternative, elm

DESCRIPTION Just as line editors pale compared to screen editors such as vi, so does Berkeley Mail when compared to the Elm Mail System, or elm. Although the Elm Mail System is not available on all Unix systems, it's widely distributed, and if you don't have it on your system, your system's vendor should be able to help out.

The basic premise of elm is that the user should be able to focus on the message, not the medium. Emphasis is placed on showing human information. The best way to show how it works is to go straight into it!

I'm probably just a bit biased about elm because I am the author of the program. The widespread acceptance of the design, however, suggests that I'm not alone in having sought a friendlier alternative to Berkeley Mail.

Another mailer with a very similar user interface is Pine. If you have access to both Elm and Pine, however, I recommend that you pick Elm because it lets you work with your mail in a much more efficient manner. Read the last section of this lesson to learn more about Pine before you decide, however!

ACTION

1. To start the Elm Mail System, enter elm:

   ```
   $ elm
   ```

   The screen clears and is replaced with this:

   ```
   Mailbox is '/usr/spool/mail/taylor' with 15 messages [ELM 2.3 PL11]


   --> 1   Dec 8  v892127@nooteboom. (52)   Re: Have you picked up
       2   Dec 7  Mickey Harris      (214)  writing environments
       3   Dec 7  Cheryl             (24)   Computer Based GRE's
       4   Dec 7  Mickey Harris      (69)   Re: Writing Lab OWL proj
       5   Dec 7  Russell Holt       (37)   flash cards
       6   Dec 7  Bill McInerney     (121)  New Additions to U.S. Dept
       7   Dec 5  Mickey Harris      (29)   Re: OWL non-stuff
   ```

   continues

21

```
    8   Dec 5   Rob Sartin          (31)    I need your address
    9   Dec 4   J=TAYLOR@MA@168ARG  (28)    Note to say HI!
OU 10   Dec 3   Linda Wei           (143)   Re: Attachments to XALT


    You can use any of the following by pressing the first char
d)elete or u)ndelete, m)ail a message, r)eply or f)orward, q)uit
    To read a message: <return>.  j=move down, k=move up,?=help

Command: _
```

The current message is indicated by the arrow (or, on some screens, the entire message line appears in inverse video). Whenever possible, elm shows the name of the person who sent the message (for example, Mickey Harris rather than mharris as in Berkeley Mail), indicates the number of lines in the message (in parentheses), and shows the subject of the message.

The last few lines on the screen indicate the options available at this point. Notice that j and k move the cursor up and down the list, just as they move up and down lines in vi.

2. To read a message, use the j key to zip down to the appropriate message and press Return. You then will see this:

```
Message 3/15  From Cheryl                  Dec 7 '98 at 4:57 pm est
                       Computer Based GRE's


I've scheduled to take the computer based GRE's in Indy on Jan. 6th.
Call me crazy but someone's got to do it.  I'll let you know how it
goes.

Do you know anyone else that has taken the GRE's this way?  I figure
there's a paper in it somewhere.....

If you have that handout from seminar in a file, could you please
send it to me?

Thanks.
```

continues

```
Command ('i' to return to index): _
```

At this point, you can use j to read the next message directly, r to reply, or i to return to the table of contents.

3. I realized that I said something in my message to Cheryl that was incorrect. I can type r here to reply to her message. Typing r causes the last few lines of the screen to be replaced with this:

```
- - - - - - - - - - - - - - - - - - - - - - - - - - - - - - - - - - - - - - - - -
Command: Reply to message                    Copy message? (y/n) n
```

To include the text of the message in your response, type y. I don't want to, so I press Return:

```
- - - - - - - - - - - - - - - - - - - - - - - - - - - - - - - - - - - - - - - - -
Command: Reply to message       To: CBUTCHER (Cheryl)
Subject of message: Re: Computer Based GRE's_
```

Now you can see the address to which the response will be sent, the name of the recipient (in parentheses), and the subject of the message. (elm automatically adds the Re prefix to the subject.) The cursor sits at the end of the subject line so that you can change the subject if you want. It's fine, so I again press Return:

```
- - - - - - - - - - - - - - - - - - - - - - - - - - - - - - - - - - - - - - - - -
Command: Reply to message       To: CBUTCHER(Cheryl)
Subject of message: Re: Computer Based GRE's
Copies To: _
```

21

No copies are needed, so I again press Return. The bottom of the screen now looks like this:

```
--------------------------------------------------------------------
Command: Reply to message      To: CBUTCHER(Cheryl)
Subject of message: Re: Computer Based GRE's
Copies to:

Enter message.  Type Elm commands on lines by themselves.
Commands include:  ^D or '.' to end, ~p to list, ~? for help.


=
```

Notice that ~p and ~? are available. In fact, all the tilde commands available in Berkeley Mail also are available in the Elm Mail System.

I enter the message and end with a .:

Just a reminder that we have that seminar tomorrow
afternoon too. See ya there?   -- Dave
.

Ending the message calls up this:

```
Please choose one of the following options by parenthesized letter: s
          e)dit message, edit h)eaders, s)end it, or f)orget it.
```

I press Return once more, and the message is sent.

4. I type i to return to the index page and q to quit.

SUMMARY There's a lot more the Elm Mail System can do to simplify your electronic mail interaction. If elm is available on your system, I encourage you to check it out further, and if it's not, try calling your vendor or a user group to see whether someone else can arrange for you to have a copy. Like the Free Software Foundation applications, elm is free. With it you even get the source code so that you can see how things are done internally if you're so inclined.

Task 21.7: A Glimpse of Pine

DESCRIPTION Elm was written primarily to make using e-mail easier than Berkeley Mail, and Pine (which stands for Pine Is Nearly Elm) was written by a team of programmers at the University of Washington to make a mailer that was even easier than Elm.

Built on the same core programs, the biggest change that you'll notice switching from Elm to Pine (or vice versa) is that Pine starts up with a screen that lets you easily pick which folder you'd like to work with, whereas Elm goes directly to your inbox.

ACTION

1. Let's start up the Pine program and see the similarity between the mailboxes.

```
Welcome to Pine ... a Program for Internet News and Email

We hope you will explore Pine's many capabilities. From the Main Menu,
select Setup/Config to see many of the options available to you. Also
note that all screens have context-sensitive help text available.

SPECIAL REQUEST: This software is made available world-wide as a
public service of the University of Washington in Seattle. In order to
justify continuing development, it is helpful to have an idea of how
many people are using Pine. Are you willing to be counted as a Pine
user? Pressing Return will send an anonymous (meaning, your real
email address will not be revealed) message to the Pine development
team at the University of Washington for purposes of tallying.

    Pine is a trademark of the University of Washington.
```

This text is only shown the first time you run Pine, but it's helpful to peruse.

2. Let's press 'space' to continue and see what happens.

```
PINE 4.21   MAIN MENU                    Folder: INBOX   15 Messages


        ?    HELP            -  Get help using Pine

        C    COMPOSE MESSAGE  -  Compose and send/post a message

        I    MESSAGE INDEX    -  View messages in current folder

        L    FOLDER LIST      -  Select a folder OR news group

        A    ADDRESS BOOK     -  Update address book

        S    SETUP            -  Configure Pine Options

        Q    QUIT             -  Leave the Pine program




    Copyright 1989-1999.  Pine is a trademark of the University of
Washington.
          [Folder "INBOX" opened with 15 messages]
? Help                    P PrevCmd                  R RelNotes
O OTHER CMDS > [ListFldrs] N NextCmd                 K KBLock
```

At this juncture, your best bet is to type **?** for information on the many possible commands available at this point.

21

SUMMARY   Needless to say, there's quite a bit more to learn about Pine, if that's the mailer that you opt to use. There's lots of online documentation, and you can always go to the University of Washington's online information center (`http://www.washington.edu/Pine/`) for the definitive word on the program.

Summary

For awhile, you've known that other users are on your computer system, and you've even learned how to find out what they're doing (with the w command). Now you know how to communicate with them, too!

Here's a word of advice: It can be frustrating and annoying to be pestered by unknown folk, so I recommend that you begin by sending mail to yourself and then to just your friends on the system. After some practice, you'll learn how net etiquette works and what is or isn't appropriate for your electronic mail.

> You can learn a lot more about network etiquette by visiting my online Network Etiquette Primer at `http://www.intuitive.com/tyu24/netiq.html`.

Workshop

The Workshop summarizes the key terms you learned and poses some questions about the topics presented in this chapter. It also provides you with a preview of what you will learn in the next hour.

Key Terms

blind carbon copy   An exact copy of a message, sent without the awareness of the original recipient.

carbon copy   An exact copy of a message sent to other people. Each recipient can see the names of all other recipients on the distribution list.

e-mail   Electronically transmitted and received mail or messages.

mail folder   A file containing one or more e-mail messages.

mail header   The To:, From:, Subject:, and other lines at the beginning of an e-mail message. All lines up to the first blank line are considered headers.

mailbox   A synonym for mail folder.

preserve Ensure that a message doesn't move out of your incoming mailbox even though you've read it.

starting flag Parameters you specify on the command line when you invoke the program.

tilde command A command beginning with ~ in Berkeley Mail or the Elm Mail System.

undelete Restore a deleted message to its original state.

Exercises

1. Use `tty` to identify your terminal device name, and then use `ls` to look at its current permissions. Do you have messages enabled or disabled? Confirm with the `mesg` command.

2. Try using the `talk` command by writing to yourself; or, if you have a friend on the system, try using `talk` to say hi and see whether the person knows how to respond.

3. Send yourself a message using `mailx`.

4. Now use Berkeley Mail to read your new message, and then save it to a file, delete it, undelete it, and save it to a mail folder.

5. Start Berkeley Mail so that it reads in the newly created mail folder rather than in your default mailbox. What's different?

6. If `elm` is available to you, try using it to read your mail. Do you like this mail program or Berkeley Mail better? Why?

Preview of the Next Hour

In the next hour, you learn about how to use the `telnet`, `ssh`, and `ftp` programs to interact with computers throughout the Internet.

21

HOUR **22**

Using `telnet`, `SSH`, and `ftp`

In the preceding hour, you learned how to use electronic mail and the `talk` program to interact with other users both on your system and elsewhere on the Internet. In this hour, you see how to use Unix tools to connect to remote systems and transfer files and programs back and forth at will.

Goals for This Hour

In this hour, you will learn about

- Connecting to remote Internet sites
- Securing connections with `SSH`
- Copying files from other Internet sites

This hour is intended to offer a quick overview of how to connect to other Unix systems on the Internet, both to transfer files and to interact directly.

Stepping Beyond Your Own System

You can do lots of things on a local Unix system, but if you're lucky, your system is hooked up to the rest of the Internet world. Unix offers some powerful tools to let you exploit your network connectivity.

Task 22.1: Connecting to Remote Internet Sites

DESCRIPTION The really fun part of Unix, and one reason that it has grown dramatically in popularity, is that it's the most connected operating system in the world. The variety of services available for users of a networked Unix machine is staggering.

The Internet can help you with three main tasks: using remote systems, sending mail to remote users, and working with remote file systems. In addition, you can find out who is logged on to any system on the Internet with `finger` and use the `talk` program to talk with someone else.

If you know that the remote site is a Unix system, the easiest way to log in to that site is to use the `rlogin` command, which has the awkward notation of `rlogin` *host* `-l` *account*. If you aren't sure about the remote operating system, use `telnet`, which is the universal program for connecting to remote computer systems. Unlike any of the other programs you've learned so far, `telnet` actually works either as a simple program you can invoke from the command line or as a sophisticated environment for connecting to various systems.

ACTION

1. First, I'll use `rlogin` to connect to a remote system and see whether I have a file there:

   ```
   $ rlogin intuitive.com
   Password:_
   ```

   By default, `rlogin` assumes that your account on the remote system has the same name as your account on your home system. If you forget to use the `-l` account option, press Return here, and it prompts for an account name:

   ```
   $ rlogin intuitive.com
   Password:
   Login incorrect
   login: taylor
   Password:_
   ```

After I enter my password, I'm logged in to the remote system:

```
Last login: Mon Jun 29 15:27:24 from 204.247.39.239

                Netcom On-line Communication Services, Inc.

We thank you for your patience while we upgrade our network to
better serve you.

" "
$
```

Using `ls` tells me what I want to know:

```
netcom $ ls
Global.Software    News/            history.usenet.Z
Interactive.Unix   Src/             login
Mail/              bin/             testme
netcom $
```

2. The `rlogin` command offers a shorthand notation for logging out of the remote system; instead of using `logout`, you can simply enter `~.` to do the job. To stop the `rlogin` session, use `~^z`. No other tilde commands are available in `rlogin`.

   I choose to log out the normal way:

   ```
   netcom $ exit
   Connection closed
   $
   ```

   Now I'm back on the original computer system.

3. The alternative way to connect to a remote computer is to use `telnet`. The easiest way to use this command is the same way you use `rlogin`. At the command prompt, specify the name of the system to which you want to connect:

   ```
   $ telnet netcom.com
   Trying...
   Connected to netcom.com.
   Escape character is '^]'.


   SunOS UNIX (netcom)

   login: _
   ```

   Notice that this way is much more like having a terminal connected to this system. I can log in, enter my password, and then have a new login session on the remote system as if I were sitting in that computer room working away.

4. Instead, though, I'm going to use the `^]` control character to switch back into the `telnet` program itself:

```
SunOS UNIX (netcom)
login: ^]
telnet > _
```

Now I enter help to see what the options are:

```
telnet> help
Commands may be abbreviated.  Commands are:

close           close current connection
display         display operating parameters
mode            try to enter line-by-line or character-at-a-time mode
open            connect to a site
quit            exit telnet
send            transmit special characters ('send ?' for more)
set             set operating parameters ('set ?' for more)
status          print status information
toggle          toggle operating parameters ('toggle ?' for more)
z               suspend telnet
?               print help information
telnet>  _
```

There are lots of possible commands. I choose to return to my connection to Netcom, however; I press Return, and I'm back at the login prompt. If I don't enter anything quickly enough, the remote system automatically drops the connection:

```
login: Login timed out after 60 seconds
Connection closed by foreign host.
$
```

To log out of the remote system, the best strategy is simply to exit the telnet session, which will drop the line automatically. If that doesn't work, the ^] sequence followed by either quit or close will do the trick.

5. To start out directly in the telnet command mode, enter the command without specifying a remote host:

```
$ telnet
telnet>  _
```

From here, connecting to the remote host is also quite simple:

```
telnet> open netcom.com
Trying...
Connected to netcom.com.
Escape character is '^]'.


SunOS UNIX (netcom)

login:  _
```

Again, I use ^] and close to close the connection.

22

SUMMARY Both the `rlogin` and the `telnet` commands are useful in different situations, but I find myself using the `rlogin` command more often because it sends much of the current environment along to the remote system. So if I have my system set for a specific type of terminal (that is, the `TERM` variable is set to a specific value), that value is automatically copied into the new environment of the remote system, which saves lots of hassle.

Task 22.2: Telnet from Windows and Macs

DESCRIPTION Another way that you can use `telnet` is to use it as a mechanism for connecting *to* the Unix machine you're working with. That's how I connect to my systems now: It's been rather a long time since I had an actual Unix terminal or computer on my desktop.

A variety of different `telnet` programs are available for both the Mac and PC, with many different options that are free. The best place to look for these free `telnet` programs is at Download.com: Just search for 'telnet' when you get there.

ACTION

1. Although I usually spend most of my time on the Macintosh platform, I do occasionally delve into the arcane Windows environment. When I'm on a Windows system and want to use a simple telnet program to connect, it turns out that there's already one included with Windows.

   A secret: The easiest way to launch your telnet program is to simply use your Web browser to find it. That's right, just enter the URL `telnet:` and it will find and launch the program you have on your system.

2. If that doesn't work, you can go to Start, Find, Files or Folders and search for "telnet" on your Windows system. It will show a number of results, and the one you want is the `telnet.exe` application. Double-click it, and you'll see a blank white window. Choose Connect, Remote System and it will look like Figure 22.1.

   As you can see, it's fairly bare bones, but enter the name of the system to which you want to connect, and it'll open a window running as a vt100 terminal. (Remember you might have to change the TERM settings in your shell to match).

3. I'll switch over to my Macintosh for a moment to show you that there are also easy (free) telnet clients for the Macintosh platform.

   On the Macintosh, however, no telnet clients are included automatically with the operating system (though there is some nice telnet software within the Unix side of Mac OS X, if you're running it). Instead, I popped over to `http://www.download.com/` and found 20 different free telnet clients listed!

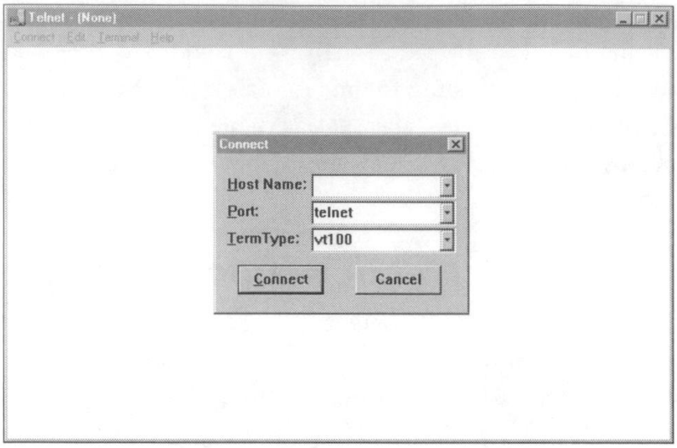

FIGURE 22.1

Windows telnet when first launched.

Of those, the two most popular are NCSA Telnet (NCSA is where they invented the Mosaic Web browser that morphed into Netscape and really started the whole Web explosion; it's the National Center for Supercomputer Applications at the University of Illinois Urbana-Champaign) and Better Telnet. My personal favorite, however, is NiftyTelnet, for its capabilities and easy configuration screens.

4. If you've downloaded any of these, you're going to start them up with a double-click and see something similar to Figure 22.2.

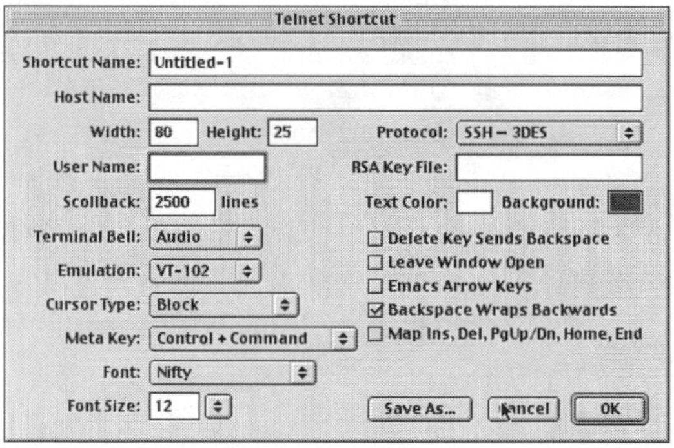

FIGURE 22.2

Macintosh NiftyTelnet when first launched.

SUMMARY   Notice here that there are many different settings for a telnet session, but I think that's a good thing. You can specify the default window size, typeface to use, and even the foreground and background colors, all in one place. Then, you can save it as a shortcut, and you're ready to go!

Task 22.3: Secure Connections with SSH

DESCRIPTION Telnet and its ilk are tremendously useful programs, but they have some inherent security problems, not the least of which is that the information between the client and the server is "in the clear." That is, if you could somehow interpose a network packet sniffer that could filter out just the telnet traffic, you could read the account/password pair and everything that's displayed on the remote users display.

Although a number of possible solutions exist for this problem, Tatu Ylönen at Helsinki University of Technology in Finland came up with the best one: SSH. *SSH* stands for *Secure Shell,* a point-to-point encrypted telnet protocol. If your server supports SSH, you should unquestionably use it. There are no downsides that I've found, and the additional security is a definite boon.

Well, there is one downside: Most SSH clients are commercial products and will cost between $50–$100 rather than the preferable free price of the telnet clients.

On the PC side, the SSH client of choice is unquestionably SecureCRT from Datafellows. You can learn more about it at `http://www.vandyke.com/`.

For Macintosh users, the best solution I've found is a version of NiftyTelnet that adds the SSH protocols. It's a bit tricky to find because of U.S. export restrictions on encryption software, but you can start your quest at Jonas Walldén's site in Sweden: `http://www.lysator.liu.se/~jonasw/freeware/niftyssh/`.

One important warning: Two incompatible versions of the SSH protocol, SSH 1 and SSH 2, can be installed on servers. If you try to connect to a secure server and it fails, try the other protocol (all SSH clients give you a choice).

ACTION

1. To connect to a secure server within SecureCRT, I must fill out a couple of fields in addition to the regular telnet information, as shown in Figure 22.3.

   As you can see, there are lots of options, many of which sound quite intimidating. The good news is that I've found that I can leave all the default settings, and that choosing the right protocol (SSH1, SSH2, regular non-encrypted telnet, and so forth) is all you need to get things working quickly.

   While you're looking at this screen, notice how many configurations and appearance options SecureCRT offers over and above the primitive telnet client that's included with Windows. I like to have things "just so" when I'm logged in, so I really appreciate being able to set color choices, default window sizes, and so forth.

FIGURE 22.3

*Details of a Secure
SSH Connection.*

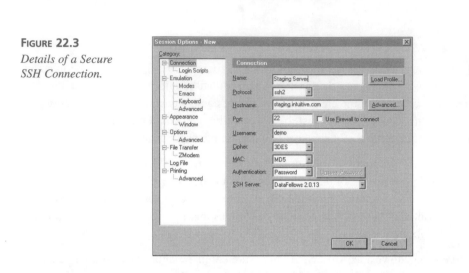

2. After you're connected to an SSH server, the client program really works almost 100% identically to a telnet client, without any apparent performance issues or other downsides.

SUMMARY The Internet has grown and become a tremendously popular place, both for nice folk offering lots of cool and compelling information and for bad people trying nefarious schemes to break in and steal information. I'm not too paranoid about things, but I like the security that I get from using SSH instead of regular telnet, and on my own servers, I only run SSH software: Regular telnet clients cannot connect at all.

My recommendation: If you have a server that supports SSH, it's definitely in your best interest to switch to an SSH client and use that instead of raw telnet.

Task 22.4: Copying Files from Other Internet Sites

The main program used to copy files on the Internet is ftp, which is named after the protocol it implements, the *file transfer protocol*. Like much of Unix, ftp can take a while to master, particularly because no effort has been made to make it at all user-friendly. Nonetheless, it functions very similarly to the telnet command; either you enter ftp to start the program and then specify the system with which you'd like to connect, or you specify the name of the system on the command line. Either way, you are prompted for an account and password; then you are dropped into ftp with the connection open and waiting.

The more sophisticated SSH clients also offer a secure file transfer protocol essentially running on top of SSH. Some security-conscious sites might not allow regular FTP and might restrict file transfer to SSH-based software.

Many sites have anonymous `ftp` capabilities. Systems allowing this connection indicate that you don't need your own computer account on that machine to be able to connect and copy files from their archives. To use these systems, enter `ftp` as the account name, and then enter your own email address as the password (for example, I'd enter `ftp` and then `taylor@intuitive.com` as my password). The most important commands available in `ftp` are summarized in Table 22.1. The most important one to remember is `bye`, which you use when you're done.

TABLE 22.1   Valuable `ftp` Commands

Command	Meaning
ascii	Set `ftp` to transfer a text (ASCII) file.
binary	Set `ftp` to transfer a binary file, probably a program or database of information.
bye	Quit the `ftp` program.
cd dir	Change the remote directory to `dir`.
close	Close the current connection.
dir	Print a listing of files in the current remote directory.
get	Transfer a file from the remote system to your local system.
lcd *dir*	Change the current directory on the local system to *dir* or to your home directory if no argument is given.
ls	List the files in the current remote directory (try this: The output is usually different than the `dir` command produces).
mget	Multiple `get`—get files with a wildcard matching capability (example: `mget *.c`).
mput	Multiple `put`—put files with a wildcard matching capability. (example: `mput *.html`)
open	Open a connection to the specified remote machine.
prompt	Control whether or not to ask for confirmation of each file transferred if using `mget` or `mput`.
put	Put a file onto the remote system from the local system. (example: `put index.html`)
pwd	Show the present working directory on the remote system.

ACTION

1. To begin, I want to pick up a file from `netcom` that I saw earlier when I used `rlogin` to look at the remote system. To start `ftp`, I use the short notation of specifying the host at the command line:

```
$ ftp netcom.com
Connected to netcom.com.
220 netcom FTP server (Version 2.1 Fri Apr 9 13:43 PDT 1996) ready.
Name (netcom.com:taylor): _
```

By default, `ftp` assumes that I want to use the same account name, which in this case I do, so I press Return and then enter my password:

```
Name (netcom.com:taylor):
331 Password required for taylor.
Password:
230 User taylor logged in.
ftp> _
```

2. Now I'm at the `ftp` program prompt, and any of the commands shown in Table 22.1 will work here. To start, I use `dir` and `ls` to list my files in different formats:

```
ftp> dir
200 PORT command successful.
150 Opening ASCII mode data connection for /bin/ls.
total 140
-rwxr-xr-x  1 taylor   users0    4941 Oct   4  1991 .Pnews.header
-rw-r--r--  1 taylor   users0    2103 Sep  30 19:17 .article
-rw-r--r--  1 taylor   users0     752 Apr  17  1998 .cshrc
drwx------  2 taylor   daemon    4096 Dec   6 14:25 .elm
-rw-r--r--  1 taylor   users0      28 Nov   5 09:50 .forward
-rw-r--r--  1 taylor   users0    1237 Dec  13 09:40 .login
-rw-r--r--  1 taylor   users0       6 Aug   6  1991 .logout
-rw-r--r--  1 taylor   users0     538 Dec   6 14:32 .newsrc
-rw-r--r--  1 taylor   users0    1610 Feb  17  1992 .plan
-rw-r--r--  1 taylor   users0       0 Aug   6  1991 .pnewsexpert
-rw-r--r--  1 taylor   users0      45 Feb   2  1993 .rnlast
-rw-r--r--  1 taylor   users0       6 Feb   8  1993 .rnlock
-rw-r--r--  1 taylor   users0   16767 Jan  27  1993 .rnsoft
-rw-r--r--  1 taylor   users0     114 Apr   6  1998 .sig
drwxr-xr-x  4 taylor   users0    4096 Nov  13 11:09 .tin
-rw-r--r--  1 taylor   users0    1861 Jun   2  1997 Global.Software
-rw-------  1 taylor   users0   22194 Oct   1  1995 Interactive.Unix
drwx------  4 taylor   users0    4096 Nov  13 11:09 Mail
drwxr-xr-x  2 taylor   users0    4096 Nov  13 11:09 News
drwxr-xr-x  2 taylor   users0    4096 Nov  13 11:09 Src
drwxr-xr-x  2 taylor   users0    4096 Nov  13 11:09 bin
-rw-r--r--  1 taylor   users0   12445 Sep  17 14:56 history.usenet.Z
-rw-r--r--  1 taylor   users0    1237 Oct  18 20:55 login
```

```
-rw-r--r--  1 taylor    users0       174 Nov 20 19:21 testme
226 Transfer complete.
1792 bytes received in 3.1 seconds (0.56 Kbytes/s)
ftp> ls
200 PORT command successful.
150 Opening ASCII mode data connection for file list.
Mail
News
bin
Global.Software
history.usenet.Z
Src
Interactive.Unix
testme
login
226 Transfer complete.
269 bytes received in 0.02 seconds (13 Kbytes/s)
ftp>
```

As you can see, `ftp` can be long-winded, particularly with the DIR output format.

> One trick for using the `ls` command within `ftp` is that if you specify a set of command flags as a second word, it works fine. Specify a third argument, however, and it saves the output of the command into a local file by that name; so `ls -1 -C` would create a file called `-C` on your system with the output of the `ls -1` command.

Because you can supply some flags to the `ls` command, I always use `-aCF` to force the output to list dot files in multiple columns and show directories, which makes the output more readable:

```
ftp> ls -aCF
200 PORT command successful.
150 Opening ASCII mode data connection for /bin/ls.
.Pnews.header*         .newsrc                Interactive.Unix
.accinfo*              .oldnewsrc             Mail/
.article              .plan                  News/
.cshrc                .pnewsexpert           Src/
.delgroups            .rnlast                bin/
.elm/                 .rnlock                history.usenet.Z
.forward              .rnsoft                login
.ircmotd              .sig                   testme
.login                .tin/
.logout               Global.Software
226 Transfer complete.
remote: -CF
287 bytes received in 0.05 seconds (5.6 Kbytes/s)
ftp>
```

3. To transfer the file login from the remote system, I can use the get command:

```
ftp> get
(remote-file) login
(local-file) login.netcom
200 PORT command successful.
150 Opening ASCII mode data connection for login (1237 bytes).
226 Transfer complete.
local: login.netcom remote: login
1281 bytes received in 0.22 seconds (5.7 Kbytes/s)
ftp>
```

This can get a bit tricky. I've just copied the login file from netcom (where I FTP'd) to the local Unix system where I'm running the ftp command itself. On the local system, I gave the file the new name of login.netcom.

4. Alternatively, I could use mget and specify a wildcard pattern similar to one I'd give the shell:

```
ftp> mget log*
mget login? y
200 PORT command successful.
150 Opening ASCII mode data connection for login (1237 bytes).
226 Transfer complete.
local: login remote: login
1281 bytes received in 0.03 seconds (42 Kbytes/s)
ftp>
```

There was only one match, so the transfer was easy. Entering anything other than y at the mget login? prompt would have resulted in the file not being transferred. The mget and mput commands are particularly useful if you want to transfer many files at once, so mget *.? would get *.c, *.h and any other source files that have a single-letter suffix to their filenames, for example.

That job was easily accomplished. Now I will look on another system in the anonymous FTP directory to see what's available.

5. To disconnect, I enter close so that I don't leave the ftp program:

```
ftp> close
221 Goodbye
ftp>
```

There are hundreds of information servers on the Internet, offering an astounding variety of information, from weather service maps to the full text of the Bible and *Alice in Wonderland* to the source listings of thousands of programs.

In this example, I want to look at the anonymous FTP archive at the Massachusetts Institute of Technology's Artificial Intelligence Laboratory. The host is called ftp.ai.mit.edu:

```
ftp> open ftp.ai.mit.edu
Connected to mini-wheats.ai.mit.edu.
220 mini-wheats FTP server (Version wu-2.4.2-academ[BETA-8](6)
Thu Jan 25 07:08:03 EST 1996)

Name (ftp.ai.mit.edu:taylor): ftp
331 Guest login ok, send your complete e-mail address as password.
Password:
230-
230-
230-Welcome to the MIT Artificial Intelligence Laboratory. If you are
230-interested in Artificial Intelligence Laboratory publications please
230-ftp to publications.ai.mit.edu.
230-
230-
230-
230 Guest login ok, access restrictions apply.
ftp>
```

Now I can use ls -CF to look around:

```
ftp> ls -CF
200 PORT command successful.
150 Opening ASCII mode data connection for /bin/ls.
-rw-r--r--  1 root     daemon     171 Aug 25  1993 .message
drwxr-xr-x  2 bruce    114        512 Sep  1  1993 ai-pubs/
dr-xr-xr-x  2 root     user       512 Jan 25  1996 bin/
drwxr-xr-x  2 root     user       512 Mar 14  1995 dev/
dr-xr-xr-x  2 root     user       512 Apr 24  1995 etc/
drwxrwxr-x 32 root     user       512 Jul 28 12:55 incoming/
drwxr-xr-x  2 root     wheel     8192 Mar 13  1995 lost+found/
lrwxrwxrwx  1 root     daemon       9 May 10  1997 people -> pub/users/
drwxrwxr-x112 root     user      2560 Sep  3 21:58 pub/
drwxr-xr-x  3 root     staff      512 Apr  8  1992 usr/
226 Transfer complete.
58 bytes received in 0.39 seconds (0.15 Kbytes/s)
ftp>
```

It looks as though there might be something of interest in the pub directory (a directory by this name usually contains public information). I use cd to change to that directory, then dir to see what's available there:

```
ftp> cd pub
250 CWD command successful.
ftp> dir
200 PORT command successful.
150 Opening ASCII mode data connection for /bin/ls.
total 21407
drwxrwxr-x  2 bergenda user       512 Mar 20  1997 6.371
drwxrwxr-x  2 caroma   user       512 Nov 25  1997 6.835
```

```
drwxrwxr-x  2 mdlm     user       512 Sep 24  1995 DHC
drwxrwxr-x  2 mdlm     user       512 Aug 24  1993 GA
drwxrwxr-x  2 loeb     user      7168 Jun 11  1996 Kennedy

lots and lots of lines

drwxr-xr-x151 root     user      2560 Oct 16  1997 users
drwxrwxr-x  2 viola    user       512 Sep  2 01:28 viola
drwxrwxr-x  3 vkumar   user       512 Aug 19 17:30 vkumar
drwxrwxr-x  2 wang     user       512 Jan 21  1997 wang
drwxr-xr-x  3 wessler  user       512 Aug  9 18:17 wessler
drwxrwxr-x  5 ddaniel  user       512 Jul 21  1994 x3j13
drwxr-xr-x  2 misha    daemon    1536 Sep 24  1996 xemacs
drwxrwxr-x  3 rst      user       512 Feb 20  1995 xplay
drwxrwxr-x  3 yip      user       512 Dec 25  1997 yip
drwxr-xr-x  2 yweiss   user       512 Feb  6  1998 yweiss
drwxr-sr-x  2 friedman user       512 Sep 11 07:01 zenirc
ftp>
```

There's quite a lot on the MIT AI Lab server, as you can see. You could explore
further with cd and dir, until you found something of interest.

6. It's time to split and check another FTP archive, this time one at Apple Computer
(ftp.apple.com):

```
ftp> close
221 Goodbye.
ftp> open ftp.apple.com
Connected to bric-a-brac.apple.com.
220 bric-a-brac.apple.com FTP server (IG Version 5.93 (from BU,
from UUNET 5.51) Sun Nov 21 14:24:29 PST 1993) ready.
Name (ftp.apple.com:taylor): ftp
331 Guest login ok, send ident as password.
Password:
230 Guest login ok, access restrictions apply.
ftp>
```

Again, ls -CF shows what files are available:

```
ftp> ls -CF
200 PORT command successful.
150 Opening ASCII mode data connection for /bin/ls.
Apple_Support_Area/  dts/              research/
Quicktime/           etc/              web/
bin/                 lib/              whymac/
devworld/            lists/
226 Transfer complete.
remote: -CF
143 bytes received in 0.01 seconds (14 Kbytes/s)
ftp>
```

I've been to this site before, and I know that a few directories down there are a lot of useful applications to help make a Macintosh friendlier for people with disabilities. Let's have a look by using the `cd` command to move:

```
ftp> cd /Apple_Support_Area/disability-solutions/shareware
250 CWD command successful.
```

You could use the `DIR` command to see what's in this directory, but I already know that there's a program called `Snap To` that I want to learn more about. I'll do a wildcard listing instead:

```
ftp> dir Snap*
200 PORT command successful.
150 Opening ASCII mode data connection for /bin/ls.
-rw-r--r--   1 0     system  30464 Mar 14 1998 Snap-To.sit.bin
-rw-r--r--   1 0     system   1070 Mar 14 1998 Snap-To.txt
226 Transfer complete.
ftp>
```

7. Any file that has a filename suffix of `.txt` is usually a good thing to start with. A handy `ftp` trick is that you can copy files directly to your screen by using `/dev/tty` as the local filename, or you can even pipe them to programs by using the pipe symbol as the first character of the destination filename:

```
ftp> get Snap-To.txt |more
local: |more remote: Snap-To.txt
200 PORT command successful.
150 Opening BINARY mode data connection for Snap-To.txt (1070 bytes).
AUTHOR:     Trevden Sherzell
NEEDS:      Any Mac running System 6.0.4 or greater.
SYSTEM 7:   Compatible

----------------
Keywords:   DEFAULT BUTTON MOUSE SNAP TO CLICK ENTER RETURN DIALOG

Snap-To is a Control Panel that snaps the cursor to the default button
whenever a dialog comes up on your screen. Simple as that.

Snap-To will increase your speed when using a Macintosh, especially if you
use dialogs often and/or have a large screen.

Snap-To's features include:

* A Control Panel interface, which allows easy customization of several of
Snap-To's features.

* The ability for Snap-To to draw default button outlines around default
buttons which normally wouldn't have them.
```

```
* Optional automatic disabling in Open and/or Save dialogs.

* The ability for Snap-To to gradually move the cursor to the default
button, instead of abruptly snapping it there.

* The ability for Snap-To to move the cursor back to its original location
after you have closed a dialog box.

* Improved snapping over version 1.0.

* Full Balloon Help.

* And more!

ShareWare - $5.
226 Transfer complete.
1070 bytes received in 0.396 secs (2.6 Kbytes/sec)
ftp>
```

Sounds like a very interesting program, but not quite what I'm looking for, so let's
move to another directory on this server.

8. A new Macintosh application called ColorFinder is available on this system in
dts/mac/hacks that I've been interested in seeing. I can move directly there with
cd, confirming that I'm where I think I am with pwd:

```
ftp> cd /dts/mac/hacks
250 CWD command successful.
ftp> pwd
257 "/dts/mac/hacks" is current directory.
ftp> ls -CF
200 PORT command successful.
150 Opening ASCII mode data connection for /bin/ls.
aetracker-3-0.hqx               lockdisk-1-0.hqx
applicon-2-1.hqx                mountalias-1-0.hqx
appmenu-3-5.hqx                 newswatcher.hqx
bison-flex.hqx                  okey-dokey-1-0-1.hqx
colorfinder.hqx                 oscar.hqx
darkside-of-the-mac-4-2.hqx     piston.hqx
drop-disk-1-0b3.hqx             snake.hqx
dropper.hqx                     switchapp-1-1.hqx
escape-dammit-0-4.hqx           system-picker-1-0.hqx
extensions-manager-2-0-1.hqx    trashman-4-0-2.hqx
flipper.hqx                     understudy.hqx
folder-icon-maker-1-1.hqx       unlockfolder.hqx
fsid.hqx                        virtual-controllers.hqx
im-mac-1-0b26w.hqx              xferit-1-4.hqx
226 Transfer complete.
remote: -CF
559 bytes received in 0.14 seconds (3.9 Kbytes/s)
ftp>
```

I check to see how big the file is; then I can use `get` to transfer it, and drop the connection with `bye`:

```
ftp> dir colorfinder.hqx
200 PORT command successful.
150 Opening ASCII mode data connection for /bin/ls.
-rw-r-xr-x  1 mjohnson archivis  43442 May 24  1991 colorfinder.hqx
226 Transfer complete.
remote: colorfinder.hqx
71 bytes received in 0 seconds (0.069 Kbytes/s)
ftp> get colorfinder.hqx
200 PORT command successful.
150 Opening BINARY data connection for colorfinder.hqx (43442 bytes).
226 Transfer complete.
local: colorfinder.hqx remote: colorfinder.hqx
43442 bytes received in 2.09 seconds (20 Kbytes/s)
ftp> bye
221 CUL8R.
$
```

Now that I'm back at the command prompt, I can use `ls` again to confirm that I've received both the `colorfinder.hqx` and the `login.netcom` files:

```
$ ls
Archives/        bin/              keylime.pie       sample3
InfoWorld/       buckaroo          login.netcom      src/
Mail/            buckaroo.confused newsample         src.listing
News/            cheryl            papert.article    temp/
OWL/             colorfinder.hqx   sample            tmp.listing
awkscript        dickens.note      sample2           who.is.who
$
```

SUMMARY   The FTP system is a terrific way to obtain information from the Internet. Thousands of systems offer various services via anonymous FTP too: Table 22.2 lists a few of the most interesting ones.

TABLE 22.2   Some Interesting `ftp` Archives

Site	Institution and Available Information
`aisun1.ai.uga.edu`	University of Georgia. Files: LISP, PROLOG, natural language processing, MS-DOS utilities.
`ftp.sfu.ca`	San Francisco University. Files: MS-DOS, Mac.
`ftp.msu.edu`	Michigan State University. Files: MS Windows.
`ftp.cs.rice.edu`	Rice University. Files: Sun-Spots, Amiga, ispell, ofiles.
`ftp.cu.nih.gov`	U.S. National Institutes of Health.
`deja-vu.aiss.uiuc.edu`	University of Illinois Urbana-Champaign. Files: Rush Limbaugh transcripts, Monty Python, humor, song lyrics, movie scripts, urban legends.

TABLE 22.2 continued

Site	Institution and Available Information
f.ms.uky.edu	University of Kentucky. Files: Mac, MS-DOS, Unix, Amiga, NeXT, 386BSD, AppleII, GNU, RFCs, various Usenet archives.
ftp.apple.com	Apple Computer. Files: Apple (Mac, II, IIgs) product information, software, developer support.
ftp.cica.indiana.edu	Indiana University. Files: Unix, MS-DOS, NeXT updates, MS Windows 3.x archive.
ftp.csc.liv.ac.uk	Liverpool University Computer Science Department. Files: Ports to HP-UX machines (especially Series 700), including X11R4 clients, GNU, recreational software, text editors, system adminis- trator tools.
ftp.eff.org	Electronic Frontier Foundation.
gatekeeper.dec.com	Digital Equipment Corporation, Palo Alto, California. Files: X11, recipes, cron, map, Modula-3.
ftp.cs.caltech.edu	California Institute of Technology. Files: GNU (Free Software Foundation).
info.umd.edu	University of Maryland. Files: government-related, books, eco- nomics, MS-DOS, Novell, Mac.
ftp.ucsc.edu	University of California, Santa Cruz. Files: amoeba, U.S. Constitution.
ftp.nsf.net	National Science Foundation Network. Files: Network informa- tion, Internet Resource Guide.
ftp.sri.com	SRI International. Files: Improving the security of your Unix system.
anise.ee.cornell.edu	Cornell University. Files: tcsh.
ftp.cc.columbia.edu	Columbia University. Files: kermit.

There's no question that the interface to ftp is awkward. The good news is that most people have a Windows or Macintosh system as their actual desktop, and there are a ton of great FTP clients for both systems. For the PC I really like FTP Explorer by Alan Chavis, at www.ftpx.com. On the Macintosh, it's hard to beat the well-designed NetFinder, written by Peter Li and Vincent Tan, which you can find at netfinder.homepage.com.

Workshop

The Workshop summarizes the key terms you learned and poses some questions about the topics presented in this chapter. It also provides you with a preview of what you will learn in the next hour.

Key Terms

anonymous FTP   A system set up to respond to `ftp` queries that does not require you to have an account on the system.

search string   The pattern specified in a search.

Exercises

1. Use `telnet` and `rlogin` to try to log in to one of the FTP server sites shown in Table 22.2. You don't have an account, so drop the connection once you see a `login:` prompt.

2. Use `ftp` to connect to `ftp.eff.org` and see what files the Electronic Frontier Foundation has made available to anonymous FTP users. Copy one onto your system, and read through it to see what you think about the organization itself.

Preview of the Next Hour

This completes your tour of the basic tools of the Internet. In the next hour, you are introduced to the basics of working with C, the primary programming language for Unix.

HOUR 23

C Programming in Unix

This hour introduces you to the wonderful set of tools available for developing programs in the C programming language within the Unix environment. C is the most commonly used language for programming Unix systems. Other common languages are C++ and Perl, but C is the oldest, and many of the most fundamental Unix concepts are derived from this language. I'll be showing you a small C program to help make FTP easier to use and demonstrating all the Unix tools available to ease development and testing. If you have some basic programming skills, you'll like what I've written, but even if not, I'll explain everything carefully and be sure not to lose you. If you don't plan on programming, I'd still encourage you to read through this lesson. With any luck, you'll have your interest piqued and decide to learn how to get the computer to jump through hoops for you by writing your own programs. It's fun. Really!

Goals for This Hour

In this hour, you learn to use the many Unix tools to help develop and debug your first program. Specifically, you learn about

- `fget`, a smarter FTP client
- Compiling the program with `cc`, the C compiler
- The invaluable `make` utility
- Additional useful C tools

First you learn how to do something sneaky with FTP to make it easier to use; then you learn how to put that into a simple C program. After that, you see the various Unix tools at work helping develop the new software.

Extending and Expanding Unix with Your Own Programs

The set of commands that Unix encompasses offers a remarkable amount of flexibility, but even with fancy shell script programming, you'll doubtless come across situations where a program is your only solution. There are two popular Unix solutions: the Perl scripting language (covered in the next hour) and the C programming language, as explored in this hour.

Task 23.1: `fget`, a Smarter FTP Client

DESCRIPTION   When you learned about the FTP program earlier in this book, you probably thought to yourself, *Sheesh, that's pretty ugly and hard to use.* Well, you're not alone, but if you're stuck on the command line, it's quite surprising that there aren't any well-distributed alternatives. The good news is that it turns out that all the commands you type when you're within FTP can be stored in a file and your session scripted, automatically doing whatever you want.

Want to have a file transferred to you at three in the morning? You can do that. More importantly, however, we can write an easier interface to FTP. The key is the `-n` flag to the `ftp` program, which says "read standard input for all the commands to use."

ACTION

1. Let's say I wanted to see what files were available on the FTP archive on
   `ftp.intuitive.com`. Here's how that would look with a regular FTP session:

```
$ ftp ftp.intuitive.com
Connected to www.intuitive.com.
220 limbo.hostname.com FTP server (Version wu-2.4.2-academ[BETA-15](1) Sat
Nov 1
 03:08:32 EST 1997) ready.
Name (ftp.intuitive.com:taylor): ftp
331 Guest login ok, send your complete e-mail address as password.
Password:
230-Please read the file README
230-  it was last modified on Sun Sep 13 18:50:12 1998 - 0 days ago
230 Guest login ok, access restrictions apply.
Remote system type is UNIX.
Using binary mode to transfer files.
ftp> dir
200 PORT command successful.
150 Opening ASCII mode data connection for /bin/ls.
total 7
drwxr-xr-x   6 root     root         1024 Sep 13 18:50 .
drwxr-xr-x   6 root     root         1024 Sep 13 18:50 ..
-rw-rw-r--   1 root     root          175 Sep 13 18:50 README
d--x--x--x   2 root     root         1024 Mar 26 23:09 bin
d--x--x--x   2 root     root         1024 Mar 26 23:09 etc
drwxr-xr-x   2 root     root         1024 Mar 26 23:09 lib
dr-xr-sr-x   2 root     ftp          1024 Sep 13 18:48 pub
226 Transfer complete.
ftp> quit
221 Goodbye.
$
```

That's a lot of information for a simple directory listing.

2. As it turns out, everything I had to type in the preceding step—all the words in
   bold—can be saved in a file and fed directly to the `ftp` program:

```
$ cat ftp-script
user ftp taylor@intuitive.com
dir
quit
$
```

The only thing I've had to add here is that you can see the password I'm using for
the "ftp" account in this interaction. For anonymous FTP interaction, you'll almost
always use your own e-mail address, but other than that, it's exactly what I typed
earlier.

23

Now the secret step: I'm going to use the `-n` flag to FTP and feed it the preceding script. Watch what happens:

```
$ ftp -n ftp.intuitive.com < ftp-script
total 7
drwxr-xr-x   6 root      root          1024 Sep 13 18:50 .
drwxr-xr-x   6 root      root          1024 Sep 13 18:50 ..
-rw-rw-r--   1 root      root           175 Sep 13 18:50 README
d--x--x--x   2 root      root          1024 Mar 26 23:09 bin
d--x--x--x   2 root      root          1024 Mar 26 23:09 etc
drwxr-xr-x   2 root      root          1024 Mar 26 23:09 lib
dr-xr-sr-x   2 root      ftp           1024 Sep 13 18:48 pub
$
```

Way cool!

3. What the `fget` program does is create the simple script shown previously on-the-fly so that you can specify the FTP server and have it automatically produce a file listing.

   I've added two other features to the `fget` program to make it as useful as possible: You can specify any directory you'd like to see on the remote system, and you can specify a file on the remote system and it will copy it into the current local directory automatically.

   Here's a synopsis of how to use `fget`:

```
$ fget

Usage: fget host:remotefile {local}
```

   If you omit the `:remotefile` portion, `fget` will produce a listing of the files on the remote system. To specify a particular directory on the remote system, replace `local` with that directory name. For example, the command `fget ftp.intuitive.com /pub` will list the contents of the `/pub` directory on that machine. Copy a file from the remote system to the local system with `fget ftp.intuitive.com:README`, or rename it as you go by using `fget ftp.intuitive.com:README new.readme`. To display a file directly on the screen, use `-` as the value for `local`.

> A handy hint: Always try to make the "usage" of your programs as helpful as possible!

4. The logic flow of the program is as follows:

```
figure out what elements the user has specified
create a temporary work file
output the 'user' line so you can log in to the server
if (remotefile is not specified)
   if (localfile is specified)
     output "cd localfile";
   output "dir"
else
   output "get remotefile localfile"
feed temporary file to "ftp" program.
```

5. The main C program, fget.c, is shown here:

```c
/**                           fget.c                      **/

/** (C) Copyright 2001, Dave Taylor. All Rights Reserved.***/

#include "fget.h"

main(argc, argv)
int argc;
char **argv;
{
        FILE *fd;
        char buffer[SLEN], username[NLEN], hostname[NLEN];
        char remotehost[SLEN], remotefile[SLEN], localfname[SLEN];

        if (argc < 2) usage();  /* too few args: usage and quit */

        splitword(argv[1], remotehost, remotefile);
             /* split host/file */

        if (argc == 2) strcpy(localfname, basename_of(remotefile));
        else           strcpy(localfname, argv[2]);

        initialize(username, hostname);
             /* get username and local host */

        if ((fd = fopen(TEMPFILE, "w")) == NULL) {
           fprintf(stderr,
"Couldn't open tempfile '%s': move into your home
 directory?\n",
              TEMPFILE);
           exit(1);
        }

        /** build the information to hand to ftp in the temp file **/

        fprintf(fd, "ascii\nuser %s %s@%s\n",
ANONFTP, username, hostname);
```

23

```
            if (strlen(remotefile) == 0) {
              if (strlen(localfname) > 0)    /* directory specified? */
                fprintf(fd, "cd %s\n", localfname); /* add 'cd' */
              fprintf(fd, "dir\n");
            }
            else    /* get a file from the remote site */
              fprintf(fd, "get %s %s\n", remotefile, localfname);

            fprintf(fd, "bye\n");

            fclose(fd);

            /* the input file is built, now to hand it to 'ftp' */

            sprintf(buffer, "ftp -n %s < %s; rm %s",
        remotehost,TEMPFILE, TEMPFILE);
            exit(system(buffer));
        }
```

I won't go into details about exactly how this works or what the individual C statements do; that's beyond the scope of this book.

What is important to notice, however, is the line #include "fget.h" at the top,
which tells the C compiler to include an additional *header file*, a clue that the program is built from more than a single *source file*.

6. Here's what fget.h looks like:

```
/**                             fget.h                         **/

/** Headers file for the FGET program.  See "fget.c" for info.
    (C) Copyright 2001, Dave Taylor, All Rights Reserved.    ***/

#include <stdio.h>

#define FTP            "ftp -n"    /* to invoke FTP in silent mode */
#define TEMPFILE       ".fget.tmp"  /* temp file for building cmds */
#define ANONFTP        "ftp"       /* anonymous FTP user account */

#define SLEN           256         /* length of a typical string */
#define NLEN           40          /* length of a short string   */

char *basename_of(), *getenv();
```

It turns out that a third file is required too: utils.c, which contains the actual subroutines initialize(), splitword(), basename_of(), and usage(). It's too long
to present here in the book, but it's easily available online: Go to
http://www.intuitive.com/tyu24/ for your own copy of all three of these files.

SUMMARY   There's more to the fget program than the snippet you've seen here, but if you
pop over to the Web site, you'll have everything you need to follow the rest of
this lesson.

Task 23.2: Compiling the Program with cc, the C Compiler

DESCRIPTION Unlike Perl, BASIC, and Unix shell scripts, C is one of a class of programming languages that must be translated into machine language before it becomes usable. The tool for translating *source code* like what's shown in the preceding listings to *executable binaries* is a compiler. Sensibly enough, the C compiler is cc.

A few different things are actually happening behind the scenes when you compile a program. The sequence is actually "add all the include files, compile the program to an intermediate object file, and then link all the object files together with any runtime libraries needed to produce the final program."

Fortunately you don't need to worry about these steps, except to know that because we're working with multiple source files, we'll need to change the default behavior of cc slightly.

ACTION

1. The C compiler has oodles of command options, but there's really only one I need to be concerned with right now. The -c flag tells the compiler to build the *object file* associated with the individual C program, but not to try to link all the runtime libraries:

```
$ cc -c fget.c
$
```

Not much output, but no output is good news: Everything worked just fine.

> You might not have the cc compiler on your system. If not, no worries; try typing gcc -c fget.c. gcc is the GNU C compiler and it's 100% functionally equivalent to cc. gcc is included with Linux, for example.

2. There's one more file to compile before I'm done. (Remember, you can get it from the book's Web site if you'd like to follow along step-by-step here.)

```
$ cc -c utils.c
$
```

Again, no problems.

23

3. A quick peek with `ls` shows what has happened:

```
$ ls -l
total 21
-rw-r--r--    1 taylor    taylor        2523 Sep 13 13:08 fget.c
-rw-r--r--    1 taylor    taylor         624 Sep 13 11:58 fget.h
-rw-rw-r--    1 taylor    taylor        1988 Sep 13 13:08 fget.o
-rw-r--r--    1 taylor    taylor        2802 Sep 13 11:58 utils.c
-rw-rw-r--    1 taylor    taylor        2592 Sep 13 11:58 utils.o
```

There are two new files: `fget.o` and `utils.o`. Those are the object files.

4. Now let's put everything together and create the `fget` program itself. Notice that I won't need the `-c` flag but will instead use the `-o` flag to specify the name of the output file (the final program to be created).

```
$ cc fget.o utils.o -o fget
$
```

Great! It worked without a problem. Now let's try it:

```
$ fget ftp.intuitive.com
total 7
drwxr-xr-x   6 root      root        1024 Sep 13 18:50 .
drwxr-xr-x   6 root      root        1024 Sep 13 18:50 ..
-rw-rw-r--   1 root      root         175 Sep 13 18:50 README
d--x--x--x   2 root      root        1024 Mar 26 23:09 bin
d--x--x--x   2 root      root        1024 Mar 26 23:09 etc
drwxr-xr-x   2 root      root        1024 Mar 26 23:09 lib
dr-xr-sr-x   2 root      ftp         1024 Sep 13 18:48 pub
```

Super!

SUMMARY Using the C compiler to put all the pieces together is easy, but as you might expect, it can become quite tedious. The more C files you have for your program, the more typing you'll end up doing, and what's worse, you're never sure that you have the very latest versions of every file unless you rebuild every one every time. That's where the `make` utility comes to the rescue.

Task 23.3: The Invaluable `make` Utility

DESCRIPTION You saw earlier that you can type the `cc` commands needed each time to rebuild the object files from the C source files you have, and then use `cc` again to create the final program—but wouldn't it be nice if there were an easier way? In particular, imagine that you have a big program that includes 3 header (`.h`) files and 16 source files. It would be a nightmare to type all those commands each time you wanted to update the program!

Instead, Unix has a great utility called `make` that enables you to define a set of rules regarding how files should be compiled and linked together and can then build them automatically.

Rules for compilation are good, but being able to keep track of the minimum amount of recompilation for any given modification to the program is really the big win for make, as you'll see.

The one price you pay is that you need to create a *Makefile*, a somewhat peculiar-looking file that defines all the rules and dependencies in your project.

ACTION

23

1. First, I need to create one of these Makefile files, which means I need to define the rule for compiling a C program. In its most basic form, it's cc -c *sourcefile*, but I'll make it more general purpose by having the compiler specified as a Makefile variable and adding another optional variable, CFLAGS, in case I want to specify any other possible compilation flags.

   It looks like this:
   ```
   CC=/usr/bin/cc
   CFLAGS=
           $(CC) $(CFLAGS) -c sourcefile
   ```

   If I specify this for the two files in the fget project, it will look like this:
   ```
   $(CC) $(CFLAGS) -c fget.c
   $(CC) $(CFLAGS) -c utils.c
   ```

2. But there's more that can be included in the Makefile—there are file dependencies. These are straightforward, thankfully: The object file or program I'm trying to create is specified, followed by a colon, followed by a list of the files that are required.

   In fact, Makefile rules (contained in a file called Makefile in the same directory as the source files) generally need to be
   ```
   target: dependencies
       commands for building the target
   ```

   Taking that into account, here are the two rules for the current project:
   ```
   CC=/usr/bin/cc
   CFLAGS=

   fget.o: fget.c fget.h
           $(CC) $(CFLAGS) -c fget.c

   utils.o: utils.c fget.h
           $(CC) $(CFLAGS) -c utils.c
   ```

   Only one more rule is needed and we've got the entire Makefile written.

These rules tell make how to create the intermediate files from the original C source files using cc, but not how to build the actual fget program. That's done with one more rule:

```
TARGET=fget

$(TARGET): $(OBJ) fget.h
        $(CC) $(CFLAGS) $(OBJ) -o $(TARGET)
```

3. Now, finally, here's the entire Makefile:

```
#
# Makefile for the FGET utility

TARGET=fget
OBJ=fget.o utils.o

CFLAGS=
CC=/usr/bin/cc

$(TARGET): $(OBJ) fget.h
        $(CC) $(CFLAGS) $(OBJ) -o $(TARGET)

fget.o: fget.c fget.h
        $(CC) $(CFLAGS) -c fget.c

utils.o: utils.c fget.h
        $(CC) $(CFLAGS)  -c utils.c
```

4. Now we can build the program with a single command: make.

```
$ make
/usr/bin/cc  -c fget.c
/usr/bin/cc  -c utils.c
/usr/bin/cc  fget.o utils.o -o fget
$
```

Now watch what happens if I try to build it again, without having made any changes to any of the C source files:

```
$ make
make: 'fget' is up to date.
```

If I make a change to the utilities source file (which I'll simulate by using the handy touch command), notice that only the minimum number of files are recompiled to build the program:

```
$ touch fget.c
$ make
/usr/bin/cc  -c fget.c
/usr/bin/cc  fget.o utils.o -o fget
```

A lot less typing!

SUMMARY When you get the hang of creating Makefiles, you'll find yourself unable to live without 'em, even for as small a project as the `fget` program. It's a good habit to learn, and it will pay dividends as your projects grow in size and complexity.

Task 23.4: Additional Useful C Tools

DESCRIPTION Between `vi` for entering programs and `cc` and `make` for building them, it seems as though programming is a breeze on Unix. In fact, a standard cycle for developing software is edit, compile, test in a loop. What's missing from this picture are the Unix test facilities, also known as *debuggers*.

Unfortunately, about a half-dozen debugging programs are available on different types of Unix systems, and they are very different from each other! The good news is that they are but one of a set of useful commands you'll want to research further as you continue to learn how to program C within the Unix environment.

ACTION

1. The easiest way to see exactly what C utilities you have on your system is to use the `man -k` command:

```
$ man -k c | wc -l
2252
```

With 2,252 matching commands, it's clear that the `man` command is showing all commands that have a letter *c* somewhere in their description. Not too useful. Instead, a more sophisticated filter is needed, one that shows only commands that include the letter *c* without any other letters on either side of it and also includes only those commands in section one of the Unix online manual—the actual interactive commands:

```
$ man -k c | grep -i ' c ' | grep 1 | wc -l
    12
```

2. Much better. Let's have a look and see what these commands are on my Linux system by removing the "word count" at the end of the pipe:

```
$ man -k c | grep -i ' c ' | grep 1
c2lout (1)            - convert C and C++ source code into Lout
cdecl, c++decl (1)    - Compose C and C++ type declarations
cproto (1)            - generate C function prototypes and convert
➥function definitions.
ctags (1)             - Generate C language tag files for use with vi
f2c (1)               - Convert Fortran 77 to C or C++
gcc, g++ (1)          - GNU project C and C++ Compiler (v2.7)
indent (1)            - changes the appearance of a C program by
➥inserting or deleting whitespace.
```

23

```
p2c (1)                   - Pascal to C translator, version 1.20
perlembed (1)             - how to embed perl in your C program
tcsh (1)                  - C shell with file name completion and command
➥line editing
imake (1)                 - C preprocessor interface to the make utility
makestrs (1)              - makes string table C source and header(s)
```

The most useful command on this list, in my experience, is the C compiler (here it's gcc).

3. If I try the same command on a different version of Unix, Solaris, you'll see that the output is quite different:

```
$ man -k c | grep -i ' c ' | grep 1
ansic (7V)                - ANSI C (draft of December 7 1988) lint
   library
cb (1)                    - a simple C program beautifier
cc (1V)                   - C compiler
cflow (1V)                - generate a flow graph for a C program
cpp (1)                   - the C language preprocessor
csh, %, @, alias, bg, break, breaksw, case, continue, default, dirs,
➥else, end, endif, endsw, eval, exec, exit, fg, foreach, glob, goto,
➥hashstat, history, if, jobs, label, limit, logout, notify, onintr,
➥popd, pushd, rehash, repeat, set, setenv, shift, source, stop,
➥suspend, switch, then, umask, unalias, unhash, unlimit, unset,
➥unsetenv, while (1) - C shell built-in commands, see csh(1)
ctrace (1V)               - generate a C program execution trace
cxref (1V)                - generate a C program cross-reference
gcc, g++ (1)              - GNU project C and C++ Compiler (v2
   preliminary)
h2ph (1)                  - convert .h C header files to.ph Perl
   header files
indent (1)                - indent and format a C program source file
lint (1V)                 - a C program verifier
mkstr (1)                 - create an error message file by massaging C
   source files
ref (1)                   - Display a C function header
tcsh (1)                  - C shell with file name completion and
   command line editing
xstr (1)                  - extract strings from C programs to
   implement shared strings
```

Quite a different result! In this case, the most useful commands are unquestionably lint and cc.

lint is an interesting program and worth using if you have access: It runs a fine-tooth comb over your program to see whether any potential problems are lurking in your coding style (for example, variables used before they're initialized) or use of functions and system libraries (for example, you call a library with an integer, but it expects a string).

The output is usually quite verbose. Experiment with different options to limit what's reported. Really clean programs have zero output from `lint`, though it can be quite a bit of work!

4. The program we haven't found yet is the debugger, and a quick peek at the man page for `gdb`, the GNU debugger, explains why:

```
$ man gdb | head -15

gdb(1)                       GNU Tools                       gdb(1)

NAME
       gdb - The GNU Debugger

SYNOPSIS
       gdb     [-help] [-nx] [-q] [-batch] [-cd=dir] [-f] [-b bps]
               [-tty=dev] [-s symfile] [-e prog] [-se prog] [-c
               core] [-x cmds] [-d dir] [prog[core|procID]]

DESCRIPTION
       The  purpose  of a debugger such as GDB is to allow you to
       see what is going on "inside" another program  while  it
```

The problem is that it isn't described as being unique to the C programming language!

> If you don't have `gdb`, look for either `cdb` or `dbx`, two of the other common debugging environments.

SUMMARY Many kinds of tools are available to help you with developing programs written in the C programming language. For me, I'd say that I end up using mostly `vi` as I edit things, `make` to hide the compilation step, and, sporadically, `gdb` to find problems while running the program itself.

Summary

Writing your own Unix commands is not only valuable, enabling you to customize the operating system to your own needs, but fun too! If you choose to pursue this avenue further, you'll be well served to look for a book on C programming in a Unix environment.

Workshop

The Workshop summarizes the key terms you learned and poses some questions about the topics presented in this chapter. It also provides you with a preview of what you will learn in the next hour.

Key Terms

executable binary   A file containing special machine instructions that let the computer directly execute the commands therein.

header file   A shared file that contains variable definitions and macro preprocessor directives. The filename usually ends with a .h suffix.

object file   An intermediate file that contains the executable command sequences from a source file but hasn't been linked with the necessary runtime libraries to work correctly. The filename usually ends with a .o suffix.

source code   A human-readable C program listing.

source file   A file containing the source to a particular set of functions or program. The filename ends with a .c suffix if it's a C program.

Exercises

First, go to the Web site http://www.intuitive.com/tyu24/ and download the files for this hour.

1. What C development commands are available on your system? Use man -k to find out.

2. Use make to build the fget program. You might have to use the which command to find out exactly where your C compiler lives and then edit the Makefile to match.

3. Use fget to list the files available at ftp.apple.com.

4. Use lint to check the quality of the code, if available.

Preview of the Next Hour

In the next hour, you learn about the Perl programming language and the many tools available on Unix to help you develop software in this cool alternative to C.

Hour **24**

Perl Programming in Unix

In the previous hour you learned about the C programming language, the underpinnings of the entire Unix operating system. C has been around for as long as Unix—more than 30 years—without any major changes. Newer languages have arisen in the meantime, languages with weird names such as Python, Eiffel, Tkl, and Perl. Each has certain strengths, but it has been my experience that knowledge of C, shell scripts, and Perl is the cornerstone of any Unix expert.

In this final hour I introduce you to the Perl language. Perl is an *interpreted* language, so it doesn't require you to use a compiler as an intermediate step in getting it to work. Perl works much more like shell scripts, which makes it easier as a development tool. However, it's worth pointing out that running lots of Perl programs simultaneously is definitely more resource-intensive than running a similar number of C programs.

Whether or not you read through the lesson on C programming, I definitely encourage you to read more about Perl. In addition to being an elegant and powerful Unix tool builder, Perl is also the programming language of choice for Web professionals. You'll learn more about CGI programming in Perl in Appendix A, "Working with Apache Server," when we talk about the Apache Web server and how it fits so gracefully into the Unix environment.

Goals for This Hour

In this hour, you learn what tools are available with the standard Perl distribution to help you develop smart, fast programs.

In this hour, you will learn about

- Exchange, a demonstration currency translator written in Perl
- Checking code quality with -w
- Online Perl documentation and information
- Other useful Perl commands

In the previous lesson we used a simple FTP front-end program as an example of what you can do in a few dozen lines of C. This lesson will offer a different program, one that enables you to do easy currency translation to prepare for travel overseas.

Perl isn't included with every Unix implementation, surprisingly. If you don't have it, or if your version of Perl is earlier than 5.0 (try perl -v to find out what version you have), then go to http://www.perl.org/ to find out about downloading a newer version.

Flexible and Powerful: Perl

Programming in C offers considerable flexibility, as you saw in the previous lesson, but C was originally designed for system-level programming tasks. Perl, by contrast, was designed to be a powerful language for string or word processing. You can most easily see the difference by exploring a programming task, so that's what we'll do in this last hour of the book.

Task 24.1: Exchange, a Demonstration Currency Translator Written in Perl

DESCRIPTION Some friends recently returned from a couple of weeks' traveling throughout Europe. Upon their return, they commented that they were baffled by the sheer variety of currencies. They're not the first to observe this, of course, but I thought "what a great Perl program to write!"

Translating currencies is simple once you get the formula and exchange rates. Here in the United States, currency values are usually presented relative to a single U.S. dollar, so the French franc might be valued at 7.052, which means that every dollar you exchange is worth 7.052 francs. Exchange $20 and it will net you 20*7.052, or 141.04FF.

The Exchange program started out life by reading in the current exchange rates for five major world currencies (U.S. dollar, Japanese yen, German deutsche mark, French franc, and British pound), prompting for an amount in U.S. dollars, and then showing what its equivalent value was in these other currencies. Much more useful, however, is the capability to translate from any one of these currencies to the other four. Further, sites are on the Internet that show the daily currency exchange rate, so ensuring up-to-date rates is another desirable program feature.

Let's see how to carry this out with Perl and Unix.

24

ACTION

1. The basic logic flow (or *algorithm* if you want to be technical about it) for the Exchange program is this:

   ```
   Read current exchange rates
   Repeat
     Ask user for an amount and currency
     Translate that into US dollars
     Show the equivalent value in all five currencies
   Until done
   ```

2. Perl supports subroutines to help develop clean, readable programs, so let's have a peek at the main code in the program:

   ```perl
   #!/usr/ bin/perl

   &read_exchange_rate;      # read the exchange rate table into memory

   # now let's cycle, asking the user for input...

   print "Please enter the amount, appending the first ";
   print "letter of the name of\nthe currency that you're ";
   print "using (franc, yen, deutschmark, pound) - \n";
   print "the default value is US dollars.\n\n";
   print "Amount: ";

   while (<STDIN>) {
   ```

```
($amnt,$curr) = &breakdown(chop($_));

$baseval = $amnt * (1/$rateof{$curr});    # translate into USD

printf("%2.2f USD, ", $baseval * $rateof{'U'});       # USA
printf("%2.2f Franc, ", $baseval * $rateof{'F'});     # France
printf("%2.2f DM, ', $baseval * $rateof{'D'});        # Germany
printf("[%2.2f Yen, and ", $baseval * $rateof{'Y'});    # Japan
printf("%2.2f Pound\n\nAmount: ', $baseval * $rateof{'P'});# UK
}
```

The first line needs to point to your Perl interpreter; an easy way to find it is to use which perl on the command line.

I've added some fancy output formatting with the print statement, but otherwise this code is quite similar to the algorithm you've already seen. Notice that the array rateof uses the first letter of the currency as an index and returns the current exchange rate relative to the US dollar (that is, $rateof{'F'} is actually 7.052).

One slick thing about Perl is that subroutines can return a list of variables, as you see demonstrated in the call to the "breakdown" subroutine, which returns both $amnt and $curr.

3. Two subroutines are included in this program, read_exchange_rate and breakdown. Let's consider them in reverse order.

   The breakdown subroutine receives the user currency entry and splits it into two parts: the numeric value and the first letter of the currency indicator, if any (the default currency is US dollars):

```
sub breakdown {
   @line = split(" ', $_);        # chop at space

   $amnt = $line[0];
   if ($#line == 1) {
     $curr = $line[1];
     $curr =~ tr/a-z/A-Z/;         # uppercase
     $curr = substr($curr, 0, 1);  # first char only
   } else { $curr = "U"; }
   return ($amnt, $curr);
}
```

I won't go into too much detail here—Perl can be somewhat overwhelming when you first start working with it—but if the subroutine is given a value such as "34.5 yen" it will return $amnt = 34.5 and $curr = 'Y'.

4. The current exchange rate is read in from an associated data file, `exchange.db`, which contains the exchange rate for the five currencies (although the exchange rate for US dollars is always 1, of course!):

```perl
sub read_exchange_rate {
  open(EXCHRATES, "<exchange.db') ||
    die "Can't find current exchange rates.\n";

  while ( <EXCHRATES> ) {
    chop; split;
    $curr = @_[0];
    $val  = @_[1];
    $rateof{$curr} = $val;
  }
  close(EXCHRATE);
}
```

Using the notation you're already familiar with from the Unix shell, Perl specifies whether files are being opened for reading or writing with the direction of the redirect arrow. Here on line two you can see that the exchange.db file is being opened for reading. The `||` die is a shorthand way of saying, if the open fails, output the error message and quit immediately.

The `exchange.db` data file looks like this:

```
P       0.594
D       1.687
F       5.659
Y       132
U       1
```

5. Here's the cool part about this program: The exchange rates can be lifted off a handy Web page automatically, to ensure that they're always current and accurate.

I accomplish that task by using the `lynx` text-based Web browser to grab a page off Yahoo Financials that has the exchange rates, then a few simple Unix commands in a pipeline to strip out the information I don't want and reformat it as needed.

It's all dropped into a shell script, `build-exchrate`:

```sh
#!/bin/sh

# Build a new exchange rate database by using the data on Yahoo

# special case for the British Pound needed...

lynx -dump http://quote.yahoo.com/m3\?u | \
   awk '/U.K./ { if (NF > 4) print "P\t"$3 }'

# now let's get the other three...
```

24

```
lynx -dump http://quote.yahoo.com/m3\?u | \
    awk '/Can/,/SFran/ { if (NF > 4) print $1"\t"$2 }' | \
    cat -v | sed 's/M-%/Y/' | \
    egrep '(U.K.|DMark|FFranc|Yen)' | \
    sed 's/U.K./P/;s/DMark/D/;s/FFranc/F/;s/Yen/Y/'

echo "U 1"
exit 0
```

To learn more about the useful `lynx` command, use `man lynx` on your system. It's a good addition to your bag of Unix tricks, particularly within scripts and programs.

 For those of you who are Web developers, `lynx` users are why you've been putting those ALT tags in your pages whenever you included any sort of images with IMG SRC. Try it and you'll see what I mean.

The output of the `build-exchrate` command is exactly the database file format, albeit to the screen rather than the data file:

```
$ build-exchrate
P       0.6854
D       2.103
F       7.052
Y       114.8
U       1
```

Creating the data file for the program is easy:

```
$ build-exchrate > exchange.db
$
```

6. Let's now try out the exchange program and see how it works!

```
$ perl exchange.pl
Please enter the amount, appending the first letter of the name of
the currency that you're using (franc, yen, deutschmark, pound) -
the default value is US dollars.

Amount: 20
20.00 USD, 141.04 Franc, 42.06 DM, 2296.00 Yen, and 13.71 Pound

Amount: 20 pounds
29.18 USD, 205.78 Franc, 61.37 DM, 3349.87 Yen, and 20.00 Pound

Amount: 20 yen
0.17 USD, 1.23 Franc, 0.37 DM, 20.00 Yen, and 0.12 Pound
```

```
Amount: 20 deutchmarks
9.51 USD, 67.07 Franc, 20.00 DM, 1091.77 Yen, and 6.52 Pound

Amount: 20 francs
2.84 USD, 20.00 Franc, 5.96 DM, 325.58 Yen, and 1.94 Pound
```

Finally, one last query: In the United States the dynamite RedHat Linux package (a great, inexpensive Unix for PC-based computers) costs about $80. It's easy to use Exchange to compute the equivalent price overseas:

```
Amount: 80
80.00 USD, 564.16 Franc, 168.24 DM, 9184.00 Yen, and 54.83 Pound
Amount:
```

To quit the program, I use ^D to send an end-of-file signal.

You can get an online copy of the Exchange program and its companion build-exchrate shell script by visiting http://www.intuitive.com/tyu24/.

24

 The Exchange program demonstrates how you can write succinct and sophisticated programs in Perl. It also demonstrates that Perl can be a wee bit confusing if you're uninitiated! That's why your best bet for learning Perl, or any other programming language, is to spend the time to find and read a good tutorial.

More importantly, the program demonstrates that it's the combination of tools—Unix commands and Perl— that enables you to really create some terrific applications.

Task 24.2: Checking Code Quality with -w

DESCRIPTION There are two main ways to run Perl programs: by typing perl followed by the name of your program (as shown previously), or by specifying program names directly on the command line. For the latter approach to work, you'll need to include #!/usr /bin/perl as the first line of your program (you can use which perl to ensure that's the correct path on your system, of course) and use chmod to make your program executable.

Whichever way you choose to invoke your Perl program, the Perl interpreter will scan the program to see whether it all makes syntactic sense, and then actually begin executing the instructions specified.

The scan performed is rudimentary, however, and catches only the most grievous of mistakes. Add a simple -w flag, however, and the interpreter looks much more closely at the program, emitting various warnings ("-w" = "warnings") for odd constructs and more.

Even Perl programs that work fine can generate quite a variety of warnings! In fact, `perl -w` is the Perl version of `lint`.

ACTION

1. I'll start by making the `exchange.pl` program executable, to save a little bit of typing:

```
$ chmod +x exchange.pl
$
```

Not much output, but no output is good news: Everything worked fine.

2. I'm going to delete the semicolon after the call to `read_exchange_rate` in the `exchange.pl` file so that you can see what happens when the Perl interpreter finds the mistake.

Done. (We'll call that an "edit between the lines," okay?)

```
$ exchange.pl
syntax error at ./exchange.pl line 7, near "print"
Execution of ./exchange.pl aborted due to compilation errors.
```

Hmm..line 7, eh? Let's use the `-n` flag to the `cat` command to see the first 10 lines, numbered:

```
$ cat -n exchange.pl | head
     1  #!/usr/bin/perl
     2
     3  &read_exchange_rate        # read exchange rate into memory
     4
     5  # now let's cycle, asking the user for input...
     6
     7  print "Please enter the amount, appending the first ";

     8  print "letter of the name of\nthe currency that you're ";
     9  print "using (franc, yen, deutschmark, pound) - \n";
    10  print "the default value is US dollars.\n\n";
```

Line 7 isn't where the problem occurs (it's on line 3), but this is a great opportunity to point out that you should never entirely trust the line numbers in compiler or interpreter error messages.

3. Now let's invoke Perl with the `-w` flag to see whether it offers more advice on what's wrong with the program:

```
$ perl -w exchange.pl
syntax error at exchange.pl line 7, near "print"
Scalar value @_[0] better written as $_[0] at exchange.pl line 43.
Scalar value @_[1] better written as $_[1] at exchange.pl line 44.
Execution of exchange.pl aborted due to compilation errors.
$
```

Alas, no help here, but it is showing two old-style lines I have in the read_exchange_rate subroutine.

4. I'm going to restore the semicolon (though I won't show that here; just use vi to add it) and run the -w flag one more time to see whether there are any additional useful suggestions:

```
$ perl -w exchange.pl
Scalar value @_[0] better written as $_[0] at exchange.pl line 48.
Scalar value @_[1] better written as $_[1] at exchange.pl line 49.
Use of implicit split to @_ is deprecated at exchange.pl line 47.
Name "main::EXCHRATE" used only once: possible typo at exchange.pl line 52.
Please enter the amount, appending the first letter of the name of
the currency that you're using (franc, yen, deutschmark, pound) -
the default value is US dollars.

Amount:
```

Wow! Lots of output, most of which is telling me that there are new, fancier ways to specify things (for example, use $_[1] instead of @_[1]).

5. Buried in all of this output, however, is a bug in the program that the Perl interpreter found:

```
Name "main::EXCHRATE" used only once: possible typo at exchange.pl
Âline 47.
```

A closer look at the read_exchange_rate subroutine shows what's wrong:

```
$ cat -n exchange.pl | tail -12
    37  sub read_exchange_rate {
    38    open(EXCHRATES, "<exchange.db") ||
    39      die "Can't find current exchange rates.\n";
    40
    41    while ( <EXCHRATES> ) {
    42      chop; split;
    43      $curr = @_[0];
    44      $val  = @_[1];
    45      $rateof{$curr} = $val;
    46    }
    47    close(EXCHRATE);
    48  }
```

Can you see the problem it has found? The open statement creates a *file handle* called EXCHRATES, which is then used in the while statement, but when I went to close the file handle, I forgot the trailing *s* and called it EXCHRATE.

An easy fix, fortunately!

SUMMARY Even the most carefully written Perl programs can have problems lurking. The -w flag isn't ideal, but you should become familiar with its use and learn how to distinguish important warnings from unimportant ones.

In this case the bug identified wouldn't have broken anything or generated any incorrect results, but if I had continued to improve Exchange, not closing the file handle could have become a significant problem down the road.

Task 24.3: Online Perl Documentation and Information

DESCRIPTION Earlier I recommended that you buy a good Perl tutorial book to learn more about the language. I'm going to revise that a bit, because the standard Perl installation includes a ton of online documentation.

ACTION

1. If you've been trying all the examples as you've been reading the lessons, you're already familiar with the standard Unix man page format and how to find the information you see there. Man pages are good for summaries of how to work with individual commands, but they're much less useful for explaining large, complex programs such as bash, the Elm Mail System, or the Perl interpreter.

   That's why the Perl documentation is broken into a staggering number of man pages:

```
$ man -k perl | grep 1
a2p (1)                  - Awk to Perl translator
perl (1)                 - Practical Extraction and Report Language
perlLoL (1)              - Manipulating Lists of Lists in Perl
perlXStut (1)            - Tutorial for XSUBs
perlapio (1)             - perl's IO abstraction interface.
perlbook (1)             - Perl book information
perlbot (1)              - Bag'o Object Tricks (the BOT)
perlbug (1)              - how to submit bug reports on Perl
perlcall (1)             - Perl calling conventions from C
perldata (1)             - Perl data types
perldebug (1)            - Perl debugging
perldelta (1)            - what's new for perl5.004
perldiag (1)             - various Perl diagnostics
perldoc (1)              - Look up Perl documentation in pod format.
perldsc (1)              - Perl Data Structures Cookbook
perlembed (1)            - how to embed perl in your C program
perlfaq (1)              - frequently asked questions about Perl
perlfaq1 (1)             - General Questions About Perl
perlfaq2 (1)             - Obtaining and Learning about Perl
perlfaq3 (1)             - Programming Tools
perlfaq4 (1)             - Data Manipulation
perlfaq5 (1)             - Files and Formats
perlfaq6 (1)             - Regexps
perlfaq7 (1)             - Perl Language Issues
perlfaq8 (1)             - System Interaction
```

```
perlfaq9 (1)         - Networking
perlform (1)         - Perl formats
perlfunc (1)         - Perl builtin functions
perlguts (1)         - Perl's Internal Functions
perlipc (1)          - Perl interprocess communication (signals,
➡fifos, pipes, safe subprocesses, sockets, and semaphores)
perllocale (1)       - Perl locale handling (internationalization
➡and localization)
perlmod (1)          - Perl modules (packages and symbol tables)
perlmodlib (1)       - constructing new Perl modules and finding
➡existing ones
perlobj (1)          - Perl objects
perlop (1)           - Perl operators and precedence
perlpod (1)          - plain old documentation
perlre (1)           - Perl regular expressions
perlref (1)          - Perl references and nested data structures
perlrun (1)          - how to execute the Perl interpreter
perlsec (1)          - Perl security
perlstyle (1)        - Perl style guide
perlsub (1)          - Perl subroutines
perlsyn (1)          - Perl syntax
perltie (1)          - how to hide an object class in a simple variable
perltoc (1)          - perl documentation table of contents
perltoot (1)           Tom's object-oriented tutorial for perl
perltrap (1)         - Perl traps for the unwary
perlvar (1)          - Perl predefined variables
perlxs (1)           - XS language reference manual
s2p (1)              - Sed to Perl translator
POSIX (3)            - Perl interface to IEEE Std 1003.1
```

Quite a few man pages, eh?

2. The good news (I think) is that the standard perl man page offers a suggested order for reading the man pages that can help overcome some of the gasping, drowning feeling you probably have right now!

For ease of access, the Perl manual has been divided into a number of sections:

```
          perl       Perl overview (this section)
          perldelta  Perl changes since previous version
perlfaq      Perl frequently asked questions

perldata   Perl data structures
perlsyn    Perl syntax
perlop     Perl operators and precedence
perlre     Perl regular expressions
perlrun    Perl execution and options
perlfunc   Perl builtin functions
perlvar    Perl predefined variables
perlsub    Perl subroutines
perlmod    Perl modules: how they work
```

24

```
perlmodlib   Perl modules: how to write and use
perlform     Perl formats
perllocale   Perl locale support

perlref      Perl references
perldsc      Perl data structures intro
perllol      Perl data structures: lists of lists
perltoot     Perl OO tutorial
perlobj      Perl objects
perltie      Perl objects hidden behind simple variables
perlbot      Perl OO tricks and examples
perlipc      Perl interprocess communication

perldebug    Perl debugging
perldiag     Perl diagnostic messages
perlsec      Perl security
perltrap     Perl traps for the unwary
perlstyle    Perl style guide

perlpod      Perl plain old documentation
perlbook     Perl book information
perlembed    Perl ways to embed perl in your C or C++ application
perlapio     Perl internal IO abstraction interface
perlxs       Perl XS application programming interface
perlxstut    Perl XS tutorial
perlguts     Perl internal functions for those doing extensions
perlcall     Perl calling conventions from C

    (If you're intending to read these straight through for
    the first time, the suggested order will tend to reduce
    the number of forward references.)
```

I find the Perl man pages overwhelming, so don't worry if this doesn't make you
want to leap online and read it all.

3. The smarter way to learn more about Perl is to read the online documentation. You
   can start at `http://www.perl.org/` or jump straight to the terrific Perl 5 Desktop
   Reference in HTML form at `http://reference.perl.com/guides/perl5.html`.

SUMMARY Start with the FAQs and the basic Perl man page, and then graduate to a book on
the subject (or even a course)—you'll be a Perl expert.

Task 24.4: Other Useful Perl Commands

DESCRIPTION There are useful pieces to the Perl environment other than just the -w flag to the
interpreter! In this section I'll highlight some special command flags worth
knowing to help you get the most out of Perl.

ACTION

1. The first new flag to learn about is the `-d` debug flag. It's documented (in detail) in `perldebug`, which you'll want to read because various debugging commands are accessible.

2. An interesting variation in debugging requires another flag, the `-e` (execute the following command) flag. It will let you actually use the Perl interpreter interactively:

```
$ perl -de 1

Loading DB routines from perl5db.pl version 1
Emacs support available.

Enter h or 'h h' for help.

main::(-e:1):   1
  DB<1> print "Hi!";
Hi!
  DB<2> q
$
```

The 1 was actually a command to the Perl interpreter, and it was because I specified `-d` for debugging that the interpreter executed the command and then stopped for input.

3. If you'll be using Perl to write Common Gateway Interface (CGI) scripts for a Web server (which I'll talk about again in Appendix A), you'll want to explore the `-T` ("taint") flag, which keeps close track of the flow of user input for security. See `perlsec` for more information.

4. Finally, no discussion of Perl can be complete without highlighting the terrific Perl developer community and its Comprehensive Perl Archive Network (CPAN). The best place to learn about it is `http://www.perl.com/CPAN-local/CPAN.html`.

24

 You can also use Perl interactively to learn about the CPAN modules available, though I've never had any luck with it myself. Try entering `perl -MCPAN -e shell`.

SUMMARY   The Perl language is well worth spending some time learning. The Unix shell offers various capabilities, but you'll undoubtedly hit the edge as you become more sophisticated; that's where Perl can really fill in the gaps.

You can find a great list of Perl books—many with reviews included—maintained by Perl guru Tom Christiansen at `http://www.perl.com/perl/critiques/index.html`.

Summary

The C programming language is the concrete foundation of the Unix operating system, but although it's powerful, it's also rigid and useless for simple tasks. Perl is a great alternative and the de facto language of the World Wide Web, and it has a fabulous developer community. I'd recommend that if you want to become a Unix genius, learn C first, but if you want to become a power user and have the ability to create top-notch CGI (Web) solutions, Perl is the way to go.

Kudos to inventor Larry Wall and his large team of co-developers!

Congratulations!

You've gotten through the entire book, all 24 hours, and you're now a bona fide Unix expert. If you follow up by using the system as much as possible for a few weeks, you'll find that the commands, option flags, and pipes all begin to come naturally. Having used Unix in various flavors for more than two decades (it's hard for me to believe, but I first logged in as a freshman in college in 1980!) I can assure you that the reason Unix hasn't changed dramatically is that it's just so darn powerful, comprehensive, and useful.

The time you spend learning to become a Unix power user will be time very well spent, whether you're aiming at becoming an OS kernel hacker or simply want to be able to make the shared Web server on which you have an account jump through hoops.

Thanks for spending your time learning Unix with me! Feel free to drop me a note if you have any questions or just want to let me know whether you found the book helpful. You can reach me, at any time, at `taylor@intuitive.com`.

Workshop

The Workshop summarizes the key terms you learned and poses some questions about the topics presented in this chapter. It also provides you with a preview of what you will learn in the next hour.

Key Terms

algorithm   The logical sequence of steps taken by a program.

file handle   An internal program variable that's used to refer to a specific file. In Perl, you'll have used an open command to associate a file handle with a file.

Exercises

First, go to the Web site http://www.intuitive.com/tyu24/ and download the files for this hour.

1. Congratulations! You just won £ 50! Use Exchange to see how much that's worth in US dollars.

2. Find and fix the bug highlighted in the exchange.pl program earlier in this lesson. Run perl -w to confirm that it's fixed.

3. Read through the Perl FAQ man pages. What do the Perl FAQ authors recommend as the forum for free Perl advice? What's a JAPH?

24

APPENDIX **A**

Working with the Apache Server

Throughout this book, you've learned how to work with Unix to increase the efficiency of your system. In the last few lessons, that has been extended to include The Great Beyond, the Internet. What you might not have realized, however, is that the history of the Internet is intimately intertwined with the Unix operating system, and to this day the vast majority of Web sites run Unix as their underlying operating system.

Various Web server packages are available for Unix, including most notably Netscape's terrific suite of commercial offerings. (The company actually produces quite a bit more than only a great Web browser.) A strong competitor to Netscape on the server side is another server that's robust, capable, easy to configure, and free: the Apache Web Server.

Goals for This Hour

In this hour, you will learn about

- Exploring Apache configuration files
- Creating a simple CGI program
- A server-side include program
- Understanding Apache log files

In the previous lesson we explored Exchange, a short Perl program that offered direct currency conversion. This time we create a couple of simple Unix CGI scripts, expand the program to become a Web-based currency exchange translator, look at a simple program to automate adding a last-modified date and time on your pages, and produce a shell script that analyzes Apache log files.

Apache is well distributed and is included with all versions of Linux, among others, but you might not have it on your system. If not, go to http://www.apache.org/ and download a copy. If you have a different server, rest assured that 90% of what's discussed in this lesson will be true for your setup, too.

Working with a Unix Web Server

You'd have to be pretty out of touch not to have been inundated by Web and Internet information in the past few years. What you might not have realized is that most Web sites you visit are running on Unix systems. Hence this added appendix; if you're learning Unix, there's a very good chance that it's so that you can work with your Web server.

Task A.1: Exploring Apache Configuration Files

DESCRIPTION One of the most delightful aspects of the online community is the sense of cooperation that I've found pervasive in the years I've been involved. This cooperation extends from the development of the Unix system itself; to the creation and group evolution of individual utilities including Perl, Emacs, Elm, Usenet, and the X Window System; to the maintenance of otherwise obsolete products.

It was out of an amalgamation of all of these that Apache was born.

In the early days of the Internet, the National Center for Supercomputer Applications (NCSA) at the University of Illinois, Urbana-Champaign, was the hub of Web development. The Web browser they invented, NCSA Mosaic, went on to great acclaim, winning industry awards and forever changing the online world. Less well known is the seminal work the NCSA team did on the underlying engine, the Web server. By early 1995, however, the popular NCSA Web server was facing obsolescence as the developers went on to other projects.

Rather than let this valuable software die from lack of attention, the Internet community came to the rescue, creating a loose consortium of programmers and developers. Consolidating a wide variety of patches, bug fixes, and enhancement ideas, they released a new, improved server they called Apache. (Get it?—"a patchy Web server.")

Zoom forward a half-dozen years and Apache is by far the most popular Web server on the World Wide Web, with over half of all Web sites running either Apache or a variant. Even better, versions of Apache are available for all major Unix platforms and even MacOS, Windows 95, 98, and NT.

> If you've had a chance to visit http://www.intuitive.com/tyu24/, you've been interacting with an Apache Web server!

Apache typically is unpacked in either /src or /usr/src, though the source distribution can live anywhere on your Unix machine. A bit of detective work and you can track down where the executable lives (the executable is the compiled program that can be run directly by the operating system, which means, yes, Apache is written in C, not Perl).

Action

1. The first step in trying to find out where your Web server lives is to see whether there's a directory called /etc/httpd on your system. If there is, you're in luck; it will have the central configuration and log files.

   If not, you can try using the ps processor status command to see whether you have an HTTP daemon (search for HTTPD) running: That will probably give you the name of the configuration file. On a Unix system running Sun Microsystems' Solaris operating system, here's what I found out:

   ```
   $ ps -ef | grep httpd | head -1
     websrv 21156  8677  0 14:51:25 ?   0:00 /opt/INXapache/bin/httpd
   ➥-f /opt/INXapache/conf/httpd.conf
   ```

   By contrast, when I ran the ps command on my Linux system (with the slightly different arguments expected: aux instead of -ef), the output is different:

   ```
   $ ps aux | grep httpd | head -1
   nobody    313 0.0 0.8 1548 1052 ? S   15:49  0:00 httpd
   ➥-d /etc/httpd
   ```

In the former case, you can see that the configuration file is specified as /opt/INXapache/conf/httpd.conf, and in the latter case, the program is using the directory /etc/httpd as the starting point to search for the configuration file. Either way, we've found the mystery configuration file and can proceed.

2. Now that you've found your configuration file, I have to warn you: There are many options you don't want to worry about or touch. If you want to change anything with the configuration of your Apache server, you'll want to study it closely first. This doesn't mean that you can't peek inside and find out a few things about your configuration, however.

Three configuration files are in most Apache installations and, confusingly, most of the configuration options we're interested in can appear in any of them. The best way to work, therefore, is to use grep across all three files at once (access.conf, srm.conf, and httpd.conf).

 CGI is the *common gateway interface*, the environment through which all Web-based programs are run by the server. They're 95% identical to a program that presents output on the screen in Unix, but they have a few added features that make them Web-friendly.

I'll start by checking to ensure that I have permission to run CGI programs, a crucial capability for creating sophisticated, interactive Web sites. The option is called ExecCGI:

```
$ grep -n ExecCGI *.conf
access.conf:16:Options Indexes FollowSymLinks ExecCGI
access.conf:24:Options  ExecCGI  Indexes
access.conf:61:Options Indexes FollowSymLinks ExecCGI
```

On this particular server, the CGI configuration elements are contained in the access.conf file. The -n flag adds line numbers, so it's easy to look at a 10-line slice centered on the first occurrence, for example:

```
$ cat -n access.conf | head -21 | tail -10
    12
    13  # This should be changed to whatever you set DocumentRoot to.
    14
    15  <Directory /web/fryeboots.com>
    16  Options Indexes FollowSymLinks ExecCGI
    17  AllowOverride None
    18  order allow,deny
    19  allow from all
    20  </Directory>
    21
```

You can see that the directory /web/fryeboots.com is configured to access indexes (for example, to look for a default file called index.html in the directory), follow symbolic links (letting the developer have more flexibility in organizing files), and execute CGI programs.

Now the question is, "Which domain is associated with the directory this defines?"

3. Our friend grep comes into play again to answer this question. What we're looking for is the root of the Web site. In Apache parlance, it's the DocumentRoot, so I'll build a two-part grep to zero in on exactly the line I want:

```
$ grep -n /web/fryeboots.com *.conf | grep DocumentRoot
httpd.conf:312:DocumentRoot /web/fryeboots.com
httpd.conf:320:DocumentRoot /web/fryeboots.com
```

4. Either one of these lines could be what I seek, so let's take a 20-line slice of the configuration file and see what's there:

```
$ cat -n httpd.conf | head -323 | tail -20
   304   ErrorLog /web/onlinepartner.com/logs/error_log
   305   TransferLog /web/onlinepartner.com/logs/access_log
   306   </VirtualHost>
   307
   308   ## fryeboots.com
   309
   310   <VirtualHost fryeboots.com>
   311   ServerAdmin webmaster@fryeboots.com
   312   DocumentRoot /web/fryeboots.com
   313   ServerName fryeboots.com
   314   ErrorLog /web/fryeboots.com/logs/error_log
   315   TransferLog /web/fryeboots.com/logs/access_log
   316   </VirtualHost>
   317
   318   <VirtualHost www.fryeboots.com>
   319   ServerAdmin webmaster@fryeboots.com
   320   DocumentRoot /web/fryeboots.com
   321   ServerName fryeboots.com
   322   ErrorLog /web/fryeboots.com/logs/error_log
   323   TransferLog /web/fryeboots.com/logs/access_log
```

Notice the ErrorLog and TransferLog values (this is where the log files that we'll examine later are being stored). As has already been shown, the home directory of this Web site can be found at /web/fryeboots.com.

5. You can also extrapolate some interesting information about an overall Apache configuration by slicing the preceding code differently. I'll show you one example.

You can identify all the domains served by an Apache Web server simply by searching for the VirtualHost line:

A

```
$ grep '<VirtualHost ' *.conf
httpd.conf:#<VirtualHost host.foo.com>
httpd.conf:<VirtualHost www.hostname.com>
httpd.conf:<VirtualHost www.p3tech.com>
httpd.conf:<VirtualHost www.rjcolt.com>
httpd.conf:<VirtualHost www.aeshoes.com>
httpd.conf:<VirtualHost www.coolmedium.com>
httpd.conf:<VirtualHost www.thisdate.com>
httpd.conf:<VirtualHost www.realintelligence.com>
httpd.conf:<VirtualHost www.marsee.net>
httpd.conf:<VirtualHost www.star-design.com>
httpd.conf:<VirtualHost www.trivial.net>
httpd.conf:<VirtualHost www.p3m.com>
httpd.conf:<VirtualHost www.touralaska.com>
httpd.conf:<VirtualHost www.nbarefs.com>
httpd.conf:<VirtualHost www.canp.org>
httpd.conf:<VirtualHost www.voices.com>
httpd.conf:<VirtualHost www.huntalaska.net>
httpd.conf:<VirtualHost www.cbhma.org>
httpd.conf:<VirtualHost www.cal-liability.com>
httpd.conf:<VirtualHost www.intuitive.com>
httpd.conf:<VirtualHost www.sportsstats.com>
httpd.conf:<VirtualHost www.videomac.com>
httpd.conf:<VirtualHost www.birthconnect.org>
httpd.conf:<VirtualHost www.birth.net>
httpd.conf:<VirtualHost www.baby.net>
httpd.conf:<VirtualHost www.chatter.net>
httpd.conf:<VirtualHost fryeboots.com>
httpd.conf:<VirtualHost www.fryeboots.com>
httpd.conf:<VirtualHost www.savetz.com>
httpd.conf:<VirtualHost www.atarimagazines.com>
httpd.conf:<VirtualHost www.faq.net>
```

I know, you're thinking, *Wow!* All those domains are on a single machine?

That's part of the beauty of Apache. It's very easy to have a pile of different domains, all serving up their Web pages from a single shared machine.

There are many kinds of configurations for Apache server installations, so don't get too anxious if you can't seem to figure out the information just shown. Most likely, if you're on a shared server, you've been told the information we're peeking at anyway. You'll know the three key answers: where all your Web pages should live in your account (probably public_html or www in your account directory), whether you can run CGI programs from your Web space (that's what the ExecCGI indicates in the preceding configuration), and where your log files are stored (often it's just httpd_log or httpd_access.log in your own directory).

The Apache Web server demonstrates all that's wonderful about the synergy created by an easy, high-speed communications mechanism shared by thousands of bright and creative people. A cooperative development effort, each release of Apache is a significant improvement over the preceding release, and Apache keeps getting better and better. And as for the price, it's hard to argue with free.

Knowing how to pop in and look at the configuration of an Apache installation is a good way to find out what capabilities you have as a user of the system. Although thousands of companies offer Web site hosting, those that actually give you all the information you want are few, so having your own tricks (and an extensive knowledge of Unix, of course) is invaluable.

Task A.2: Creating a Simple CGI Program

DESCRIPTION Now I know where the files associated with my Web site live (the `DocumentRoot` directory in the configuration file), and I have ascertained that I have CGI execution permission (`ExecCGI`). It's time to exploit this information by creating a simple CGI program that's actually a shell script, to demonstrate how Unix and the Web can work hand in hand.

ACTION

1. First off, a very basic CGI script to demonstrate the concept:

```
$ cat hello.cgi
#!/usr/bin/perl -w
print "Content-type: text/html\n\n";
print "<h1>Hello there!</h1>\n";
exit 0;
$ chmod a+x hello.cgi
```

When this is invoked from within a Web browser, as with `http://www.intuitive.com/tyu24/hello.cgi`, the results are as shown in Figure A.1.

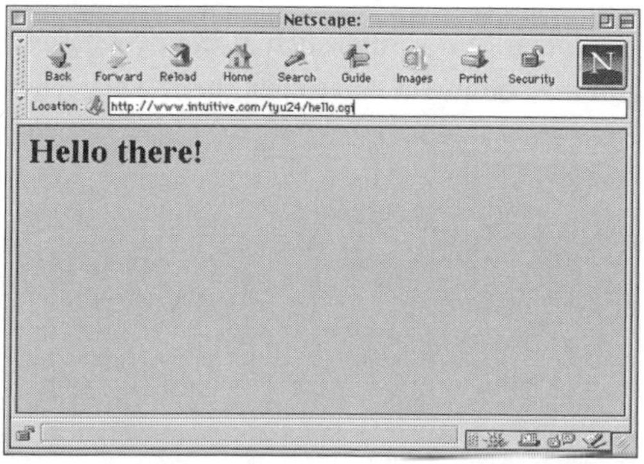

FIGURE A.1

Hello there—our first CGI program.

A

Not very exciting, but it's a skeleton for developing considerably more complex programs.

2. Let's jump to a more complex CGI script, one that's actually a Unix shell script. This time the layout will be quite similar, but I'm going to include the output of an `ls` command and then add a timestamp with `date`, too:

```
$ cat files.cgi
#!/bin/sh -f
echo "Content-type: text/html"
echo ""
echo "<h2>This directory contains the following files:</h2>"
echo "<PRE>"
ls -l
echo "</PRE>"
echo "<h4>output produced at"
date
echo "</h4>"
exit 0
```

The output is considerably more interesting, as shown in Figure A.2.

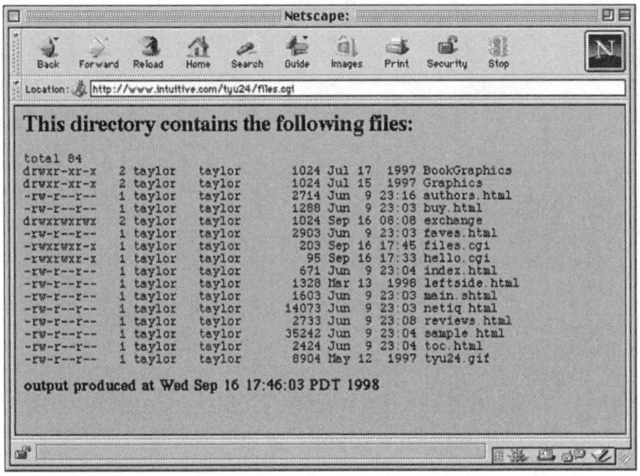

FIGURE A.2

A file listing and the current date and time.

3. It's useful to know that CGI scripts such as the two shown here can also be executed directly on the command line to test them while you're working in Unix:

```
$ cat hello.cgi
Content-type: text/html

<h1>Hello there!</h1>

$ cat files.cgi
Content-type: text/html
```

```
<h2>This directory contains the following files:</h2>
<PRE>
total 84
drwxr-xr-x   2 taylor   taylor    1024 Jul 17  1999 BookGraphics
drwxr-xr-x   2 taylor   taylor    1024 Jul 15  1999 Graphics
-rw-r--r--   1 taylor   taylor    2714 Jun  9 23:16 authors.html
-rw-r--r--   1 taylor   taylor    1288 Jun  9 23:03 buy.html
drwxrwxrwx   2 taylor   taylor    1024 Sep 16 08:08 exchange
-rw-r--r--   1 taylor   taylor    2903 Jun  9 23:03 faves.html
-rwxrwxr-x   1 taylor   taylor     203 Sep 16 17:45 files.cgi
-rwxrwxr-x   1 taylor   taylor      97 Sep 16 17:50 hello.cgi
-rw-r--r--   1 taylor   taylor     671 Jun  9 23:04 index.html
-rw-r--r--   1 taylor   taylor    1328 Mar 13  2000 leftside.html
-rw-r--r--   1 taylor   taylor    1603 Jun  9 23:03 main.shtml
-rw-r--r--   1 taylor   taylor   14073 Jun  9 23:03 netiq.html
-rw-r--r--   1 taylor   taylor    2733 Jun  9 23:08 reviews.html
-rw-r--r--   1 taylor   taylor   35242 Jun  9 23:04 sample.html
-rw-r--r--   1 taylor   taylor    2424 Jun  9 23:04 toc.html
-rw-r--r--   1 taylor   taylor    8904 May 12  1999 tyu24.gif
</PRE>
<h4>output produced at
Wed Feb 14 17:50:46 PDT 2001
</h4>
$
```

This can be incredibly helpful with debugging your CGI programs as you develop them.

4. Now let's peek at the new `exchange.cgi` program that offers the currency conversion program on a Web page.

I'm not going to include the code here because the script has evolved into a rather extensive program (much of which deals with receiving information from the user within the Web environment through QUERY_STRING, a topic beyond the scope of this book).

Check out the exchange rate Web page for yourself. Go to
http://www.intuitive.com/tyu24/exchange/.

Here's a teaser, however:

```
$ head -33 exchange.cgi
#!/usr/bin/perl

&read_exchange_rate;      # read exchange rate into memory
```

A

```
# now let's cycle, asking the user for input...

print "Content-type: text/html\n\n";

print "<HTML
TITLE>Currency Exchange Calculator</TITLE>\n";
print "<BODY BGCOLOR=white LINK='#999999' VLINK='#999999'>\n";
print "<CENTER
h1>Foreign Currency Exchange Calculator</h1>\n";

$value = $ENV{"QUERY_STRING"};              # value from FORM

if ( $value ne undef ) {

  ($amnt,$curr) = &breakdown();

  $baseval = $amnt * (1/$rateof{$curr});

  print "<CENTER
TABLE BORDER=1 CELLPADDING=7
TR>\n";
  print "<TH>U.S.Dollars</TH
TH>French Franc</TH>\n";
  print "<TH>German Mark</TH
TH>Japanese Yen</TH>\n";
  print "<TH>British Pound</TH
/TR>\n";
  print "<TR>\n";

  printf("<TD>%2.2f USD</TD>", $baseval * $rateof{'U'});
  printf("<TD>%2.2f Franc</TD>", $baseval * $rateof{'F'});
  printf("<TD>%2.2f DM</TD>", $baseval * $rateof{'D'});
  printf("<TD>%2.2f Yen</TD>", $baseval * $rateof{'Y'});
  printf("<TD>%2.2f Pound</TD
/TR
/TABLE>\n ", $baseval * $rateof{'P'});
}
```

Figure A.3 shows what the program looks like when you've entered an amount to be converted and the program is showing the results.

SUMMARY I'll be honest with you. Learning the ins and outs of CGI programming within the Unix environment is complex, and you'll need to study for a while before you can whip off CGI scripts that perform specific tasks. Throw in a dose of interactivity, where you glean information from the user and produce a page based on his data, and it's 10 times more complex.

FIGURE A.3

*One hundred yen isn't
what it used to be.*

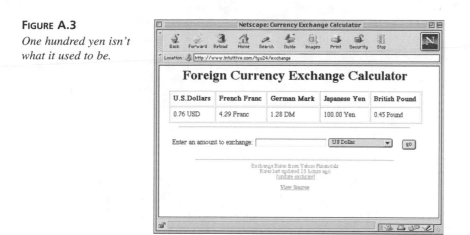

If you want to learn more about Web programming and HTML, which you're seeing throughout these examples, I suggest you read another book of mine, a bestseller: *Creating Cool HTML 4 Web Pages*. You can learn more about it online (of course) at `http://www.intuitive.com/coolweb/`.

Task A.3: A Server-Side Include Program

DESCRIPTION The capability to have CGI programs that are shell scripts, Perl programs, or even extensive C programs adds a great degree of flexibility, but sometimes you just want to add a tiny snippet to an existing HTML page. That's where server-side includes (SSI) can come in handy.

Many sites are configured to prevent you from using the SSI capability for security reasons, so you might not be able to follow along exactly in this portion of the lesson. Those sites that do allow SSI almost always insist on a `.shtml` suffix, rather than the usual `.html` suffix. That tells the Web server to parse each line as the page is sent to the user.

ACTION

1. Here's a common task you might have encountered in a Web project: letting visitors know the date and time when each page was last modified. Sure, you can add the information explicitly on the bottom of each page and then hope you'll remember to update it every time you change the page, but it's more likely that this will be just another annoying detail to maintain.

Instead, let's automate things by using a server-side include in all the HTML files, a single line that automatically checks and displays the last modified time for the specific file. This is a perfect use for a small C program and a call to a library function called `strftime`.

Here's the C source to `lastmod.c`, in its entirety:

```
/**                     lastmod.c                     **/

/** This outputs the last-modified-time of the specified file in
    a succinct, readable format.

    From the book "Teach Yourself UNIX in 24 Hours" by Dave Taylor
**/

#include <sys/stat.h>
#include <unistd.h>
#include <time.h>
#include <stdio.h>

main()
{
        struct stat stbuf;
        struct tm   *t;
        char    buffer[32];

        if (stat(getenv("SCRIPT_FILENAME"), &stbuf) == 0) {
          t=localtime(&stbuf.st_mtime);
          strftime(buffer, 32, "%a %b %d, %y at %I:%M %p", t);
          printf( "<font size=2 color=\"#999999\">");
    printf("This page last modified %s</font>\n", buffer);          }
        exit(0);
}
```

The environment variable `SCRIPT_FILENAME` is quite helpful for SSI programming; it always contains the name of the HTML file that contains the reference. That is, if you have a page called `resume.html` on the file system `/home/joanne/public_html`, `SCRIPT_FILENAME` contains `/home/joanne/public_html/resume.html`.

2. A server-side include is always referenced by its full filename, and the general format is to embed the reference in an HTML comment:

```
<!--#exec cmd="/web/bin/lastmod" -->
```

That's all that's needed in the HTML source file to automatically add a "last modified" entry to a Web page.

3. For an example of how to use this, here are the last 14 lines of the main HTML page for *Sams Teach Yourself Unix in 24 Hours*:

```
$ tail -14 main.shtml
<P>
<hr width=40% noshade size=1>
<font size=2>
You're visitor
<!--#exec cmd="/web/bin/counter .counter"-->
to this site
</font>
<P>
<!--#exec cmd="/web/bin/lastmod"-->
</CENTER>
<P>
</BODY>

</HTML>
```

Notice that the filename suffix is .shtml to ensure that the Web server scans the file for any possible server-side includes. Also notice that the counter on the bottom of the page is *also* a server-side include.

Figure A.4 shows how the bottom of this page looks when it's delivered within a browser. Notice that the SSI lastmod sequence generates the entire phrase last modified, as well as the date.

FIGURE A.4

Server-side includes enhance Web pages.

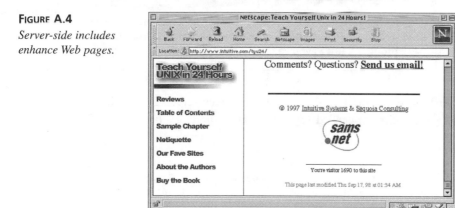

SUMMARY Between server-side includes and CGI programs, you can start to see how really knowing the ins and outs of your Web server can reap great benefits in creating a dramatic and smart Web site.

There's one more area to consider with Web server interaction before this lesson is over, however: analyzing traffic logs and extracting traffic data.

A

Task A.4: Understanding Apache Log Files

DESCRIPTION Whether or not you choose to explore the capabilities of the Apache Web server for delivering custom pages through CGI programming or server-side includes, you'll undoubtedly want to dig through your Web site log files to see what has been going on. The good news is that you're running the best environment for accomplishing the task: Unix.

The wide set of tools and commands available within Unix makes analyzing the otherwise cryptic and usually quite long log files a snap.

ACTION

1. On most shared Web servers, you have a file located in your home directory called `httpd.log`, `httpd_access.log`, or something similar. If you're lucky, the log file is actually broken down into its two components: errors and fulfilled requests.

   On my system, that's exactly how it works. I'm curious to learn more about the traffic that was seen on the `www.trivial.net` Web site recently.

   > Interested in computer trivia? Then Trivial Net is a great site to visit, at www.trivial.net. Even better, the site is built around both C- and Perl-based CGI programs, just as you've seen in this lesson.

   After I move into the Trivial Net area on the Web server, I know that the traffic is all kept in a directory called `logs`. Within that directory, here are the files available

   ```
   $ ls -l
   total 19337
   -rw-r--r--  1 taylor   taylor    9850706 Sep  1 00:08 access_log
   -rw-r--r--  1 taylor   taylor    4608036 Sep  1 00:08 agent_log
   -rw-r--r--  1 taylor   taylor       5292 Sep  1 00:08 error_log
   -rw-r--r--  1 taylor   taylor    5253261 Sep  1 00:08 referer_log
   ```

   As you can see, not only are there an `access_log` and an `error_log`, which contain the fulfilled and failed access requests, respectively, but there also are two additional logs. The `agent.log` log records the Web browsers that visitors used when visiting the site, and `referer_log` records the page that users were viewing immediately prior to visiting the Trivial Net site.

2. These are pretty huge files, as you can see. The `access_log` file is 9.8 megabytes. A quick invocation of the `wc` command and you can see the number of lines in each file instead:

```
$ wc -l *
 104883 access_log
 104881 agent_log
     52 error_log
 102047 referer_log
 311863 total
```

The good thing to notice is that there are only 52 lines of error messages encountered during the month of use, against 104,883 "hits" to the site.

3. Let's start by peeking at the error_log to see what exactly was going on:

```
$ head -10 error_log
[Sat Feb  1 02:28:55 2001] lingering close lost connection to client
hertzelia-204-51.access.net.il
[Sat Feb  1 03:52:22 2001] access to /web/trivial.net/robots.txt
failed for heavymetal.fireball.de, reason: File does not exist
[Sat Feb  1 06:50:04 2001] lingering close lost connection to client
po90.snet.ne.jp
[Sun Feb  2 15:39:14 2001] access to /web/trivial.net/robots.txt
failed for barn.farm.gol.net, reason: File does not exist
[Sun Feb  2 17:16:34 2001] access to /web/trivial.net/robots.txt
failed for nahuel.ufasta.com.ar, reason: File does not exist
[Sun Feb  2 19:20:55 2001] access to /web/trivial.net/robots.txt
failed for c605d216.infoseek.com, reason: File does not exist
[Sun Feb  2 21:13:12 2001] access to /web/trivial.net/playgame.cgi'
failed for saturn.tacorp.com, reason: File does not exist
[Sun Feb  2 21:58:05 2001] access to /web/trivial.net/robots.txt
failed for as016.cland.net, reason: File does not exist
[Mon Feb  3 03:21:54 2001] access to /web/trivial.net/robots.txt
failed for mail.bull-ingenierie.fr, reason: File does not exist
[Mon Feb  3 08:58:26 2001] access to /web/trivial.net/robots.txt
failed for nahuel.ufasta.com.ar, reason: File does not exist
```

The information in the [ ] indicates the exact time and date of the failed request, and the last portion indicates the actual error encountered.

4. Because we're using Unix, it's easy to extract and count the failed access requests to ensure that there are no surprises in the other 42 lines of the file:

```
$ grep 'File does not exist' error_log | cut -d\  -f9
/web/trivial.net/robots.txt
/web/trivial.net/robots.txt
/web/trivial.net/robots.txt
/web/trivial.net/robots.txt
/web/trivial.net/playgame.cgi'
/web/trivial.net/robots.txt
/web/trivial.net/robots.txt
/web/trivial.net/robots.txt
/web/trivial.net/robots.txt
/web/trivial.net/robots.txt
```

A

```
/web/trivial.net/robots.txt
/web/trivial.net/robots.txt
/web/trivial.net/picasso
/web/trivial.net/robots.txt
/web/trivial.net/robots.txt
/web/trivial.net/robots.txt
/web/trivial.net/robots.txt
```

By using the ever-helpful cut command to extract just the ninth word in each line, coupled with a grep command to extract the File does not exist error message, I've extracted just the list of bad files. Now let's create a standard pipe for this kind of work: Sort the list, pipe the results to the uniq program (with the -c prefacing a count of the occurrences of each unique line), and then feed that to another invocation of sort, this time using a reverse numeric sort (-rn) to list the most commonly failed filenames first:

```
$ grep 'File does not exist' error_log | cut -d\  -f9 | \
sort | uniq -c | sort -rn
     16 /web/trivial.net/robots.txt
      1 /web/trivial.net/playgame.cgi'
      1 /web/trivial.net/Picasso
```

You could easily make this an alias or drop it into a shell script to avoid having to type all this each time.

5. Let's get to the more interesting log file, however: the access_log that contains all the successful traffic events:

```
$ head -10 access_log
ppp-206-170-29-29.wnck11.pacbell.net - - [01/Feb/2001:00:12:01 -0700]
"GET / HTTP/1.0" 200 2976
ppp-206-170-29-29.wnck11.pacbell.net - - [01/Feb/2001:00:12:02 -0700]
"GET /animated-banner.gif HTTP/1.0" 200 3131
ppp-206-170-29-29.wnck11.pacbell.net - - [01/Feb/2001:00:12:02 -0700]
"GET /play-the-game.gif HTTP/1.0" 200 1807
ppp-206-170-29-29.wnck11.pacbell.net - - [01/Feb/2001:00:12:02 -0700]
"GET /signup-now.gif HTTP/1.0" 200 2294
ppp-206-170-29-29.wnck11.pacbell.net - - [01/Feb/2001:00:12:03 -0700]
"GET /buy-the-book.gif HTTP/1.0" 200 1541
ppp-206-170-29-29.wnck11.pacbell.net - - [01/Feb/2001:00:12:04 -0700]
"GET /kudos.gif HTTP/1.0" 200 804
ppp-206-170-29-29.wnck11.pacbell.net - - [01/Feb/2001:00:12:05 -0700]
"GET /intsys.gif HTTP/1.0" 200 1272
204.116.54.6 - - [01/Feb/2001:00:18:04 -0700] "GET /animated-banner.gif
HTTP/1.0" 200 3131
204.116.54.6 - - [01/Feb/2001:00:18:04 -0700] "GET /play-the-game.gif
HTTP/1.0" 200 1807
204.116.54.6 - - [01/Feb/2001:00:18:04 -0700] "GET /signup-now.gif
HTTP/1.0" 200 2294
$
```

You can see the basic layout of the information, though a bit of explanation will prove very useful. There are some fields you probably won't care about, so focus on the first (which indicates what domain the user came from), the fourth (the time and date of the access), the seventh (the requested file), and the ninth (the size, in bytes, of the resultant transfer).

For example, the first line tells you that someone from pacbell.net requested the home page of the site (that's what the / means in the request) at 12 minutes after midnight on February 1, and the server sent back 2,976 bytes of information (the file index.html, as it turns out).

6. Every time an element of a Web page is accessed, a record of that event is added to the access_log file. To count the number of page views, therefore, simply use the -v (exclusion) feature of egrep (the regular expression brother of grep) to subtract the GIF and JPEG image references, and then count the remainder:

```
$ cat access_log | egrep  -v '(.gif|.GIF|.jpg|.JPG|.jpeg|.JPEG)' \
  | wc -l
  43211
```

This means that of the 104,883 hits to the site (see the output from wc earlier in this lesson), all but 43,211 were requests for graphics. In the parlance of Web traffic experts, the site had 104,883 hits, of which 43,211 were actual page views.

7. This is where the cut program is going to prove critical, with its capability to extract a specific field or word from each line. First, let's quickly look at the specific files accessed and identify the top 15 requested files, whether they be graphics, HTML, or something else:

```
$ cat access_log | cut -d\  -f7 | sort | uniq -c | \
  sort -rn | head -15
  39040 /playgame.cgi
  13255 /intsys.gif
  12282 /banner.gif
   7002 /wrong.gif
   4464 /right.gif
   3998 /Adverts/computerbowl.gif
   3506 /
   2736 /play-the-game.gif
   2692 /animated-banner.gif
   2660 /signup-now.gif
   2652 /buy-the-book.gif
   2624 /kudos.gif
   1623 /final-score.gif
    621 /forget.gif
    411 /Results/3.gif
```

Interesting results: the `playgame.cgi` program was by far the most commonly accessed file, with the Intuitive Systems graphic a distant second place. More entertainingly, notice that people were wrong almost twice as often as they were right in answering questions (7,002 for `wrong.gif` versus 4,464 for `right.gif`).

8. One more calculation. This time, I'm going to use another great Unix utility: `awk`. In many ways, `awk` is a precursor to Perl that isn't as flexible or robust. However, in this case it's perfect for what we want: a summary of the total number of bytes transferred for the entire month. Because `awk` can easily slice a line into individual fields, this is a piece of cake:

```
$ cat access_log | awk '{sum+=$10} END{print sum}'
325805962
$
```

The quoted argument to `awk` is a tiny program that adds the value of field 10 to the variable `sum` for each line seen and, when it's done with all the lines, prints the value of the variable `sum`.

To put this number in context, it's 325,805,962 bytes, or about 300 megabytes of information in 30 days (or 10 megabytes/day).

SUMMARY The previous examples of using various Unix tools to extract and analyze information contained in the Apache log files demonstrate not only that Unix is powerful and capable, but also that knowing the right tools to use can make some complex tasks incredibly easy. In the last example, the `awk` program did all the work, and it took only a second or two to add up a line of numbers that would overwhelm even the most accomplished accountant.

Summary

I really like the Apache Web server, in case that fact hasn't become clear as you've read through this lesson. It's not only a wonderful software package, but also a great testament to the value of the Internet itself, a key factor in the continued success of the Apache development team. Free software isn't inferior to expensive packages, and in many cases it's quite a bit better.

Again, please visit `http://www.apache.org/` to learn more about the Apache project and learn about how you can download your own Web server for your computer.

Workshop

The Workshop summarizes the key terms you learned and poses some questions about the topics presented in this chapter. It also provides you with a preview of what you will learn in the next hour.

Key Terms

CGI (common gateway interface)   The environment through which all Web-based programs are run by the Web server.

daemon   A program that's run by the operating system itself; it acts as a request server for a specific protocol. Apache runs as httpd, a Web request server.

regular expression   A pattern-matching expression that uses a wide variety of special characters to indicate sequences, selectors, and so on.

Exercises

First, go to the Web site `http://www.intuitive.com/tyu24/` and explore the examples shown in this hour.

1. Congratulations! You just won £150! Use the Web-based version of Exchange to see how much that's worth in Japanese yen.

2. Poke around on your system and determine whether an httpd daemon is running. If so, find the configuration files and peek inside to identify where the source HTML files live in the file system.

A

INDEX

Symbols

& (ampersand), 322, 349-350, 419

&& (double ampersands), 322

* (asterisk), 68, 131, 162-163, 317
    * expansion, 395
    filenames, 44
    regular expressions, 171

@ (at sign), 44, 68

\@ value (system prompts), 309

` (back quote), 125, 317, 405, 411

\ (backslash), 49, 175, 317, 351, 387

\; (backslash, semicolon), 387

[ ] (brackets), 165, 321, 352

^ (caret), 203, 344

^ (regular expression notation), 171-172, 176-177

: (colon), 173, 184, 201, 285, 293, 367, 463

: (colon) commands (vi editor), 190, 224-229, 250

:! command (vi editor), 243-244, 247

:- syntax (shells), 315-316

:= character (shells), 315

= command, 144

, (comma), 232

{ command (vi editor), 249

} command (vi editor), 246, 249

{ } (curly braces), 387

[^] control, 437-438

$ (dollar sign), 28, 174, 232, 237, 293, 314, 344, 350
    regular expression notation, 171
    regular expression notation for egrep command, 176
    shell commands, 300

$ command (vi editor), 202, 214

$ motion command (vi editor), 240

$ prompt (shells), 186

$$ shell variable, 284

. (dot), 51, 175, 395
    directory, 53-55, 59
    files, 60, 67

PATH environment variable, 290

regular expressions, 171, 176

shells, 293

.. (dot dot)
    directory, 53-55, 59
    shorthand, 71

! (exclamation point), 33, 270, 300, 320

! command (vi editor), 243-249, 267, 270

!! (double exclamation points)
    bash shell command, 304
    shell commands, 300-302

!! command (vi editor), 245, 249

!$ (exclamation point and dollar sign)
    bash shell command, 304
    shell commands, 300, 303

!* (exclamation point and asterisk)
    bash shell command, 304
    shell commands, 300, 303

!n bash shell command, 304

F

search paths, 60
search strings, 453
searching
    directories, 387
    with emacs editor,
        267-270
    file patterns, 177-178
    file systems, 386
    files, 167-170, 218-224
    text, 232-235
search PATH, 92-93
sections (manual), Perl programming online documentation, 479-480
Secure Shell (SSH). 441-442
SecureCRT, 441
security
    account names, 27
    passwords, 29-32
    systems, logging in and
        out, 26-29
sed command, inline editing, 341-346
sed stream editor, 246, 368
semicolon (;), 124, 308, 387
sending e-mail messages,
    416, 421-427
separator characters (directories), 48-49, 59
Sequent workstation, ps
    command, 359
server side include (SSI)
    programs on Apache Web
    Server, 495-497
servers. See Apache Web
    Server
set commands (shells), 293
:set number command (vi
    editor), 250
settings
    directory permissions,
        95-98
    file permissions, 90-95
sh shell, 279-280
SHELL environment variable, 56, 289

shell programs, 6, 9-10
    $ (dollar sign), 293, 314
    $ prompt, 186
    $$ variable, 284
    : (colon), 293
    :- syntax, 315-316
    := character, 315
    . (dot), 293
    #270 command, 299
    #271 command, 299
    #279 command, 299
    alias command, 306
    alias word=commands,
        305
    aliases, 125-127, 372
    bash, 279-282, 287, 314,
        327
        !! (double exclamation
            points) command,
            304
        !$ (exclamation point
            and dollar sign) command, 304
        !* (exclamation point
            and asterisk) command, 304
        !n command, 304
        ^a^b command, 304
        .bashrc file, 292-294
        command aliases,
            304-306
        command histories,
            298-304
        command table, 298
        configuration files,
            292-294
        custom prompts, setting, 308-310
        finding on systems,
            283
        history mechanisms,
            298-304
        home directories, 292
        internal variables, 291
        power aliases, 307-308
        .profile file, 292-294
    -bash, 356-357
    /bin directory, 283

    Bourne (sh), 4, 125,
        279-280
    Bourne Again (bash), 279,
        281
    Bourne, Steven, 280
    build-exchrate, downloading, 475
    C (csh), 279-281
        commands, 93
        environment variables,
            299
        processes, 346
        tcsh version, 282
    case command, 323
    checking availability on
        systems, 283
    choosing, 286-288
    chsh command, 286, 298
    commands, 279-281
        ! (exclamation point),
            300
        !! (double exclamation
            points), 300-302
        !$ (exclamation point
            and dollar sign), 300,
            303
        !* (exclamation point
            and asterisk), 300,
            303
        $ (exclamation point),
            300
        bash functions,
            326-330
        blocks, 321, 331
        building, 314
        comparison functions,
            318-321
        conditional expressions, 321-324
        fc -1, 298
        looping expressions,
            324-326
        numbers, 311
        rn, 300
        variables, 314-317
    comments, # (pound sign),
        294
    conditional expressions,
        331